D1356088

Research in Networked Learning

Series Editors
Vivien Hodgson
David McConnell

More information about this series at http://www.springer.com/series/11810

Christopher Jones

Networked Learning

An Educational Paradigm for the Age
of Digital Networks

 Springer

Christopher Jones
Liverpool John Moores University
Liverpool, Merseyside, UK

Research in Networked Learning
ISBN 978-3-319-01933-8   ISBN 978-3-319-01934-5   (eBook)
DOI 10.1007/978-3-319-01934-5

Library of Congress Control Number: 2015935430

Springer Cham Heidelberg New York Dordrecht London

Printed on acid-free paper

Springer International Publishing AG Switzerland is part of Springer Science+Business Media (www.springer.com)

Foreword

Chris Jones' *"Networked Learning: An Educational Paradigm for the Age of Digital Networks"* is a very welcome contribution to the Springer Series in Research in Networked Learning.

This book is a major contribution to the field of networked learning and provides the most comprehensive examination and analysis to date of its place in education in a networked society. As Chris Jones comments in his conclusion, at root the book argues for a relational view of learning through which networked learning can deal with the new mobility and from which networked learning can take its next steps by designing educational opportunities for citizens in an increasingly complex network society. In this book Chris Jones clearly identifies and differentiates networked learning as a specific field of research and scholarship that is broadly based on social theories of learning.

The book explores the relationship between digital and network technologies, learning and social life. We are not aware of any other book on networked learning that does what Chris Jones does here, nor of any book that does it so thoroughly. He examines the broad themes of networks, networking and networked learning as seen or experienced by institutions, through the use of infrastructures (the socio-material contexts), as well as perspectives and experiences of the human elements of academics and students. It's a broad sweep, taking the reader through the major components of networked learning as we experience them today.

In the book Chris Jones provides a critique of political and policy issues within the scope of the broad background picture relating to infrastructures. The changing roles, contexts and expectations of the academic are illuminated. The book broadens and contextualises contemporary issues in our understanding of networked learning. Issues covered range across the role of the university and position of academics in networked learning, restructuring of the academic role in teaching and digital scholarship, through to topical developments such as MOOCs and adoption and use of Learning Analytics, as well as examining the learner and the learner's experience as real embodied students within networked learning. These topics are drawn together in a way that makes logical, progressive sense, moving from the big and broad issues and perspectives, to the local and human ones. In doing this, Chris Jones situates networked learning in a spectrum of important issues that surround, support and make networked learning possible.

This monograph is a major critical analysis of networked learning that stands out as possibly the most significant statement on the subject currently available.

Vivien Hodgson
David McConnell

Contents

1   Introduction: The Long View—Technology, Learning
    and Social Life..   1
    Why Networked Learning?...   3
    Alternatives to Networked Learning...   6
        e-Learning...   8
        Technology-Enhanced Learning   9
        Disambiguation of Networked Learning..   11
    Key Ideas in Networked Learning   12
    References...   14

Part I   Theories and Concepts in Networked Learning

2   The Age of Digital Networks   19
    Change   19
        Society, Economy and Politics...   20
        Technology and Change...   23
    Technology and Society   23
        Technology, Determinism and Social Shaping   25
        Affordances and Constraints..   27
        Criticisms of Affordances   31
    Knowledge, Technology and Society..   35
        Knowledge, Work and Network Society...   35
        Network Society...   36
        Work..   38
        Knowledge   40
    Conclusions..   41
    References...   42

3   Theories of Learning in a Digital Age 47

An Accepted Canon? 49

Behaviourism 50

Cognitivism.. 51

Constructivism 52

Alternative Views of Learning 55

Pragmatism 55

Social/Situated Learning 57

Computer-Supported Collaborative Learning....................................... 60

The Phenomenographic Tradition.. 63

Newer Theories and Networked Learning 64

Conclusions: The Issues Arising from Learning Theory for Networked
Learning 67

There Is No Specific Learning Theory for Networked Learning........... 67

Design and Indirect Design.. 68

Disaggregation of the Teaching Function 70

Practice... 71

References.. 72

4   A Network of Network Theories... 79

What Is a Network? 80

Scientific and Mathematical Frameworks... 81

Random Networks 81

Small Worlds... 81

Scale-Free Networks and Hierarchical Networks................................. 83

Social Networks 87

Networked Individualism... 90

Technologies as Actants and Agents.. 91

Criticisms of ANT.. 94

Emergence and Intentionality 96

The Significance of Network Theories for Networked Learning 99

References.. 99

Part II   Agents and Actors in Networked Learning

5   Networked Learning and Institutions.. 107

Institutions and the Changing Nature of Work 108

Team Working, Instability and Change... 109

The University and the Digital.. 110

The University and Learning Analytics 112

Learner Analytics... 114

Enterprise Resource Planning.. 117

Openness, Open Educational Resources and the University 120

Institutional Supports for Openness.. 124

The University and the Challenge of MOOCs... 126
Conclusions.. 131
References.. 132

6 **The Infrastructures**.. 137
Infrastructure... 139
Information Infrastructures.. 140
Infrastructures for Learning... 144
Infrastructure and Levels 146
Institutional Infrastructures... 150
Universal Service Infrastructures.. 152
Hybrid Infrastructures.. 158
Cloud Computing and Hybrid Infrastructures 159
Conclusions.. 161
References.. 163

7 **Academics and Digital Networks**.. 169
Disciplines, Scholarship and Digital Technology 171
Digital Scholarship.. 174
A 'New' Invisible College?... 178
Pedagogy and the Scholarship of Teaching and Learning 180
Para-Academics and the Emergence of the New Professionals............... 185
E-Research and the Digital Humanities... 186
Conclusions.. 190
References.. 191

8 **The Learner and Digital Networks**.. 197
Early Work on Students and Technology.. 198
The Net Generation and Digital Natives... 200
A Generational Divide? 204
Relationships Between Technology Use in Society and in Education 206
Design and Alternative Accounts of Technology 208
Affordance, Agency and Causation 209
Spaces and Places 210
Learners at the Interface.. 212
Student Experience and Design 213
The Student/Learner Experience.. 214
Students and Their Experiences of Technology.. 217
References.. 218

9 **Networked Learning: A New Paradigm?**.. 225
Key Concept 1: Affordance 226
Key Concept 2: Agency 228
Key Concept 3: Assemblage... 231
The Future of Networked Learning 234
The Political Nature of Networked Learning... 235

Suggestions for a Research Agenda... 237
Data and Educational Infrastructures.. 238
Following the Actor in a Digital Ecology 238
Future Issues and Developments in Networked Learning 240
References.. 241

Index.. 245

Chapter 1
Introduction: The Long View—Technology, Learning and Social Life

This book is about networked learning and it offers a different way of thinking about the relationship between digital and network technologies and learning.[1] In the author's lifetime digital and networked technologies have developed from large-scale technologies marginal to everyday lives, deployed in sizeable organisations, to items the public carry in our pockets and use routinely in our everyday lives. My personal working life tracks some of the more recent changes. In my first job (in 1966) I worked in a commercial laundry that was still powered by a single source with power delivered to the washing machines and spinners via a power shaft and belts. While I worked there a new machine was installed that took washing in at one end and delivered it at the other end washed and spun. It was a large washing machine of the modern kind only horizontal in layout and large in size. What intrigued me most and led me to talk to the Swiss technician installing the machine was its computerised control. By pressing large numbered keys the machine could be programmed to carry out various washes. The laundry work, largely done by hand loading and moving between various washing and drying machines was to be brought into a single computerised machine. I did not understand it then, but the work of the laundry was being 'informated' (Zuboff 1988) and the kind of simple labour I was being employed to carry out was being made redundant. Much of the discussion in that era concerned the effects that computers might have on the labour process, particularly in relation to skill (Braverman 1974). This discussion took place largely in the context of mainframe computers, sometimes networked with white collar work distributed in remote locations working at 'dumb' terminals.[2]

---

[1] Networked and digital is used throughout this volume to characterise current technologies in a general way. Networks exist independently of digital technologies and computing can take analogue and quantum forms. Digital and networked describes the contemporary form of 'new' technologies and tries to avoid over generalisation.

[2] Those younger than the author might need to know that a dumb terminal was a workstation that had no self-contained processing power, it preceded the personal computer. The terminal was local but the processing power was remote at the mainframe computer.

© Springer International Publishing Switzerland 2015
C. Jones, *Networked Learning*, Research in Networked Learning,
DOI 10.1007/978-3-319-01934-5_1

When I first went to university in the early 1970s 'the' computer was in its own building separate from normal university life. It was considered so special it was guarded by selected student volunteers during a student protest (a 'sit-in' that occupied university administration buildings). In my first job following university I encountered a 24 h computer room with separate staff working on a 7-day 24 h shift cycle to service a large computer. In the mid-1970s I found myself working for a large UK electricity supply company in what would now be described as a call centre. The computer looked much as desktop computers look now although interactions were using a command line interface and not the visual interfaces commonly used now. The mainframe was in another city some 35 miles (50 km) away but I could call up customers' accounts and deal with them via the telephone in a way that has become familiar, but was then quite a novelty. Paper-based accounts held on paper files had just been replaced for one side of the business, monthly accounts; one half of the office was still paper-based dealing with another kind of account. This transition in white collar work from paper-based systems to electronic systems is now at least 40 years old but it has not affected all aspects of work and many universities remain at least partially paper-based in their administrative and academic work.

The move from mainframe computer systems to the personal computer (PC) began on a wide scale in the mid-1980s with the introduction of the Apple 11 and other similar devices. While microcomputers began to emerge in the late 1970s with the Apple 11, it was the introduction of the IBM personal computer and the Apple Macintosh PCs with a graphical user interface that began to lead to a significant expansion (Allan 2001). These work-related changes were accompanied by a range of home computers, game consoles and education-related developments (e.g. the BBC microcomputer was introduced to schools in the UK and the Phillips P2000 in the Netherlands). The development of the computer was related to the wider development of the networks connecting them. From the mainframe computing of the late 1960s and 1970s, the 1980s saw a move towards both PCs and network connections. In the very early 1990s I was introduced to the Internet by a local union educator as part of a process to bring local union officers up to speed with technological developments. The union's offices were being equipped with PCs and we were shown how to connect to Manchester Host (Fourkas 2002), a community informatics project's server which allowed onward access to other networks. This was my first view of the Internet. I have to say that at the time it was less than impressive, without a graphical user interface and limited in the kinds of information available. I found it difficult to imagine how I would use it. At the same time I was studying for an Open University (UK) degree by distance learning. This was largely conducted via paper-based resources and broadcast TV with a small number of local seminars and annual summer schools. It did however involve visits to a computer lab at a local higher education college. These computers were networked although the work we did was computer-assisted learning using the PC as a local device.

This book is a product of that rapid sociotechnical change introduced along with networked digital computers and how it is implicated in changes in education. Education and learning do not stand apart from society and the kind of educational systems we have are engaged in a complex interaction with technologies often developed elsewhere in society and frequently for very different purposes. My first university post was in an institution that based its learning infrastructure on Lotus Notes, a business groupware built for corporations which had been adapted for university use. The kind of learning that is demanded by society and for society is an obviously political question, deeply affected by who can choose and what they can choose from. The period in which digital and networked technologies have spread to all aspects of social life is the same historical period in which communist governments fell across Eastern Europe, and new forms of capitalism came to dominate the world economy. It is also an historical period in which global processes of integration, the economic development of large populations in newly developing areas of the world, and large migrations of people have taken place. For the first time in history more than half the world's entire population live in urban centres and the globe is now a truly bourgeois society. I make these points to emphasise that networked learning is about learning in this world, a world that is an assemblage of people and machines, of politics and economics, and large historical forces in which education and learning only form one small but essential part. My engagement with networked learning is concerned with learning conditioned by its interaction with this emerging society and the political choices that have to be made at all levels of organisation when technology and education come together.

Why Networked Learning?

This book enters a congested field with many books already in existence, some dating back many years, so why should a reader bother with this one? Educational technology has been the subject for many years to wide-eyed enthusiasm and boosterism (see for example on MOOCs Barber et al. 2013). Each new technology is promoted by its advocates as requiring a radical break from the past and the revolution in education is always just around the corner. There are a smaller number of doom mongers who see only bad things in the same educational technologies advocated by the boosters (see for example Brabazon 2002, 2007). Networked learning by contrast stands as a critical research-based strand which adopts neither of these positions. Networked learning casts a cold hard eye on the evidence, informed by a set of flexible but robust values that I claim should inform education. Research in networked learning is interested in praxis, action in the world informed by theory, and also an engagement in practice informed by a notion of what is good. Research led and interested in empirical work networked learning is concerned with values (Hodgson et al. 2012). The idea of the network is another central reason to engage with networked learning. I claim that the metaphor of networks, as well as their actual existence and processes, help to cohere a research field with a distinct focus and research agenda (Jones 2004). It has been well argued that networks can be seen as the defining feature of contemporary social life and the basis of a network society (Castells 2000 [1996]; Van Dijk 1999 [1991]).

This book is useful because the tradition of networked learning has grown strongly over the past 15 years into a robust and productive area of research and it has informed some significant areas of successful design and development. However there is no single book that sets out the field from a single perspective. There are several edited collections (Steeples and Jones 2002; Goodyear et al. 2004; Dirckinck-Holmfeld et al. 2009, 2012; Hodgson et al. 2012) but no single authored text. There are books that are close to networked learning (Ellis and Goodyear 2010), but networked learning is frequently confused with other approaches to technology and learning and sometimes even otherwise well-informed academic work assumes that networked learning is just another term that equates with e-learning, technology-enhanced learning (TEL) and a number of other general terms.

This book is addressed to a number of different audiences:

1. *Research communities.* This book is concerned with community, cooperation, collaboration, participation, dialogue, networked and digital technology in education. Researchers concerned with these issues will find something of value in networked learning.
2. *Teachers.* Educational professionals who undertake teaching will find this book useful in situating how their practices are changing and being changed by the introduction of digital and networked technologies.
3. *The new (emergent) professions.* Learning technologists, educational technologists and educational developers, all those in para-academic roles who will find in networked learning a critical research-based approach that takes design and development seriously.
4. *Designers and developers.* The ideas in this book can help inform those who design and develop technologies for use in education and for learning.
5. *Policy makers* at all levels. This book can help inform those staff who work in senior positions in universities, government, think tanks and policy bodies. It is a book for national and international bodies involved in representing the university sector and the staff that work in that sector.
6. *Students.* This book will help students at all levels to understand the ways digital and networked technologies interact with and co-construct contemporary education and learning.
7. *Opinion formers.* This book can help journalists and others in the media who report on education to differentiate between different sources. Media often report startling claims and make sweeping claims based on limited resources. Support for these claims can be found in, academic, non-academic, and 'grey' literature,[3] and discrimination between sources is essential.

---

[3] Grey literature abounds in this area, often written by academics these are reports and publications that are not peer reviewed. They are important because they can be produced and spread quickly to keep up with a fast moving field, but they are not scientific literature because of the lack of peer review and their potential disconnect from a body of acknowledged literature. In current conditions blogs are a very good example of grey literature and its potential strengths and weaknesses.

The claim that I make in this book is that networked learning is not just another term for a common academic field it is a different way of thinking about the relationships between digital and networked technologies and the processes of learning and education.

The core definition of networked learning is:

> …learning in which information and communications technology (ICT) is used to promote connections: between one learner and other learners, between learners and tutors; between a learning community and its learning resources.

The key term in this definition is *connections* and the emphasis is on the interactions between people mediated by technology and between people and resources. This basic definition was included in the book I co-edited with Chris Steeples in 2002 and it grew out of earlier project work as reported by Goodyear (2014). The team involved with the Networked Learning in Higher Education project and the organisers of the networked learning conference series agreed to standardise their citations of the definition by referencing the definition to a chapter by Goodyear et al. (2004). This core definition has provided a degree of stability for researchers, allowing for the development of a coherent body of work with a common focus. Inevitably there are differences of emphasis and there has been some discussion about the nature of the field and the question of definition (see McConnell et al. 2012; Dohn 2014). The core definition, having proved remarkably resilient in a fast changing field, remains a cornerstone for the networked learning conference series in many research studies, edited collections and this book series.

Carvalho and Goodyear (2014), p. 11 provide an additional section from the original definition which states that:

> Some of the richest examples of networked learning involve interaction with on-line materials and with other people. But the use of on-line materials is not a sufficient characteristic to define networked learning.

This is an important feature of networked learning because although the definition includes information and communication technology, and it makes technological mediation a necessary condition, it also made mediated human activity a core component. Networked learning was never conceived of as purely interaction with content made available via digital networks. This point is further emphasised by examining the complete definition provided by the JISC-funded project Networked Learning in Higher Education[4] which includes the following:

> The interactions between people in networked learning environments can be synchronous, asynchronous or both. The interactions can be through text, voice, graphics, video, shared workspaces or combinations of these forms. Consequently the space of possibilities for networked learning, and the space of potential student experiences, is vast.

This section, although somewhat dated in style, displays some of the reasons why the definition has been so robust. It was never tied to any one particular technology, or any specific feature of the available technologies apart from their potential for interactivity. At that time Internet connections were still limited,

---

[4] Networked Learning in Higher Education: http://csalt.lancs.ac.uk/jisc/definition.htm

especially away from university premises, but the definition included the possibilities for interaction using features that have since then become commonplace e.g. the use of video. These three short sections when taken together provided a suitable starting point for a research field that sits within, but is not coincident with, the broad subject area of educational technology. The next section looks at the main alternative definitions found in educational technology and argues that networked learning has clear advantages over the alternatives for the development of a field of research and in encouraging a critical engagement with design and development.

Alternatives to Networked Learning

Technology and learning have been intertwined from the beginning of human civilisation and Plato reported that Socrates was concerned that the introduction of written texts would degrade previously important skills such as memorisation and rhetoric (Plato 2008). The written word, taken from its context was thought to be inferior to spoken words which could be attuned to the speaker's awareness of the settings in which they would be uttered. Thoughts could remain silent if they would be of either no use or counterproductive in a particular situation, but the written word had no such sensitivity to where it would be taken up. Writing is an early example of the remediation of thought and its consequences for learning were contested when it was introduced. Other technological innovations were perhaps less dramatic and also less contentious. Perhaps the most ubiquitous piece of educational technology, the chalkboard (blackboard), was invented at the beginning of the nineteenth century in Scotland and used almost simultaneously in the United States at West Point (Krause 2007; Wylie 2012). The slate had been used previously but the innovation lay in being able to use the board to present to an entire class. This was not simply a technical change and Wylie (2012) has illustrated the way that the chalkboard was integrated into classroom practice by way of manuals providing guidance on the ways the board could be used. The chalkboard is now rarely thought of as an educational technology. However Andrews and Haythornthwaite (2007) discuss its recent reincarnation as the interactive whiteboard and point out that the focus in research has too often been on the technology itself and not on broader questions of adoption and implementation, and the use of the whiteboard alongside other complementary technologies. Cuban's work provides a link between modern technologies including computing and the long history of technology and learning (Cuban 1986, 2001; Tyack and Cuban 1995). Cuban's work shows that the practices of teaching and learning are highly resilient and the ways that established practices have to provide substantial resistance to changes said to be the consequences of the technology itself. Educational technology is a broad domain and it has generated many arguments that are repeated anew in the context of the recent waves of digital and networked technology. In this long historical process the terms and definitions we use are important for delimiting the areas of study and the kinds of research and development that are encompassed.

Learning technology has emerged as more than an academic research field and it encompasses new job roles and emerging professional bodies (see Chap. 7). There is an overabundance of terms that have been used to discuss the use of new (generally digital and networked) technologies for teaching and learning. Early terms such as teaching machines (Skinner 1958) and telematics (Selinger and Pearson 1999) still have some resonance, and broader approaches can still be influential, especially in some parts of the world e.g. instructional design in the United States (Reigeluth 1999). Some terms focus on particular technologies such as mobile/Internet/Web-based and computer-assisted-*learning*; others focus on process such as online/distance/blended and flexible *learning*. Within this field there is a general recognition that two broad ways of thinking can be discerned. There are those who focus on a broadcast model of distribution and an acquisition model of learning and there are those who favour dialogue, participation and discussion as the model for learning (Sfard 1998; Weller 2007). There are also fashions in the use of these terms and terms such as virtual learning, cyberspace and the information superhighway, which were once popular but are less common now. Of all the terms that have been used perhaps the two most common are e-learning and in Europe, Technology-Enhanced Learning (TEL). There are of course some significant, relevant and more specific expressions and theories associated with the educational technology research area and one of the more developed is Computer-Supported Collaborative Learning (CSCL). This approach is not dealt with in the Introduction; however, a discussion can be found later in Chap. 3.

Key issues that help to discriminate between the many approaches and the cut-paths through the thicket of terminology are:

1. The theory of technology

   a. Is technology seen as an independent force driving change, or as socially shaped and co-constructed by its design and its context when it is taken into use?
   b. Are the technology and its features seen as defining its educational use?

2. The underlying theory of learning

   a. Is learning a process of delivery or is it an interactive process that involves participation through dialogue?
   b. Are learning processes seen as primarily individual, social or sociomaterial in character?

Networked learning has its own particular views on these issues which are developed throughout this volume, and it is the combination of these which give networked learning a distinct critical position in relation to the other dominant terms and the theories associated with them. There are a small number of other terms that roughly approximate to the approach taken by networked learning. One of the more interesting and recent of the alternatives is the idea of connected learning (Ito et al. 2013; Kumpulainen and Sefton-Green 2014; Sefton-Green 2014). Connected learning is in some ways complementary to networked learning because it concentrates on young people between 12 and 18 years of age, whereas networked learning generally focuses on learning in higher education and in professional development which in both cases are concerned with people largely older than 18.

e-Learning

Probably the most widely used expression that has been used to describe the field concerned with digital and networked technologies for education and learning is e-learning. It has been given a variety of definitions by policy makers, practitioners and academic researchers. An example of a policy definition is that given by the UK government in 2003:

> If someone is learning in a way that uses information and communication technologies ICTs, they are using e-learning. They could be a pre-school child playing an interactive game; they could be a group of pupils collaborating on a history project with pupils in another country via the Internet; they could be geography students watching an animated diagram of a volcanic eruption their lecturer has just downloaded; they could be a nurse taking her driving theory test online with a reading aid to help her dyslexia—it all counts as e-learning (Department for Education and Skills 2003, p. 4).

Used in this way e-learning lacks precision and simply describes all and any uses of ICT for learning. More theoretically informed uses of the term also lack precision and can be accompanied by a revolutionary rhetoric suggesting the necessity of rapid change. For example Garrison and Anderson (2003) state:

> …e-learning is not simply another technology or add-on that will be quietly integrated or ultimately rejected… e-learning represents a very different category and mode of communication… E-learning will inevitably transform all forms of education and learning in the twenty-first century (Garrison and Anderson 2003, pp. 1–2).

This slightly breathless approach provides no real definition of e-learning but hints at it being connected to a process of educational reform placed in contrast to a persistent 'transmission model' of education. This approach can be found repeatedly in writing about educational technology and its effects on institutions, academics and students, and this is explored further in subsequent chapters. The significant issue here is that networked learning tries to avoid this kind of hype and work in this tradition seeks to maintain a critical stance towards the object of research. This makes it quite different to this kind of use of the term e-learning.

There are those who retain the term e-learning but use it more critically and distance themselves from many of the uses the term e-learning has been put to (see for example Andrews and Haythornthwaite 2007). Andrews and Haythornthwaite note that e-learning is a compound term made up of two elements and that:

> The 'e' of e-learning has a longer history than many will assume, including long term efforts to capture voice and images, and to store and transmit those recordings. With each capture—from records to CDs, from film to DVD, conversation to chat—there are trade-offs in quality, interactivity, and transferability: trade-offs that mark both the pros and cons of technology mediation (Andrews and Haythornthwaite 2007, p. 3).

This quote illustrates an important issue often lost in discussions of e-learning. E-learning blurs a boundary, the boundary between digital and analogue technologies. The 'e' in e-learning is electronic and belongs as much to the world of Telstar and McLuhan as it does to the digital age. Andrews and Haythornthwaite go on to identify the 'e' in e-learning with digital computing and networks but this is not clear in the term they use. Networked learning is preferable to this use of the term e-learning precisely because it locates itself specifically in digital and networked technology and it focuses on a main characteristic of these technologies, their interactivity and connectivity.

So e-learning is an imprecise term, used in a variety of ways in different contexts (Guri-Rosenblit and Gros 2011). Guri-Rosenblit and Gros note that the lack of a precise and widely accepted definition of e-learning causes misunderstanding and robust debate between researchers and an effect on research outcomes by blurring and confusing the specific detail of what is under discussion. For these reasons and others, e-learning is now challenged by another commonly used phrase, TEL

Technology-Enhanced Learning

TEL has become common place in some areas, especially Europe, but definitions are uncommon and it is not clear that those who use the term share an understanding of what it might mean. The EU-funded network of excellence (Kaleidoscope) was constructed around the term TEL and produced a book summing up the networks outlook, but it is not possible to find in that book a concise definition of what TEL might mean (Balacheff et al. 2009). While there is no definition, the book does set out the sources for the research field:

> We believe it is reasonable to say that TEL has grown out of five main areas of research:
> 1. The design area—a focus on the design and co-evolution of new learning activities.
> 2. The computational area—a focus on what technology makes possible.
> 3. The cognitive area—a focus on what the individual can learn under certain conditions in different types of contexts.
> 4. The social and cultural area—a focus on meaning-making, participation, and changes in activities in schools, universities, workplaces, and informal settings.
> 5. The epistemological area—a focus on how the specificities of the domain impact the design and use of technologies.
>
> All these areas contribute to the overall understanding of TEL (Balacheff et al. 2009, p. vii).

Of course the book itself stands as a contribution to defining the term, but its use in this context is something of a catch-all, an expression that adds little to the generally used expression educational technology. A significant strength of the approach is that there is a conscious attempt to make TEL an interdisciplinary activity building links and synergies between technologically oriented and human-oriented research activities in computer science, psychology and the social sciences. The work begun in the network described by Balacheff et al. (2009) has been continued in a new network (STELLAR) that brought together elements of Kaleidoscope with another preceding EU network Prolearn. A report of the activity of the new network continues to use TEL as the defining term but persists in not supplying a concise definition (Sutherland et al. 2012). Interestingly at the time of writing this chapter, despite all the efforts of Kaleidoscope and STELLAR, the TEL Thesaurus does not contain a dictionary entry for Technology-Enhanced Learning.[5]

---

[5] http://www.tel-thesaurus.net/wiki/index.php/TEL_Dictionary_entries

Kirkwood and Price reviewed the use of TEL in education, and they conclude that the most common use of the phrase considers it synonymous with equipment and infrastructure. They quote from the Higher Education Funding Council for England (HEFCE 2009) who provides a definition of TEL as:

Enhancing learning and teaching through the use of technology.

The same HEFCE document makes available the reasoning behind their change of terminology from e-learning to TEL:

The first edition of our strategy talked about e-learning, but in the past three years, terminology, practice and contexts have developed. The term 'e-learning' can now sometimes be too narrowly defined to describe fully the widespread use of learning technology in institutions. We think it is more appropriate to consider how institutions can enhance learning, teaching and assessment using appropriate technology (HEFCE 2009, p. 1).

One important feature of this account is the shift in focus from the use of technology for learning to an institutional perspective, something I address in Chap. 5. The normative inclusion of 'enhancement' in TEL is clearly displayed, and this is a problem for those wishing to use the expression for research purposes because TEL assumes some kind of benefit from the use of technology. HEFCE identifies three levels of potential benefits of TEL:

* *Efficiency*—existing processes carried out in a more cost-effective, time-effective, sustainable or scalable manner.
* *Enhancement*—improving existing processes and the outcomes.
* *Transformation*—radical, positive change in existing processes or introducing new processes (HEFCE 2009, p. 2).

Although the term enhancement is central to this definition, Kirkwood and Price note that the meaning of 'enhanced' in TEL is often taken for granted and generally used uncritically and in ways that leave its meaning opaque. This led them to conclude that:

The term TEL is too often used in an unconsidered manner…This review has highlighted variations in both the purpose of TEL interventions and the ways that **enhancement** has been conceived. Underpinning this is a conflation of two distinct aims:

> * Changes in the **means** through which university teaching happens; and
> * Changes in **how** university teachers teach and learners learn (Kirkwood and Price 2014, p. 26).

Bayne (2014) explicitly references the review by Kirkwood and Price and argues that her critical approach to TEL differs because she argues that TEL is not a term that requires better definition because it is fundamentally flawed because it carries with it a set of discursive limitations and deeply conservative assumptions. Using a variety of theoretical perspectives, Bayne critiques the way technology is underdefined in TEL and described in essentialist and instrumental terms. Bayne also criticises TEL for being related to an unquestioned dependence on humanistic values and the idea that the humans can be perfected via technological enhancement and scientific progress. Bayne's third argument concerns learning and the way the discussion of learning is very often really concerned with education and the institutional, political and legal contexts that education is enmeshed with. The arguments Bayne advances are of significance to networked learning and in the chapters that follow which discuss technology, issues of agency, symmetry between humans and machines, and the importance of sociomaterial assemblages in education are considered (Chaps. 4 and 6). However the question of learning is embedded in the definition of networked learning and the issues Bayne raises need careful consideration in the networked learning community. They are touched on in later chapters, especially Chap. 3, but I do not think that learning is a problem of equal significance to the others Bayne raises. I agree that learning has become a way to downplay the institutional, infrastructural and political aspects of education but I try to demonstrate that the use of the term learning is no bar to their full and proper inclusion in networked learning.

Disambiguation of Networked Learning

Beyond the general terms applied to learning technology there are other terms related to networked learning that need to be mentioned in order to set out clearly the relationships they have to the discussion found in this book. One of the oldest and most visible by way of published outputs is the phrase Asynchronous Learning Networks (ALN) (Hiltz et al. 2007). The history of ALN overlaps with networked learning as it is developed in this book. However the specific focus on asynchronous technologies limits its scope in ways that networked learning does not. Networked learning can involve the use of computer networks by learners who are co-located and working together in real time. Synchronous technologies form a full part of the approaches taken by researchers in networked learning, but they are excluded from research in ALN.

> ...online courses that primarily rely on synchronous audio or video presentation or chat are not ALN because these require learners and instructors to be available to communicate at the same time (Hiltz et al. 2007, p. 56).

A second feature of the use of ALN is that it requires interactivity and interaction in social networks and communities. This aspect draws it closer to networked learning because both approaches exclude learning that does 'not include substantial and rapid interactivity with others' (Hiltz et al. 2007, p. 56). The link is reinforced by a common concern with cooperative and collaborative forms of learning and an extension of that via networks, not only conceived of as technical systems but to the social networks enabled by the technologies. Some of the earliest writing acknowledged as part of the history of networked learning comes from the tradition that uses the designation ALN (Hiltz and Turoff 1978; Harasim et al. 1995), but the history diverged as the Sloan Foundation helped to establish a conference series focused on ALN and the Journal of Asynchronous Learning Networks which developed a more narrowly devised area of research and practice to that developed using the alternative formulation networked learning.

Another term used by authors in this tradition that has a wider influence is the expression learning networks (Harasim et al. 1995). Their definition was that:

...learning networks are groups of people who use CMC [Computer-Mediated Communication] networks to learn together at the time, place, and pace that best suits them and is appropriate to the task (Harasim et al. 1995, p. 4).

The link to ALN is clearly visible in this definition but the same phrase is used elsewhere with varying meanings (Downes 2007; Haythornthwaite and De Laat 2010; Carvalho and Goodyear 2014). Downes for example identifies learning networks with a general case elaborated from the Personal Learning Environments (PLE) and writes:

Taken together, the ideas that underlie the PLE—learning in communities, creation over consumption, and context over class—constitute an instance of a more general approach that may be characterized as 'learning networks' (Downes 2007, Online).

This definition is quite different to Harasim et al. and the tradition of ALN which is much more focused on conventional classes and university courses than the approach advocated by Downes who's work went on to inform the first generation of cMOOCs (see Chap. 5). The use of the term by those more closely associated with the networked learning community has been to identify the characteristics of the network structures and the practices taking place in them. In this usage networked learning is the general phenomenon and the learning network is the particular set of interactions in a specific learning network (for example, see Haythornthwaite and De Laat 2010). Goodyear and Carvalho (2014) add greater precision to this approach and link their definition directly back to the work of Harasim et al. and the limitations that they see in the original definition. Their argument suggests that learning networks need to be a focus for networked learning research because of the idea of *indirect design,* a key theoretical contribution of networked learning (see Chap. 4). Indirect design argues that learning cannot be designed directly and that it can only be designed *for.* The significance of this is that actual learning networks can be investigated and analysed so that they can inform the future designs of those elements (tasks, spaces, tools and organisations) open to design activity. Indirect design requires the building up of a repertoire of properly understood examples that illustrate and simplify the complex processes and assemblages in which networked learning takes place.

Key Ideas in Networked Learning

A number of key ideas are developed in the main chapters of this book in particular affordance, agency and assemblage and these are returned to in the concluding chapter. The main areas covered in the subsequent chapters are:

- The relationships between technology, society and change.
  - Technological determinism, social shaping and sociomateriality.
  - The relationships between technology, academic work and learning.

- The concept affordance and its potential for use in networked learning.

    - As a way of stabilising dynamic relations.
    - Related to issues of design.

- Design for learning, the notion of indirect design,

    - Intentionality and emergence in complex systems
    - Big data and analytics in learning

- The relationships between humans, artefacts and machines in networked learning

    - Symmetry and asymmetry
    - Thinking in terms of levels—macro-meso-micro

- Infrastructure and its role in networked learning

    - Infrastructures for learning
    - Universal, institutional and hybrid infrastructures

- The politics and policy options related to networked learning

    - Technology design and deployment as political choices
    - Policy and institutional factors in networked learning

The book is structured in two parts with the first dealing with the three main components in an understanding of networked learning. In Part I Chap. 2 deals with the world in which networked learning is one small part. This chapter concentrates on the processes of change, and technological change in particular, and the ways it can be understood. It also discusses the kind of society that is emerging and the idea of a network society. It discusses the idea of affordance and how it can be used to provide a solid basis for understanding technological change. Chapter 3 examines learning and asks the question whether networked learning has its own pedagogy. The classic theories of learning are discussed and assessed in relation to networked learning. This chapter also considers the question of whether networked learning either needs or has its own pedagogy. Chapter 4 explores some of the different ways networks can be understood. This chapter surveys mathematical theories of learning, social network analysis and actor-network theory (ANT). It finds some key concepts in each of these different ways of thinking about networks that can be fruitfully applied to networked learning. Taken together these three chapters provide a thorough grounding in the basic elements required for a comprehension of networked learning.

The second part of the book looks in detail at some of the key areas of activity that are implicated in any occurrence of networked learning. Chapter 5 examines the institutions within which networked learning takes place, primarily the university as the location for higher education and the idea of the 'digital university'. The institutions that support higher education are also the location for changes in the use of data for analytic purposes and for new arrangements for generating open resources and open and online courses. Chapter 6 explores the infrastructures through which networked learning is supported. It discusses the different forms that infrastructures take when used in supporting learning and it makes distinctions between universal service infrastructures, institutional infrastructures and a growing category of hybrid infrastructures, such as Cloud-based services that are integrated into institutions. The following two chapters focus on two key groups of people involved in networked learning, the students and academic staff. Chapter 7 investigates the changing roles and activities of academic staff and discusses the idea of digital scholarship. It also includes a discussion of the growth of para-academic roles such as learning technologists and educational developers. Chapter 8 explores some of the common discourses about students and their changing place in networked learning. It provides a critical assessment of the net generation and digital natives discourse and concludes that this persistent set of ideas is an inadequate way of thinking about students and their relationships with technology. The chapter also sets out alternative ways of thinking about the issues that change in technologies and new cohorts of young students do give rise to. It stresses that age is only one important factor amongst others and that there is no evidence of any generational break between a group of young students and their older teachers.

References

Allan, R. A. (2001). *A history of the personal computer: The people and the technology*. Ontario, CA: Allan Publisher.

Andrews, R., & Haythornthwaite, C. (Eds.). (2007). *Sage handbook of e-learning research*. London: Sage.

Balacheff, N., Ludvigsen, S., De Jong, T., Lazonder, A., Barnes, S., & Montandon, L. (Eds.). (2009). *Technology-enhanced learning*. Berlin, Germany: Springer.

Barber, M., Donnelly, K., & Ritzvi, S. (2013). *An avalanche is coming: Higher education and the revolution ahead*. London: IPPR. Retrieved from http://www.ippr.org/publication/55/10432/an-avalanche-is-coming-higher-education-and-the-revolution-ahead

Bayne, S. (2014). What's the matter with 'technology enhanced learning'? *Learning, Media and Technology, 40*(1), 5–20. doi: 10.1080/17439884.2014.915851. Retrieved from http://dx.doi.org/10.1080/17439884.2014.915851

Brabazon, T. (2002). *Digital hemlock: Internet education and the poisoning of teaching*. Sydney, NSW: University of New South Wales Press.

Brabazon, T. (2007). *The university of Google*. Aldershot, England: Ashgate.

Braverman, H. (1974). *Monopoly capitalism*. New York: Monthly Review Press.

Carvalho, L., & Goodyear, P. (Eds.). (2014). *The architecture of productive learning networks*. New York: Routledge.

Castells, M. (2000). *The rise of the network society* (2nd ed.). Oxford, England: Blackwell (Original work published 1996).

Cuban, L. (1986). *Teachers and machines: The classroom use of technology since 1920*. New York: Teachers College Press.

Cuban, L. (2001). *Oversold and underused: Computers in the classroom*. Cambridge, MA: Harvard University Press.

Department for Education and Skills. (2003). *Towards a unified e-learning strategy: Consultation document*. Nottingham: DFES. Retrieved from http://webarchive.nationalarchives.gov.uk/20130401151715/http://www.education.gov.uk/publications/eOrderingDownload/DfES-0455-2003.pdf

Dirckinck-Holmfeld, L., Hodgson, V., & McConnell, D. (Eds.). (2012). *Exploring the theory, pedagogy and practice of networked learning*. New York: Springer.

Dirckinck-Holmfeld, L., Jones, C., & Lindström, B. (Eds.). (2009). *Analysing networked learning practices in higher education and continuing professional development*. Rotterdam, The Netherlands: Sense Publishers, BV.

Dohn, N. (2014). Implications for networked learning of the 'practice' side of social practice theories—a tacit-knowledge perspective. In V. E. Hodgson, M. De Laat, D. McConnell, & T. Ryberg (Eds.), *The design, experience and practice of networked learning* (pp. 29–49). Heidelberg, Germany: Springer.

Downes, S. (2007). Learning networks in practice. In D. Ley (Ed.), *Emerging technologies for learning*. London: BECTA. Retrieved from http://nparc.cisti-icist.nrc-cnrc.gc.ca/npsi/ctrl?acti on=rtdoc&an=8913424&lang=en

Ellis, R., & Goodyear, P. (2010). *Students' experiences of e-learning in higher education: The ecology of sustainable innovation*. New York: Routledge.

Fourkas, V. (2002). The development and operation of virtual manchester(s), 1989-2001: A research report. *Online Planning Journal*. Retrieved from http://www.casa.ucl.ac.uk/planning/ articles61/vrmanchester.pdf

Garrison, D. R., & Anderson, T. (2003). *E-learning in the 21st Century: A framework for research and practice*. London: RoutledgeFalmer.

Goodyear, P. (2014). Productive learning networks: The evolution of research and practice. In L. Carvalho & P. Goodyear (Eds.), *The architecture of productive learning networks* (pp. 23–47). London: Routledge.

Goodyear, P., Banks, S., Hodgson, V., & McConnell, D. (2004). *Advances in research on networked learning*. London: Springer.

Goodyear, P., & Carvalho, L. (2014). Introduction: Networked learning and learning networks. In L. Carvalho & P. Goodyear (Eds.), *The architecture of productive learning networks* (pp. 3–22). London: Routledge.

Guri-Rosenblit, S. & Gros, B. (2011). E-learning: Confusing terminology, research gaps and inherent challenges. *The Journal of Distance Education*, 25(1). Retrieved from http://www.ijede.ca/ index.php/jde/article/view/729/1206

Harasim, L., Hiltz, S. R., Teles, L., & Turoff, M. (1995). *Learning networks: A field guide to teaching and learning online*. Cambridge, MA: MIT Press.

Haythornthwaite, C. & De Laat, M. (2010). Social networks and learning networks: Using social network perspectives to understand social learning. In L. Dirckinck-Holmfeld, V. Hodgson, C. Jones, D. McConnell, & T. Ryberg (Eds.), *Proceedings of the 7th International Conference on Networked Learning* (pp. 183–190), 3–4 May 2010, Aalborg, Denmark. Retrieved from http://networkedlearningconference.org.uk/past-proceedings/index.htm

Higher Education Funding Council for England (2009). *Enhancing learning and teaching through the use of technology: A revised approach to HEFCE's strategy for e-learning*. Bristol: Higher Education Funding Council for England. Retrieved from http://www.hefce.ac.uk/pubs/ hefce/2009/09_12/09_12.pdf

Hiltz, S. R., & Turoff, M. (1978). *The network nation—human communication via computer* (1st ed.). Reading, MA: Addison-Wesley [Revised Edition. Cambridge, MA: MIT Press, 1993].

Hiltz, S. R., Turoff, M., & Harasim, L. (2007). Development and philosophy of asynchronous learning networks. In R. Andrews & C. Haythornthwaite (Eds.), *Sage handbook of e-learning research* (pp. 55–72). London: Sage.

Hodgson, V., McConnell, D., & Dirckinck-Holmfeld, L. (2012). The theory, practice and pedagogy of networked learning. In L. Dirckinck-Holmfeld, V. Hodgson, & D. McConnell (Eds.), *Exploring the theory, pedagogy and practice of networked learning* (pp. 291–305). New York: Springer.

Ito, M., Gutiérrez, K., & Livingstone, S. et al. (2013). *Connected learning: An agenda for research and design*. Irvine, CA: Digital Media and Learning Research Hub. Retrieved from http:// dmlhub.net/sites/default/files/ConnectedLearning_report.pdf

Jones, C. (2004). Networks and learning: Communities, practices and the metaphor of networks. *The Association for Learning Technology Journal, 12*(1), 82–93.

Kirkwood, A., & Price, L. (2014). Technology-enhanced learning and teaching in higher education: What is 'enhanced' and how do we know? A critical literature review. *Learning, Media and Technology, 39*(1), 6–36.

Krause, K.-L. (2007). Who is the e-generation and how are they fairing in higher education. In J. Lockard & M. Pegrum (Eds.), *Brave new classrooms: Democratic education and the Internet* (pp. 125–139). New York: Peter Lang.

Kumpulainen, K., & Sefton-Green, J. (2014). What is connected learning and how to research it? *International Journal of Learning and Media, 4*(2), 7–18.

McConnell, D., Hodgson, V., & Dirckinck-Holmfeld, L. (2012). Networked learning: A brief history and new trends. In L. Dirckinck-Holmfeld, V. Hodgson, & D. McConnell (Eds.), *Exploring the theory, pedagogy and practice of networked learning* (pp. 3–24). New York: Springer.

Plato. (2008). *Phaedrus* (B. Jowett, Trans.). Project Gutenberg. Retrieved from http://www.gutenberg.org/ebooks/1636

Reigeluth, C. M. (Ed.). (1999). *Instructional-design theories and models: A new paradigm of instructional theory* (Vol. 2). Mahwah, NJ: Lawrence Erlbaum Associates.

Sefton-Green, J. (2014). Introduction: Innovative methods for researching connected learning. *International Journal of Learning and Media, 4*(2), 1–5.

Selinger, M., & Pearson, J. (Eds.). (1999). *Telematics in education: Trends and issues.* Bingley, England: Emerald Group.

Sfard, A. (1998). On two metaphors for learning and the dangers of choosing just one. *Educational Researcher, 27*(2), 4–13.

Skinner, B. F. (1958). Teaching machines. *Science, 128*(3330), 969–977.

Steeples, C., & Jones, C. (Eds.). (2002). *Networked learning: Perspectives and issues.* London: Springer.

Sutherland, R., Eagle, S., & Joubert, M. (2012). *A vision and strategy for technology enhanced learning: Report from the STELLAR network of excellence.* Retrieved from http://www.teleurope.eu/pg/file/read/152343/a-vision-and-strategy-for-technology-enhanced-learning-report-from-the-stellar-network-of-excellence

Tyack, D., & Cuban, L. (1995). *Tinkering toward utopia: A century of public school reform.* Cambridge, MA: Harvard University Press.

Van Dijk, J. (1999). *The network society.* London: Sage (Original work published 1991).

Weller, M. (2007). *Virtual learning environments: Using, choosing and developing your VLE.* Abingdon, England: Routledge.

Wylie, C. D. (2012). Teaching manuals and the blackboard: Accessing historical classroom practices. *History of Education: Journal of the History of Education Society, 41*(2), 257–272.

Zuboff, S. (1988). *In the age of the smart machine: The future of work and power.* New York: Basic Books.

Part I
Theories and Concepts
in Networked Learning

Chapter 2
The Age of Digital Networks

This chapter examines the kind of society that has developed alongside digital and networked technologies and it discusses the role of technology and of digital technology in that society. Digital and networked technology is a recent development in terms of human history and even in terms of modern and contemporary history (Dyson 2012). What kind of society is associated with these new technologies and is that society significantly different from previous societies? How does technology interact with society? These questions have a strong relationship to learning and the way learning is located in a wider social context. The societies that emerged in the late twentieth and early twenty-first century relied on the education of vast new workforces and the reconfiguration of the existing workforces in already economically developed regions. Networked learning emerged as an idea in the context of these rapid changes, changes to social, economic and political structures and changes with regard to technologies. It is an unanswered question as to what the relationships are between one set of changes and the other. Technology arises from and is designed in society, for the existing society or its imagined future. However once deployed in the world, technologies take on a life of their own changing the societies they emerged from, often in unexpected ways, and spreading to societies that did not design or envisage a future with that technology. In these ways technologies can have a revolutionary role in social change but one that is highly contested. Do technologies drive change or are they outcomes of social processes of change? Perhaps they are both.

Change

Change is a constant and the early twentieth century was defined by wars and revolutions which continued to have ripple effects into the late twentieth century and on into the early twenty-first century. So the claim here is not that change is unique to the past 50 years rather the aim is to locate the emergence and development of the

© Springer International Publishing Switzerland 2015
C. Jones, *Networked Learning*, Research in Networked Learning,
DOI 10.1007/978-3-319-01934-5_2

idea of networked learning in a period of significant change in two potentially discrete areas, (a) society/economy/politics and (b) technology. I say potentially discrete
areas because there are few if any who would dispute the connection between one
sphere and the other, even though there are large and significant debates about what
the relationships between the two might be. For purposes of clarity the section begins
by outlining the significant changes that have taken place in society, the economy and
politics. The timescale is largely within the last 50 years; that is the period dating
from the mid-1960s, although reference is made to developments prior to that time.
This timescale is related to my personal development as much as it is to a periodiza-
tion of history because this is the time period in which the I began to be self-aware
and to engage in thinking about the issues raised in this chapter.

Society, Economy and Politics

In the mid-1960s the world was thought to be divided into blocks and it was rarely
thought of as a world system. The capitalist 'West' faced the Communist 'East' and
the others were variously described as the 'Third World' or self-organised into the
'non-aligned' movement. There has been significant debate about the ways that
military expenditure in this period interacted with the development of e-learning
(Friesen 2009, 2010). As I write globalisation is an assumption and the world system of capitalism is almost universal, there are no blocks and Communist China is
as much a part of the global market economy as any other state. Beyond the market
are just one or two 'pariah' states, such as North Korea. In the mid-1960s political
choices were made between entire systems and ideologies whereas now choices
seem to be technical and managerial rather than driven by ideological demands. The
one line on the map that still embodies the old system is the demilitarised zone
between the two Koreas, one capitalist, the other a local version of Stalinist self-
sufficiency, Juche.

The second key difference between the mid-1960s and today is the level of development of what was described in the 1960s as the 'Third World'. Development has
been uneven but there is rapid growth in most if not all major parts of the world.
Development has occurred most strikingly in China, but it is evident across East
Asia in South Korea, Singapore and increasingly Vietnam, Malaysia, Indonesia and
beyond. The designation, BRIC countries has been applied to Brazil, Russia, India
and China in an attempt to capture the growing economic powers in a single term
(O'Neil 2001). Since the designation of these emerging economies, a variety of new
terms have been coined to identify groups of other emergent nation states, most
recently MINT, Mexico, Indonesia, Nigeria and Turkey . Without delving into the
details of the developments that have taken place in different states and regions, two
key features are relevant to networked learning. The first is globalisation and the
second is the homogenisation of market cultures. Globalisation is not a smooth
process and the 'clash of civilisations' (Huntington 1993) is a claim made highlight-
ing frictions between broadly aggregated cultural blocks facing an increasingly

globalised world. Without accepting the cultural claims of Huntington, the tensions of globalisation are nevertheless clearly being played out in wars, revolts and insurrections (currently in Iraq, Ukraine, the Syrian civil war and a range of other conflicts). At the level of the market economy many global cities can be interchanged and the major shops and suppliers found on the streets and shopping Malls frequently remain the same wherever they are situated. Labour processes are also exported to new regions, not only in factories but also in services including fast-food outlets in a process described as a McDonaldisation (Ritzer 1993), which affects patterns of consumption as much as production.

Globalisation has led to the growth of cities and urban areas and around 2008/2009 the proportion of the world's population residing in urban areas increased to more than 50 % of the total population, with about 50 % of those in urban areas residing in urban areas with populations between 100 and 500 thousand. The growth of towns and cities is not currently at its most rapid, and rates of growth in urban populations seem to have peaked in the 1950s according the World Health Organisation.[1] This growth in urban populations was achieved in part by large-scale migration. Internal migrations took place within states and external migration has also taken place between states and regions of the world. The International Organisation For Migration estimates that just over 3 % of the world's population are migrants, amounting to 214 million people. The number and proportion of migrants has begun to fall in most areas of the world with only the United States and the former USSR showing an increase. The increase in the former USSR is largely a result of the redrawn boundaries following the demise of the Soviet Union.[2] In educational terms the internal movement of labour and the growth of urban areas have increased educational possibilities and the options available for study. Migration is linked not only to the movement of labour but also to the movement of students and the growth of a world market in education, either through the movement of students to educational establishments, or the building of overseas educational institutions in the developing world.

The globalisation and development of the world economy has taken place in the political and economic context of an apparent resurgence of market capitalism, often described using the term neoliberalism (Fuchs 2008; Harvey 2005). Neoliberalism has come to mean the kind of deregulated capitalism first implemented following the coup and dictatorship of Pinochet in Chile in the mid-1970s and it includes an open market, a dominant private sector and a minimal state. These characteristics and the broad neoliberal agenda later became associated with Anglo Saxon capitalism by association with the political policies and open endorsements of Ronald Reagan (USA) and Margaret Thatcher (UK). While neoliberal capitalism has dominated intellectually it is important to note that in practice the state has continued to have an enormously important, if not dominant role, even in those

---

[1] Figures obtained from the World health Organisation: http://www.who.int/gho/urban_health/situation_trends/urban_population_growth_text/en/

[2] Figures obtained from the International organisation for Migration: http://www.iom.int/cms/en/sites/iom/home/about-migration/factsDOUBLEHYPHENfigures-1/global-estimates-and-trends.html

countries adopting an explicitly neoliberal agenda. Indeed some commentators have noted that the new world system is 'socialism for the rich' in which:

> Even though the ideology of the Establishment passionately abhors statism, business elites are completely dependent on the largesse of the state (Jones 2014, p. 179).

Education, and how it is paid for, is a key part of this contradiction between state support for the infrastructure of business and private enterprise and a laissez-faire market ideology. More broadly the world continues to show signs of what the Economist and some left wing and Marxist analysts call 'state capitalism' (Economist 2012). Many enterprises in the world economy are state owned rather than privately owned and the state continues to dominate in some spheres of economic activity by regulation, via state investment companies, and direct legislation. The interplay of market and state is an important feature of education which largely remains either in state control or under strict regulation by the state. This issue is closely related to the process of globalisation and the internationalisation of education because large multinational companies (e.g. Pearson and Laureate) are interested in entering the previously state dominated national education systems, especially the higher education sector.

Related to the dominance of neoliberal capitalism and the revised role for the state that comes with it, inequality has increased in the twenty-first century (Picketty 2014). Picketty argues that capital accumulates more rapidly than the economy in capitalist societies and that this pattern, visible in the nineteenth century, has reasserted its dominance since the 1980s when neoliberal policies led to the lifting of controls on capital. In brief, Picketty argues that financial inequality is rising and it is doing so at a very dangerous pace. Castells who is so closely associated with the idea of network society has long argued that the rise of the information society is closely connected to rising inequality and social exclusion at a global scale (Castells 2000a). Castells presents an image of simultaneous development and underdevelopment, social inclusion and exclusion, taking place both within states and between states at a global level. His argument concludes that despite the evidence of rapid development, and as a consequence of global processes related to network society, there is a growth in poverty and misery in the world at large.

A further aspect of politics and society is the interplay between markets, hierarchies and networks (Thompson et al. 1991). The overall changes in the structure of the economy and the political ideas informing recent developments are reflected in new policy and management styles and structures (Rhodes 1997). Networks have become a focus for analysis as a counterpoint to simple hierarchies and markets (Castells 2000b/1996; Van Dijk 1999/1991). Bureaucracy and classic hierarchical forms of organisation are familiar forms in popular discourse and we are also familiar with the mechanisms of the market. It is less common to think of networks as an alternative form of coordination with their own mechanisms, such as relations of trust and cooperation. Networks are not an exclusive form and markets and hierarchies can be thought of, and described as types of networks. They can also be described as containing various networks and networks in this view are just one way of describing and analysing the coordination of social life (Thompson et al. 1991). Rhodes draws our attention to another common term used in contemporary debate about political systems, governance. Rhodes focuses on what he describes as the mesolevel of analysis located within a macrolevel theory of the state (1991). The kind of policy networks Rhodes describes conform to the neoliberal minimal state, the related development of 'New Public Management', and self-governing interorganisational networks that can span public bodies or combine a mix of public and private entities. The hollowing out of the state that Rhodes points to is a process that goes both upward and downward, upward to multinational bodies, including formal political bodies such as the European Union, and downward to new agencies at a local, regional, and substate level. This concern with new forms of public management and mesolevels of organisation will be developed in later chapters in relation to networked learning.

Technology and Change

Technology and social change have a close but disputed relationship, with technology often described in ways that suggest it has an autonomous existence independent of society. Although currently associated with a Californian free-wheeling neoliberal (if not libertarian) capitalism, the technology of computing has its roots in Second World War cryptography and the military-industrial complex of the Cold War (Dyson 2012). Technology in the early twenty-first century carries with it the political and economic debates of the late twentieth century, both in its origins and in its supposed effects. The technology that is now taken for granted is in fact a combination of ideas that arise separately. The idea that information can be coded into zeroes and ones dates back to the seventeenth century and mathematical work by Hobbes and Leibniz (Dyson 1999, 2012). The calculating device goes back to designs by Babbage and there were mechanical computing devices constructed as recently as the 1950s (Dyson 1999). In 1835 Babbage even conceived of a mechanical communications network operating over steel wires with repeater stations acting as nodes every 5 miles and foresaw that the physical movement of paper might be supplanted by telegraphic communication (Dyson 1999). What we now take to be the 'computer' and related information and communication technologies are an evolutionary outcome, an aggregation of ideas and technological forms that could have developed differently. It was not until after the Second World War that the technology even settled on a digital rather than an analogue form and there are those who want to return to analogue computing today (Dyson 2012). Technology has its own separable history, but the relationship between that history and broader social change forms the basis of much of the section that follows.

Technology and Society

The change in technology has a link to changes in society but the nature of that link has been a subject of intense speculation. Earlier theories that focused on the effects of technology on society were challenged by theories that focused on the effects of society on the design and development of technology. Before examining these debates it is worth pausing for a moment to consider what we mean when we use the term technology and where technology fits into thinking about politics and society. A standard dictionary definition of the word usually includes the idea of an applied art or craft and the usage of science for practical purposes. One of the features of technology currently discussed is the relationship of technology to the material world. It is clear that hammers, wrenches and even digital devices such as tablet computers are material technologies, but it less clear that entities such as computer programmes and organisational protocols are also material technologies. This of course matters to networked learning. The question of whether technology can be 'immaterial' is important because we are an era in which there is an explosion of apparently immaterial technology. The collection of standards and protocols that underpin the Internet and World Wide Web are examples of what is claimed to be immaterial technology. Firstly it is important to note that technologies, even when apparently immaterial rely on material infrastructures, cables and servers or papers and pens, because to be a technology means having a capacity to extend over space and time. These technologies are material in the sense that they exhibit spatial (location and mass) and temporal (stability) attributes. Secondly technologies are increasingly capable of manipulating matter so that even the matter which composes a technology can now be designed or manipulated to provide desired characteristics. Thirdly the material and the technological are not coextensive, not all material artefacts are technologies, even if all technologies are material in some part. So it is clear that matter has an important place in discussing technology, but its place is currently contested and I will return to the question of materiality and technology at various stages in the book (For a fuller discussion of these issues see Leonardi et al. 2012).

Reviewing the use of the term technology in organisational research and more broadly in general usage Orlikowski and Scott (2008) argued that:

> Developing a singular or definitive definition of technology is… inherently problematic, and it may be more useful to understand this term as theoretically and historically contingent (ibid, p. 437).

In place of providing a particular definition Orlikowski and Scott chose to point to the definitions found in existing literature. This approach suggests an historical dimension to defining the term, with technology having particular meanings for different discourses and at different times. Arthur adds to this historical dimension by offering a distinct evolutionary approach to technology. He argues that technologies have a combination principle; they are composed of combinations of existing technologies and they are evolutionary in the sense that they are related by their ties of common descent from prior technologies. After arguing that current definitions of technology are not only diverse but also in conflict with each other Arthur provides three complementary definitions of technology (Arthur 2009). He argues that three definitions are required to cover this single term because they point to different categories of technology, each with their own origins and evolutionary paths. The definitions Arthur provides are:

1. Technology as a means to fulfill a human purpose
2. Technology as an assemblage of practices and components
3. Technology as the entire collection of devices and engineering practices available to a culture (adapted from Arthur 2009, p. 28)

Although I accept Orlikowski and Scott's caution about the difficulties in providing a definition I find the triple definition provided by Arthur useful and I will return to it in later chapters of the book particular when discussing infrastructure and the use of the term assemblage (Chaps. 6 and 9). Its importance lies in the evolutionary processes it identifies in all three definitions. Furthermore the three-part definition addresses issues raised by the significant variation scale when discussing different technologies and the variability of the term in day-to-day use while it adds a useful layer of precision to thinking about the term technology.

Technology is not only varied because of its historical and evolutionary nature but also because technologies are the outcome of political processes (Winner 1986). Feenberg (1991) argues that:

> … technology is not a destiny but a scene of struggle. It is a social battlefield, or perhaps a better metaphor would be a parliament of things on which civilizational alternatives are debated and decided (Feenberg 1991, p. 14).

Feenberg's argument that technologies are a site of social struggle, challenges the view that technology is simply a means to an end. In educational terms the idea that technology is a means to an end gives rise to the idea that technologies can 'deliver' something, for example content or pedagogy without affecting what is delivered. Feenberg's argument is that technology has influence and for the reason it should be opened up to politics because democratic principles require *technological* as well as political change. Technology in this view is not determining nor is it neutral because it is part of a politically charged and contested process. Feenberg's argument raises the much broader question of whether technology has effects or whether conversely it is socially shaped and reflects its origins.

Technology, Determinism and Social Shaping

Technological change is often seen as arising independently in society and then having an impact on other dependent domains. In this common sense argument, technology is seen as having discernible effects and of being a force that can change society in definable ways (Selwyn 2011). Technology to have this autonomous capacity is also described as standing outside of normal social processes and being driven by its own internal logic. This is what is meant by the term technological determinism. Technological determinism can be articulated in either hard or soft forms. Hard forms of determinism argue that technology changes society directly whereas softer forms argue that technologies imply social changes but indirectly, often through better ways to adopt or integrate the technology. Examples of direct determination in education include the idea of 'digital natives' being the direct consequence of the large-scale introduction of digital technologies (see Chap. 8). Examples of soft determinism argue that if educators are to work with digital and networked technologies then one or another specified approach is better than the alternatives. Soft determinism argues that in some way the technology requires a defined kind of practice to accommodate it. Technological determinism in either form is widely criticised and it is currently a largely discredited academic outlook (Oliver 2011). However it remains common in policy discussion and in popular discourse about particular technological innovations, for examples see Jones (2011) for a discussion of technological determinism in relation to the digital native thesis.

In part in reaction to the prevalence of determinism an alternative set of theories were developed, inspired by the sociology of scientific knowledge (SSK) (Barnes et al. 1996). These various theories were brought together under the banner of the social shaping of technology (MacKenzie and Wajcman 1999). Despite the variations between a number of contending outlooks all of them argued that technologies were created, designed and used within a particular society and that the kinds of technologies that emerged reflected the societies they came from in significant ways.

> Technologies do not have a momentum of their own at the outset that allows them to pass through a neutral social medium. Rather they are subject to contingency as they pass from figurative hand to hand, and so are shaped and reshaped (Bijker and Law 1992, p. 8).

The banner of social shaping disguises a variety of underpinning standpoints and one of the most pervasive of these is social constructivism (Brey 1997; Leonardi and Barley 2010). Social constructivism is a broad philosophic standpoint that has also had a significant influence in learning theory (see Chap. 3). Social constructivism is also a contested theory, even by some of those who are called social constructivists by others, for example Latour (Latour 2005; Harman 2009). The idea of social shaping was closely related to the development of an area of social science specifically focused on studies of science and technology (SST). This area is also described variously as the Social Construction of Technology (SCOT) (Pinch and Bijker 1987) and Science and Technology Studies or Science, Technology and Society (STS) (Hacket et al. 2008). A core belief held by these different approaches was the need for detailed empirical studies of technology, its design, development and use. Some versions of SST are based on strong ontological and epistemological positions. The early origins of SST in the sociology of scientific knowledge linked the idea to the relativism of what was called 'the strong programme' (Bloor 1991 [1976]). More recently relativism has been developed in terms of ontologies (Mol 2002; Van Heur et al. 2013; Woolgar and Lezauan 2013). On the opposing side there are amended forms of realism (e.g. critical realism) and the very particular realism claimed by Latour (Harman 2009; Latour 2005). Some of these theories are dealt with more fully elsewhere in Chaps. 3 and 4, but for the discussion here the most important feature of these developments was the way social shaping directed attention towards either the social forces affecting the design and development of technologies, and /or the ways in which technologies once designed were taken up by their users (Hacket et al. 2008).

The recent turn towards materiality and the sociomaterial has added to the discussion of technology by pointing to the ways in which technologies have to be considered as material as well as social in character (Fenwick 2012; Fenwick et al. 2011). In this view the material is more than a context which is to be interacted with, or tools to be used to enable certain outcomes, the material is an active force shaping practice. The material turn moves on from the social and cultural turn and the social shaping of technology and it also coincides with a debate about ontology in the study of technology. The idea of materiality and its relationship to ontology are discussed further in relation to learning (Chap. 3) and in the context of ANT (Chap. 4). A crude but illuminating sequence can be elaborated in which the move from technological determinist concerns with the *effects* of technology leads on to ideas about the social shaping of technology. Social shaping places an emphasis on the ways that technologies come to be the way that they are and the ways that technologies are taken up. The emphasis is on the *design* and development of technologies and the ways that they are subsequently deployed and taken into use. The material turn adds a further consideration by offering the possibility of a *co-construction* between materials, material technology and social practice throughout the lifetime of a technology. In this view technologies have their own history and evolve (Arthur 2009), and technologies are an imbrication of humans and things, of intentionality and material agency. Inevitably this displaces the human actor from centre stage and draws attention to a range of forces including humans, non-humans (animals, machines and things) and assemblages of humans and non-humans (complex sociotechnical systems). In this view technologies are just one kind of material artefact and because they are material they are resistant, or pushback, when they interact with other technologies, with people and with assemblages of the two. In actor-network theory things are thought of as actants or actors in their own right with agency of their own. Technology when considered in its material aspect can be thought of as including the social in its origins and in the ways it is used, and at the same time as having *effects* that allow for (afford) and/or constrain certain practices (Cornford and Pollock 2002).

Affordances and Constraints

Technologies as material entities are designed with purposes in mind and they embody properties and features that are intended to be taken up in particular kinds of use. As Hutchby noted:

> The concept of affordance has been applied to technology in the sense that: technologies possess different affordances, and these affordances constrain the ways that they can possibly be 'written' or 'read' (Hutchby 2001, p. 447).

In Hutchby's approach technologies 'possess' affordances but as I have already argued the properties of technologies are not themselves determinants of the uses made of them. However later I discuss the ways that certain features of technologies can become available as affordances or constraints in use, and the ways that the presence of these features makes certain kinds of practice more or less likely to occur than others. The idea of affordance and the related idea of constraint have been used to reintroduce the role of technology as having effects on social life. Change related to technology ceases to be a purely socially driven and intentional process and social action is seen to take place in material contexts that have implications for the range of options that are available. Affordances and constraints can be thought of as *relational* properties that are not essential characteristics of an object, technological artefact or system, rather they are thought of as emerging from the interactions between different elements. This way of thinking is rooted in a Gibson's work and a broadly ecological stance. The ecological outlook provided Gibson with a basis for describing relationships in a way that cuts across traditional dualities such as subject and object (Gibson 1977, 1986/1979). Affordances provide an account of environmental attributes as relative to a living organism, affordances don't simply reside in the environment they are affordances *for* this or that organism. The implication is that the idea of affordance places subjective interpretations into relationship with an objective physical world.

> The affordance of something does not change as the need of the observer changes. The observer may or may not perceive or attend to the affordance, according to his needs but the affordance, being invariant is always there to be perceived. An affordance is not bestowed upon an object by a need of an observer and his (sic) act of perceiving it. The object offers what it does because it is what it is (Gibson 1986/1979, pp. 138–139).

In this account affordances are relational but also real, independent of the act of perception. This allows for an affordance to be latent (hidden), a possibility in the environment even if it is not actually perceived (Gaver 1991, 1996). An example of a latent affordance is one in which there is no perceptual indication that the affordance exists. It could be nested, hidden beneath an affordance that can be perceived or simply arrived at by chance. A hidden door or draw in a piece of furniture is a case of an affordance being deliberately obscured, but available to those who know of its existence, or potentially stumbled on by chance. The idea of affordance thus has both a relational focus and a realist implication.

The idea of affordance was popularised by Norman's application of the term to the design and use of artefacts (Norman 1988) and the concept of affordance became integrated into studies of Human–Computer Interaction (HCI). The significance of Norman's work was the application of the idea of affordance to the design of everyday things. Here was a theory that looked for ways to make the technologies and artefacts we meet all the time, such as doors and microwave ovens, understandable and usable. Norman like Gibson was very concerned with the visible structure of things and how design could render itself visible (or audible in some cases). Gibson's concept of affordance differs in significant ways from Norman's application of the term (1990, 1999).

...the term affordance refers to the perceived and actual properties of the thing, primarily those fundamental properties that determine just how the thing could possibly be used (Norman 1988, p. 9).

Norman develops an essentialist approach in which affordances are fundamental properties, whereas Gibson makes no such distinction because he views affordance as being relational between things and their potential users. The affordances of the same stone can be as a vantage point to a small mammal, a heat source to a reptile and a hiding place to an insect. Norman removes this relational aspect and makes affordance a fixed property. Secondly Norman makes affordance relative to perception. Gibson holds that although relational an affordance is fixed and does not vary with the needs of the observer. For Norman affordance becomes a dualist concept in which perception takes on a different role because affordances are fundamental to the thing and the user is active in perceiving those already determined affordances. Norman's interpretation of affordance led to disagreements about the ontological nature and the epistemological status of an affordance. One fundamental difference concerns whether a distinction should be drawn between 'real affordances' and 'perceived affordances' (Norman 1999).

The designer cares more about what actions the user perceives to be possible than what is true. Moreover, affordances, both real and perceived, play very different roles in physical products than they do in the world of screen-based products. In the latter case, affordances play a relatively minor role: cultural conventions are much more important (Norman 1999, p. 39).

For Norman affordances were fundamental features and perception revealed them, the 'real' affordance was the functionality, the perceived affordance was the way this was identified and accessed. It is notable in the context of networked learning that the spur to clarifying this distinction was the design of computer interfaces which Norman noted relied strongly on cultural conventions.

Gaver like Norman took the idea of affordance away from its origin in ecological perception and applied it to technology and HCI. He argued that affordances were properties of the world that were related to people's interactions in ways that were compatible and relevant. In this way he retained Gibson's relational concerns because a real affordance was not a fundamental feature of a thing, it was those aspects of a thing relevant and compatible with the related person. Gaver drew a distinction between affordances that were perceptible and those that were hidden and false. A perceived affordance could be accessed directly whereas hidden or false affordances could lead to mistakes (Fig. 2.1).

Perhaps the most interesting contribution Gaver made was to analyse complex actions in relation to affordance and to suggest that they could be understood in terms of 'groups of affordances that are sequential in time or nested in space' (Gaver 1991, p. 79). The idea of sequential affordance is that action on a perceptible affordance can lead on to information about a previously unperceived or hidden affordance so that an affordance can be revealed over time. Gaver (1991) also develops the idea of affordances being nested that is of affordances being grouped in space.

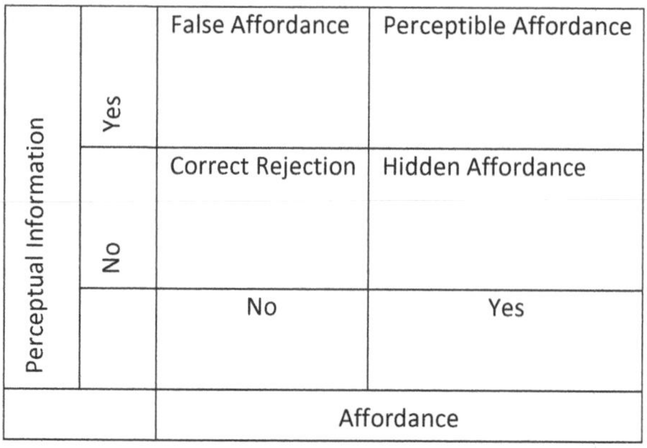

		False Affordance	Perceptible Affordance
Perceptual Information	Yes		
		Correct Rejection	Hidden Affordance
	No		
		No	Yes
		Affordance	

Fig. 2.1 Separating affordances from the information available about them. Adapted from Gaver (1991), p. 80

> ...the nested affordance offers itself as an end in itself and as a means towards realizing another affordance (Gaver 1991, p. 94).

A very useful summary and discussion of the development of the idea of affordance and its application to HCI can be found in McGrenere and Ho (2000).

McGrenere and Ho (2000), emphasise the need to re-introduce and further develop the original Gibsonian concept of affordance by acknowledging that an expanded notion of affordance was required which acknowledged the existence of varying degrees of affordance (McGrenere and Ho 2000). Torenvliet observed that Gibson's view was that affordance was a characteristic of the environment that existed relative to an object, but that it existed independently of perception (Torenvliet 2003). Gibson's approach was based on the idea of direct perception, the idea that there is a perception-action link and the relationship between organism and environment was not mediated by cognitive processes. It is important to note that the idea of direct perception does not rule out learning:

> Direct perception depends on the actor's 'picking up' the information that specifies the affordance and may depend on the actor's experiences and culture. Let us be clear, the existence of the affordance is independent of the actor's experiences and culture, whereas the ability to perceive the affordance may be dependent on these. Thus, an actor may need to learn to discriminate the information in order to perceive directly. In this way learning can be seen as a process of discriminating patterns in the world, rather than one of supplementing sensory information with past experience (McGrenere and Ho 2000, p. 180).

The idea of direct perception remains controversial and Gregory, for example, argues that perception is indirect (Gregory 1997; Gregory and Wallace 2001/1963). Gregory and Wallace report a case study of a person who had been blind from 10 months who regained his sight after 50 years (Gregory and Wallace 2001/1963). They argued that although the subject of the case came to use vision, his ideas of the world arose from touch and there was a 'direct' transfer of information from touch to vision once sight was regained.

> We may conclude that this case does provide evidence of transfer of perceptual information from the tactual sphere to the visual modality. This seems somewhat at variance with the evidence from studies of cross-modal transfer in animals and we can only speculate as to the reasons for the discrepancy. It maybe that language is the decisive factor (Gregory and Wallace 2001/1963, p. 37)

The importance of this finding is that it suggests a history, that perceptions at one point in time are related to previous experiences, even when those experiences involve senses related to another mode (touch rather than vision). Gregory's general position is that perception depends very largely on knowledge derived from past experience (Gregory 1997).

It should be noted that Gregory's argument does not contradict the position outlined by McGrenere and Ho (above) who acknowledge that perception could indeed be influenced by prior learning. An example of the potential importance of historical experience when dealing with newer technologies was provided by Kaptelinin and Hedestig (2009). Using the concept of affordance they pointed out the difficulties that occurred when teacher activity, grounded in previous and different practices, was carried over into a new learning environment based on the decentralised use of videoconferencing. The case study suggested that most of the breakdowns they observed could be explained as being the result of 'hidden' affordances (there were possibilities for action but they are not perceived by the participants) and 'false' affordances (the participants perceived non-existent possibilities for action). They argued that the separation of affordance from perception and culture was incompatible with the thrust of Gibson's approach. Drawing on the case study they demonstrated that the knowledge and skills teachers had developed in previous settings were mobilised in the new technologically mediated one. In this case study the way teachers drew on this prior knowledge often led to breakdowns in the new setting.

Criticisms of Affordances

The concept of affordance and the related idea of constraint have been discussed in various contexts and the focus here is on the challenges that have focused clearly on technology (see for example Hutchby 2001; Rappert 2003; Hutchby 2003). Two articles stand out in this regard in terms of educational technology, Oliver (2005) and Derry (2007). Oliver argues that the concept of affordance has drifted and that it is now too ambiguous to be useful. He goes on to say that because the concept has its origins in ecological perception, and primitive claims about animal-object relations, it has little direct relevance to interactions between a person and a specific artefact. Oliver sets out the essentials of Gibson's position on affordance and then articulates what he considers to be the three available accounts that could make sense of Gibson's claim that affordances are neither objective nor subjective. He finds none of these accounts satisfactory concluding later that:

> One line of development is consistent with Gibson's original position, although arguably these refinements have not countered problems with its relevance to learning. This tradition is positivistic and essentialist, at odds with contemporary educational thought (Oliver 2005, p. 410).

Later Oliver suggested in his discussion of technological determinism that:

Affordance neatly illustrates the concept of technological determinism, which has been widely explored in the field of science and technology studies. This is the belief that technology shapes society in some way... (Oliver 2011, p. 374)

Oliver argues that any account based on Gibson's version of affordance is going to be essentialist, positivist and technological determinist. All in all this is quite a charge sheet and Oliver explicitly references one of my own early attempts to clarify the use of the term:

Jones (2005) argues that it is possible to overcome these difficulties by emphasising the nondualist, realist and relational nature of affordances. However, this position does not address either of the two main critiques offered. No ontological explanation is provided of what this relationship between animal and environment consists of... Second, the assumption that a totalising 'view from nowhere' can be inferred from specific perceived instances fails to account for the idea that affordances might exist but never be perceived, and is also an epistemologically suspect inferential move (Oliver 2005, p. 410).

In these arguments I think Oliver misses some fundamental points that have their roots in Gibson's own accounts and these are magnified by the way Oliver overlays his argument with an explicit preference for constructivist accounts, positioned against a weak positivist opponent. Firstly Gibson's own account is relational without invoking cognition. That is an affordance is only an affordance *for* something or someone and it is therefore relational in character. A technology can have an affordance for teachers and different affordances for a student. Secondly because in Gibson's account an affordance has reality apart from the perception of the affordance there is no problem in principle with an affordance 'never' being perceived. Furthermore Oliver positions the argument as being between positivist or constructivist alternatives and fails to see the possibility of a third option, one offered by sociomateriality (for more on this see Chap. 4). I think one aspect of Oliver's conflation of affordance with technological determinism is that he fuses materialism with determinism, although it is well known that the equation of materialism with determinism is not a sustainable position (Leonardi and Barley 2008). I argue below that the idea of affordance can allow for a non-deterministic understanding of the ways in which technologies, although socially constructed, are real and have material effects or consequences.

Derry's argument is that the term affordance has moved from its specific place in ecological psychology into a loosely defined vernacular use. Derry noted that affordance was used in an essentialist manner which suggested affordances were inherent in technologies.

Rather than speaking in general terms of how ICT may offer or afford opportunities when used within carefully designed educational contexts, the authors prefer the use of the technical noun 'affordance', a word made up by Gibson to communicate the possibility of direct perception of meaning. This alters the focus of attention and contributes to the view that technologies can offer educational advantages independently of the individuals engaging with them for specific purposes (Derry 2007, p. 504).

Derry's critique draws on a strong version of Gregory's argument about indirect perception which suggests that a prerequisite of perception is prior knowledge leading to predictive hypotheses (Derry 2007). It also slides away from Gibson's own accounts when it suggests affordance leads to the 'direct perception of meaning'. Gibson was concerned with action, not meaning and he expresses strong opinions with regard to accounts of perception which rely on meaning. It is central to a Gibsonian account that affordances have real qualities that remain invariant whatever the observer's requirements. Indeed Oliver in his own critique of Gibson drew attention to this when he notes that Gibson's view was that:

> The world is specified in the structure of the light that reaches us, but it is entirely up to us to perceive it (Gibson 1986/1979, p. 63).

Oliver's conclusion is that this is a comment about the transparency of information and he goes on to say that Gibson begs the question about what the relationship consists of in the interaction between organism and environment.

My own reading of Gibson is that his suggestion is that the relationship is real, that both parts are real entities, separate from each other and neither party is dependent on the other perceiving it. However an affordance requires complementarity between the parties. In perceptual terms if there is light emission or reflection from one then the other party needs receptors to 'see' it. It also requires complementarity between the parties for there to be a relationship and an affordance at all. Gibson's original notion of affordance relied on the possibilities for action in an environment. The objective properties of the setting are relational to the action possibilities of an actor or agent but the properties of the setting are independent of the perceptions, needs and intentions of the actor or agent. The same set of objective properties can have quite different affordances for the same agent, for example water in a lake can afford swimming and it can also afford drowning to the same person. Perception, needs and intentions might be independent of any particular affordance, but they are usually closely related. In Gibson's ecological theory, affordances were not important in themselves but they provided a basis for his account of perception. The role affordances have taken in relation to studies of technology in HCI and educational technology is quite different to this original usage. Gibson's theory made no distinction between different kinds of organism, e.g. between humans and animals and by extension the theory of affordance can be extended beyond organisms to machines and hybrid assemblages of humans and machines. This is consistent with Gibson's insistence that there is only 'one world' and that:

> It is a mistake to separate the natural from the artificial as if there were two environments: artefacts have to be manufactured from natural substances. It is also a mistake to separate the cultural environment from the natural environment, as if there were a world of mental products distinct from the world of material products. There is only one world, however diverse, and all animals live in it, although we human animals have altered it to suit ourselves (Gibson 1986/1979, p. 130).

Gibson's conception of affordance provides a starting point for a conception of affordance that is useful when examining educational technology from the standpoint of the materiality of networked learning. However the role of culture, history and memory need further consideration for a more consistent application to the use of technology for learning.

Kaptelinin and Nardi write from a Human–Computer Interaction (HCI) background but HCI, like networked learning, is a field concerned with advanced, rapidly developing mediational means and the limitation they identify significantly undermines Gibson's theory of affordance in terms of its ability to serve as a theoretical foundation for studying the action possibilities offered by technologies to humans (Kaptelinin and Nardi 2012). They propose that to understand technological affordances it is necessary to adopt a mediated human action perspective. Significantly in the context of arguments presented in this volume they acknowledge that their approach is currently focused on individual action and that the next step would be to extend the approach to collective action. This is especially so in the context of networked learning.

Kaptelinin and Nardi's approach provides a useful link between the Gibsonian conception of affordance and theories of action with advanced technology. The activity theory influenced view of affordance is non-essentialist, non-dualist and it is critical of both an information processing (cognitivist) and a simple direct understanding of perception. They argue that affordances can be discerned as a set of potentials in a relationship between different elements of a setting whether or not the prospective user of an affordance perceives or understands their meaning. This view of affordance suggests that it is possible to analytically discern features of a technology in relation to potential users apart from the actual understandings and perceptions of particular groups of users. As a consequence this allows the theory to explain the potential for the use of the term hidden affordance. A significant difference between my own view and that offered by Kaptelinin and Nardi is that they do not clearly distinguish between the properties or features of a technology and its affordances. In contrast I argue that a technology has describable properties or features, but these are not in themselves affordances. Affordances are relational between the properties and features of the technology and the properties or features of the organism, person or machine making interacting with it. A second difference I have with Kaptelinin and Nardi is that they restrict their conception of affordance to human action and I argue that this is problematic when dealing with complex technologies that have forms of secondary agency or when dealing with hybrids or assemblages composed of humans and machines. While their argument holds broadly it is possible to think of circumstances in which human–machine combinations are the actors and in which the second order nature of affordance is still relevant.

Although the idea of affordance when applied to educational technology has been criticised for being inconsistently and often inappropriately applied (Oliver 2005; Derry 2007; Wright and Parchoma 2011) I want to conclude this section by providing a defence of the term. My argument is that affordance is a necessary and useful term because it points to the materiality of technology and the limits this materiality places on interpretation. Affordance is a term that can bridge the division between objectivist realism and relativist constructivism. As Hutchby puts it, the technologies materiality constrains the ways it can be read or written (2001). Hutchby argued that technologies *possess* affordances and this approach feeds into the essentialising of what I argue is a relational property between the technology and the user. However both the relationship and the affordance have reality and they can constrain activity in the way Hutchby suggests. The reality is not possessed by the technology alone but it resides in the relationship between the technology and its user(s). It is this separation between the technology and the affordance which is critical because this is the reason why affordance, properly understood, is far from the determinist caricature portrayed by Oliver (2011). Gibson's original notion of affordance relied upon a relatively simple conception of activity and there is a useful critique of the way affordance has been interpreted, arising from activity theory, which provides a more sophisticated account of action (Kaptelinin and Nardi 2012).

Knowledge, Technology and Society

The previous sections have briefly examined the way that society has changed in the past 50 years and the way technologies have also undergone a process of change. The arguments have been non-deterministic and it has been argued that social change has not been caused or determined by technology but equally technology has not been the outcome of social processes alone. Instead the chapter has argued for an emergent materialism, an understanding of technology as having material form that has a co-constructive role with social practice in an historical and evolutionary development. The final step in the argument was to review the idea of affordance and to argue that this concept can provide the basis for understanding how technology, understood as material, can afford or constrain activity. This final main section of the chapter leads on towards Chap. 3 which examines theories of learning, by exploring how the changes in society and technology have been implicated in the production, storage and distribution of knowledge in society. The entire period covered by this book has seen popular descriptions of society focused on 'information' and knowledge with various kinds of theories about what has been characterised as the information society (Webster 2006). More recent theories have been focused, by advocates and critics, not simply on information but the contemporary infrastructure that supports information flows, the Internet, Web and more recently Web 2.0 (see for example, Fuchs 2008; Rainie and Wellman 2012; Bakardjieva 2005; Morozov 2011, 2013). In what follows there is a key issue that develops from the earlier accounts of change in society and the economy, and in technological change, and that issue is choice. If society and technology are neither determined nor determining what are the choices that can be made and who can make them? Will these choices reply on individuals, the crowd, or collective organisations?

Knowledge, Work and Network Society

There is a long-standing debate in the social sciences about whether contemporary society can be classified by the relationships society has to information (Webster 2006). Starting with ideas about an economy moving from reliance on material goods to one based on knowledge (Drucker 1969) and a shift from an industrial economy to one based on services requiring information as a resources rather than muscle, power or energy (Bell 1973). The idea moved on to the post-industrial society (Touraine 1971) which emphasised the production of symbolic goods rather than either material goods or services. Eventually it could be argued that:

> It is widely acknowledged that knowledge has become the principle force of production over the last few decades (Lyotard 1984, p. 5).

For Lyotard the post-industrial economy was accompanied by what he described as a post-modern culture. The importance of this developing and wide-ranging body of ideas, which I have barely touched on above, is to draw out the way it places at centre stage the role of knowledge in society and the economy. This theoretical thrust should not be accepted uncritically and many of the predictions based on such theories look distinctly odd to a contemporary eye. For example Lyotard having made the case for the centrality of knowledge goes on to say on the very same page that because of these changes the gap between the developed and developing countries will grow ever wider. In light of the subsequent growth of China and the other BRIC countries this now seems to be a major error because the capacity to distribute knowledge and the spread of new technologies (not simply cheap labour) has enabled enormous economic development in the following 30 years. The following sections will review perhaps the most pertinent and most developed version of the theories of an information society, the idea of Network Society (Castells 2000b/1996; Castells 2001; Van Dijk 1999/1991). The sections explore how knowledge is implicated in contemporary society, how work and the workforce are evolving and the way machines, specifically those using digital and networked technologies are imbricated (interwoven like tiles overlapping on a roof) in these changes.

Network Society

The change described by Castells using the phrase network society suggests that it is not just that education and learning are required for work in an Internet- and Web-based economy, but that network society also changes the character of the learning that is required. Learning via networks can be moved from retention to learning-to-learn. As access to information becomes more available the learner needs to develop the capacity to know what to learn, how to discriminate between sources, how to retrieve, process and reuse information and knowledge for the task in hand. This view of the relationship between network society and knowledge is similar to that found in the work of Van Dijk (1999/1991), although Van Dijk expresses some concerns about the tendency towards technological determinism found in Castells work. It also provides a direct link to the development of the idea of networked learning. Early writers in the field of networked learning had a vision that went beyond education and learning and described a 'Network Nation' (Hiltz and Turoff 1978). These authors were amongst the first wave of writers focused on the possibilities of online or networked learning. They envisaged ways in which the then new information and communications technologies could be applied to education and learning in novel ways that took learning out of the classroom (see Harasim 2012, pp. 84–87 for a brief history from a US perspective). Network society impacts on knowledge and learning by: (a) changing the amount of information that is available; (b) by changing the type of much communication to multimodal texts; (c) by changing the ways that educational and learning practices can be conducted.

The publication of Manuel Castells trilogy The Information Age over the years 1996–1998 took the understanding of the way knowledge, information, technology and society interacted on from earlier discussions of information society (Webster 2006). Whatever the flaws of this work it was the culmination of 25 years social research and it is all-encompassing in its scale and ambition. The term network society derives both from the first volume of Castells' trilogy (2000b/1996) and the work of Van Dijk (1999/1991). The idea has since been taken up widely and it informs a wide variety of topics including education. Castells introduced the term informationalism to identify:

> The action of knowledge upon knowledge itself as the main source of productivity (Castells 2000b/1996, p. 17),

He argues that this change modifies both the economy and society, but he does not go on to suggest that the new arrangements mean the end of capitalism. In the new economy, profit seeking private ownership of the means of production and the market still prevail. This socioeconomic system might be networked but it remains capitalist. Informational capitalism via its network structure combines enormous flexibility with global extension, well beyond the possibilities of previous periods of capitalism.

> It is a hardened form of capitalism in its goals but it is incomparably more flexible than any of its predecessors in its means. It is informational capitalism, relying on innovation-induced productivity and globalisation-oriented competitiveness to generate wealth, and to appropriate it selectively. It is more than ever, embedded in culture and tooled by technology. But, this time, both culture and technology depend on the ability of knowledge and information to act upon knowledge and information, in a recurrent network of global exchanges (Castells 2000/1998, p. 369).

Castells 'it should be noted' does not suggest that the forces of capitalism and technology, or the forces of individuals and the state, can set the agenda by themselves. He also credits change to the social movements of the late 1960s and those following them up to the present day.

The network society is a society in which the core social activities and structures are organised via electronically processed information networks. The network society cannot be reduced to either networks or to social networks, because both networks and social networks have long histories which predate digital technologies. The defining characteristics of network society are the kinds of social networks which process and manage information using micro-electronics-based digital technologies. It is important to note that Castells also distances himself from radical notions of an information or knowledge society because information and knowledge have been decisive in all aspects of previous societies. The defining characteristic of network society requires the necessary but not sufficient condition of digital networks. These digital technologies are described as social outcomes and not as an autonomous development. In relation to the Internet Castells points out that:

> The history of the Internet provides ample evidence that the users, particularly the first thousands of users, were, to a large extent, the producers of the technology (Castells and Cardoso 2005, p. 3).

A second defining feature of network society is its global nature. Networks are extensible and do not respect boundaries, the network society is based on global networks, but these do not extend to all people. While network society covers the entire planet and influences all global developments, currently the majority of the world's population remain excluded in network society (this despite rapid changes such as the extensive diffusion of mobile telecommunications in the most remote and economically deprived regions). Inequality and exclusion remain problems in network society, both within and between states. The network society is not set out as a goal or an objective, it is proposed as a description of the logic and morphology of contemporary society. The approach adopted by those who describe society in terms of networks, has been criticised by Fuchs as presenting the problems found in network society as inevitable and something which people have to adapt to rather than challenge and change (Fuchs 2008). My personal view is that some of Fuchs' criticisms seem to ignore the link made by Castells between the network society and contemporary capitalism. For example Fuchs argues that networks are characteristic of all systems noting that:

> The historically novel quality is that in more and more systems, such as the economy, polity and the Internet, we find transnational actors that operate on a global scale; they are trans-national/global networks (Fuchs 2008, p. 101).

Although Fuchs prefers to call this 'transnational/global capitalism' he seems to be emphasising exactly the points made by Castells and I think the term network society is more than adequate when used in the ways Castells suggests. However it is worth adding a cautionary note that network society can be used in ways that do suggest a technological determinism in which large-scale forces drive social change and choice and agency can be downplayed (See for example Rainie and Wellman 2012). It is also important to remember that the restructuring of relations via digital networks is a complex mixture of inclusion and exclusion, both between populations (classes and peoples) within individual states and between states. Overall the importance of network society is the way that it stresses the significance of knowledge in the development of information technologies, a reliance on digital networks, and the radical restructuring of capital on a global scale.

Work

Zuboff (1988) linked the growth of information technology to changes in the workforce and coined the term 'informating' to describe the properties of new technologies in the context of a paper processing mill.

What is it, then, that distinguishes information technology from earlier generations of machine technology? As information technology is used to reproduce, extend, and improve upon the process of substituting machines for human agency, it simultaneously accomplishes something quite different. The devices that automate by translating information into action also register data about those automated activities, thus generating new streams of information (Zuboff 1988, p. 9)

The informating of educational processes has recently become a major focus for policy makers and researchers in educational technology with the development of learning analytics (see Chap. 5). Barley and Orr (1997) explicitly build on this characterisation of the new work process and they go further by identifying a growing sector of the workforce which relies on the manipulation of symbols to carry out their work. The development of digital and networked infrastructure has resulted in the emergence of an increasing number of technical occupations with a specific relationship to scientific knowledge. They argue that such technical work sits at the intersection of craft and science and it combines attributes of both mental and manual skills which need to exist inseparably even if their coexistence is not always comfortable. Barley and Orr refer to the process that leads to this coexistence as technisation:

By technization, we mean to characterize the emergence of work which is comparatively complex, analytic, and even abstract, because it makes use of tools that generate symbolic representations of physical phenomena and that often mediate between workers and the objects of their work (Barley and Orr 1997, p. 5).

They note that effective technical practice relies heavily on theoretical or abstract knowledge which is often used to justify requiring technicians to obtain relevant degrees from postsecondary educational institutions. However in practice, critical skills and judgments are contextually situated and formal knowledge is only a small part of what is required to be a skilful technical practitioner. These aspects of the new workforce are related to developments in learning theory explored in Chap. 3 in terms of social and situated accounts of learning. They are also related to the development of para-academic roles (e.g. learning technologists and educational developers) in higher education and this is explored further in Chap. 7.

More recently Hardt and Negri (2005) have drawn attention to the growth of immaterial labour; that is:

...labor that creates immaterial products, such as knowledge, information, communication, a relationship or an emotional response (ibid, p. 108)

This general term actually captures two different kinds of work, one which is concerned with the production of symbols, codes, ideas, texts etc. and the other with affective labour, the production of relationships, a good attitude and social skills. In this way of thinking the work remains material; it is the products or outputs from the work process which are immaterial. Fuchs argues that this approach is problematic in the way that it splits the world into material and immaterial forms (Fuchs 2008). I would agree with this criticism and add that the idea of 'immaterial' products does not do justice to many of the areas of work that Hardt and Negri include in their analysis. The generation of texts and ideas is very much a sociomaterial practice with products often taking a material form. Equally communication involves embodied people and media through which they communicate, both of which are material in their own ways (Ihde 2002). The 'products' of communication are increasingly captured and made material by the informating processes identified by Zuboff. Even affective labour's outputs are usually materially embedded. The 'have a good day' encounter in a coffee shop is part of a complex and designed sociomaterial practice, involving the persons interacting in a controlled and designed exchange that obtains its meaning, not just from the appropriate actions of the worker, but from the entire material context. Nevertheless immaterial labour draws attention to another kind of shift in the workforce requiring different kinds of knowledge and learning.

Knowledge

In this context the important element for networked learning is the relationship between network society and knowledge. Castells argues that while knowledge is not the defining character of network society, increased access to information means that education and life-long learning become essential resources for achievement in work and for personal development (Castells 2001). I am not of course equating information with knowledge, but noting that the flow of information can enable construction of knowledge. Indeed Castells argues that the increased availability of information reinforces the need to shift from learning to learning-to-learn and to enhance the capacity to transform information into knowledge and knowledge into action. The increased flow of information is also related to the 'attention economy' which means that an ability to select between sources based on a very limited reading is an essential practical element of our day-to-day lives (Goldhaber 1997). Säljö (2010) argues that in an attention economy education and learning require an ability to select between sources, and learners must therefore direct their attention in ways that mean they have to disregard much of what is available to them. The need to disregard parts of the increased flow of information has been accompanied by a shift in the forms that this information takes with communication increasingly multimodal in form.

The focus on the ability to read a text and to discriminate between them has led Säljö to draw on Kress (2003) to make a distinction between 'reading as interpretation' and 'reading as design'. In reading as interpretation the meaning is there in every word and the task is to be able to read the text and to interpret and transform what is clearly present in it. In multimodal texts he claims that the emphasis shifts from telling to showing and the task for the reader is to impose order and to select for relevance, a practice he calls 'reading as design'. In Säljö's view, reading becomes an act of participation and the reader has greater flexibility in interpretation and is able to produce a version of a multimedia text for their own purposes. This argument firstly directs attention to the multimodal forms available in digital networks and secondly it places an emphasis on the practices of decoding text.

In combination, these two movements, from an information poor to an information rich environment and from reading as interpretation to reading as design have the potential to change the place of knowledge and the characteristics of learning in network society.

Säljö's also argues that digital and networked technologies don't enable or improve learning in a linear sense. Digital technology isn't a quick fix for the existing system boosting performance. Digital technologies change what we mean by learning and our expectations of what it means to know something. This argument is consistent with the idea of learning-to-learn as used by Castells and builds on the idea of reading as design. Overall digital technologies change what we mean by learning, from reproduction of what is already known to being able to transform what is already known into something new, with the potential to have an impact in the world. Säljö's account draws explicitly on the notion of affordance and it is framed in terms of choice and possibilities. The change in learning identified by Säljö is not an inevitable outcome of technological development it is a process of change in which multiple levels of choice impact on the final outcomes.

Conclusions

The underlying theme of this chapter has been change. Change in society, change in technology and the consequent change that arises when these two aspects are brought together in a network society. The way that change has been discussed is to emphasise the weaknesses of determinist, specifically technological determinist, arguments and this raises the question of the politics of change. Change in network society arises in a number of ways, and these all involve choice and the choices have a political dimension. Change can be individual in character, although this kind of change is often overhyped. Humans always exist as social beings and a society rich in technology is socially complex. The changes that affect network society are often if not always collective in nature. The collective could be a 'crowd' a loosely linked grouping in which individuals act in their own interests but generate an overall collective response (Watts and Strogatz 1998). This kind of change is rare because social life is generally historical in character and collective responses usually lead to organisations that persist over time and once organisations are constituted they act back on their members. This reflexive kind of collective self-organisation is the stuff of politics and of democratic politics in particular. It is also a foundation of organisational and social politics because it leads to self-organisation in professional bodies, and in interest and pressure groups. It should not be forgotten that the design and deployment of technology also has a politics, and technology is a site of struggle involving a 'parliament of things' (Feenberg 1991). Choice and political and policy processes rely on a degree of stability and the concept of affordance can be useful in providing a degree of permanence in changing circumstances. There is then a 'politics' of networked learning, even if networked learning is generally not concerned with Politics in the party political sense of the term.

There is a small literature that addresses the question of the politics of networked learning directly (Jones 2001, 2002; Land 2006; Greener and Perriton 2005; Levinsen and Nielsen 2012). In the broader field of educational technology there has been an increasing interest in a critical and political focus (see for example Nespor 2011; Selwyn and Facer 2013). McConnell, Hodgson and Dirckinck-Holmfeld do not mention politics directly in their brief history of networked learning, but they do refer to the role of critical pedagogy and the ethics of learning:

> The various scholars and practices associated with networked learning have an identifiable educational philosophy that has emerged out of those educational theories and approaches that can be linked to radical emancipatory and humanistic educational ideas and approaches (McConnell et al. 2012, p. 15).

In the conclusions to the same volume Hodgson et al. (2012) extend this and overtly discuss the political positioning of networked learning in relation to ontology and epistemology. They argue that networked learning questions the nature of society and how new knowledge is developed, emphasising collaboration and sharing as both a pedagogical and social goal. However overall networked learning has rarely engaged with the broader political landscape sketched by Selwyn and Facer (2013) and this is becoming a more pressing concern in the current global recession because of the severe pressures placed on higher education by economic conditions.

References

Arthur, W. B. (2009). *The nature of technology: What it is and how it evolves*. London: Allen Lane.

Bakardjieva, M. (2005). *Internet society: The internet in everyday life*. London: Sage.

Barley, S. R., & Orr, J. E. (1997). *Between craft and science: Technical work in US settings*. Ithaca, NY: Cornell University/ILR Press.

Barnes, B., Bloor, D., & Henry, J. (1996). *Scientific knowledge: A sociological analysis*. London: Athlone Press.

Bell, D. (1973). *The coming of post-industrial society: A venture in social forecasting*. New York: Basic Books.

Bijker, E., & Law, J. (Eds.). (1992). *Shaping technology/building society: Studies in sociotechnical change*. Cambridge, MA: MIT Press.

Bloor, D. (1991). *Knowledge and social imagery* (2 ed.). Chicago: University of Chicago Press. (Original work published 1976).

Brey, P. (1997). Social constructivism for philosophers of technology: A shopper's guide. *Society for Philosophy and Technology, 2*(3–4), 56–78.

Castells, M. (2000). *The end of the millennium* (2nd ed.). Oxford, England: Blackwell. (Original work published 1998).

Castells, M. (2000a). The rise of the fourth world. In D. Held & A. McGrew (Eds.), *The global transformations reader: An introduction to the globalization debate* (pp. 348–354). Cambridge, England: Polity Press.

Castells, M. (2000b). *The rise of the network society* (2nd ed.). Oxford, England: Blackwell (Original work published 1996).

Castells, M. (2001). *The internet galaxy: Reflections on the internet, business, and society*. Oxford, England: Oxford University Press.

Castells, M., & Cardoso, G. (Eds.). (2005). *The network society: From knowledge to policy.* Washington, DC: Johns Hopkins Center for Transatlantic Relations.

Cornford, J., & Pollock, N. (2002). The university as a 'resourceful constraint': Process and practice in the construction of the virtual university. In M. R. Lea & K. Nicoll (Eds.), *Distributed learning: Social and cultural approaches to practice.* London: RoutledgeFalmer.

Derry, J. (2007). Epistemology and conceptual resources for the development of learning technologies. *Journal of Computer Assisted Learning, 23*(6), 503–510.

Drucker, P. (1969). *The age of discontinuity: Guidelines to our changing society.* London: Heinemann.

Dyson, G. (1999). *Darwin among the machines.* London: Penguin.

Dyson, G. (2012). *Turing's cathedral: The origins of the digital universe.* London: Allen Lane.

Economist. (2012). The rise of state capitalism. *Economist.* Retrieved January 21, 2012, from http://www.economist.com/node/21543160

Feenberg, A. (1991). *Critical theory of technology.* New York: Oxford University Press.

Fenwick, T. (2012). Matterings of knowing and doing: Sociomaterial approaches to understanding practice. In P. Hager, A. Lee, & A. Reich (Eds.), *Practice, learning and change: Practice-theory perspectives on professional learning* (pp. 67–83). Dordrecht, The Netherlands: Springer.

Fenwick, T., Edwards, R., & Sawchuk, P. (2011). *Emerging approaches to educational research: Tracing the sociomaterial.* London: Routledge.

Friesen, N. (2009). *Re-thinking e-learning research: Foundations, methods and practices.* New York: Peter Lang.

Friesen, N. (2010). Ethics and the technologies of empire: e-learning and the US military. *AI & Society, 25*(1), 71–81.

Fuchs, C. (2008). *Internet and society: Social theory in the information age.* New York: Routledge.

Gaver, W. W. (1991). Technology affordances. *Proceedings of CHI'91, New Orleans, LA, April 28–May 2, 1991* (pp. 79–84). New York: ACM.

Gaver, W. W. (1996). Situating action II: Affordances for interaction: The social is material for design. *Ecological Psychology, 8*(2), 111–129.

Gibson, J. J. (1977). The theory of affordances. In R. Shaw & J. Bransford (Eds.), *Perceiving, acting and knowing.* Hillsdale, NJ: Erlbaum.

Gibson, J. J. (1986). *The ecological approach to visual perception.* Mahwah, NJ: Lawrence Erlbaum Associates (Original work published 1979).

Goldhaber, M. H. (1997). The attention economy and the net. *First Monday, 2*(4). Retrieved from http://firstmonday.org

Greener, I., & Perriton, L. (2005). The political economy of networked learning communities in higher education. *Studies in Higher Education, 30*(1), 67–79.

Gregory, R. (1997). Knowledge in perception and illusion. *Philosophical Transactions of the Royal Society: Biological Sciences, 352,* 1121–1127. Retrieved from http://www.richardgregory.org/papers/knowl_illusion/knowledge-in-perception.doc

Gregory, R., & Wallace, J. G. (2001). *Recovery from early blindness—A case study.* Reproduced from Experimental Psychology Society Monograph No. 2 1963. (Original work published 1963). Retrieved from http://www.richardgregory.org/papers/index.htm

Hacket, J. E., Amsterdamska, O., Lynch, M., & Wacjman, J. (2008). *Handbook of science and technology studies* (3rd ed.). Cambridge, MA: MIT Press.

Harasim, L. (2012). *Learning theory and online technologies.* New York: Routledge.

Hardt, M., & Negri, A. (2005). *Multitude: War and democracy in the age of empire.* London: Hamish Hamilton.

Harman, G. (2009). *Prince of networks: Bruno Latour and metaphysics.* Melbourne, VIC: Re. Press. Retrieved from http://re-press.org/books/prince-of-networks-bruno-latour-and-metaphysics/

Harvey, D. (2005). *A brief history of neoliberalism.* Oxford, England: Oxford University Press.

Hiltz, S. R., & Turoff, M. (1978). *The network nation—Human communication via computer* (1st ed.). Reading, MA: Addison-Wesley [Revised edition, Cambridge, MA: MIT Press, 1993].

Hodgson, V., McConnell, D., & Dirckinck-Holmfeld, L. (2012). The theory, practice and peda-gogy of networked learning. In L. Dirckinck-Holmfeld, V. Hodgson, & D. McConnell (Eds.), *Exploring the theory, pedagogy and practice of networked learning* (pp. 291–305). New York: Springer.

Huntington, S. P. (1993). The clash of civilizations? *Foreign Affairs, 72*(3), 22–49.

Hutchby, I. (2001). Technologies, texts and affordances. *Sociology, 35*(2), 451–456.

Hutchby, I. (2003). Affordances and the analysis of technologically mediated interaction: A response to Brian Rappert. *Sociology, 37*(3), 581–588.

Ihde, D. (2002). *Bodies in technology* (Electronic mediations, Vol. 5). Minneapolis, MN: University of Minnesota Press.

Jones, C. (2001) Do technologies have politics? The new paradigm and pedagogy in networked learning. In *Technology pedagogy and politics—What next?*, Mount Royal College, Calgary, AB, May 4–5, 2001. Retrieved from http://oro.open.ac.uk/33381/

Jones, C. (2002). The politics of networked learning (Symposium 8). In S. Banks, P. Goodyear, V. Hodgson, & D. McConnell (Eds.), *Networked learning 2002: A research based conference on e-learning in higher education and lifelong learning.* Sheffield, England: University of Sheffield. Retrieved from http://www.networkedlearningconference.org.uk/past/nlc2002/pro-ceedings/symp/08.htm

Jones, C. (2005). Who are you? Theorising from the experience of working through an Avatar. *E-learning, 2*(4), 415–426.

Jones, C. (2011). Students, the net generation and digital natives: Accounting for educational change. In M. Thomas (Ed.), *Deconstructing digital natives* (pp. 30–45). New York: Routledge.

Jones, O. (2014). *The establishment: And how they get away with it.* London: Allen Lane Press.

Kaptelinin, V., & Hedestig, U. (2009). Breakdowns, affordances and indirect design. In L. Dirckinck-Holmfeld, C. Jones, & B. Lindström (Eds.), *Analysing networked learning prac-tices in higher education and continuing professional development.* Rotterdam, The Netherlands: Sense Publishers, BV.

Kaptelinin, V., & Nardi, B. (2012). Affordances in HCI: Toward a mediated action perspective. In *Proceedings of the 2012 ACM Annual Conference on Human Factors in Computing Systems* (pp. 967–976). New York: ACM.

Kress, G. (2003). *Literacy in the new media age.* London: Routledge.

Land, R. (2006). Networked learning and the politics of speed: A dromological perspective. In S. Banks, V. Hodgson, C. Jones, B. Kemp, D. McConnell, & C. Smith (Eds.), *Proceedings of the Fifth International Conference on Networked Learning 2006.* Lancaster, England: Lancaster University. Retrieved from http://www.networkedlearningconference.org.uk/past/nlc2006/abstracts/pdfs/P16%20Land.pdf

Latour, B. (2005). *Reassembling the social: An introduction to actor-network theory.* London: Routledge.

Leonardi, P. M., & Barley, S. R. (2008). Materiality and change: Challenges to building better theory about technology and organizing. *Information and Organization, 18*, 159–176.

Leonardi, P. M., & Barley, S. R. (2010). What's under construction here? Social action, materiality, and power in constructivist studies of technology and organizing. *The Academy of Management Annals, 4*(1), 1–51.

Leonardi, P. M., Nardi, B. A., & Kallinikos, J. (Eds.). (2012). *Materiality and organising: Social interaction in a technological world.* Oxford, England: Oxford University Press.

Levinsen, K. T., & Nielsen, J. (2012). Innovating design for learning in the networked society. In L. Dirckinck-Holmfeld, V. Hodgson, & D. McConnell (Eds.), *Exploring the theory, pedagogy and practice of networked learning* (pp. 237–256). New York: Springer.

Lyotard, J-F. (1984). *The postmodern condition: A report on knowledge* (G. Bennington, & B. Massumi, Trans.). Manchester, England: University of Manchester Press.

MacKenzie, D., & Wajcman, J. (1999). *The social shaping of technology* (2nd ed.). Buckingham, England: Open University Press.

McConnell, D., Hodgson, V., & Dirckinck-Holmfeld, L. (2012). Networked learning: A brief his-tory and new trends. In L. Dirckinck-Holmfeld, V. Hodgson, & D. McConnell (Eds.), *Exploring the theory, pedagogy and practice of networked learning* (pp. 3–24). New York: Springer.

McGrenere, J., & Ho, W. (2000). Affordances: Clarifying and evolving a concept. In *Proceedings of graphics interface 2000* (pp. 179–186). New York: ACM. Retrieved from http://www.dgp. utoronto.ca/~joanna/papers/gi_2000_affordances.pdf

Mol, A. (2002). *The body multiple: Ontology in medical practice*. Durham, NC: Duke University Press.

Morozov, E. (2011). *The net delusion: How not to liberate the world*. London: Allen Lane.

Morozov, E. (2013). *To save everything click here: Technology, solutionism and the urge to fix problems that don't exist*. London: Allen Lane.

Nespor, J. (2011). *Technology and the politics of instruction*. Abingdon, England: Routledge.

Norman, D. (1988). *The psychology of everyday things*. New York: Basic Books.

Norman, D. A. (1990). *The design of everyday things*. New York: Doubleday.

Norman, D. (1999). Affordance, conventions, and design. *Interactions, 6*(3), 38–42.

O'Neil, J. (2001). *Building better global economic BRICs*. Global economics paper No. 66. London: Goldman Sachs. Retrieved from http://www.goldmansachs.com/our-thinking/archive/archive-pdfs/build-better-brics.pdf

Oliver, M. (2005). The problem with affordance. *E-Learning, 2*(4), 402–413.

Oliver, M. (2011). Technological determinism in educational technology research: Some alternative ways of thinking about the relationship between learning and technology. *Journal of Computer Assisted Learning, 27*(5), 373–384.

Orlikowski, W. J., & Scott, S. V. (2008). 10 sociomateriality: Challenging the separation of technology, work and organization. *The Academy of Management Annals, 2*(1), 433–474.

Piketty, T. (2014). *Capital in the twenty-first century* (A. Goldhammer, Trans.). Cambridge, MA: Harvard University Press.

Pinch, T., & Bijker, W. (1987). The social construction of facts and artifacts: Or how the sociology of science and the sociology of technology might benefit each other. In W. Bijker, T. Hughes, & T. Pinch (Eds.), *The social construction of technological systems: New directions in the sociology and history of technology* (pp. 17–50). Cambridge, MA: MIT Press.

Rainie, L., & Wellman, B. (2012). *Networked: The new social operating system*. Cambridge, MA: MIT Press.

Rappert, B. (2003). Technologies, texts and possibilities: A reply to Hutchby. *Sociology, 37*(3), 565–580.

Rhodes, R. A. W. (1997). *Understanding governance: Policy networks, governance, reflexivity and accountability*. Buckingham, England: Open University Press.

Ritzer, G. (1993). *The McDonaldization of society*. London: Sage.

Säljö, R. (2010). Digital tools and challenges to institutional traditions of learning: Technologies, social memory and the performative nature of learning. *Journal of Computer Assisted Learning, 26*(1), 53–64.

Selwyn, N. (2011). *Schools and schooling in the digital age: A critical analysis*. London: Routledge.

Selwyn, N., & Facer, K. (Eds.). (2013). *The politics of education and technology: Conflicts, controversies, and connections*. New York: Palgrave McMillan.

Thompson, G., Frances, J., Levačić, R., & Michell, J. (1991). *Markets, hierarchies and networks: The coordination of social life*. London: Sage.

Torenvliet, G. (2003). We can't afford it! The devaluation of a usability term. *Interactions, 10*, 12–17.

Touraine, A. (1971). *The post-industrial society: Tomorrow's social history: Classes, conflicts and culture in the programmed society*. New York: Random House.

Van Dijk, J. (1999). *The network society*. London: Sage (Original work published 1991).

Van Heur, B., Leydesdorff, L., & Wyatt, S. (2013). Turning to ontology in STS? Turning to STS through 'ontology'. *Social Studies of Science, 43*(3), 341–362.

Watts, D. J., & Strogatz, S. H. (1998). Collective dynamics of 'small-world' networks. *Nature, 393*(6684), 440–442.

Webster, F. (2006). *Theories of the information society* (3rd ed.). London: Routledge.

Winner, L. (1986). Do artifacts have politics? In L. Winner (Ed.), *The whale and the reactor: A search for limits in an age of high technology* (pp. 19–39). Chicago: University of Chicago Press (Reprinted in D. MacKenzie, & Wajcman, J. (Eds.), (1999). The social shaping of technology (2nd Ed., pp. 28–40). London: Open University Press).

Woolgar, S., & Lezauan, J. (2013). The wrong bin bag: A turn to ontology in science and technology studies? *Social Studies of Science, 43*(3), 321–340.

Wright, S., & Parchoma, G. (2011). Technologies for learning? An actor-network theory critique of 'affordances' in research on mobile learning. *Research in Learning Technology, 19*(3), 247–258.

Zuboff, S. (1988). *In the age of the smart machine: The future of work and power*. New York: Basic Books.

Chapter 3
Theories of Learning in a Digital Age

In the previous chapter I outlined the kind of society that has emerged in conjunction with the rise of digital networks. In this chapter I will examine the kinds of theories of learning that might be applicable in such a society and explore how theories of learning are changing. A society based on digital networks has clearly changed the kinds of labour that are required in the economy and this shift in the demand for labour has an influence on the kinds of learning that are required. The hidden curriculum of an industrial society was the organisation of time and space in the factory system and this led to structuralist and functionalist accounts of education that emphasised how the educational system prepared people for working lives within the factory system (e.g. Willis 1977). A limitation on the scope of the chapter is that it largely deals with learning at the post compulsory level, focused largely on higher education, as I explain below. Higher education has not been exempted from the processes affecting education as a whole and although higher education is focused on highly qualified sections of the workforce it has been argued that historically the educational system prepared the university educated for certain kinds of scientific and technical labour and the command and control positions in the state's governance and administration (see Margolis 2001; Bourdieu 1988). A starting point for this chapter is the term learning and the way digital and networked technologies intertwine with social forms in contemporary universities, corporate training and continuing professional development. Digital and networked technologies play a part in forming and reforming work, social life and higher education. It is this complex and dynamic mix of work, social life and the higher education system that we need to understand alongside the different theories of education and learning.

The focus of this book is consistently on networked learning in the post compulsory sector. This could be workplace learning, professional and lifelong learning but most centrally it is focused on learning at university level. One critical reason for this restriction is that learning at the post compulsory level is concerned with more than the transfer, transmission or internalisation of knowledge that is already in circulation in society. The university remains a main site for the production of new knowledge, despite challenges, and indeed the higher degrees conferred by

© Springer International Publishing Switzerland 2015

C. Jones, *Networked Learning*, Research in Networked Learning,

DOI 10.1007/978-3-319-01934-5_3

universities contain the requirement that the candidates for such degrees have made a significant contribution to knowledge. University education can be seen as part of the transition from schooling in an authorised canon of knowledge to a critical understanding of existing bodies of knowledge and the eventual production of new knowledge. The potential for challenges—related to digital and networked technologies—to the university's dominance in this role as producer of knowledge are explored further in Chaps. 5 and 7.

This chapter does not take a particular view of learning, indeed it argues that one of the strengths of networked learning is its flexibility in allowing for different ways of thinking about learning. In this way this chapter differs from other accounts of networked learning that privilege one tradition of learning theory or another. For example McConnell et al. (2012) provide a brief history of networked learning in which they state:

> The development of networked learning has largely been influenced by understanding of developments in technology to support learning alongside thinking stemming from the traditions of open learning and other radical pedagogies and humanistic educational ideas from the likes of Dewey, Freire, Giroux and Rogers (McConnell et al. 2012, p. 4).

There is clearly a relationship between ideas drawn from some of these thinkers to networked learning, and these ideas have informed individuals who have been key in developing the academic area, but they have not to date been the main sources of inspiration for many of the theories of learning which have been regularly drawn on by networked learning researchers. The chapter returns to this point in its conclusions and the author takes the view that because learning is a complex matter, one that is universal across human societies, it cannot be reduced to any single or simple definition (for a recent collection of contemporary learning theory see Illeris 2009). This means that this chapter will examine a number of competing and at times overlapping theories that often draw on traditional understandings of learning, even though networked learning can be thought of as a relatively new phenomenon. Illeris notes that:

> During the last 10–15 years, learning has become a key topic, not only for professionals and students in the areas of psychology, pedagogy and education, but also in political and economic contexts. One reason for this is that the level of education and skills of nations, companies and individuals is considered a crucial parameter of competition in the present globalised market and knowledge society (Illeris 2009, p. 1).

Learning is therefore not something that can be understood in isolation, abstracted from the contemporary contexts of learning, or as independent of the development of each social system and its economic conditions. The focus of the chapter is on contemporary theories of learning and their relationships to a networked and digital setting. I should be clear that I do not work from any particular date or deadline for a theory to qualify as relevant, although the theories explored in this chapter are contemporary in the broad sense that they are currently applied and relevant to a contemporary context. The chapter explores a relational view of learning, one that suggests that learning cannot be reduced to the person, an individualised cognition, nor can it be reduced to a context, a social view of learning that ignores the already established characteristics of the learner (Ellis and Goodyear 2010; Haythornthwaite and De Laat 2011).

Learning has become the lens through which educational processes have been understood. As noted by Illeris (2009) learning has become a key topic and the attention paid to learning signifies a shift from previous ways of discussing higher education and education more broadly. Previous thinkers developed theories of education, even though many are now remembered as learning theorists (e.g. Dewey 1986a/1933, 1986b/1938). Dewey wrote about the school, the classroom, and the role of the teacher in addition to the process of learning. It is in this tradition that this chapter will locate itself, focusing on learning but placing it in the wider context of the teaching and learning process, and the social and material settings in which learning takes place. The chapter takes a broadly indirect view of learning (Ellis and Goodyear 2010; Beetham and Sharpe 2013) and argues that learning can be designed *for* but never directly designed (see also Wenger 1998). This key concept will be developed later in the chapter but it is related to the idea that learning must be seen in a social and material context, rather than as an internal or private process. Learning always involves the brain and body of the person but it is not an individual process. It has a relational character, interrelated with the social and material world in which the person is located.

An Accepted Canon?

There is a standard way of discussing theories of learning in relation to new technologies and that is to frame the discussion in terms of a sequence moving from behaviourism to cognitivism and then on to constructivism (e.g. Lowyck 2013). This framing has recently been applied by one of the early writers to use the term networked learning Harasim (2012). This standard classification organises twentieth-century learning theory as a progression, even though the different perspectives it identifies are in many ways still in competition. Furthermore examples of each approach can be found in current practice and in contemporary literature (see for example Kirschner et al. 2004). An alternative classification has been applied by Mayes and de Freitas (2013) who follow Greeno et al. (1996) by identifying three clusters of broad perspectives in educational theory with fundamentally different assumptions. These are associationist, cognitive and situative perspectives. This alternate classification does not map neatly on to behaviourism, cognitivism and constructivism, despite the middle term (cognitivism) remaining the same. This chapter will initially consider the standard view of a progression of learning theories, outlined by Harasim and Lowyck, prior to moving on to examine a range of other approaches that don't fit neatly into this somewhat simplistic tripartite scheme. It is necessary to locate networked learning and the theories of learning it draws on in relation to this standard account because it is so pervasive in educational discourse.

Behaviourism

Behaviourism arose in the early twentieth century and its roots lie in the work of Pavlov and the idea of conditioning (Harasim 2012). The approach was scientific in the sense of the term that is currently viewed as 'scientism'. That is it has a narrow focus on objective knowledge and a refusal to include in scientific discourse internal states and accounts of these states as mind or experience, which is an approach behaviourism's adherents dismissed as 'mentalism'. Key figures in behaviourism include Watson (1913), Thorndike (1911) and Skinner (1958). Watson recognised no boundary between humans and animals (brutes) and reinforced the objectivist and experimental basis of behaviourism by firmly locating it within psychology and emphasising the prediction and control of behaviour.

Behaviourism has at its core a design-focused way of thinking. The experimental stress on prediction and control, developed by Thorndike's connectionist school of behaviourism, emphasised the role of habit and the usefulness of stimulus response pairings in establishing behavioural patterns. The connectionist use of association reinforced the general behaviourist notion that learning could be explained without reference to any states that were not directly observable. It is of course Skinner's name that is now most associated with the relationship between behaviourism and the use of technology in education (Skinner 1954). A key development introduced by Skinner was the notion of operant conditioning (Skinner 1953). Pavlov had made use of direct stimuli such as the use of a bell to positively reinforce behaviours in dogs. Skinner extended this notion to emphasise how behaviour could be modified with both positive and negative reinforcement. Skinner's notion of operant conditioning was that active behaviour operated upon the environment to generate consequences, and it allowed for a feedback loop in which the pattern of rewards or punishment could feedback onto future behaviours.

Behaviourism has been widely criticised from a number of different perspectives and in many ways it is currently used to set up a subsequent progression of ideas about learning and learning with technology in particular. For example the idea of a stimulus response pairing, while simplified in laboratory experiments, can easily be confounded in a complex natural environment such as a classroom. However care needs to be taken with this tendency towards blanket criticism because some of the basic ideas, sketched out above, are still current and relevant in education. As Wilson and Myers noted:

> Recall that behaviorism was once a reform movement with a core commitment to active learning. To fully appreciate the contribution of behaviorism, we would need to understand what the behaviorists were trying to reform, and what they brought to the table? Proponents of programmed instruction were dedicated to making instruction more individually tailored and effective in accomplishing its objectives. A full range of media and technologies were organized into new designs for instruction. Traditional methods such as teacher-centered classrooms and lectures were precisely what behaviorists were trying to reform (Wilson and Myers 2000, p. 60).

There are ideas drawn from behaviourism that are still relevant today. Firstly behaviourism has a focus on the learner, even though it is often dismissed as teacher-centred.

Secondly behaviourism has a focus on design and the idea that learning occurs through modifications in behaviour. The idea of active learning with rapid if not immediate feedback on outcomes is still practiced, most notably in the idea that learning processes should be carefully analysed and planned in terms of intended outcomes (Mayes and de Freitas 2013). The use of learning objectives linked to strategies for instruction and crafted forms of assessment is still embedded in many institutional and national regulatory systems and regimes. Implicitly it informs some of the more recent experiments with learning analytics. Behaviourism remains a theory concerned with the design of learning, but it remains relevant and can still be an influence in educational technology. Networked learning rejects the idea that the subjective aspect of human activity can be ignored and the neglect of intentionality inherent in the use of the term behaviour; however, it remains interested in some common areas such as design and a planned approach to learning.

Cognitivism

Cognitivism which became the dominant paradigm in psychology, and arguably in education, in the mid-twentieth century has its origins in theories that were critical of behaviourism and its 'black box' approach to questions of the mind and internal mental states (Harasim 2012). Cognitivism and behaviourism have a complex relationship because elements of behaviourist thinking were retained in later cognitivist psychology (Harasim 2012). In a simplified account one can say that cognitivism was concerned with determining the mental states and processes that were assumed to take place in the mind between stimulus and response. Cognitivism can be seen as a continuation of the debate between behaviourism and mentalism in psychology and philosophy, and it led to the acceptance of accounts of internal states, introspection, mental models, schema and schemata. Cognitivism accepted the folk vocabulary of thinking, imagining and conceiving in a way that the objectivist and scientific approach of behaviourism would not allow. A key development allowing cognitivism to replace behaviourism as the dominant psychological paradigm was the rise of the digital computer. By analogy the computer was used to demonstrate the application of an information processing model of the brain and the metaphor of the mind as a computer.

The mind as computer was brutally captured in the phrase attributed to Marvin Minsky the founder of Artificial Intelligence—the human brain is 'a meat machine'. While cognitivism cannot be reduced to the mind as machine metaphor, it can be associated with the idea that the brain and mind were related to each other in ways that resembled the relationship between the hardware and software found in digital computers (Harasim 2012). Just as computers encode and process data using short-and long-term memory so it is argued does the mind/brain by encoding symbols and the procedures for processing them. Cognitive theories address issues concerning how information is received, organised, stored and retrieved. Learning from this perspective is concerned with what the learners know and how they come to acquire knowledge.

The acquisition of knowledge is described as a mental activity that requires coding and structuring by the learner and the learner takes an active part in the learning process. The idea of cognition as information processing has had a significant impact on cognitive psychology, educational practice and the development of educational technology. In particular, cognitivism had an impact because of the way it viewed knowledge acquisition as a process of developing expertise, and the development of a framework for understanding (Mayes and de Freitas 2013). The influence of this account in terms of expertise and broader cognitivist influences can be seen in technological applications such as intelligent tutoring systems (ITS) and artificial intelligence (AI).

The idea of mental representation and structured knowledge in cognitivist thinking is one way in which the learner is active in the process of acquiring knowledge. Mental models are assumed to be personal, internal models of an external reality which are mobilised to interact with the world. Mental models and schemata are hypothetical mental structures that represent generic concepts in memory, they are plans, scripts or programmes that are presumed to be generalisations or stereotypical instances created through experience and learning. The break with behaviourism lies in this use of internal states to explain behaviour. However there is a continuity with behaviourism in the retention of a largely objective conception of the external world and an individualist notion of learning. The continuities between behaviourism and cognitivism in education can be seen in the work of Gagné and the various editions of his book *Conditions of Learning* (1965). Although Gagné represented continuity he also represented a break in that he took research away from the laboratory and into real-world settings. His impact in educational technology was largely by way of his role in developing instructional design as a field concerned with the systematic design of learning processes and evaluation (Gagné et al. 1992).

For networked learning the influence of cognitivism has been limited but there are some elements that have a continuing relevance. Firstly there is a concern with the thinking and intentions of learners. Networked learning still has an interest in what happens in the brain and an interest in what can be called the mind (Goodyear and Carvalho 2014; Ellis and Goodyear 2010). Secondly cognitivism continues to have an influence in networked learning because of its application in a number of cognate fields dealing with the uses of technology in education. This has been explicitly mentioned with regard to instructional design and AI but it is also a continuing influence in Computer-Supported Collaborative Learning.

Constructivism

In the standard view of learning theory constuctivism is positioned as following on, both intellectually and temporally, from behaviourism and cognitivism, although it is acknowledged that it has its roots in thinkers who were contemporary with each other and predate much of the work in both of the other traditions, Piaget (1896–1980) and Vygotsky (1896–1934). The central ideas of constuctivism are that knowledge is created by people, either as individuals or as part of groups, through experiencing the world and reflecting upon those experiences. In this view knowledge is constructed by the knower and as a consequence it does not exist externally and independently of the knower(s) and knowledge cannot simply be transmitted and received. Let me be clear this account does not ignore the encoding of knowledge into artefacts (books, procedures, multimedia etc.) that can be circulated and exist separately from their originators, it suggests that the encoded knowledge they carry has to be decoded and re-created by those (individual and collective) who wish to access that knowledge. In this way constructivism marks a significant break with the objectivism found in both behaviourism and cognitivism.

Constructivism is often subdivided between individual or 'cognitive' and social forms and the origin of these two different perspectives are ascribed to Piaget and Vygotsky respectively. This simple account is acknowledged to be suspect because Piaget can be described as a social constructivist while Vygotsky had a role in the development of Soviet psychology (Daniels 2010; Cole and Wertsch 1996). The distinction drawn between individual and social constructivism is more one of convenience, allowing psychological and social accounts to be brought together under a single constructivist banner without any apparent contradiction. The characteristics of constructivist learning theory can be summarised as:

- Knowledge is not transferred or acquired it has to be constructed and understood
- Constructivism can be both social and individual and it can assist in bridging a divide between individual and social views of learning
- It is active and requires the activity of the learner either as an individual or as a member of a group

In addition to this list Harasim (2012) argues that constructivism differs from behaviourism and cognitivism by having a particular approach to epistemology (see also Jonassen 1991). It is this link with epistemology that can make constructivism, viewed as a learning theory, difficult to grasp because educational ideas become entwined with philosophical arguments that extend beyond epistemology and touch on the nature of reality itself. In the more radical epistemology associated with constructivism it is not simply knowledge that is constructed but 'reality' itself, and from this perspective there are as many realities as there are ways of knowing. Constructivism was developed and associated with the work of Bruner (1986) and later Von Glasersfeld (1984). Bruner's constructivism is active and learning is viewed as a process in which learners construct new ideas or concepts based upon their current or prior experience and knowledge. While Bruner is a major figure in the development of constructivism he is also a bridge to cognitivism and in his early writing he shared many of the ideas found in mainstream cognitive thinking. In his later work Bruner became sharply critical of cognitivism and more closely aligned with theories that focused on the cultural and social contexts in which education takes place (Bruner 1996). In this later form Bruner's ideas are often ascribed to social constructivism but Bruner's work is often refreshingly non-aligned in relation to learning theory, despite Bruner being widely considered one of the major figures in the development of constructivism.

> There is not one kind of learning. It was the vanity of a preceding generation to think that
> the battle over learning theories would eventuate in one winning over all the others. Any
> learner has a host of learning strategies at command. The salvation is in learning how to go
> about learning before getting irreversibly beyond the point of no return (Bruner 1985, p. 8).

Von Glasersfeld became associated with 'radical' constructivism. Radical constructivism emphasised the epistemological understanding of constructivism and suggested a form of relativism:

> The revolutionary aspect of Constructivism lies in the assertion that knowledge cannot and
> need not be 'true' in the sense that it matches ontological reality, it only has to be 'viable'
> in the sense that it fits within the experiential constraints that limit the cognizing organism's
> possibilities of acting and thinking (Von Glasersfeld 1989, p. 162).

Adaptation to an environment and pragmatic usefulness were emphasised rather than a notion of truth and reality. Harasim argues that behaviourism and cognitivism are identified with an 'objectivist' epistemology whereas constructivism is said to be subjective in character and dependent on individual and social perceptions, interpretations and agreed conventions. This reduction of opponents of constructivism to a simple and mechanical realism characterised as 'objectivism' ignores those traditions in which reality is retained as external to the knower even though a simple correspondence perspective on knowledge and reality is rejected (e.g. critical realism, Archer 1995).

My own view is that this elision of learning theories with epistemology is an oversimplification and it has seriously limiting consequences. The sequence of epistemologies in this glossed history of learning theory implies a progression from objectivism to constructivism, whereas accounts of the development of epistemology could be given in a number of alternative ways, for example in relation to modernism and post-modernism, or realism and relativism. Lankshear et al. (2000) suggest that there is a standard view of epistemology which dates back to Plato, which they summarise as 'justified true belief'. In this interpretation both objectivism and constructivism fall within this standard view which Lankshear et al. argue is challenged by the possibilities inherent in new, largely Internet-based technologies. Furthermore the standard ordering of learning theories by linking them to underlying epistemologies is challenged by the sequence of learning theories outlined by Mayes and de Freitas (2013) because in their account they incorporate constructivism within cognitivism and replace the third position in the standard sequence (behaviourism-cognitivism-constructivism) with a 'situative' perspective. Mayes and de Freitas comment that:

> Increasingly mainstream cognitive approaches to learning and teaching have emphasised
> the assumptions of constructivism: that understanding is gained through an active process of
> creating hypotheses and building new forms of understanding through activity (ibid, p. 21).

If the standard view is correct how can these two epistemologically opposed outlooks sit together so happily in the way that Mayes and de Freitas suggest? This disagreement points to a major problem with simplified accounts of learning theory which focuses on an implied progression from behaviourism to either constructivism or a situative perspective—they do not accord with the history of ideas, they exclude significant trends in educational theory and muddle together approaches with quite different ways of seeing the world and quite different practical implications.

In recent years constructivism has possibly been the most influential of the three mainstream approaches to learning theory. The kind of constructivism that has been most influential has been social in character and there is a slight difference in the ways that constructivism has developed in the United States and Europe. European approaches to learning theory are happier to speak and write in terms of sociocultural theory and about situated learning whereas approaches from the United States are more likely to use the term constructivism to cover similar issues. The most important inheritance from constructivism in networked learning is the situation of learning in social practice and in the interactions between people and their social settings.

Alternative Views of Learning

This chapter now explores some of the alternative ways of thinking that do not sit comfortably in the accounts provided by either Harasim or Mayes and de Freitas. The exploration begins with pragmatism and the work of Dewey (1859–1952) and the way this outlook retains its influence (Garrison and Anderson 2003; Koschmann 2002; Vanderstraeten and Biesta 2006). It goes on to look at the varieties of what might be summarised as social and situated views of learning, including the ideas of communities of practice (Wenger 1998), legitimate peripheral participation (Lave and Wenger 1991), cultural historical activity theory (CHAT) and expansive learning (Engeström 1987), and CSCL which was at one time portrayed as a new paradigm for learning (Koschmann 1996). These theories continue to have a significant influence on networked learning. This exploration also examines another broad outlook that doesn't fit in with standard views, the study of approaches to learning and teaching alongside ideas such as constructive alignment and phenomenography (Prosser and Trigwell 1999; Biggs 1999; Marton 1981; Marton and Booth 1997; Richardson 1999). The review of alternative theories then concludes with some current contending ideas for framing a new paradigm of learning, connectivism (Siemens 2005) and the sociomaterial approach and actor-network theory (Fenwick et al. 2011; Fenwick and Edwards 2010)

Pragmatism

Pragmatism is a broad philosophical movement which has its own view of epistemology and knowledge, although the particular pragmatic view is often confused with constructivism. In relation to education and learning it is most associated with Dewey and the idea of learning through experience (1916/1980). Pragmatists reject the idea that knowledge describes, represents, or mirrors reality, but significantly pragmatists are not relativist and they believe judgements can still be made between better and worse accounts of the world. Pragmatists developed a philosophy in which knowledge is related to an understanding of the world gained through prediction, action, and problem-solving. Pragmatists contend that the nature of knowledge, science and belief are best viewed in terms of their practical uses. Dewey's (1916/1980) body of work emphasises action and experience, although his use of experience is quite distinct and can easily be confused with more recent accounts of experience and experiential learning (Elkjaer 2009).

> Experience is both the process of experiencing and the result of the process. It is in experience, in transaction, that difficulties arise, and it is with experience that problems are resolved by inquiry. Inquiry (or critical and reflective thinking) is an experimental method by which new experience may be had not only through action but also by using ideas and concepts, hypotheses and theories as 'tools to think with' in an instrumental way (Elkjaer 2009, p. 75).

Dewey's educational approach is based on the use of inquiry as a method for generating working hypotheses that anticipate consequences which can then be tested in action. In this sense it is based on a generalisation of the experimental method and it is guided by imagination, creativity and a future orientation (Dewey 1986a/1933, 1986b/1938). It stands apart from constructivism because of the way in which knowledge and cognition are only parts of the interaction with the world envisaged in the inquiry method.

> Two conclusions important for education follow. (1) Experience is primarily an active–passive affair; it is not primarily cognitive. But (2) the measure of the value of an experience lies in the perception of relationships or continuities to which it leads up. It includes cognition in the degree in which it is cumulative or amounts to something, or has meaning (Dewey 1916/1980, p. 147).

Experience for Dewey involved knowledge as only one part of interaction with the world (other aspects being emotion, aesthetics and ethics) and experience was both subjective and objective, involving cultural practice and not simply individualised minds.

Pragmatism retains an influence on education and learning (Elkjaer 2009; Garrison and Anderson 2003) through pragmatist epistemology and debates between contemporary philosophers with a relevance to education that draw on pragmatism (Rockwell 2003). Dewey is also drawn on for more recent developments in educational thinking such as Kolb's model of experiential learning (Miettinen 2000). Pragmatism can also seem to have some very strange bedfellows. Koschmann noted that Dewey in an address to the 25th anniversary American Psychological Society praised the work of an early behaviourist:

> ...Dewey argues for the inclusion of the social in psychological research. As examples of psychologists who had already made moves in this direction, he cited approvingly William James, the British psychologist McDougall, and his colleague at Columbia, E. L. Thorndike! Dewey goes on to applaud efforts by Thorndike and others to introduce statistical methods and behaviorism into the study of social aspects of cognition (Koschmann 2000, p. 314).

The point being made here is not to suggest that Dewey endorsed behaviourism in any significant way, but to note that the clear separation that is often made between competing theories is not always as clear or as clean as it is suggested. Dewey and the pragmatists were supporters of the scientific method, something which post-positivists in the current era might find odd. Koschmann in this discussion clearly shows how Dewey differed from Thorndike, but he draws attention to the fact that the originators of two very different traditions in the early years of the twentieth century were close enough to require differentiation.

Social/Situated Learning

The most important approach not properly accounted for in the standard view of a progression from behaviourism to cognitivism and onward to constructivism is what Mayes and de Freitas described as the 'situative' view of learning (Mayes and de Freitas 2013). The ideas of Jean Lave and Etienne Wenger, captured by the terms legitimate peripheral participation and communities of practice have been highly influential in educational technology (Lave 2011; Lave and Wenger 1991; Wenger 1998). Equally a set of theories based on Vygotsky's activity theory have been highly influential in educational research and practice, in particular Yrjö Engeström's work on CHAT and his theory of expansive learning (Engeström 1987, 1999). What unites these theories is a social view of learning, but they emerged with distinct differences and some apparent contradictions between them. There is also a link that unites pragmatism with these theories and that is the idea of practice.

Jean Lave located her work as social, cultural and historical but placed it in contrast to much that has been encompassed by the term constructivism:

> I take issue with some work characterized in this way, for it either maintains overly simple boundaries between the individual (and thus the 'cognitive') and some version of a world 'out there', or turns to a radical constructivist view in which the world is (only) subjectively or intersubjectively constructed. Learning, it seems to me, is neither wholly subjective nor fully encompassed in social interaction, and it is not constituted separately from the social world (with its own structures and meanings) of which it is part. This recommends a decentered view of the locus and meaning of learning, in which learning is recognized as a social phenomenon constituted in the experienced, lived-in world, through legitimate peripheral participation in ongoing social practice; the process of changing knowledgeable skill is subsumed in processes of changing identity in and through membership in a community of practitioners; and mastery is an organizational, relational characteristic of communities of practice (Lave 1991, p. 64).

The term communities of practice was originally developed by Lave and Wenger (1991) and the stress at that time was on legitimate peripheral participation, a process abstracted from the observation of craft workers, which involved the movement of a novice at the periphery towards mastery at the centre of a practice. Etienne Wenger developed the idea of legitimate peripheral participation, formed jointly with Jean Lave, into the full framework of communities of practice (Wenger 1998). As he did so he further abstracted the concept, minimising its link to preindustrial notions of apprenticeship and applied it to modern managerial practice (Wenger et al. 2002).

Communities of practice have since become one of the standard lenses through which learning and teaching in a technologically rich environment is viewed. A community of practice is a group of people who share a concern, a set of problems or an interest (passion) for a topic and who then deepen their knowledge and expertise by having an ongoing interaction (Wenger et al. 2002). The process Wenger identified is an ongoing dialectical interaction between reification and participation that involves the formation of identity. This dialectical relationship is evidenced in the duality between reification and participation which is illustrated using a yin- and yang-like tension within a unity (Wenger 1998, p. 63). In its initial formulation Wenger identified three features of a community of practice, joint enterprise, mutual engagement, and a shared repertoire (Wenger 1998). While the idea of community of practice has become widespread Wenger has always insisted that his conception involves 'learning, meaning and identity' with the last term being often the least emphasised by those inspired by the idea of a community of practice. Wenger emphasised that the process of active participation in a community of practice involves learning; and the formation of identity is understood as both a shared identity as a group, and the person's identity within the group.

Wenger has in recent years developed his view of networks and their relationship to communities of practice. In his 1998 book Wenger referred to networks in a number of footnotes to distinguish them from communities in the sense that he used the term. More recently he has taken up the position that communities of practice are special cases of networks; that is that all communities of practice are networks but not all networks are communities of practice (Wenger et al. 2011).

> We prefer to think of community and network as two aspects of social structures in which learning takes place.
>
> • The network aspect refers to the set of relationships, personal interactions, and connections among participants who have personal reasons to connect. It is viewed as a set of nodes and links with affordances for learning, such as information flows, helpful linkages, joint problem solving, and knowledge creation.
> • The community aspect refers to the development of a shared identity around a topic or set of challenges. It represents a collective intention—however tacit and distributed—to steward a domain of knowledge and to sustain learning about it (Wenger et al. 2011, p. 9).

This newer formulation is explicitly related to social networks enabled by digital and networked technologies. In some ways the adoption of the idea of communities of practice by educational technology researchers and practitioners is odd because the initial research that led to the development of this perspective was so clearly located in the observation of craft workers (tailors in West Africa), working in conditions that did not include modern technologies and digital and networked technologies in particular. The issue of the craft basis and preindustrial origins of the idea of a community of practice is one of the points of difference between theories based on communities of practice and those drawing on activity theory and CHAT (Engeström 2007).

Both Lave and Engeström draw on aspects of Marxist theory (Lave 2011). Lave emphasised alienation and the commodity form in her work, whereas Engeström has a more explicit and fully developed link to Marxism via Vygotsky and the activity theory tradition originally developed in the Soviet Union (Lave 1991; Engeström 1987). In Engeström's work there is reference to the pivotal idea of contradictions as being a key instrument for change and the central focus of the theory is the activity system, rather than singular activities. The theory of expansive learning based on this approach is concerned with learning at the level of collectives and networks rather than individuals. The problems which expansive learning is concerned with often cannot be fixed by individuals alone, but only socially by the collaboration and cooperation of groups. In addition the case made for expansive learning is that 'standard' views of learning are concerned with the transmission, understanding of, and preservation of what is already known.

> Standard theories of learning are focused on processes where a subject (traditionally an individual, more recently possibly also an organization) acquires some identifiable knowledge or skills in such a way that a corresponding, relatively lasting change in the behavior of the subject may be observed. It is a self-evident presupposition that the knowledge or skill to be acquired is itself stable and reasonably well defined. There is a competent 'teacher' who knows what is to be learned (Engeström 2009, p. 58).

By way of contrast, expansive learning is concerned with entire activity systems, and with generating through cultural change and learning new patterns of activity.

The theory of expansive learning is historically located and it has a specific positioning with regard to the changing nature of work:

> The increasingly societal nature of work processes, their internal complexity and interconnectedness as well as their massive volumes in capital and capacity, are making it evident that, at least in periods of acute disturbance or intensive change, no one actually quite masters the work activity as a whole, though the control and planning of the whole is formally in the hands of the management (Engeström 1987, pp. 113–114).

The theory of expansive learning thus sits in a framework of analysis that deals with the inner contradictions of capitalist production in a way that the ideas of communities of practice do not. Another feature of expansive learning is its concern with 'horizontal' rather than vertical processes. In his criticism of communities of practice Engeström argues that the movement from novice to master remains a vertical process and he also argues that Vygotsky's work is vertical in character (Engeström 2007). Engeström argues that the theory of expansive learning takes a different stance and is concerned with the horizontal plane and sideway moves, in which thinking is not moving vertically between abstract scientific concepts and everyday thinking. Sideway moves are argued to be creative re-conceptualisations of the problem, setting new agendas and new ways of working.

Despite these important differences there are explicit connections that link the idea of a community of practice with the idea of an activity system:

> An activity system is a complex and relatively enduring 'community of practice' that often takes the shape of an institution. Activity systems are enacted in the form of individual goal-directed actions. But an activity system is not reducible to the sum total of those actions. An action is discrete, it has a beginning and an end. Activity systems have cyclic rhythms and long historical half-lives (Engeström 2005, p. 219)

Both outlooks take learning away from the isolated individual and locate it in social processes which involve groups, social dynamics and culture. The kind of learning covered by these theories ranges from the acquisition of already established bodies of knowledge and practice, especially in relation to communities of practice, to the way new knowledge is generated via contradictions within current social practices identified by activity theory. The approach taken by social and situated views of learning is self-consciously related to the changing status and nature of work. Social and situated learning is less concerned with training, for example in the military, which might continue to draw on behaviourist and cognitivist approaches to instructional design (Harasim 2012). The focus of social and situated learning is on the kinds of flexibility and the creative application of knowledge found in professional and highly skilled technical work. It is this kind of education that is found in universities, but which is not confined to educational institutions, and it can also be found in continuing professional development (Hansson 2002), professional and management learning (Hodgson and Watland 2004), and informal settings (Boud and Middleton 2003). Networked learning sits firmly in this tradition with much of its focus being on higher education and on learning in professional, technical and informal settings (Jones and Dirckinck-Holmfeld 2009). Networked learning also has a close relationship to another area of research and practice that has its roots in social and situated views of learning, Computer-Supported Collaborative (Cooperative) Learning (CSCL).

Computer-Supported Collaborative Learning

Computer-Supported Collaborative Learning (CSCL) is an interesting area in relation to other social theories of learning because of its clear and explicit link with information and communication technologies. CSCL in some ways runs parallel with networked learning and like networked learning, CSCL has a loose relationship to learning theory, with work located in the research area being informed by a number of different learning theories. However I have located CSCL as a social learning theory because of its specific relationship with collaboration and cooperation. The development of CSCL is related to earlier work concerned with cooperative and collaborative learning which was based on non-technologically mediated settings (Slavin 1990; Johnson and Johnson 1999). Furthermore one of the founders of the networked learning conference series published a book titled *Computer-Supported Cooperative Learning* shortly before he helped launch the networked learning conference series (McConnell 1994).

CSCL is also related to the cognate field of Computer-Supported Collaborative Work (CSCW), but the two traditions have developed separately with separate journals and conferences which have had little overlap, although individual researchers have crossed over between both fields. There is also a current attempt to develop a linked field in CSCL learning at work (Goggins et al. 2013). CSCL is clearly a term with varied interpretation, so much so that an early edited collection chose to use

CSCL as a designation in its own right because some were so uncomfortable with the expansion, Computer-Supported Collaborative Learning (Koschmann 1996). CSCL is then something of a contested term, but one with a strong and distinctive tradition that once laid claim to be a new paradigm (Koschmann 1996). Something of the richness of the tradition can be seen in the proceedings of the conference series and a book series (Kirschner et al. 2004; Wasson et al. 2003; Spada et al. 2011; Rummel et al. 2013). It can also be seen in recent summaries (Goodyear et al. 2014).

There are some authors who make a distinction between cooperative and collaborative learning (Crook 1994; Dillenbourg 1999) while others only make a distinction between individualistic learning and learning involving either cooperation or collaboration (Jones et al. 2007; Johnson and Johnson 2008). In so far as a distinction between the two terms can be maintained, cooperation has most often been applied to a division of labour, in which individuals achieve their aims by mutual assistance, whereas collaboration has implied a stronger commitment to joint aims as well as mutual assistance (Jones et al. 2007). A second feature that has been used to distinguish between the different kinds of group organisation has been the role of authority (Jones et al. 2007). McConnell has argued that cooperative learning situations can be divided between those in which an external authority, usually the teacher, enforces cooperation by structure and rewards, and those where the learners choose cooperation without external intervention (McConnell 1994). A popular definition found in CSCL is that collaborative learning is:

> A *situation* in which *two or more* people *learn* or attempt to learn something *together* (Dillenbourg 1999, p. 2, emphasis in original).

CSCL builds on these definitions of collaborative learning by applying itself to settings in which computer technologies play a significant role (Goodyear et al. 2014). CSCL can involve learners working at a distance from each other with the computer technology providing a primary or only means of interacting. However CSCL can also be used to describe situations in which learners are co-present, as long as the technology plays a significant role in supporting collaborative activities (Goodyear et al. 2014).

Despite the variations between them, advocates of CSCL generally hold a social or situated view of learning (for example Stahl 2003). This strand of thinking about CSCL does not rely on a claim that cooperation or collaboration is a more efficient or a more effective learning process whereas others who draw on research in cooperative and collaborative learning argue that collaborative learning is a superior, or more effective, form of learning (see for example Johnson and Johnson 1999; Johnson and Johnson 2008). Collaborative learning from a social or situated perspective can come close to the meaning of learning in general, because *all* learning can be described as a social activity. When collaborative learning is understood as social learning it becomes a descriptive enterprise setting out how people learn *in* and *through* social activity. A key aspect of this is the claim that:

> CSCL research has the advantage of studying learning in settings in which learning is observably and accountably embedded in collaborative activity. Our concern, therefore, is with the unfolding process of meaning-making within these settings, not so-called 'learning outcomes' (Koschmann 2001, p. 19).

This claim that CSCL makes learning observable and accountable was originally motivated by an ethnographic or ethnomethodological understanding of accountability. In contemporary conditions accountability has moved beyond that to another quite different conception. It now coexists with a managerial concern with accountability and a much more general claim about learning based on computing which has developed using the term learner analytics (Ferguson 2012). This managerial sense of accountability also extends beyond group learning at a relatively small scale to include whole institution processes (McCluskey and Winter 2012). This alternative understanding of accountability as learner analytics is dealt with more fully in Chap. 5.

CSCL is the closest approach to networked learning and there are significant overlaps in terms of researchers active in both fields and in terms of ideas (Goodyear et al. 2014; Dirckinck-Holmfeld et al. 2009; Steeples and Jones 2002). For this reason it is important to draw attention to some of the divergences between them. CSCL tends to deal with smaller scale interactions (Goodyear et al. 2014; Jones 2013). Networked learning usually has a focus on tens to hundreds (if not thousands in distance mode), whereas CSCL can include quite small-scale interactions such as small groups and dyads. CSCL has a clear focus on a particular kind of interaction, collaboration, whereas networked learning has a focus on connections which can take many forms and include both strong and weak links (Jones 2004, 2013). Furthermore networked learning tends to focus on readily available public technologies rather than technologies designed for a particular purpose (for a related discussion of this issue see Nespor 2011). Much of the research in CSCL is concerned with software specifically designed for education and collaboration, sometimes designed for a particular setting (Jones 2013; Tchounikine 2011). Tchounikine for example refers to software not designed for an educational purpose as 'basic software' (Tchounikine 2011), however networked learning is often concerned with the educational use of just such basic software. The focus on small-scale and purposively designed software may pose a challenge for CSCL in the context of Web 2.0 (Dohn 2009) because Web 2.0 involves large-scale network effects and the ability to interact in, and contribute to, large groups (Kafai and Peppler 2011; Goodyear et al. 2014). This challenge arises because CSCL has previously concerned itself with tool and application development and Web 2.0 technologies and contemporary processes suggest a change of focus to whole infrastructures and the use of universal services. Jahnke (2009) observed that Web 2.0 applications:

> Transform social systems (e.g. social groups, universities) into socio-technical systems, where socially and technically supported relationships are highly interwoven (Jahnke 2009, p. 287).

Networked learning concerns itself rather more with these large-scale infrastructures and the levels between microlevel interactions and macrolevel social and technical conditions (Jones et al. 2006; Jones and Dirckinck-Holmfeld 2009). Some of these issues are developed further in later chapters dealing with institutions (Chap. 5) and infrastructure (Chap. 6).

The Phenomenographic Tradition

There is one further major influence on networked learning that does not fit comfortably in the sequential standard view of learning theory and that is phenomenography and the somewhat broader tradition of research that can be identified with the idea of approaches to learning and teaching. Networked learning has an explicitly relational approach which prioritises connections between elements and in this it finds a compliment in the relational approach to learning found in phenomenography (Ellis and Goodyear 2010). Ference Marton described phenomenography as:

> The empirical study of the differing ways in which people experience, perceive, apprehend, understand, or conceptualize various phenomena in, and aspects of, the world around them (Marton 1994, p. 4424).

Phenomenography aims to describe qualitatively different ways of experiencing phenomena with the objective of illuminating the *variations* in ways of experiencing networked learning (Marton and Booth 1997; Laurillard 1993). Phenomenography is a non-dualist approach based on experience in the world (Marton and Booth 1997). It differs from phenomenology because it is an empirical project, and it has generated an extensive literature concerning the learner experience (Marton and Säljö 1976a, b; Entwistle and Ramsden 1983; Biggs 1987; Marton et al. 1997; Ramsden 2002) and teachers' conceptions of teaching and how these conceptions relate to the students experience of learning (Prosser and Trigwell 1999).

From an approach to learning perspective, experience is characterised as the internal relationship that is constituted between persons and phenomena. The non-dualist characterisation of experience facilitates a second-order research perspective which involves studying the experience of learning, rather than learning itself, and the outcome of the research is expressed in qualitative descriptions of the variations found in these experiences of learning (Marton et al. 1993). Typically these qualitative descriptions are in the form of collective instances, or pools of meaning, rather than accounts of individual experiences. The outcomes of the research in this tradition are associated with the widespread use of the idea of 'deep' and 'surface' learning (Haggis 2009) and they became associated with both a qualitative research tradition and one concerned with Approaches to Study which used quantitative survey instruments such as the Approaches to Study Inventory (ASI) (Entwistle and Ramsden 1983). In many ways this general understanding of learning in terms of approaches/conceptions/outcomes became an orthodox policy perspective in the UK and Australia informing aspects of the training of teachers in higher education, national student surveys and government policies. Haggis (2003) noted the development of approaches to learning research and its incorporation into educational policy has led to the generalisation of context-specific elements of learning and a removal of the relational aspect of the original approach (Haggis 2003).

Phenomenography remains a powerful and useful approach and one that when used in a manner that retains its relational and context-sensitive original form has much to offer networked learning research (see for example Ellis and Goodyear 2010). An interesting feature of the phenomenographic and approaches to study literature is the way it cannot be easily contained in a standard model of the progress of learning theory because it allows for both a psychological and a social reading. Ellis and Goodyear argue that learning remains an individual process and that what goes on 'between a person's ears' is still important for the learning process (Ellis and Goodyear 2010, p. 6). They suggest that an ecological framework can locate student difficulties so that they are identified as a mismatch with their environment rather than being seen as individual characteristics which are persistent, context-free, personal failings. This use of ecology in this way has a clear relationship with ideas of balance and equilibrium which are in turn associated with functionalism and later with ideas of cybernetics and self-regulation. It stands in sharp contrast to the idea of contradiction found in activity theory and the idea that it is through an imbalance or contradiction that learning takes place and knowledge moves forwards.

Phenomenography also stands distinct from social and situated views of learning, locating itself in a more individualistic tradition, but it cannot be subsumed under the labels of behaviourism, cognitivism or constructivism. It stands out for its grounding in a distinct relational and monist tradition of research that emphasises *approaches*, rather than fixed characteristics or styles, related to the contexts they arise in. It is this location of the person-in-context that opens phenomenography up to a social reading, in which personal characteristics are provisional and they can be altered by interventions from outside e.g. by the design of technologies, social settings and environments. Phenomenography when viewed from both an individualist and a social reading is concerned with what students (and teachers) do and their activity in the world. This emphasis on context and activity leads to a design impulse that can be found in the idea of 'constructive alignment' (Biggs 1999) and the idea of indirect design (Goodyear 2001, 2005) which is addressed later in this chapter.

Newer Theories and Networked Learning

There are newer contending theories that have an influence in networked learning. Not all can be explored in this chapter and there is only sufficient space to briefly consider two of the most significant, sociomaterialism, specifically actor-network-based theories (Fenwick et al. 2011; Fenwick and Edwards 2010; Hannon 2013) and connectivism (Siemens 2005; Downes 2006; Kop and Hill 2008). A notable and relevant omission in this section is the role of dialogue and dialogicality (Bakhtin 1981, 1986; Koschmann 1999; Wegerif 2013) which has a distinct tradition related to social and situated views of learning and activity theory. A second notable exception that has received recent attention in networked learning is the role of critical theory (Selwyn and Facer 2013; Jandrić and Boras 2015).

Connectivism

Connectivism argues that the starting point for learning occurs when knowledge is actuated through the process of a learner connecting to, and providing information in, a networked learning community. The idea of connectivism is closely linked to the idea of networked learning because several of the authors writing about connectivism also identify their work using the term networked learning (Siemens 2005; Downes 2006). Connectivism stresses two important skills that contribute to learning namely the ability to seek out information, and the ability to filter information (Kop and Hill 2008). Connectivism locates itself in the standard progression of learning theories, behaviourism, cognitivism and constructivism, adding itself as the next (fourth) step that is required as a response to digital and networked technologies:

> Behaviorism, cognitivism, and constructivism are the three broad learning theories most often utilized in the creation of instructional environments. These theories, however, were developed in a time when learning was not impacted through technology (Siemens 2005).

There is something distinctly odd about this claim because all three prior learning theories had their own distinct links to technology: Behaviourism in relation to teaching machines, cognitivism by way of the information processing model, and constructivism due to its focus on artefacts, including technological artefacts.

The learning process that connectivism describes is cyclical and learners who have connected to a network to share and find new information subsequently modify their beliefs and then afterward when they connect to a network (the same one or another) to share and find new information they begin the process again. In this account learning occurs via connections so that learning can be optimised by identifying the properties of effective networks. In connectivism it is the formation of connections between nodes that constitute knowledge, and skilful learning involves the ability of a learner to construct and traverse networks. As a consequence in some ways of thinking about connectivism the learning *is* the network.

There are those who argue that connectivism is not a learning theory (Kop and Hill 2008; Bell 2011). Clarà and Barberà (2013a, b) argue that connectivism is seriously underdeveloped as a theory and that it has yet to be properly scrutinised in terms of peer review. They note that connectivism is currently elaborated on blog posts, non-peer-reviewed Internet articles, books compiling the previous two items and MOOC courses. None the less Clarà and Barberà treat connectivism as if it was a coherent theory and they argue that there are three important problems with connectivism, namely the lack of a solution to the learning paradox, the underconceptualisation of interaction and the inability to explain concept development (2013b). Downes (2013) has fiercely defended his position with regard to connectivism arguing that the link that Clarà and Barberà (2013b) make with the work of Ilich (1970) is unwarranted and that their criticisms are mistaken. I think the current status of connectivism is underdeveloped and it cannot be regarded as a developed learning theory. However there are some interesting aspects of connectivism that warrant further attention, specifically the conception of learning as connections and an ability to navigate networks. Some of Clarà and Barberà's criticisms seem to miss their mark, for example by confusing interaction with connection, but there is substance in other arguments they make, in particular the criticism that connectivism has an inadequate way of accounting for human development. Connectivism has had important impacts, not least in the development of MOOCs and this alone makes connectivism significant for networked learning and some of the issues in relation to connectivism are developed further in Chap. 5.

Sociomaterialism

The sociomaterial perspective argues that it is necessary to rethink theoretical conceptions about the material and:

> ...how matter comes to matter in the social and personal mix-specifically in terms of educational processes and educational research (Fenwick et al. 2011, p. viii)

The four main areas the authors draw upon to develop a sociomaterialist perspective are CHAT, ANT, complexity theory and theories of spaciality. Connectivism also draws on some of the same intellectual sources as these in chaos and complexity theories. The unifying claim made for the term sociomaterialism is that all of these four areas have similarities in the ways that they conceptualise knowledge and capacities as being emergent from the webs of interconnections between heterogeneous entities, both human and non-human. The 'material turn' that is outlined in sociomaterialism has implications for education, and the claim that it is relevant to learning theory may also be important, but both of these claims are entangled in a larger theoretical framework. The larger claims are in terms of a 'relational materiality' that understands matter not as discrete reified objects but as *effects* of dynamic indeterminate processes. The implications of this are temporal as well as material because the real becomes an effect of a specific balance of forces between different actors at a particular point in time. These claims cannot be dealt with properly in this chapter which is concerned with learning theory, but they are examined more fully in the following chapter dealing with ANT as one kind of network theory relevant to networked learning.

Sociomaterialism and learning are part of a research programme that has a somewhat descriptive character concerned with how learning might be portrayed.

> Humans and what they take to be their learning and social processes do not float, distinct, in 'contexts' of practice that are a background of material stuff and spaces. The things that assemble these contexts, the actions and bodies that are part of these assemblages, are continuously acting upon each other to bring forth objects and knowledge. These objects might be taken by a casual observer as natural and given—as a 'context'. But a more careful analysis notes that these objects, including objects of knowledge, are very messy, slippery and indeterminate (Fenwick 2012, p. 70).

As outlined by Fenwick et al. (2011) sociomateriality does not have a single unified definition of learning. Indeed the authors celebrate the multiple and contested positions that are held by the different feeder theories and they make no attempt to synthesise them. For this reason alone it is difficult to summarise sociomaterial perspectives on learning or to treat these perspectives as being a 'learning' theory or possibly even being 'a' theory at all.

Conclusions: The Issues Arising from Learning Theory for Networked Learning

The field of learning theory is extensive and well developed so this chapter has only been able to focus on those areas that have had an extensive and direct influence on research in networked learning. Even then there are theories that some of the origi- nators of the idea of networked learning have drawn on, such as critical, humanistic and radical pedagogy, which other than Dewey are not fully accounted for here (see McConnell et al. 2012; Hodgson et al. 2014; Jandrić and Boras 2015). The final section of this chapter examines some of the issues that arise from this review and ends with those questions that networked learning still has to fully address.

There Is No Specific Learning Theory for Networked Learning

Haythornthwaite and Andrews (2011) reflected on the position they had taken ear- lier which argued that the field of 'e-learning' was not sufficiently mature to gener- ate a 'grand theory' (Andrews and Haythornthwaite 2007). By 2011 they felt they could give a clear answer that 'yes' a new theory of e-learning was required and that it needed its own theoretical treatment. The term e-learning is imprecise and covers many areas that would not be included in a consideration of networked learning (e.g. standalone computing) but the question as to whether the introduction of new technologies requires a new theory of learning (or e-learning for that matter) is clearly of relevance to networked learning because networked learning is by defini- tion concerned with the introduction of information and communication technolo- gies into the process of learning. My conclusion differs to that of Haythornthwaite and Andrews because I do not think that networked learning requires a new 'grand theory' but I do concur that there are new elements to learning that uses information and communication technologies and that these new elements may require new theories. My disagreement is in terms of an encompassing theory of e-learning or networked learning. My view is that learning is too slippery and complex a term to have a single theoretical solution and the addition of networked and digital tech- nologies only adds to that complexity.

This does not mean that networked learning is neutral in relation to theories of learning. Networked learning has a broadly social approach but it doesn't exclude accounts of the individual in their social and material context. My own personal views are more social than some others in the field who derive their views of net- worked learning from a psychological or radical pedagogical origin (for example Goodyear 2002; Ellis and Goodyear 2010; McConnell et al. 2012). This does not stop us working closely together and indeed our research suggests that many prac- titioners show little of the divergence in their day-to-day practice that might be expected from their different overt theoretical positioning. In some ways theory is a neglected area in research concerned with educational technology which generally focuses on technological change and design issues (Bennett and Oliver 2011). Networked learning has a clear view that theory and theoretically informed research are central to the successful use of technologies in education and learning, but I argue that the need for theory is not answered by proposing a new theory of learning or limiting networked learning to one approach or theory of learning.

Design and Indirect Design

The idea that learning can be designed is implicit in the tradition of instructional design and it goes beyond the question of a theory of learning because it deals with the role of the teacher and pedagogy (Harasim 2012; Illeris 2009; Koschmann 1996). It has also informed a large body of recent work that describes itself as learning design (Koper and Tattersall 2005; Conole 2013). Learning design has developed into two different forms, often indicated by capitalisation such that Learning Design has a distinctly different emphasis to learning design. Learning Design used in a strong sense of the term relies on assumptions that assume learning itself can be designed.

- Learning can be improved by making the conditions of optimal learning explicit (Koper 2005, p. 3)
- The quality of a unit of learning depends largely on the quality of the learning design (Koper 2005, p. 4)
- A learning designer's basic task is to design a course that meets a set of learning objectives (Koper 2005, p. 4)
- Learning design knowledge consists of a series of rules following the 'if situation, then method' (Koper 2005, p. 19)

Such a view of design runs counter to much recent work concerning the process of design more generally (Suchman 2007, 2011). Design from an anthropological point of view results in plans that in and of themselves do not dictate the activity that flows from them. Instead designs become one of a number of resources for action that need to be mobilised in context. This is a fundamental point and it cannot be addressed by finding a special category of 'situated' plans or designs. All designs, all plans remain resources for action and no particular approach to design can avoid the consequences. Learning design in the second sense of the term acknowledges this and often incorporates a notion of design for learning rather than design of learning (Beetham 2013; Beetham and Sharpe 2013; Jones 2013; Goodyear and Carvalho 2013).

The theories of learning that have been discussed in this chapter incorporate both implicit and explicit notions of teaching and pedagogy (for a discussion of how these might relate see Beetham 2013). The approaches to learning tradition, for example, includes a branch dealing explicitly with approaches to teaching (Hativa and Goodyear 2002; Prosser and Trigwell 1999) and how approaches to teaching relate to approaches to learning (Richardson 2005). At a time when learning can sometimes be placed in opposition to teaching it is worth emphasising the importance of the reflexive and self-conscious activity of pedagogy understood as guidance to learn. Teaching is not always conducted by a teacher and this aspect is explored below in terms of the teaching function, which although it might once have been embodied in a single person, is now often dispersed and located in a number of persons and/or material or technological artefacts. This book while it concerns net-worked *learning* considers learning as a practical accomplishment that takes place in material and social contexts. As such learning is as much concerned with the practice of pedagogy and teaching as it is with learning itself. Furthermore peda-gogy and teaching, while they are not directly design activities, both involve aspects of design. Pedagogy and teaching, like design in general, are practical activities involving abstract theory and a praxis, understood as practical activity with an ethi-cal or moral dimension.

Networked learning is a complex domain in which groups of humans interact with, through and around technologies. Like many other complex systems net-worked learning is not deterministic in character, but it still has a degree of regular-ity or self-similarity, leading to repeated patterns of interaction that are recognisably similar, even if they are not exact replications of each other. If learning cannot be directly designed the questions then arise as to what can be designed in such com-plex systems and what kinds of limits there are to design. In previous work I have made use of an early figure derived from Peter Goodyear's work (Fig. 3.1), which sets out a set of relationships between tasks and activities, space and place and organisation and community. In this figure the elements open to design, tasks, space and organisation have a distinct if indirect relationship to those aspects which can be designed for but are not open to direct design: activities, places and communities.

While limited this conceptualisation is helpful because it emphasises that some of the elements are open to design in a way that is reminiscent of the conceptualisa-tion of affordance in Chap. 2. In this case the potentially listable features are not the properties of a technology but they are the designable components of an environ-ment for learning. In both the conceptualisation of affordance and of an indirect

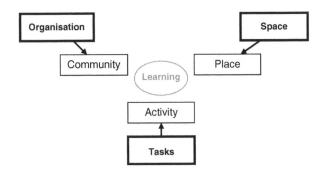

Fig. 3.1 Indirect approach to learning (Goodyear 2001)

approach to learning the enactment of these features is a relational property between the designed elements and active agent(s) taking up these potentials. This way of viewing affordance and design is in contrast to the application of the term to learning design by Conole (2013). Conole uses affordance in a way that implies that affordances themselves, rather than features or properties, can be designed into technologies and that affordances can be listed in a taxonomy and made available for use.

> Identification of the positive affordances of technologies and any associated constraints can … be used as a means of making informed design decisions in terms of using a particular technology in a specific learning context. For example, to promote student reflection, the affordances checklist can be used in terms of considering the extent to which different tools might promote this (Conole 2013, p. 89).

There is a second feature of the figure derived from Goodyear which I have always found intriguing and that is the isolated nature of the central element learning. The suggestion in this figure is that not only are the activities, places and communities in which learning takes place indirect in terms of design, there is no definite relationship indicated between these enacted elements and the learning we may wish to engender. Design and the possibilities and limits of design form important aspects of later chapters when design is examined in relation to institutions and infrastructures. The institutional and infrastructural aspects of networked learning are intimately connected to the way the teaching function has been redistributed across networks using digital technologies.

Disaggregation of the Teaching Function

The introduction of digital and network technologies can have an influence on who teaches, how teaching is configured and the balance between the different elements in the teaching process e.g. between active teaching processes and those encoded into educational resources. Distance education has illustrated these processes prior to and following the widespread use of digital and networked technologies (McAndrew and Weller 2005) but the introduction of new technology has increased the pace of change and the spread of practices once restricted to distance learning to other kinds of institutions, often under the terms blended or flexible learning (Oliver and Trigwell 2005). The development of learning resources that can be used independently of a teacher has been the hallmark of correspondence courses but in recent years the idea of learning objects (Friesen 2004) and open educational resources (Wiley 2006) has spread the practice of designing resources for either independent use or use beyond the context for which the resources were originally designed (Pegler 2011, 2013). The practice in distance learning of employing part-time teaching only staff is long-standing but the more recent large-scale use of adjunct (US) or sessional (UK) staff in whole-time place-based institutions raises some of the same issues. For example how is it possible to maintain common standards of teaching when courses can pass on from the staff who originated them to staff who have no ownership of the course design (Asensio et al. 2001)? The role of the teacher has been questioned by the spread of MOOCs, Massive Open Online Courses, in which a small number of instructors run courses attended by large numbers of students (Daniel 2012). In some courses other students or additional volunteers take on some of the moderation or teaching functions, but in large part the course participants have to be self-motivated and self-organised (Daniel 2012). Mitra has promoted the idea of 'minimally invasive education', by which he means teaching with a much reduced presence and role for the teacher (Mitra 2000). However Mitra's ideas are theoretically underdeveloped and the related studies implementing his ideas largely focus on children rather than adult learners. Overall two significant issues need to be addressed by networked learning concerning the teaching function. Firstly whether there is a fundamental requirement for a teaching function when dealing with adult learners and to what degree teaching interventions are required. Secondly what kinds of choices are enabled by the introduction of digital and networked technologies in terms of the disaggregation of the teaching function? The answers to these questions involve choices that need to be made at various levels, by students, academic staff and institutions.

Practice

As previously noted networked learning while not having any one particular learning theory is not neutral in relation to theories of learning and it tends towards what might be broadly described as social theories of learning. Social theories of learning are associated with communities of practice exemplified by the works of Wenger and Lave (Lave 1991; Lave and Wenger 1991; Wenger 1998) and they are associated with activity theory and the CHAT particularly associated with Engeström (2009). Broadly these social learning theories depend on an understanding of learning as a practice, an array of human activity, embodied and mediated by artefacts, hybrids and natural objects (Schatzki 1996; Schatzki et al. 2001). This idea of practice builds upon earlier work by Wittgenstein (Schatzki 1996; Bourdieu 1988, 1990). It is intimately related to the idea of indirect design and designing for learning and it raises a number of questions that will be addressed in the chapters that follow. Firstly the degree to which practice is a social phenomenon or a sociomaterial one remains a point of discussion (Hannon 2014). Furthermore some authors argue that a focus on social practice can downplay the practice aspect in favour of the social and that it is not possible to know in advance what sense—if any—participants will make of whatever they might have learned when they engage in other practice settings (Dohn 2014). The link between learning and practice also provides a bridge to broader concerns with organisations and this will be taken up in Chaps. 5 and 6 in relation to institutions and infrastructure (e.g. Orlikowski 2000; Jones and Dirckinck-Holmfeld 2009).

References

Andrews, R., & Haythornthwaite, C. (Eds.). (2007). *Sage handbook of e-learning research.* London: Sage.

Archer, M. (1995). *Realist social theory: The morphogenetic approach.* Cambridge, England: Cambridge University Press.

Asensio, M., Whatley, J., & Jones, C. (2001). Taking over someone else's design: Implications for the tutor's role in networked learning. *The Association for Learning Technology Journal, 9*(3), 65–74.

Bakhtin, M. M. (1981). *The dialogic imagination: Four essays* (C. Emerson, & M. Holquist, Trans.). Austin, TX: University Of Texas Press.

Bakhtin, M. (1986). In C. Emerson, & M. Holquist (Eds.), *Speech genres and other late essays* (V. W. McGee, Trans.). Austin, TX: University of Texas Press.

Beetham, H. (2013). Designing for active learning in technology-rich contexts. In H. Beetham & R. Sharpe (Eds.), *Rethinking pedagogy for a digital age: Designing for 21st century learning* (2nd ed., pp. 31–48). London: Routledge.

Beetham, H., & Sharpe, R. (Eds.). (2013). *Rethinking pedagogy for a digital age: Designing for 21st century learning* (2nd ed.). London: Routledge.

Bell, F. (2011). Connectivism: Its place in theory-informed research and innovation in technology-enabled learning. *International Review of Research in Open and Distance Learning, 12*(3), 98–118.

Bennett, S., & Oliver, M. (2011). Talking back to theory: The missed opportunities in learning technology research. *Research in Learning Technology, 19*(3), 179–189.

Biggs, J. B. (1987). *Student approaches to learning and studying.* Melbourne, VIC: Australian Council for Educational Research.

Biggs, J. B. (1999). *What the student does: Teaching for quality learning at university.* Buckingham, England: Open University Press.

Boud, D., & Middleton, H. (2003). Learning from others at work: Communities of practice and informal learning. *Journal of Workplace Learning, 15*(5), 194–202.

Bourdieu, P. (1988). *Homo academicus.* Cambridge, England: Polity Press.

Bourdieu, P. (1990). *The logic of practice* (R. Nice, Trans.). Cambridge, England: Polity Press.

Bruner, J. (1985). Models of the learner. *Educational Researcher, 14*(6), 5–8.

Bruner, J. (1986). *Actual minds, possible Worlds.* Cambridge, MA: Harvard University Press.

Bruner, J. (1996). *The culture of education.* Cambridge, MA: Harvard University Press.

Clarà, M., & Barberà, B. (2013a). Learning online: Massive open online courses (MOOCs), connectivism, and cultural psychology. *Distance Education, 34*(1), 129–136.

Clarà, M., & Barberà, B. (2013b). Three problems with the connectivist conception of learning. *Journal of Computer Assisted Learning, 30*(3), 197–206. doi:10.1111/jcal.12040.

Cole, M., & Wertsch, J. V. (1996). Beyond the individual-social antinomy in discussions of Piaget and Vygotsky. *Human Development, 39,* 250–256.

Conole, G. (2013). *Designing for learning in an open world.* New York: Springer.

Crook, C. (1994). *Computers and the collaborative experience of learning.* London: Routledge.

Daniel, J. (2012). Making sense of MOOCs: Musings in a maze of myth, paradox and possibility. *Journal of Interactive Media in Education.* Retrieved from http://jime.open.ac.uk/2012/18

Daniels, H. (2010). Vygotsky and psychology. In U. Goswami (Ed.), *The Wiley-Blackwell handbook of childhood cognitive development* (2nd ed.). Oxford, England: Wiley-Blackwell.

Dewey, J. (1916). Democracy and education: An introduction to the philosophy of education. In J. A. Boydston (Ed.), *Middle works 9.* Carbondale, IL: Southern Illinois University Press (Original work published 1980).

Dewey, J. (1986a). How we think: A restatement of the relation of reflective thinking to the educative process. In J. A. Boydston (Ed.), *Later works 8* (pp. 105–352). Carbondale, IL: Southern Illinois University Press (Original work published 1933).

Dewey, J. (1986b). Logic: The theory of inquiry. In J. A. Boydston (Ed.), *Later works 12.* Carbondale, IL: Southern Illinois University Press (Original work published 1938).

Dillenbourg, P. (Ed.). (1999). *Collaborative learning: Cognitive and computational approaches.* London: Pergamon.

Dirckinck-Holmfeld, L., Jones, C., & Lindström, B. (Eds.). (2009). *Analysing networked learning practices in higher education and continuing professional development.* Rotterdam, The Netherlands: Sense Publishers, BV.

Dohn, N. (2009). Web 2.0: Inherent tensions and evident challenges for education. *International Journal of Computer-Supported Collaborative Learning, 4*(3), 343–363.

Dohn, N. (2014). Implications for networked learning of the 'practice' side of social practice theories—A tacit-knowledge perspective. In V. E. Hodgson, M. De Laat, D. McConnell, & T. Ryberg (Eds.), *The design, experience and practice of networked learning* (pp. 29–49). Heidelberg, Germany: Springer.

Downes, S. (2006). Learning networks and connective knowledge. *Instructional Technology Forum: Paper 92.* Retrieved from http://it.coe.uga.edu/itforum/paper92/paper92.html

Downes, S. (2013). *On the three or four problems of connectivism.* Retrieved from http://halfanhour.blogspot.ca/2013/10/on-three-or-four-problems-of.html

Elkjaer, B. (2009). Pragmatism: A learning theory for the future. In K. Illeris (Ed.), *Contemporary theories of learning: Learning theorists... in their own words* (pp. 74–89). London: Routledge.

Ellis, R., & Goodyear, P. (2010). *Students experiences of e-learning in higher education: The ecology of sustainable innovation.* New York: Routledge.

Engeström, Y. (1987). *Learning by expanding: An activity theoretical approach to developmental research.* Helsinki, Finland: Orienta-Konsultit Oy. Retrieved from http://lchc.ucsd.edu/mca/Paper/Engestrom/expanding/toc.htm

Engeström, Y. (1999). Activity theory and individual and social transformation. In Y. Engeström, R. Miettinen, & R.-L. Punamäki (Eds.), *Perspectives on activity theory.* Cambridge, England: Cambridge University Press.

Engeström, Y. (2005). *Developmental work research: Expanding activity theory in practice.* Berlin, Germany: Lehmanns Media.

Engeström, Y. (2007). From communities of practice to mycorrhizae. In J. Hughes, N. Jewson, & L. Unwin (Eds.), *Communities of practice: Critical perspectives* (pp. 41–54). Abingdon, England: Routledge.

Engeström, Y. (2009). Expansive learning: Toward an activity-theoretical reconceptualization. In K. Illeris (Ed.), *Contemporary theories of learning: Learning theorists... in their own words* (pp. 59–73). London: Routledge.

Entwistle, N. J., & Ramsden, P. (1983). *Understanding student learning.* London: Croom Helm.

Fenwick, T. (2012). Matterings of knowing and doing: Sociomaterial approaches to understanding practice. In P. Hager, A. Lee, & A. Reich (Eds.), *Practice, learning and change: Practice-theory perspectives on professional learning* (pp. 67–83). Dordrecht, The Netherlands: Springer.

Fenwick, T., & Edwards, R. (2010). *Actor network theory in education.* London: Routledge.

Fenwick, T., Edwards, R., & Sawchuk, P. (2011). *Emerging approaches to educational research: Tracing the sociomaterial.* London: Routledge.

Ferguson, R. (2012). Learning analytics: Drivers, developments and challenges. *International Journal of Technology Enhanced Learning, 4*(5/6), 304–317.

Friesen, N. (2004). Three objections to learning objects and e-learning standards. In R. McGreal (Ed.), *Online education using learning objects* (pp. 59–70). London: Routledge Falmer.

Gagné, R. M. (1965). *The conditions of learning* (1st ed.). New York: Holt, Rinehart and Winston.

Gagné, R. M., Briggs, L. J., & Wager, W. W. (1992). *Principles of instructional design* (4th ed.). New York: Holt, Rinehart and Winston.

Garrison, D. R., & Anderson, T. (2003). *E-learning in the 21st century: A framework for research and practice.* London: Routledge Falmer.

Goggins, S. P., Jahnke, I., & Wulf, V. (2013). *Computer-supported collaborative learning at the workplace: CSCL@Work.* New York: Springer.

Goodyear, P. (2001). *Effective networked learning in higher education: Notes and guidelines (Deliverable 9).* Bristol, England: Joint Information Systems Committee (JISC). Retrieved from http://csalt.lancs.ac.uk/jisc/docs/Guidelines_final.doc

Goodyear, P. (2002). Psychological foundations for networked learning. In C. Steeples & C. Jones (Eds.), *Networked learning: Perspectives and issues* (pp. 49–75). London: Springer.

Goodyear, P. (2005). Educational design and networked learning: Patterns, pattern languages and design practices. *Australian Journal of Educational Technology, 21*, 82–101.

Goodyear, P., & Carvalho, L. (2013). The analysis of complex learning environments. In H. Beetham & R. Sharpe (Eds.), *Rethinking pedagogy for a digital age: Designing for 21st century learning* (2nd ed., pp. 49–63). London: Routledge.

Goodyear, P., & Carvalho, L. (2014). Introduction: Networked learning and learning networks. In L. Carvalho & P. Goodyear (Eds.), The architecture of productive learning networks (pp. 3–22). London: Routledge.

Goodyear, P., Jones, C., & Thompson, K. (2014). Computer-supported collaborative learning: Instructional approaches, group processes and educational designs. In J. M. Spector, M. D. Merrill, J. Elen, & M. J. Bishop (Eds.), *Handbook of research on educational communications and technology* (4th ed., pp. 439–451). New York: Springer.

Greeno, J. G., Collins, A. M., & Resnick, L. (1996). Cognition and learning. In D. C. Berliner & R. C. Calfee (Eds.), *Handbook of educational psychology*. New York: Simon & Schuster Macmillan.

Haggis, T. (2003). Constructing images of ourselves? A critical investigation into 'approaches to learning' research in higher education. *British Educational Research Journal, 29*(1), 89–104.

Haggis, T. (2009). What have we been thinking of? A critical overview of 40 years of student learning research in higher education. *Studies in Higher Education, 34*(4), 377–390.

Hannon, J. (2013). Incommensurate practices: Sociomaterial entanglements of learning technology implementation. *Journal of Computer Assisted Learning, 29*(2), 168–178.

Hannon, J. (2014). Making the right connections: Implementing the objects of practice into a network for learning. In V. E. Hodgson, M. De Laat, D. McConnell, & T. Ryberg (Eds.), *The design, experience and practice of networked learning* (pp. 67–85). Heidelberg, Germany: Springer.

Hansson, T. (2002). Leadership by activity theory and professional development by social construction. *Systemic Practice and Action Research, 15*(5), 411–436.

Harasim, L. (2012). *Learning theory and online technologies*. New York: Routledge.

Hativa, N., & Goodyear, P. (Eds.). (2002). *Teacher thinking, beliefs and knowledge in higher education*. Dordrecht, The Netherlands: Kluwer.

Haythornthwaite, C., & Andrews, R. (2011). *E-learning theory and practice*. London: Sage.

Haythornthwaite, C., & De Laat, M. (2011). Social network informed design for learning with educational technology. In A. D. Olofsson & J. O. Lindberg (Eds.), *Informed design of educational technologies in higher education: Enhanced learning and teaching* (pp. 352–374). Hershey, PA: IGI Global.

Hodgson, V. E., & Watland, P. A. (2004). Researching networked management learning. *Management Learning, 35*(2), 99–116.

Hodgson, V. E., De Laat, M., McConnell, D., & Ryberg, T. (Eds.). (2014). *The design, experience and practice of networked learning*. Heidleberg, Germany: Springer.

Ilich, I. (1970). *Deschooling society*. New York: Harper and Row. Retrieved from http://www.preservenet.com/theory/Illich/Deschooling/intro.html

Illeris, K. (2009). *Contemporary theories of learning: Learning theorists… in their own words*. London: Routledge.

Jahnke, I. (2009). The process of digital formalisation in sociotechnical learning communities— Needed or overloaded? In C. O'Malley, D. Suthers, P. Reimann, & A. Dimitracopoulou (Eds.), *Proceedings of the 9th International Conference on Computer Supported Collaborative Learning: CSCL2009: CSCL practices* (Vol. 1, pp. 287–291). Rhodes, Greece: University of the Aegean.

Jandrić, P., & Boras, D. (Eds.). (2015). *Critical learning in digital networks*. New York: Springer.

Johnson, D., & Johnson, R. (1999). *Learning together and alone: Cooperative, competitive and individualistic learning* (5th ed.). Boston: Allyn & Bacon.

Johnson, D., & Johnson, R. (2008). Cooperation and the use of technology. In J. M. Spector, M. D. Merrill, J. van Merrienboer, & M. Driscoll (Eds.), *Handbook of research on educational communications and technology* (3rd ed., pp. 1017–1044). New York: Taylor & Francis.

Jonassen, D. H. (1991). Objectivism vs constructivism: Do we need a new philosophical paradigm. *Educational Technology Research and Development, 39*(3), 5–14.

Jones, C. (2004). Networks and learning: Communities, practices and the metaphor of networks. *The Association for Learning Technology Journal, 12*(1), 82–93.

Jones, C. (2013). Designing for practice: A view from the social sciences. In H. Beetham & R. Sharpe (Eds.), *Rethinking pedagogy for a digital age: Designing for 21st century learning* (2nd ed., pp. 204–217). London: Routledge.

Jones, C., Cook, J., Jones, A., & De Laat, M. (2007). Collaboration. In G. Conole & M. Oliver (Eds.), *Contemporary perspectives in e-learning research* (pp. 174–189). London: Routledge Falmer.

Jones, C., & Dirckinck-Holmfeld, L. (2009). Analysing networked learning practices: An introduction. In L. Dirckinck-Holmfeld, C. Jones, & B. Lindström (Eds.), *Analysing networked learning practices in higher education and continuing professional development* (pp. 1–27). Rotterdam, The Netherlands: Sense Publishers, BV.

Jones, C., Dirckinck-Holmfeld, L., & Lindström, B. (2006). A relational, indirect, meso-level approach to CSCL design in the next decade. *International Journal of Computer Supported Collaborative Learning, 1*(1), 35–56.

Kafai, Y. B., & Peppler, K. A. (2011). Beyond small groups: New opportunities for research in computer-supported collective learning. In H. Spada, G. Stahl, N. Miyake, & N. Law (Eds.), *Connecting computer-supported collaborative learning to policy and practice: CSCL2011 conference proceedings* (Long papers, Vol. I, pp. 17–24). Hong Kong, China: The University of Hong Kong.

Kirschner, P. A., Martins, R. L., & Stribos, J. W. (2004). CSCL in higher education. In J.-W. Strijbos, P. Kirschner, & R. Martens (Eds.), *What we know about CSCL: And implementing it in higher education*. Boston: Kluwer.

Kop, R., & Hill, A. (2008). Connectivism: Learning theory of the future or vestige of the past? *International Review of Research in Open and Distance Learning (IRRODL), 9*(3). Retrieved from http://www.irrodl.org/index.php/irrodl/article/view/523/1103

Koper, R. (2005). An introduction to learning design. In R. Koper & C. Tattersall (Eds.), *Learning design: A handbook on modeling and delivering networked education and training* (pp. 3–20). Berlin, Germany: Springer.

Koper, R., & Tattersall, C. (Eds.). (2005). *Learning design: A handbook on modeling and delivering networked education and training*. Berlin, Germany: Springer.

Koschmann, T. (Ed.). (1996). *CSCL: Theory and practice of an emerging paradigm*. Mahwah, NJ: Lawrence Erlbaum Associates.

Koschmann, T. (1999). Toward a dialogic theory of learning: Bakhtin's contribution to understanding learning in settings of collaboration. In C. Hoadley (Ed.), *Proceedings of Computer Support for Collaborative Learning* (pp. 308–313). Mahwah, NJ: Lawrence Erlbaum.

Koschmann, T. (2000). The physiological and the social in the psychologies of Dewey and Thorndike: The matter of habit. In B. Fishman & S. O'Connor-Divelbiss (Eds.), *Fourth international conference of the learning sciences* (pp. 314–319). Mahwah, NJ: Erlbaum.

Koschmann, T. (2001). Revisiting the paradigms of instructional technology. In G. Kennedy, M. Keppell, C. McNaught, & T. Petrovic (Eds.), *Meeting at the crossroads. Proceedings of the 18th Annual Conference of the Australian Society for Computers in Learning in Tertiary Education* (pp. 15–22). Melbourne, VIC: Biomedical Multimedia Unit, The University of Melbourne. Retrieved from http://www.ascilite.org.au/conferences/melbourne01/pdf/papers/koschmannt.pdf

Koschmann, T. (2002). Dewey's contribution to the foundations of CSCL research. In *CSCL'02 Proceedings of the Conference on Computer Support for Collaborative Learning: Foundations for a CSCL Community* (pp. 17–22), Boulder, CO.

Lankshear, C., Peters, M., & Knobel, M. (2000). Information, knowledge and learning. *Journal of Philosophy of Education, 34*, 17–40.

Laurillard, D. M. (1993). *Rethinking University teaching: A framework for the effective use of educational technology*. London: Routledge.

Lave, J. (1991). Situating learning in communities of practice. In L. Resnick, J. Levine, & S. Teasley (Eds.), *Perspectives on socially shared cognition* (pp. 63–82). Washington, DC: APA.

Lave, J. (2011). *Apprenticeship in critical ethnographic practice*. Chicago: University of Chicago Press.

Lave, J., & Wenger, E. (1991). *Situated learning: Legitimate peripheral participation*. Cambridge, England: Cambridge University Press.

Lowyck, J. (2013). Bridging learning theories and technology-enhanced environments: A critical appraisal of its history. In J. M. Spector, M. D. Merrill, J. Elen, & M. J. Bishop (Eds.), *Handbook of research on educational communications and technology* (4th ed., pp. 3–20). New York: Springer.

Margolis, E. (Ed.). (2001). *The hidden curriculum in higher education*. London: Routledge.

Marton, F. (1981). Phenomenography—Describing conceptions of the World around us. *Instructional Science, 10*, 177–200.

Marton, F. (1994). Phenomenography. In T. Husen & T. N. Postlethwaite (Eds.), *The international encyclopedia of education* (2nd ed., pp. 4424–4429). Oxford, England: Pergamon.

Marton, F., & Booth, S. (1997). *Learning and awareness*. Mahwah, NJ: Lawrence Erlbaum Associates.

Marton, F., Dall'Alba, G., & Beaty, E. (1993). Conceptions of learning. *International Journal of Educational Research, 19*, 277–300.

Marton, F., Hounsell, D., & Entwistle, N. (1997). *The experience of learning: Implications for teaching and studying in higher education*. Edinburgh, Scotland: Scottish Academic Press.

Marton, F., & Säljö, R. (1976a). On qualitative differences in learning 1: Outcome and process. *British Journal of Educational Psychology, 46*, 4–11.

Marton, F., & Säljö, R. (1976b). On qualitative differences in learning 11: Outcome as a function of the learner's conception of task. *British Journal of Educational Psychology, 46*, 115–127.

Mayes, T., & de Freitas, S. (2013). Technology-enhanced learning: The role of theory. In H. Beetham & R. Sharpe (Eds.), *Rethinking pedagogy for a digital age: Designing for 21st century learning* (2nd ed., pp. 17–30). London: Routledge.

McAndrew, P., & Weller, M. (2005). Applying learning design to supported open learning. In R. Koper & C. Tattersall (Eds.), *Learning design: A handbook on modelling and delivering networked education and training* (pp. 281–290). Berlin, Germany: Springer.

McCluskey, F., & Winter, M. (2012). *The idea of the digital University: Ancient traditions, disruptive technologies and the battle for the soul of higher education*. Washington, DC: Policy Studies Organisation/Westphalia Press.

McConnell, D. (1994). *Implementing computer supported cooperative learning*. London: Kogan Page.

McConnell, D., Hodgson, V., & Dirckinck-Holmfeld, L. (2012). Networked learning: A brief history and new trends. In L. Dirckinck-Holmfeld, V. Hodgson, & D. McConnell (Eds.), *Exploring the theory, pedagogy and practice of networked learning* (pp. 3–24). New York: Springer.

Miettinen, R. (2000). The concept of experiential learning and John Dewey's theory of reflective thought and action. *International Journal of Lifelong Education, 19*(1), 54–72.

Mitra, S. (2000). *Minimally invasive education for mass computer literacy*. Paper presented at the CRIDALA 2000 conference, Hong Kong, China, June 21–25, 2000. Retrieved from http://www.hole-in-the-wall.com/docs/Paper01.pdf

Nespor, J. (2011). Devices and educational change. *Educational Philosophy and Theory, 43*(Suppl. 1), 15–37.

Oliver, M., & Trigwell, K. (2005). Can 'blended learning' be redeemed? *E-learning, 2*(1), 17–26.

Orlikowski, W. J. (2000). Using technology and constituting structures: A practice lens for studying technology in organizations. *Organization Science, 11*(4), 404–428.

Pegler, C. (2011). *Reuse and repurposing of online digital learning resources within UK higher education: 2003–2010.* PhD Thesis, The Open University. Retrieved from http://oro.open.ac.uk/32317/

Pegler, C. (2013). The influence of open resources on design practice. In H. Beetham & R. Sharpe (Eds.), *Rethinking pedagogy for a digital age: Designing for 21st century learning* (2nd ed., pp. 145–161). London: Routledge.

Prosser, M., & Trigwell, K. (1999). *Understanding learning and teaching: The experience in higher education.* Buckingham, England: Society for Research into Higher Education and Open University Press.

Ramsden, P. (2002). *Learning to teach in higher education* (2nd ed.). London: Routledge.

Richardson, J. T. E. (1999). The concepts and methods of phenomenographic research. *Review of Educational Research, 69*(1), 53–82.

Richardson, J. T. E. (2005). Students' approaches to learning and teachers' approaches to teaching in higher education. *Educational Psychology, 25*(6), 673–680.

Rockwell, T. (2003). Rorty, Putnam and the pragmatist view of epistemology and metaphysics. *Education and Culture, 14*(1), 8–16.

Rummel, N., Kapur, M., Nathan, M., & Puntambekar, S. (Eds.) (2013). *To see the world and a grain of sand: Learning across levels of space, time, and scale: CSCL 2013 conference proceedings* (Vol. 1—Full papers & symposia). International Society of the Learning Sciences.

Schatzki, T. R. (1996). *Social practices: A wittgensteinian approach to human activity and the social.* Cambridge, England: Cambridge University Press.

Schatzki, T., Knorr-Cetina, K., & von Savigny, E. (Eds.). (2001). *The practice turn in contemporary theory.* London: Routledge.

Selwyn, N., & Facer, K. (Eds.). (2013). *The politics of education and technology: Conflicts, controversies, and connections.* New York: PalgraveMcMillan.

Siemens, G. (2005). Connectivism a theory of learning for the digital age. *International Journal of Instructional Technology and Distance Learning, 2*(1). Retrieved from http://www.itdl.org/Journal/Jan_05/article01.htm

Skinner, B. F. (1953). *Science and human behavior.* New York: Macmillan.

Skinner, B. F. (1954). The science of learning and the art of teaching. *Harvard Educational Review, 24*, 86–97.

Skinner, B. F. (1958). Teaching machines. *Science, 128*(3330), 969–977.

Slavin, R. (1990). *Cooperative learning: Theory research and practice.* Englewood Cliffs, NJ: Prentice Hall.

Spada, H., Stahl, G., Miyake, N., & Law, N. (Eds.). (2011). *Connecting computer-supported collaborative learning to policy and practice: CSCL2011 Conference Proceedings* (Vol. 1). Hong Kong, China: The University of Hong Kong.

Stahl, G. (2003). Meaning and interpretation in collaboration. In B. Wasson, S. Ludvigsen, & U. Hoppe (Eds.), *Designing for change in networked learning environments: Proceedings of the international conference on computer support for collaborative learning (CSCL'03)* (pp. 523–532). Bergen, Norway: Kluwer. Retrieved from http://GerryStahl.net/cscl/papers/ch20.pdf

Steeples, C., & Jones, C. (Eds.). (2002). *Networked learning: Perspectives and issues.* London: Springer.

Suchman, L. (2007). *Human-machine reconfigurations: Plans and situated actions* (2nd ed.). Cambridge, England: Cambridge University Press.

Suchman, L. (2011). Anthropological relocations and the limits of design. *Annual Review of Anthropology, 40*, 1–18.

Tchounikine, P. (2011). *Computer science and educational software design: Resources for multidisciplinary work in technology enhanced learning.* Heidelberg, Germany: Springer.

Thorndike, E. L. (1911). *Animal intelligence.* New York: Macmillan.

Vanderstraeten, R., & Biesta, G. (2006). How is education possible? Pragmatism, communication and the social organisation of education. *British Journal of Educational Studies, 54*(2), 160–174.

Von Glasersfeld, E. (1984). An Introduction to radical constructivism. In P. Watzlawick (Ed.), *The invented reality*. New York: Norton.

Von Glasersfeld, E. (1989). Constructivism in education. In T. Husen & T. N. Postlethwaite (Eds.), *The international encyclopedia of education* (Vol. 1, pp. 162–163). Oxford, England: Pergamon Press.

Wasson, B., Ludvigsen, S., & Hoppe, U. (Eds.). (2003). *Designing for change in networked learning environments: Proceedings of the International Conference on Computer Supported Collaborative Learning 2003*. Dordrecht, The Netherlands: Kluwer.

Watson, J. B. (1913). Psychology as the behaviourist views it. *Psychological Review, 20*, 158–177.

Wegerif, R. (2013). *Dialogic: Education for the internet age*. London: Routledge.

Wenger, E. (1998). *Communities of practice: Learning, meaning, and identity*. Cambridge, England: Cambridge University Press.

Wenger, E., McDermott, R., & Snyder, W. (2002). *Cultivating communities of practice: A guide to managing knowledge*. Boston: Harvard Business School Press.

Wenger, E., Trayner, B., & De Laat, M. (2011). *Promoting and assessing value creation in communities and networks: A conceptual framework*. Heerlen, The Netherlands: Rapport 18, Ruud de Moor Centrum, Open University of the Netherlands. Retrieved from http://wenger-trayner.com/wp-content/uploads/2011/12/11-04-Wenger_Trayner_DeLaat_Value_creation.pdf

Wiley, D. (2006). Open source, openness, and higher education. *Innovate Journal of Online Education, 3*(1). Retrieved from http://citeseerx.ist.psu.edu/viewdoc/download?doi=10.1.1.18 6.5388&rep=rep1&type=pdf

Willis, P. E. (1977). *Learning to labour: How working class kids get working class jobs*. Farnborough, England: Saxon House.

Wilson, B. G., & Myers, K. M. (2000). Situated cognition in theoretical and practical context. In D. H. Jonassen & S. M. Land (Eds.), *Theoretical foundations of learning environments* (pp. 57–88). Mahwah, NJ: Lawrence Erlbaum.

Chapter 4
A Network of Network Theories

The previous chapter examined the relationship of networked learning to learning theory, this chapter examines the second major term and the ideas that currently inform our understanding of networks and how that affects networked learning. The chapter brings together a number of different theoretical approaches to networks from different intellectual traditions and explores what kinds of insights they can offer in developing a theory of networked learning. The chapter begins by discussing what a network might be. Networks are spoken about as if there was a single or simple definition which was common to all network theories. Only a little investigation reveals this is not the case, so the chapter begins with a brief outline of the way networks are described and discussed in a general way, prior to embarking on a more detailed discussion of three sources of network theory. The three sources drawn on in this chapter are: scientific and mathematical theories and descriptions; social networks and social network analysis (SNA); actor-network theory (ANT).

The popular discourse around networks has coined memorable phrases such as 'small worlds', 'six degrees of separation' (Buchanan 2002; Watts 2003) and the 'wisdom of crowds' (Surowieki 2005) and it often has a direct relationship to academic literature (Rainie and Wellman 2012). One of the names that stand out in popularising a scientific and mathematical understanding of networks that has become meshed into the popular discourse is Albert-Lázló Barabási. In *Linked: The New Science of Networks* (2002) he took a serious understanding of the mathematics behind contemporary understandings of networks and articulated these with everyday examples that allowed readers to find their relevance to a wide range of social and natural settings. Because of the embedding of these popular ideas any discussion of networks is likely to meet some already entrenched metaphors and impressions of what networks are composed of and of the kinds of effects that network organisation can be expected to lead to. This chapter begins by setting out and clarifying some of the basic ideas about networks before examining three main areas of network theory relevant to networked learning, scientific and mathematical conceptions of networks, SNA and ANT.

© Springer International Publishing Switzerland 2015
C. Jones, *Networked Learning*, Research in Networked Learning,
DOI 10.1007/978-3-319-01934-5_4

What Is a Network?

Network theory in mathematics is related to graph theory and the representation of objects some of which are connected by links. In mathematical terms these are often referred to as vertices and edges. Vertices are the nodes of a network and they are the objects that can be connected by edges or links. A basic representation of such a network is in Fig. 4.1 below in which vertices or nodes are represented by numbered circles and the edges or links by straight lines.

This mesh or net-like structure will be familiar to most readers and it may be the underlying impression that most readers rely on when they think of a network. Network theory dates back to the eighteenth century and a famous paper concerning the *Seven Bridges of Königsberg* by Euler (Barabási 2002). Euler demonstrated that there was no route around the city that allowed a person to cross each bridge only once (see Fig. 4.2). The key point for the purpose of this chapter was the abstraction of a real-world problem, crossing Königsberg's seven bridges only once, into an abstract representation and mathematical proof.

Fig. 4.1 Public domain.
Created 'neato'. *Source—*
http://en.wikipedia.org/wiki/
File:6n-graf.svg

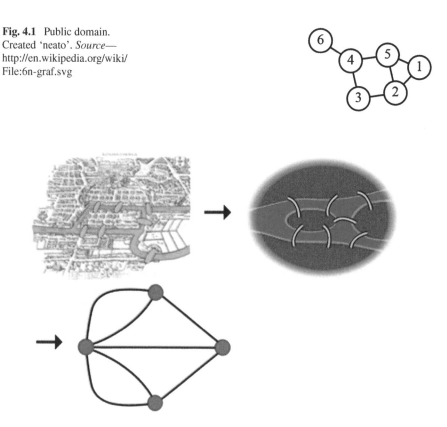

Fig. 4.2 Public domain Wikimedia commons

Since the early origins of network analysis there have been several relatively recent key developments, three of which will be explored here. Firstly the idea of random networks (Erdős and Rényi 1959; Gilbert 1959), secondly the idea of small worlds (Milgram 1967; Watts and Strogatz 1998) and thirdly and most recently the idea of scale-free networks (Barabási 2002).

Scientific and Mathematical Frameworks

Random Networks

The idea of random networks draws together statistical probability and graph theory. It was initially developed independently by Erdős and Rényi (1959) and Gilbert (1959). The theory suggests that although webs of connections that arise in a multitude of different contexts are necessarily varied, a simplified framework could be developed to represent all the sorts of complex graphs. In this framework the simplest way a network could be generated was random, and this way of under-standing networks viewed them as fundamentally random. Its importance was that it explained how starting from a simple aggregation of individual and unconnected nodes it was possible to move to a single interconnected cluster. In the social terms that are more familiar in networked learning, this theory covered a process in which a group of individuals when brought together develop interconnections between themselves, starting with a single link, and move from a fragmented aggregate to an organised community. The random networks that this framework describes were not neat regular graphs, they were abstracted representations of the messy complex systems that could be found in the real world. In regular graphs each node has the same number of links. A mesh composed of perpendicular lines forming a square lattice has nodes with four links. In a beehive structure, or hexagonal lattice, each node has three links (Barabási 2002). The regularity and neatness of such ordered patterns is what is absent from real-world complex networks and the introduction of the theory of random networks took graph theory out into the messy world of social gatherings and natural processes. The idea of random networks was until relatively recently the dominant idea and the complex networks found in the real world were viewed as fundamentally random.

Small Worlds

The random network framework of Erdős and Rényi had some clear limitations. It did not account for the clustering found in real-world networks and it did not account for the development of hubs with a large number of links. It is the first of these limi-tations that the idea of small worlds addresses, the clustered nature of many real-world networks. In popular thinking small worlds are linked to the idea of six degrees

of separation and this idea was developed, although not originated[1] in the work of
Milgram (1967) and added to by Granovetter (1973). Milgram set about testing
empirically whether the assumption of a random network applied to human relations
by estimating (a) the number of people that each person in the United States knew
(average 500) and (b) what the chances were, if randomly distributed, of any two US
citizens knowing one another (1 in 200,000) and (c) if linked by 2 intermediate
acquaintances, the odds of being linked become better than 50–50. Intrigued by this
mathematical projection Milgram set about exploring the result by an experimental
procedure. The experiment involved randomly chosen residents in Wichita, Kansas
or Omaha, Nebraska being asked to deliver a folder to one of two randomly selected
targets. For Kansas participants the target was the wife of a divinity professor in
Sharon Massachusetts and for Nebraska participants it was a stockbroker in Boston.
The finding was that any two randomly assigned persons could be linked by a median
chain length of five intermediates. This was a surprising result and it has become a
popular cultural reference by way of the phrase 'six degrees of separation', although
Milgram did not use that phrase and it has been attributed to a play of that name by
John Guare (Barabási 2002). Six degrees of separation should not be taken literally
but the idea that networks allow for relatively short steps between different nodes on
the network is highly important. It suggests that people can be connected in this way,
but documents can also be linked via their URLs on the Web, and the Web itself can
be shown to have the characteristics of a small world (Barabási 2002).

Small worlds are not confined to social networks but the idea of clustering was
something most obvious in social analysis. The mathematical development of the
idea of six degrees of separation was accomplished by Watts and Strogatz (1998).
Watts and Strogatz identified two independent structural features affecting small
world features in networks: firstly the clustering coefficient; a measure of how many
interconnections exist between nodes in a network, and secondly the distance; the
number of links in a path between nodes. The random networks described by Erdős
and Rényi exhibit a short distance between nodes and a low clustering coefficient.
In small-world networks, Watts and Strogatz showed a short distance between nodes
but a much higher clustering coefficient than randomness would allow. The small-
world networks described by Watts and Strogatz took network theory closer to real-
world networks and began to answer one of the weaknesses of a theory based on
random networks, the fact that they did not account for local clustering. Watts and
Strogatz had shown that with a high degree of clustering, in which each node is highly
connected to its near neighbours, a few weak ties connecting random nodes could
dramatically shorten the average distance between nodes, making it a small world.

Granovetter (1973) had added to the debate by discussing the strength of different
ties or links between nodes in a network. Strength was defined not in relation to the
character of the link between two nodes but in the structure of the wider network.
A strong tie was one which described two nodes with a connection that also shared
ties with others in their networks. A weak tie was one in which the two nodes shared
some links in their wider network and the absence of any shared ties would be a

---

[1] For an account of the ideas origins in the work of the Hungarian writer Karinthy see Barabási (2002).

limiting case. The idea of the strength of ties disrupts the notion of random networks in which all nodes share the same number of links. Grannoveter's work on the strength of weak ties suggested that the spread of ideas, just as the delivery of a folder, depended not so much on close contacts but on acquaintances, or 'weak ties'. These more casual links play an important part in the ability of more tightly knit communities and groups to communicate with each other. It is these looser ties that are the bridges to the wider world. This idea of groupings and clusters connected by weak links contrasts with the idea of a random network in which links are entirely random and do not have different strengths. The idea of weak and strong ties in networked learning has been explored by Jones et al. (2008). The importance of weak ties in networked learning lies in their ability to bridge between tight clusters that each may contain knowledge valuable to the other clusters linked to by a weak tie.

In Watts' view networks are everywhere: the brain is a network of neurons; social organisations are networks of people and the economy is a network of markets (Watts 1999). Network representations can be applied to ecosystems, the Internet and the Web. The distinct element of Watt's view is that many of these networks can be described as small worlds. In small-world networks local actions can have global consequences and the relationships between the local and the global are highly dependent on the network structure. Perhaps most importantly small worlds inhabit a region between random networks and the ordered networks represented by the lattices and beehive structures mentioned earlier. Watts proposes a class of networks, small worlds, which abstractly represents the clustering and tie lengths found in real-small-world networks. The importance of this for networked learning lies in the implications these descriptions have for how network structures can influence the formation of communities and patterns of cooperation and collaboration. In relation to cooperation the game theory prisoners dilemma was drawn on by McConnell to support the theory of CSCL (2000, p. 6) and this same dilemma also formed the basis for one of the chapters in Watts' book about small worlds (Watts 1999, Ch. 8).

Scale-Free Networks and Hierarchical Networks

Small worlds answered one of the weakness left by the description of random networks, the gap concerning clustering. It left another major weakness that remained to be addressed which was how hubs formed in networks. A hub is a node in a network with a high number of links or ties with other nodes. Hubs are an extension of, and an extreme example of, weak links and the tasks that they can perform. Nodes with many links can perform the role of being a connector, and the existence of nodes with anomalously large numbers of ties provides a major challenge to the conception of random networks. Barabási (2002) described how finding that the Web had a small number of hubs was a shock. There was a further surprise that the Web was not an exception and an examination of a diverse range of networks revealed that they too had hubs, something that ran counter to both the idea of a random network and small worlds. Barabási argues that hubs dominate the structure of all the networks in which they are present, making such classes of networks look like small worlds. In scale-free networks hubs acting as connectors create short paths between all nodes in a system.

Scale-free networks display a power law distribution. That is, those nodes with only a few links are numerous, but a few nodes have a very large number of links. Those not familiar with mathematics or network (graph) theory may not have heard of a power law distribution but they may have been introduced to a normal distribution or bell curve, a distribution that would characterise a random network. If the links between nodes were distributed randomly you'd expect the outcome of a plot mapping the number of connections that each node has (its degree) against the frequency of the occurrence of a node with a particular number of connections (degree) to be the familiar bell curve of the normal distribution. In this curve the mean of the number of links would be the most common node type and the poorly or exceptionally connected node would be the exceptions. Unlike the bell curve distribution a power law distribution does not have a central maximum, instead a histogram displaying a power law is a continuously decreasing curve (see Fig. 4.3). This curve describes many nodes with few links and a small number of nodes with many links and each has an exponent, a figure capturing the number of highly linked nodes relative to the less connected.

> The number of nodes with exactly k links follows a power law, each with a degree exponent that for most systems varies between two and three (Barabási 2002, p. 69).

The random network described by the normal distribution of the bell curve decays more quickly and it does not describe nodes with very high numbers of links and the majority of nodes have a similar number of links with deviations from the average being rare. It is this feature that means that random distributions have a characteristic 'scale', the node connectivity of the average node. Power law distributions do not have an average or characteristic node and they contain extremes from rare well-connected hubs to numerous small nodes with few links, they are as a consequence scale-free.

Scale-free networks predict that such networks will have several large hubs which fundamentally define the network topology. The rationale behind this kind of distribution rests on some simple propositions. Firstly networks grow through what are described as preferential attachments so that when new nodes are added to a network the new nodes link to preexisting nodes. Secondly the probability of linking to a preexisting node is higher if it already has a large number of attachments. It is from these simple processes, growth and preferential attachments that scale-free networks develop. This pattern of growth and preferential attachment provides a basis for an historical dimension to networks and their emergent structures. It also suggests an order as opposed to the randomness in earlier descriptions of networks, but an order that is not completely regular. For this reason Barabási suggests that scale-free networks: 'are the parent signatures of self-organisation in complex systems' (Barabási 2002, p. 77). A further characteristic of scale-free networks is their robustness. Scale-free networks, even more than random networks, cope well with the removal of many nodes and they are resistant both to attack and to errors.

Bell curve and scale free distributions (Plus Maths)
(text for Y axis "Number of nodes with k links)

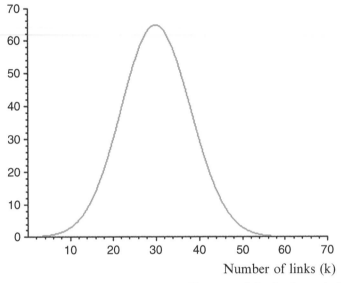

The normal distribution or bell curve

(text for Y axis "Number of nodes with k links)

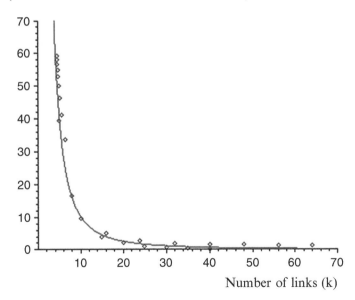

Fig. 4.3 Bell curve and scale-free distributions (Plus Maths). A scale-free distribution adhering to a power law. (The *black circles* represent a data set from a typical scale-free network. All points lie on or close to the *blue line*, which is the graph of a function of the form ax^-k. The degree distribution adheres to a power law). Adapted from: Reference: Freiberger, M. (2007) Network News. *+Plus magazine* http://plus.maths.org/content/network-news

Fig. 4.4 Hierarchical
network model. Source
Wikimedia commons GNU
free documentation licence
http://en.wikipedia.org/wiki/
File:Hierarchical_network_
model_example.png

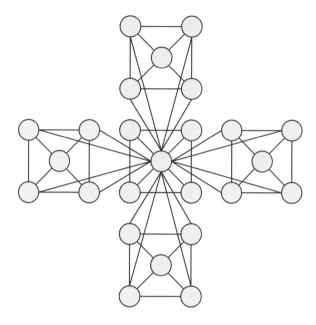

In addition to being scale-free most real-world networks also display a high
degree of clustering. This clustering is consistent with the predictions of scale-free
networks once a hierarchical organisation is introduced into the network model. The
presence of the hierarchical structure helps to reinterpret the role of hubs in complex
networks. The theory predicts a modular topology with self-nesting groups of nodes
in clusters with dense interconnections (Fig. 4.4). Clusters of nodes with strong
interrelationships such as work groups, communities are related in a hierarchical
structure.

> In hierarchical networks, the degree of clustering characterizing the different groups fol-
> lows a strict scaling law, which can be used to identify the presence of a hierarchical orga-
> nization in real networks. We find that several real networks, such as the World Wide Web,
> actor network,[2] the Internet at the domain level, and the semantic web obey this scaling law,
> indicating that hierarchy is a fundamental characteristic of many complex systems (Ravasz
> and Barabási 2003, p. 1).

If scale-free networks introduce a dynamic and historical element to networks,
hierarchy in networks implies patterns of power and influence.

The scientific and mathematical tradition of network analysis provides tools of
analysis and description that can be applied to large flows of data. Network analysis
can be applied to large networks, such as those generated by large online and distance courses and more recently MOOCs.

---

[2]This use of actor network does not refer to Actor-Network Theory but to networks composed of
actors e.g. the Kevin Bacon game in which actors are connected to Kevin Bacon in a few steps.

Social Networks

SNA has a relatively long history (Freeman 2004) that is loosely related to aspects of the development of mathematical network theory outlined above. As previously noted some of the key figures in network theory were also contributors to the development of SNA (Milgram 1967; Granovetter 1973). SNA is a developed field with handbooks (Scott 2000) providing guidance on methods and introductory texts that cover both the practical questions of implementation and the theoretical development of the field (Degenne and Forsé 1999). It has been connected with the development of networked learning through a common interest in the development of community and online community in particular (Wellman et al. 1996). More recently the idea of 'networked individualism' has been drawn on for the understanding of the network society and networked learning (Castells 2000/1996; Jones 2004; Jones and Dirckinck-Holmfeld 2009; Rainie and Wellman 2012; Wellman et al. 2003). A key link in this connection has been the work of Haythornthwaite (2002, 2006, 2010) who worked and wrote with Wellman, but who also became active in networked learning (Haythornthwaite and De Laat 2010). An early adopter of SNA in networked learning was De Laat (2006) who applied SNA to examine group cohesion and interaction patterns. Jones et al. (2008) drew on Grannoveter's notion of the strength of weak ties in a networked learning context and SNA has also been applied to relations between people and the analysis of these relations by way of the texts and resources they interact with (Haythornthwaite and Gruzd 2008, 2012). More recently this latter approach has provided a link to the developing area of learner analytics (Schreurs et al. 2013; De Laat and Prinzen 2014).

The SNA approach builds on the principles of analysis from network or graph theory but it also draws heavily on sociology and communications theory for an understanding of interpersonal, organisational and communal relations. A focus of this approach is how relationships between people and organised groups of people form networks and how these networks affect access to opportunities such as jobs, knowledge and information, physical goods and services. Haythornthwaite and De Laat (2010) identify the basic building blocks of SNA as: actors, ties, relations and networks. Care should be taken not to understand an actor in these building blocks as simply an individual. Actors in networks can be organised groups and they are not necessarily individual people or even people at all. Indeed actors can sometimes be computer agents and sociomaterial forms of mediated human–human or hybrid human–machine configurations, animals, insects or a combination of these elements (Fig. 4.5).

Haythornthwaite and De Laat are cautious about the inclusion of these inanimate and hybrid forms of actors and state:

> However, there is little work at this stage that has applied social network analysis to include objects, and interpretations of the social aspects of networks that include mixed and/or inanimate objects will require careful thought (Haythornthwaite and De Laat 2010, p. 185).

These hybrid and non-human forms of actors are discussed more fully in the next section dealing with ANT and related sociomaterial and post-human approaches.

Actors

- Nodes in the network
- Examples: Students and instructors in a class, informal learnings in an online forum; co-workers in an organization; organizations in an industry or region

Relations

- Lines in the network--Connect actors in **one** specific kind of interaction
- Directed (giving or receiving), **OR** undirected (sharing)
- Examples: sharing information; giving social support; teaching and learning

Ties

- Also lines in the network: total connection between actors, comprised of one or more relations
- Strong ties (many, important, different, plus intimate relations) or weak ties (few relations)

Networks

- Configuration of sets of actors and their ties
- Reveals key actors (star), positions (broker), roles (technological guru) **AND** connectivity, centralization, cliques, isolates
- Can be rabust, solid, enduring, based on many nodes, sustaining social capital **OR** sparse, fragile, temporory, dependent on critical nodes
- Co-located and distributed
- Center on work, social and/or learning relations

Social Network Basics

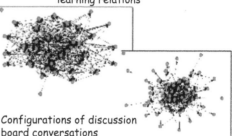

Configurations of discussion board conversations

Fig. 4.5 Social network basics. *Source* Haythornthwaite and De Laat (2010), p. 184. Open source

For the remainder of this section the focus is on more traditional social relations involving person to person and organisational relations between persons and organised groups and between organised groups.

In SNA terms the actors form the nodes of a network and the ties between these nodes are known as relations. The relations between actors can be single or multiple, frequent or infrequent, optional or required, personal or impersonal. Once actors have a minimum of one relationship they are tied and the ties can vary between weak and strong ties as discussed earlier. Weak ties can be infrequent, unimportant or incidental whereas strong ties are based on multiple relations that might involve reciprocity, trust and a degree of self-disclosure. Actors and the relations between them form networks. These networks can be drawn and represented in sociograms, and the visualisations generated can form a major part of SNA, ranging from simple line drawings to mathematically complex renderings and visually stimulating images. Early sociograms in the field of networked learning were developed from studying online learning interactions by Henri (1992) who derived 'communicograms' depicting degrees of interactivity in computer conferences from content analytic data. For examples of visualisations see De Laat et al. (2007) and Dawson et al. (2010).

We have already noted how the existence of weak ties can provide bridges between groups that are primarily tightly bound in communities and collaborative groups.

This is one feature of network structure that has a clear set of implications for networked learning but the implications of strong ties are equally important and relate to those learning theories that identify cooperation, collaboration, community and interaction including dialogue as important. So far so good, because these kinds of network patterns are well researched and at least partially understood. Recently the growth in scale of learning interactions, for example, in MOOCs (Massive Open Online Courses), has led to the growth of an interest in the kinds of emergent network patterns arising at scale (Daniel 2012; Clow 2013). Clow notes that participation rates in MOOCs look more like marketing figures and describes the pattern as a funnel of participation, a pattern which although fat-tailed is not a power law distribution:

> The funnel of participation is a real, significant phenomenon in MOOCs and related courses. Compared to formal learning, there tends to be much higher rates of drop-out, and steeply unequal patterns of participation (Clow 2013, Online).

Furthermore there is an increasing interest in institutional approaches to learner analytics, also at scale, and less concerned with personal interactions and more with institutional level structures and interventions, for example to manage and prevent the course and institutional dropout of students (McCluskey and Winter 2012). McCluskey and Winter (2012) also argue that argue the new combined sources of data enabled by digital technologies provide new opportunities for institutional governance based on data analysis, an alternative to both managerial bureaucracy and collegial academic governance, something examined more fully in Chap. 5. The interaction between the collection of information in digital systems and the organised representation by way of analytics suggests that networked and digital technologies are beginning to 'informate' educational processes in ways previously seen in more conventional industries (Zuboff 1988).

SNA having its roots in mathematical theories of networks and graphs is applicable to any connection between nodes. Networked learning is of course more specific, and it requires a more careful consideration of both the actors and relationships that form learning networks. Haythornthwaite and De Laat (2010) suggest networked learning would be interested in questions such as 'Who learns from whom? What do people learn from each other? How learning interactions between pairs support or configure the knowledge held in a network?' (ibid, p. 187–188). This fails to include an essential element of networked learning, and indeed many forms of learning, the relationship between learners and their resources. From an SNA perspective they suggest what are termed 'two-mode networks' in which common exposure to an event (attending a lecture, reading a text etc.) can provide the basis for a common understanding. Schreurs and De Laat (2014) and De Laat et al. (2014) state that networks need to be about something, they are topic-based and simple peer-to-peer relations don't explain their meaning until there is an understanding of what these relations are about. They present a network awareness tool that helps to identify two-mode networks in which content and people are combined. In a two-mode network, events provide one dimension and people the other. Representations can be developed to show networks based on common participation in a lecture or online event or common reading patterns. Such an analysis can expose important structural components of online courses, for example patterns of logging into or reading texts contained in MOOC platforms.

Networked Individualism

SNA has also led to new ways to conceptualise interactions between people that have implications for dominant theories of learning. Wellman (Wellman et al. 2003; Wellman 2001) and Castells (2000/1996) have described the form of sociality in network society as 'networked individualism' (Castells 2001, p. 129). The idea of networked individualism and network society is directly related via Wellman to early ideas informing the development of networked learning through the work of Hiltz and Turoff (1978). The idea of networked individualism is connected to changes in the contemporary economy organised around global networks. These economic relations imply on the one hand an increasing interdependence and cooperation and on the other hand a work process that is increasingly individualised. Network organisation suggests a dynamic tension between integration and fragmentation. The macrosocial question of a new network sociality and the growth of networked individualism raise fundamental questions about the relationships between the network society and the organisation of learning (see Chap. 2). At a micro- or mesolevel, networked individualism also pointedly raises critical questions about learning theories that are based on notions of community, cooperation and collaboration (Jones 2004).

Jones et al. (2006) writing in the context of CSCL argued that the tensions between networks and more communal and collaborative forms of organisation represented a challenge to conventional theories of learning that required investigation in future research. Wittel (2001) sharply contrasted the notion of network sociality with prevailing ideas about community.

> Community entails stability, coherence, embeddedness and belonging. It involves strong and long-lasting ties, proximity and a common history or narrative of the collective. Network sociality stands counterposed to Gemeinschaft. It does not represent belonging but integration and disintegration...In network sociality, social relations are not 'narrational' but informational; they are not based on mutual experience or common history, but primarily on an exchange of data and on 'catching up' (Wittel 2001, p. 51).

Ryberg and Larsen (2008) argued that the tensions between the metaphor of networks on one side, and Communities of Practice and collaboration on the other do not necessarily lead to a direct opposition between them. However the tensions between a network view and ideas of community and collaboration suggest theoretical and methodological challenges to widely accepted ideas. For example Ryberg and Larsen argue that it is difficult to circumscribe a network and as a consequence define the unit of analysis. The problem of defining and describing network boundaries is a recurrent issue because network organisation has an extensible form. Ryberg and Larsen also suggest that it might be useful to clarify the meaning that ties have in a network by the use of the conception of identity. Their suggestion extends the idea of a tie derived from network theory by drawing on identity, which was an idea already present in Wenger's (1998) conception of a community of practice. Identity formation in these two contexts does not need to have the same processes underlying it. The idea of community suggests proximity and the development of identity through a common (even if imagined) history and narrative whereas networks suggest a more fragmented engagement (Wittel 2001). Presence and proximity in networked environments become forms of remote and mediated 'tele-presence' and 'tele-proximity' relying on interactional means to achieve identity formation (Jones 2005).

SNA takes mathematical graph and network theory and applies it to a largely human world. Although SNA can include material and non-human actors it is primarily concerned with human interactions and their relationship to network structures and processes. SNA provides methods for research and analysis and these are increasingly being drawn on for administrative and managerial purposes in education via learner analytics. SNA has also generated a language for describing networks in social terms and concepts such as networked individualism that challenge existing ways of thinking about the kinds of relationships involved in learning. There remains a gap in this way of thinking about networks and it relates to the difficulty within SNA of analysing the non-human elements of the network. The use of two-mode networks was introduced above to explain how to include the resources used by learners and learning communities. This allows SNA to include the basic definitional elements included in the original definition of networked learning but it leaves out the material elements and processes included in the network itself. As noted in Chap. 3 and earlier in this chapter, there is one network theory that is clearly focused on the material actors in networks, ANT and it is to this theory the chapter now turns.

Technologies as Actants and Agents

ANT has begun to receive attention in educational research because research using this framework brings to the fore the material and takes the human and the social away from a privileged and central position in both education and educational research (Fenwick and Edwards 2010). ANT is a difficult area to pin down and authors in this tradition emphasise the variation and revisability of the ANT framework. Fenwick and Edwards (2010) talk about ANT as an array of practices for approaching the complexity of the world rather than as a coherent theory or body of work and ANT tradition has been described using a number of alternative names, for example the 'sociology of translation' (Callon 1986a) and 'material semiotics' (Law 2008). Law argues that ANT is a set of:

> Tools, sensibilities, and methods of analysis that treat everything in the social and natural worlds as a continuously generated effect of the webs of relations within which they are located (Law 2008, p. 141).

This complicated sentence set out by Law will need to be unpacked later, because it carries more than the usual baggage in its construction of the world, both human and material, as effects of webs of relations. ANT is more than simply a theory of how the material interpenetrates the world, or a theory of networks, it holds within itself a radical philosophical outlook that is at least a comment on epistemology and probably a radical ontology which brings into question both realism and relativism as usually understood (Harman 2009). A proper discussion of ANT would extend beyond the bounds of a single section of a book dealing with networked learning, however because of its increasing influence in this area a limited and at times hesitant engagement with ANT is necessary in the following pages.

From the introduction provided above it can be seen that ANT has a very different character from the two preceding network theories. Although it speaks in terms of networks and webs ANT has its own terminology and it does not repeat, or easily map on to terms used in either network and graph theory or SNA. ANT in this sense stands as an isolated outcrop in this chapter, more closely related to social theory, science and technology studies (STS), and philosophy than other network theories. Learning from an ANT perspective becomes a network effect not a cognitive process or a personal or social achievement. Applications to education, although currently gathering pace, are not new and Fox in particular has written about the potential of ANT in relation to networked learning (Fox 2000, 2002, 2005, 2009). ANT developed as a perspective in the sociology of science and technology and the key figures in this early development were Callon and Latour (Callon and Latour 1981; Callon and Law 1982; Callon 1986a, b and Latour 1990, 1991, 2005).

One of the key attractions of ANT for those interested in networked learning is the prospect of being able to integrate the material technologies and media into a framework that encompasses people and machines in a symmetrical way. An example of the ways the material is included can be seen in the following:

> In an effort to bring Web technologies to critical enquiry, they are treated as key participants in this study. The participant list, therefore, included postings; avatars; tool bars; emoticons; archives; community member profiles; viruses; hyperlinks; the delete button; passwords and the technology that delivers postings, such as e-mail, discussion forum or RSS feed. Human actants include "newbies", "wannabies, colleagues, "big names", celebrities, competitors, posers, lurkers, employment recruiters, clients, friends, strangers and online paparazzi." (Thompson 2012)

Material technologies are not included in a vague and general way as they are in some other kinds of literature dealing with educational technologies. Readers are not introduced to the 'Web', the 'Internet' or 'Web 2.0', as if such gross aggregates of technologies could be causative. Rather the reader is introduced to lists of human and non-human participants who form assemblages, entanglements of actors in a symmetrical balance. Importantly the technologies and the humans are both 'participants', equal in their place in the enquiry. To explore the complex field of ANT further I will explore some of these key concepts, including symmetry, and the way it is used in the quotation above.

Symmetry is perhaps both the most attractive element and the most controversial in relation to ANT. Symmetrical analysis holds that that the material and non-human elements of any network should be treated analytically in the same way as the social and human elements (Law 1992). Society and the social, so important to the development of networked learning are not seen as preexisting objects of study but as emergent outcomes of networks. The social is 'reassembled' (Latour 2005) out of various forms of association between human, non-human and hybrid entities. The world, both social, and natural is performed and ANT aims to elucidate how these assemblages and entanglements are formed and how they hold together in associations that produce effects. Agency in this framework is an outcome of a network, a network effect and not an inherent property of any particular kind of agent, either human or machine. Humans are treated no differently to non-humans and in the networks between them both are capable of exerting force and through their mutual associations they co-constitute the different elements of the network. ANT provides an approach that allows researchers to trace the way things come together, act and become durable, a research approach that begins by following the actor (Latour 2005).

A second important term in ANT is translation, the process in which one element stands in for another or many others (Callon 1986a, b; Callon and Law 1982). The term translation suggests an analogy with language in which one word can stand in for another or a sign or symbol stands in for one or many others. So important is this term that Latour tells us one alternative to the designation ANT that he considered was the 'sociology of translation'.

> We have now reached the very birthplace of what has been called 'actor-network-theory' or, more accurately, 'sociology of translation'-unfortunately the label never held in English (Latour 2005, p. 109).

Translation in ANT describes the links, the connections between actors. Translation is not a force or another actor it is the dynamic transformation and association that takes place between actors:

> So, the word 'translation' now takes on a somewhat specialized meaning: a relation that does not transport causality but induces two mediators into coexisting (ibid 2005, p. 108).

It can be seen from the above that ANT is not a standard network theory, although it includes the term network and actors could be subsumed under the term nodes, and translations under the terms link or tie. ANT has a philosophical edge and its terminology is tightly bound and particular because it is related to an ontology, an understanding of the way the world is. The chapter returns to this point later and shows how these debates about the nature of reality have fed into the more practical and pragmatic approach of networked learning.

The account of translation is also relevant to the idea of network that informs ANT. Networks in ANT diverge from the accounts found in other key texts in network theory, SNA or in accounts of network society (Latour 1996). Networks in ANT trace actors, and actors are not actors in this framework unless they have effects. Networks are dynamic and they check how much energy and movement researcher's reports are able to capture.

> The consequence is that you can provide an actor-network account of topics which have in no way the shape of a network—a symphony, a piece of legislation, a rock from the moon, An engraving. Conversely, you may well write about technical networks—television, e-mails, satellites, salesforce—without at any point providing an actor-network account (ibid, p. 131).

The positive contribution of ANT, beyond its inclusion of the material in social accounts, lies in its unsettling focus on change. The world ANT described is precarious and does not abide by traditional notions of cause and effect. The entities commonly worked with dissolve into assemblies of different elements, the elements themselves when unpacked are not essential items, but only further assemblies of entities that could be further divided and explored. Learning Management Systems, modules, teachers, curricula, policies etc. have to be traced through the negotiations and associations that entangle them to be able to account for their effects. The question then becomes how do we account for the apparent stability and sedate order we perceive around us? In an ANT account the precarious stability of things requires continuous ongoing work to sustain it.

A term used in ANT to describe stabilised assemblages is 'black box'. Black box is a term already introduced in relation to behaviourism in which it was used to argue that external behaviour, described in terms of stimulus and response, was what was important and that what occurred internally, in the mind or brain, could be safely ignored and treated as a 'black box'. More generally a black box applies to any device, system or object that can be considered in terms of its input, output and the frequency of transfers between them, without any knowledge of its inner workings. In ANT black box is applied to those stabilised networks that are outcomes of the precarious and dynamic processes described above using the terms translation and networks. In ANT terms, the world consists of the effects of dynamic networks of translations between actors, and these have effects. When stable these assemblages can be treated as black boxes and the processes that produce the effects can be ignored. This applies at all levels and the ANT world could be thought of as a set of Russian dolls going up and down in scale infinitely. Each stable black box can be shown to be an assembly of other actors each of which can be treated as black boxes. These component black boxed actors are the outcomes of processes, more or less transient in time, which sustain their apparent stability. The stability of all black boxes can be understood and traced by following the actors.

Criticisms of ANT

ANT is not without its critics and debates about some of the fundamental issues raised by ANT have been rehearsed at the networked learning conference. For example in 2012 a symposium session included papers coming from an ANT perspective alongside more traditional STS and network theoretical and realist accounts (Jones 2012). Drawing on Mol (2002) Oliver argued that it was to be expected that multiple 'realities' would be created by our practices (Oliver 2012).

> This is the plot of my philosophical tale: that ontology is not given in the order of things, but that, instead, ontologies are brought into being, sustained, or allowed to wither away in common, day-to-day, sociomaterial practices (Mol 2002, p. 6).

Oliver argued that such an approach gave up correspondence accounts of truth, and allowed a practice lens to be turned back on the process of research. Mol's praxeology, Oliver suggested, drew attention to the way in which research is an enactment of particular realities and it highlighted the limits of our accounts. My own view emphasised the need for at least some provisional stability and a notion of reality independent of the researcher as a basis from which to judge between different and alternative accounts. The claim I make is that a correspondence account of truth is a poor opponent and that realist accounts do not require there to be simple correspondence. The argument presented in this form resembles a simple realist–relativist dialogue but Latour's own position is more complex than that.

Latour argues that his position is that nothing by itself is either reducible or irreducible to anything else (Harman 2009). This relational stance allows him to claim a kind of realism and deny the charge of relativism. For Latour the human and world do not need to be brought into a relationship with each other because they are always, and inextricably, intertwined. ANT is not a form of social constructivism because the world does not depend on the human presence for its constitution. Reality does not require a human observer because objects and things can have relationships whether or not humans observe them. So far so realist, but there are times when Latour and ANT stray into relativist positions, for example Latour's position with regard to Pasteur's description of microbes. Latour suggests that after the description of microbes the history of events prior to that discovery are themselves altered by the discovery and then retrofitted with the subsequent knowledge of microbes. Harman remarks that:

The problem here is that Latour focuses on a human actor, Pasteur (ibid, p. 84).

This is not a necessary position for relational thinking because the interaction of objects can exist independently of Pasteur, but the slide is an easy one to make when adopting an ANT form of analysis. ANT while formally holding a specific kind of realist stance is often absorbed into wider post-modern discourses in which a radical relativism is central, this despite Latour having being criticised in STS circles for failing to take a sufficiently relativist stance (Bloor 1999).

A second criticism of ANT is important for networked learning and that is the way that ANT is thought to downgrade intentionality. This critique has been articulated in Activity Theory criticisms of ANT (Kaptelinin and Nardi 2006). Activity theory criticism focuses on symmetry because ANT treats all actors as being on the same level, human and non-human alike. Activity theorists agree that material things can have agency and that traditional accounts that restrict agency to humans are inadequate. However they argue against pure symmetry and they claim that humans are a significantly different kind of actors because they are motivated by their intentions. At its most basic this can be expressed as an existential choice, a billiard ball hit by another moving across a table will, on interacting with the other, have a predictable outcome, whereas a human being faced with complying with an instruction or being shot can always refuse to comply and accept the consequences. There seems to be a fundamentally different quality to an interaction at this human level to interactions between material non-human objects. Kaptelinin and Nardi (2006) point to the scientific work investigating strange particles, particles that were difficult to observe until the invention of the bubble chamber. Drawing on Pickering's (1993) account of this scientific development they discuss the 'mangle of practice':

Now I can talk about the mangle. In a restricted sense, the dialectic of resistance and accommodation... is what I mean by the mangle of practice. "Mangle" here is a convenient and

suggestive short-hand for the dialectic: for me, it conjures up the image of the unpredictable
transformations worked upon whatever gets fed into the old-fashioned device of the same
name used to squeeze the water out of the washing. "Mangle" can also be used as a verb: I
want to say, for example, that the contours of material agency are mangled in practice,
meaning emergently transformed and delineated in the dialectic of resistance and accommodation. In a broader sense, though, I take the mangle to refer not just to this dialectic but
to an overall image of practice that encompasses it to the worldview, if you like, that sees
science as just described, as an evolving field of human and material agencies reciprocally
engaged in the play of resistance and accommodation (Pickering 1993, p. 567).

This dialectical understanding allows for the mutual transformation of objects
(human or non-human) when they come into relation with each other, but it differentiates between two kinds of agency, one human and one material. Kaptelinin and
Nardi want to go a step further than Pickering and to argue that in human and material interactions the object does not change (Kaptelinin and Nardi 2006, p. 240). The
activity theoretical position is that the material world is not changed in the interaction whereas Pickering allows for the material to also be mangled in practice.

These debates might seem a long way from the more practical concerns of day-
to-day practice in networked learning but they have important implications. The
nature of judgement is affected by the discussion of reality and ontology found in
ANT. I want to resist the idea that there are multiple realities and to maintain the
view that there is a real world beyond human conceptions of it that has a uniformity
that can be used as a reference point in relation to which understandings can be
discussed and judged. This puts me in clear opposition to some of the more radical
positions that have emerged from ANT. Secondly I want to keep a dialectical understanding of intentionality but I think that human agency is always entangled with
material agency, so that the distinction between human and material agency is a
mistake made by both Pickering and Kaptelinin and Nardi. However I think that
there is a hint in Pickering that can help solve the puzzle of intentionality, because
there is a real problem here for ANT. I think that emergence might suggest that at
certain points of scale the equalisation between all actors in ANT fails. It fails
because at some levels of complexity there are phase changes that occur which are
related to the emergent properties of complex systems. One of these phase changes
comes with animals and it is the emergence of intentionality which is most fully
expressed in human action, activity, culture and practice.

Emergence and Intentionality

Emergence is the idea that the whole is more than the sum of its parts in particular
that at each level of complexity new and often unexpected qualities emerge that can't
in any simple or straightforward way be reduced to the known properties of the con-
stituent parts (Clayton and Davies 2006). Emergence is thus counterposed to reductionism which argues that properties of complex systems can be explained by the
characteristics of the elements the system is composed of, for example matter in

Fig. 4.6 Mandelbrot set.
Source Wikimedia commons
http://en.wikipedia.org/wiki/
File:Mandel_zoom_00_
mandelbrot_set.jpg. GNU
Free Documentation licence.
Created by Wolfgang Beyer

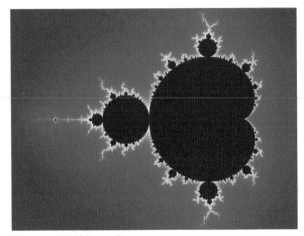

Source Wikimedia commons

terms of atoms or life in terms of molecular mechanisms. Reductionism accounts for a phenomena by appealing to the properties of the next level down. Network theory, chaos, self-organisation and a number of other subjects suggest that complexity cannot be reduced to the parts of a system or built up as exact replications from their component parts. The image suggested by emergence is of a Mandelbrot like fractal set, a system of self-similarity rather than one based on exact replication (see Fig. 4.6).

Fractal images are generated by simple rules from which complexity emerges but from the boundary of order. There are strong and weak versions of both approaches. Weak approaches suggest that reductionism and emergence are useful methodologies. Strong approaches take a more ontological stance which suggests that either reductionism or emergence is simply the way the world is. Hence views can be characterised as forms of methodological reductionism or ontological reductionism. Similarly there is a case for methodological emergentism or ontological emergentism. Methodological emergentism suggests that some things can only be properly understood by direct inspection or simulation and that it is not possible to deduce from the principles governing a class of systems how any specific example will behave. Methodological emergentists, even in a strong form, accept that reductionism can work in causally closed systems in which there are no additional principles that are not already implicit in lower level rules. However they go on to argue that there are open systems that cannot be treated in this way in which:

(a) Global principles interact with microlevel dynamics.
(b) The system is non-deterministic (e.g. quantum mechanics).
(c) The basic level of the system is intrinsically imprecise and cannot be fully or accurately measured.

Emergence, as a consequence of these features, poses a challenge to traditional sciences and opens up new areas for development, such as the development of 'laws of complexity'. Perhaps most importantly in the context of networked learning, emergence could have an important place in relation to understandings of consciousness and intentionality. It may also have a role to be explored in later chapters in understanding large and complex sociotechnical systems in education and at the level of global sociotechnical infrastructures.

Emergence offers a way of thinking about intentionality that does not require an analytic separation of the world into human and non-human agents. If the world is conceived of as being composed of complex entanglements of human and non-human agents, intentionality can still separate out certain kinds of agents, for example those occurring at the human level. Consider for the moment the understanding that quantum physics has provided of the world at subatomic level. Matter is reconceived as a form of energy $E = MC^2$, atoms are disaggregated and shown to be composed of a whole menagerie of increasingly strange particles. Yet at the level that most of us live and work, classic Newtonian physics still works. We know Newtonian physics is not a full understanding but, when planning and working with matter at a scale above the subatomic, the uncertainty and indeterminacy of the subatomic world can usually be ignored. This is a change moving down in scale. At a lower level the world is indeterminate and uncertain, yet the world at the scale above is not, even though it is composed of indeterminate elements. It is this kind of change which is associated with scale that I am thinking about in relation to intentions.

Emergence also supports the idea that thinking about networked learning needs to be concerned with levels. ANT has a weak conception of levels. Latour for example states that: 'Scale is the actor's own achievement' (Latour 2005, p. 185). He goes on to dismiss the idea of scale understood as a well ordered zoom of macro-meso-microlevels. In some respects this is to be expected of a network understanding because networks do not respect boundaries and a network has the potential to extend out in any and all directions and at any level or scale. There is the potential then for an actor considered at a microlevel to interact with an actor at the macrolevel and vice versa. Latour does not disregard levels entirely, although he restricts them to the world of common sense, but he clearly takes the position that scale should not be taken for granted and that any measurement implied by scale should be suitable for the purposes to which it is put. I think these points can be absorbed without relinquishing the use of scales and levels as long as they are explicitly relational, such that macro in one instance can be micro in another and that in general each level identified is only thought of as an abstraction enabling analysis and not a feature of the world. In addition there are the previously identified dialectical points at which quantity turns into quality and a phase change occurs. There is life and nonlife, even though the boundary is blurred. There is consciousness, and there are nonconscious states even though there are definitional and descriptive problems in formulating these and the state of consciousness is itself a classic human–non-human entanglement. Therefore despite the problems of defining the extent and boundaries of networks, and despite the nature of networks being their extensibility, thinking in terms of levels can provide a useful practical lens, and they are an essential component for thinking about the phase changes that occur, including those separating non-intentional and intentional actors.

The Significance of Network Theories for Networked Learning

Network theories straddle the classic sciences-humanities divide, and they subvert many recent social science preferences for the specifically human and cultural, emphasised in the 'cultural turn' (Jameson 1998), by re-introducing elements of the material and of structure into contemporary discourse (Fenwick et al. 2011). While this chapter has been concerned with networked theory there are a range of interventions that reconsider the place of humans and humanity in the world, from post-humanism (Hayles 1999) to the idea of the anthropocene (Crutzen and Stoermer 2000). These ideas displace the human on one hand and on the other simultaneously reinforce the importance of humanity in relation to the world. A key area for consideration in networked learning is the question of agency in an understanding of the world that displaces the specifically human and places a greater emphasis on the material, the technological and human machine hybrids and assemblages. The question of agency will be more fully explored in the concluding chapter of this book. The question of agency also relates to the concluding arguments of the preceding chapters. Agency is intimately connected with the relational account of affordance in Chap. 2 and it is also connected to the idea of practice as outlined in Chap. 3. Network theories are not simply metaphors for how the contemporary world organises, nor are they just descriptions. These theories carry with them indications of the areas for development in theories of networked learning. The application of the thinking outlined in the previous Chapters in Part I of this volume is now explored in relation to various different locations in education and learning. In the following chapter the application of the ideas found in Part 1 is in relation to the institution, primarily the University but also corporate and private bodies concerned with continuing and professional development. The subsequent chapters take up the role of infrastructure the changing place of the academic and the learner in the context of networked learning. In all of these chapters the idea of networks informed by various aspects of networked theory will be central.

References

Barabási, A.-L. (2002). *Linked: The new science of networks*. Cambridge, MA: Perseus.
Bloor, D. (1999). Anti-Latour. *Studies in the History and Philosophy of Science Part A, 30*(1), 81–112.
Buchanan, M. (2002). *Nexus: Small worlds and the groundbreaking science of networks*. New York: W.W. Norton.
Callon, M. (1986a). Some elements of a sociology of translation: Domestication of the scallops and the fishermen of St Brieuc Bay. In J. Law (Ed.), *Power, action and belief: A new sociology of knowledge?* (pp. 196–223). London: Routledge.

Callon, M. (1986b). The sociology of an actor-network: The case of the electric vehicle. In M. Callon, J. Law, & A. Rip (Eds.), *Mapping the dynamics of science and technology: Sociology of science in the real World* (pp. 19–34). London: Macmillan.

Callon, M., & Latour, B. (1981). Unscrewing the big leviathan: How actors macrostructure reality and how sociologists help them to do so. In K. D. Knorr-Cetina & A. V. Cicourel (Eds.), *Advances in social theory and methodology: Toward an integration of micro- and macro-sociologies* (pp. 277–303). Boston: Mass/Routledge/Kegan Paul.

Callon, M., & Law, J. (1982). On Interests and their transformation: Enrolment and counter-enrolment. *Social Studies of Science, 12,* 615–625.

Castells, M. (2000). *The rise of the network society* (2nd ed.). Oxford, England: Blackwell (Original work published 1996).

Castells, M. (2001). *The internet galaxy: Reflections on the internet, business, and society.* Oxford, England: Oxford University Press.

Clayton, P., & Davies, P. (Eds.). (2006). *The re-emergence of emergence: The emergentist hypothesis from science to religion.* Oxford, England: Oxford University Press.

Clow, D. (2013). MOOCs and the funnel of participation. In *Third Conference on Learning Analytics and Knowledge (LAK 2013),* 8–12 April 2013, Leuven, Belgium. Retrieved from http://oro.open.ac.uk/36657/1/DougClow-LAK13-revised-submitted.pdf

Crutzen, P. J., & Stoermer, E. F. (2000). The 'Anthropocene'. *Global Change Newsletters, 41,* 17–18.

Daniel, J. (2012). Making sense of MOOCs: Musings in a maze of myth, paradox and possibility. *Journal of Interactive Media in Education.* Retrieved from http://jime.open.ac.uk/2012/18

Dawson, S., Bakharia, A., & Heathcote, E. (2010). SNAPP: Realising the affordances of real-time SNA within networked learning environments. In L. Dirckinck-Holmfeld, V. Hodgson, C. Jones, D. McConnell, & T. Ryberg (Eds.), *Proceedings of the 7th International Conference on Networked Learning,* 3–4 May 2010, Aalborg, Denmark (pp. 125–133). Retrieved from http://networkedlearningconference.org.uk/past-proceedings/index.htm

De Laat, M. F. (2006). *Networked learning.* Apeldoorn, England: Politie Academie.

De Laat, M. F., Lally, V., Lipponen, L., & Simons, P. R. J. (2007). Patterns of interaction in a networked learning community: Squaring the circle. *International Journal of Computer-Supported Collaborative Learning, 2*(1), 87–104.

De Laat, M., & Prinzen, F. (2014). Social learning analytics: Navigating the changing settings of higher education. *Research & Practice in Assessment, 9*(2), 51.

De Laat, M. F., Schreurs, B., & Sie, R. (2014). Utilizing informal teacher professional development networks using the network awareness tool. In L. Carvalho & P. Goodyear (Eds.), *The architecture of productive learning networks.* London: Routledge.

Degenne, A., & Forsé, M. (1999). *Introducing social networks.* London: Sage.

Erdős, P., & Rényi, A. (1959). On random graphs I. *Publicationes Mathematicae Debrecen, 6,* 290–297.

Fenwick, T., & Edwards, R. (2010). *Actor network theory in education.* London: Routledge.

Fenwick, T., Edwards, R., & Sawchuk, P. (2011). *Emerging approaches to educational research: Tracing the sociomaterial.* London: Routledge.

Fox, S. (2000). Communities of practice, Foucault and actor-network theory. *Journal of Management Studies, 37*(6), 853–868.

Fox, S. (2002). Studying networked learning: Some implications from socially situated learning theory and actor-network theory. In C. Steeples & C. Jones (Eds.), *Networked learning: Perspectives and issues* (pp. 77–91). London: Springer.

Fox, S. (2005). An actor-network critique of community in higher education: Implications for networked learning. *Studies in Higher Education, 30*(1), 95–110.

Fox, S. (2009). Contexts of teaching and learning: An actor-network view of the classroom. In G. Biesta, R. Edwards, & M. Thorpe (Eds.), *Rethinking contexts for learning and teaching* (pp. 31–43). London: Routledge.

Freeman, L. C. (2004). *The development of social network analysis: A study in the sociology of science.* Vancouver, British Columbia, Canada: Empirical Press.

Gilbert, E. N. (1959). Random graphs. *Annals of Mathematical Statistics, 30*(4), 1141–1144.
Granovetter, M. S. (1973). The strength of weak ties. *The American Journal of Sociology, 78*(6), 1360–1380.
Harman, G. (2009). *Prince of networks: Bruno Latour and metaphysics.* Melbourne, VIC: Re Press. Retrieved from http://re-press.org/books/prince-of-networks-bruno-latour-and-metaphysics/
Hayles, N. K. (1999). *How we became posthuman: Virtual bodies in cybernetics, literature, and informatics.* Chicago: University of Chicago Press.
Haythornthwaite, C. (2002). Strong, weak and latent ties and the impact of new media. *The Information Society, 18*(5), 385–401.
Haythornthwaite, C. (2006). Facilitating collaboration in online learning. *Journal of Asynchronous Learning Networks, 10*(1), 7–24.
Haythornthwaite, C. (2010). Social networks and information transfer. In M. J. Bates & M. N. Maack (Eds.), *Encyclopedia of library and information sciences* (3rd ed., Vol. 6, pp. 4837–4847). New York: Taylor & Francis.
Haythornthwaite, C., & De Laat, M. (2010). Social networks and learning networks: Using social network perspectives to understand social learning. In L. Dirckinck-Holmfeld, V. Hodgson, C. Jones, D. McConnell, & T. Ryberg (Eds.), *Proceedings of the 7th International Conference on Networked Learning*, 3–4 May 2010, Aalborg, Denmark (pp. 183–190). Retrieved from http://networkedlearningconference.org.uk/past-proceedings/index.htm
Haythornthwaite, C., & Gruzd, A. (2008). Analyzing networked learning texts. In V. Hodgson, C. Jones, T. Kargidis, D. McConnell, S. Retalis, D. Stamatis, & M. Zenios (Eds.), *Proceedings of the Sixth International Conference on Networked Learning*, Halkidiki, Greece (pp. 136–143). Lancaster, England: Lancaster University. Retrieved from http://networkedlearningconference.org.uk/past-proceedings/index.htm
Haythornthwaite, C., & Gruzd, A. (2012). Exploring patterns and configurations in networked learning texts. In *Proceedings of the 45th Hawaii International Conference on System Sciences (HICSS)*, 4–7 January, Maui, HI. Retrieved from http://www.computer.org/csdl/proceedings/hicss/2012/4525/00/4525d358.pdf
Henri, F. (1992). Computer conferencing and content analysis. In C. O'Malley (Ed.), *Collaborative learning through computer conferencing* (pp. 117–136). Berlin, Germany: Springer.
Hiltz, S. R., & Turoff, M. (1978). *The network nation—Human communication via computer* (1st ed.). Reading, MA: Addison-Wesley [Revised Edition. Cambridge, MA: MIT Press, 1993].
Jameson, F. (1998). *The cultural turn: Selected writings on the postmodern 1983–1998.* London: Verso.
Jones, C. (2004). Networks and learning: Communities, practices and the metaphor of networks. *The Association for Learning Technology Journal, 12*(1), 82–93.
Jones, C. (2005). Who are you? Theorising from the experience of working through an avatar. *E-Learning, 2*(4), 415–426.
Jones, C. (2012). The place of technology in networked learning. In V. Hodgson, C. Jones, M. De Laat, D. McConnell, T. Ryberg, & P. Sloep (Eds.), In *Proceedings of the 8th International Conference on Networked Learning*, 2–4 April 2012, Maastricht, NL (pp. 438–463). Retrieved from http://networkedlearningconference.org.uk/past-proceedings/index.htm
Jones, C., & Dirckinck-Holmfeld, L. (2009). Analysing networked learning practices: An introduction. In L. Dirckinck-Holmfeld, C. Jones, & B. Lindström (Eds.), *Analysing networked learning practices in higher education and continuing professional development* (pp. 1–27). Rotterdam, The Netherlands: Sense Publishers, BV.
Jones, C., Dirckinck-Holmfeld, L., & Lindström, B. (2006). A relational, indirect, meso-level approach to CSCL design in the next decade. *International Journal of Computer Supported Collaborative Learning, 1*(1), 35–56.
Jones, C., Ferreday, D., & Hodgson, V. (2008). Networked learning a relational approach—Weak and strong ties. *Journal of Computer Assisted Learning, 24*(2), 90–102.
Kaptelinin, V., & Nardi, B. A. (2006). *Acting with technology: Activity theory and interaction design.* Cambridge, MA: MIT Press.

Latour, B. (1990). Drawing things together. In M. Lynch & S. Woolgar (Eds.), *Representations in scientific practice* (pp. 19–68). Cambridge, MA: MIT Press.

Latour, B. (1991). Technology is society made durable. In J. Law (Ed.), *A sociology of monsters* (pp. 103–131). London: Routledge.

Latour, B. (1996). On actor-network theory: A few clarifications and more than a few complications. *Soziale Welt, 47*, 369–381. Retrieved from http://www.bruno-latour.fr/sites/default/files/P-67%20ACTOR-NETWORK.pdf

Latour, B. (2005). *Reassembling the social: An introduction to actor-network theory*. London: Routledge.

Law, J. (1992). Notes on the theory of the actor network: Ordering, strategy and heterogeneity. *Systems Practice, 5*, 379–393.

Law, J. (2008). Actor network theory and material semiotics. In B. S. Turner (Ed.), *The new Blackwell companion to social theory* (pp. 141–158). Malden, MA: Blackwell.

McCluskey, F., & Winter, M. (2012). *The idea of the digital University: Ancient traditions, disruptive technologies and the battle for the soul of higher education*. Washington, DC: Policy Studies Organisation/Westphalia Press.

McConnell, D. (2000). *Implementing computer supported cooperative learning* (2nd ed.). London: Kogan Page.

Milgram, S. (1967). The small World problem. *Psychology Today, 2*, 60–67.

Mol, A. (2002). *The body multiple: Ontology in medical practice*. Durham, NC: Duke University Press.

Oliver, M. (2012). Learning with technology as coordinated sociomaterial practice: Digital literacies as a site of praxiological study. In V. Hodgson, C. Jones, M. De Laat, D. McConnell, T. Ryberg, & P. Sloep (Eds.), *Proceedings of the 8th International Conference on Networked Learning*, 2–4 April 2012, Maastricht, The Netherlands (pp. 440–447). Retrieved from http://networkedlearningconference.org.uk/past-proceedings/index.htm

Pickering, A. (1993). The mangle of practice: Agency an emergence in the sociology of science. *American Journal of Sociology, 99*, 559–589.

Rainie, L., & Wellman, B. (2012). *Networked: The new social operating system*. Cambridge, MA: MIT Press.

Ravasz, E., & Barabási, A.-L. (2003). Hierarchical organisation in complex networks. *Physical Review E, 67*(2), 026112.

Ryberg, T., & Larsen, M. C. (2008). Networked identities—Understanding relationships strong and weak ties in networked environments. *Journal of Computer Assisted Learning, 24*, 103–115.

Schreurs, B., & De Laat, M. (2014). The network awareness tool: A web 2.0 tool to visualize informal networked learning in organizations. *Computers in Human Behavior, 37*, 383–394.

Schreurs, B., Teplovs, C., Ferguson, R., De Laat, M., & Buckingham Shum, S. (2013). Visualizing social learning ties by type and topic: Rationale and concept demonstrator. In *Third Conference on Learning Analytics and Knowledge (LAK 2013)*, 8–12 April 2013, Leuven, Belgium, ACM (pp. 33–37).

Scott, J. (2000). *Social network analysis: A handbook* (2nd ed.). London: Sage.

Surowieki, J. (2005). *The wisdom of crowds: Why the many are smarter than the few*. New York: Anchor Books.

Thompson, T. L. (2012). Who's taming who? Tensions between people and technologies in cyberspace communities. In L. Dirckinck-Holmfeld, V. Hodgson, & D. McConnell (Eds.), *Exploring the theory, pedagogy and practice of networked learning* (pp. 157–172). New York: Springer.

Watts, D. J. (1999). *Small worlds: The dynamics of networks between order and randomness*. Princeton, NJ: Princeton University Press.

Watts, D. J. (2003). *Six degrees: The science of a connected age*. London: Norton.

Watts, D. J., & Strogatz, S. H. (1998). Collective dynamics of 'small-world' networks. *Nature, 393*(6684), 440–442.

Wellman, B. (2001). The rise of networked individualism. In L. Keeble (Ed.), *Community networks online*. London: Taylor & Francis.

Wellman, B., Quan-Haase, A., Boase, J., Chen, W., Hampton, K., & Isla de Diaz, I. et al. (2003). The social affordances of the internet for networked individualism. *Journal of Computer-Mediated Communication, 8*(3). Retrieved from http://jcmc.indiana.edu/issues.html

Wellman, B., Salaff, J., Dimitrova, D., Garton, L., Gulia, M., & Haythornthwaite, C. (1996). Computer networks as social networks: Collaborative work, telework and virtual community. *Annual Review of Sociology, 22,* 213–238.

Wenger, E. (1998). *Communities of practice: Learning, meaning, and identity.* Cambridge, England: Cambridge University Press.

Wittel, A. (2001). Towards a network sociality. *Theory, Culture & Society, 18*(6), 51–76.

Zuboff, S. (1988). *In the age of the smart machine: The future of work and power.* New York: Basic Books.

Part II
Agents and Actors in Networked Learning

Chapter 5
Networked Learning and Institutions

This chapter examines networked learning from the standpoint of the institutions in post-compulsory education. It will briefly examine the nature of work and the relationship work has with learning and the university. However the primary focus will remain on the university. The university remains central to modern societies because it provides an institutional solution to the problem of developing and conserving knowledge that has a universal role in grasping reality and at the same time it is dedicated to circulating that knowledge and making it, at least in principle, universally available. The rise of digital and networked technologies raises questions for some commentators about whether the institutions that grew up in earlier periods of economic and technological development are still fit for purpose. Beyond technology there are other contemporary challenges to the university posed intellectually by postmodernism (see Fuller 2009) and economically by changing financial constraints. The economic constraints have arisen firstly from the longstanding 'fiscal crisis of the state' (O'Connor 1973) and the neoliberal political and economic response (Harvey 2005; Fuchs 2008) and more recently by the banking crisis and the following period of austerity in advance industrial countries (Shattock 2010). Overall the changes that are influencing the university come from a number of intertwined sources: from globalisation and the internationalisation of the student body; from the spread of higher education to an increasingly large proportion of the population, inelegantly called 'massification'; and from the main focus of this book changes in technology and the constraints and opportunities this gives rise to.

There is a growing literature that imagines that technologies will undermine if not eliminate traditional educational institutions and the university in particular (for example see Tapscott and Williams (2010) and Barber et al. 2013). These claims take a number of forms, most recently articulated in terms of MOOCs (Daniel 2012). They also involve issues that will be dealt with more fully in following chapters. The idea of a new net generation of digital natives will be explored in Chap. 8 and the claims about the digital scholar will be explored in Chap. 7. The main focus of this chapter is the ways technologies affect the nature of work and work organisations, both within the university as a workplace and in the university's relationships with other organisations and wider populations. The arguments for institutional change based on changes

© Springer International Publishing Switzerland 2015
C. Jones, *Networked Learning*, Research in Networked Learning,
DOI 10.1007/978-3-319-01934-5_5

in technology are accompanied by others that argue, independently of technology, for universities to be businesses with significant consequences:

> The recent drive, to have universities mimic business firms as generators of intellectual property, amounts to no less than a campaign of institutional dismemberment, in which the university's research function is severed from the teaching function. (Fuller 2009, p. 5)

This chapter accepts that technological arguments are choices informed by a number of separable arguments about economic and political structures and it does not take the continued existence of the university as an institution for granted. It explores whether those who argue that technology is 'disruptive' are deploying technological arguments or masking social and economic choices with technological imperatives and it asks what weight can be given to arguments that suggest the days of the traditional university are numbered.

Institutions and the Changing Nature of Work

In Chap. 2 changes in society and technology were outlined and related to the changing place of learning and knowledge in the economy. This section takes this one step further by examining these changes in relation to the institutional context of work. The changes that have taken place in production methods have led to a series of accounts and a set of descriptions applied to newer production techniques to distinguish them from earlier forms. The mid-to-late twentieth-century system of mass production has been identified with assembly line production and the term Fordism. This system, based on Taylorism and scientific management was identified with higher wages and high productivity leading to a virtuous circle of production and consumption at a mass scale. The late twentieth-century production system has been variously described as Post-Fordism (Lash and Urry 1987) and flexible specialisation (Piore and Sabel 1984). The change to Post-Fordist systems of production signalled a move away from uniform large-scale mass production to production that is more tailored to specific consumption needs with a degree of personalisation, enabled by systems of just-in-time batch production and rapid logistic chains for distribution at a global scale. For a recent critical discussion of these trends and theories see Stuart et al (2013). In the service sector the rhythm has been slightly different with batch production being linked to a Taylorisation of the production process and what has been described as the McDonaldisation of society (Ritzer 1993). These new systems of production have affected different sectors in a variety of ways. McDonaldisation has become a byword for low-wage and low-skill jobs, while modular and batch production often requires the employment of high-wage and high-skill workers.

Most of this institutional change has occurred in the market facing sectors, whether publicly or privately owned. However the state sector has had its own transformations by way of New Public Management, driven by the demands of more for less and the introduction of quasi markets in a financially constrained public sector (Lane 2002). In both the market and tax funded public sector there has been a further transformation based on the application of networked and digital technologies on a large scale. To summarise these changes in a short section is extremely difficult and what follows is necessarily limited in scope. However a few key areas of change relevant to institutional issues are listed below.

1. The move to 'team' working and the requirement for new forms of cooperation and collaboration at work, both collaboration in teams and collaboration between teams and organisations (Engeström 2008).
2. The contradictory process of de-skilling and re-skilling of the workforce as new technologies are introduced (Braverman 1974).
3. The move from machines automating work to machines that also 'informate' the work process (Zuboff 1988).
4. The development of complex networks in production (and reflected in governance) by way of global logistics chains and the integration of independent and semi-independent producers in modular networks (Neilson et al. 2014).
5. The rise of independent professionals and consultants able to connect with their peers with greater ease, at a larger scale and on a continuing basis (De Laat, Schreurs, and Nijland 2014).

This by no means exhaustive list gives an indication of some of the institutional pressures affecting learning. Some of these affect what is learned and the way it is learned, e.g. team working as well as institutional ways of working in the university. Some like the informating of processes affect the future workforce being educated and the internal processes of the university. An assumed demand for learners and workers with the soft skills required for team working has been a recurrent issue in public policy (see for example Miles and Trott 2011). The changing labour market with a shifting pattern of requirements for skilled labour unsettles traditional disciplinary and subject-based specialisms. The development of big data derived from the informating process has brought about demands for new methods and skills that are required to manage, to represent and to understand the flows of data. Finally complex global networks have introduced the need for new networked management techniques and the development of cultural sensitivities in global corporations and between large corporations and a myriad of small suppliers and consultants distributed across the world.

Team Working, Instability and Change

The use of teams and the development of collaborative and cooperative forms of working give rise to new organisational and institutional forms. The striking thing about these arrangements has been their relatively transitory nature. Organisations and institutions are often thought of in terms of their stability but some newer organisational forms celebrate their fleeting nature. Engeström et al (1999) argue that the term knotworking is a suitable description for unstable situations in which there is an active process of construction of relations, in the moment, leading to a constantly changing configuration of people and artefacts:

In a series of recent studies, we have encountered numerous examples of this type of work organization. We call it knotworking. The notion of knot refers to a rapidly pulsating, distributed and partially improvised orchestration of collaboration between otherwise loosely connected actors and activity systems (Engeström et al. 1999, p. 346)

The idea of knotworking describes a historically new and emerging way of organising work but it is also connected by Engeström (2005) to learning. A key feature of knotworking is the lack of a centre of control and in this it resembles network forms of organisation. Engeström places teams and knotworking between the two dominant historical forms of organisation, hierarchies and markets, arguing that knotworking is a transitional form:

The notion of co-configuration and knotworking are but initial attempts to sketch the contours of knowledge- and innovation- driven production. Organisations break through into this poorly charted gray zone, where they face constant disturbances, ruptures and unanticipated learning imperatives. (Engeström 2008, p. 20)

The unstable organisational context also gives rise to what Engeström describes as a radical new landscape of widely dispersed, fluctuating and weakly bounded community forms (Engeström 2007). He argues that these features are particularly evident in new forms of peer or social production, for example the Open Source movement and he introduces the concept of mycorrhizae to capture the quality of these new forms of organisation. Engeström acknowledges that his use of mycorrhizae is related to Deleuze and Guattari (1987) and the idea of rhizome which was deployed to indicate a horizontal and multidirectional pattern of organisation in contrast to hierarchical, top-down and tree-like forms. Engeström argues that his use of mycorrhizae builds upon this organic metaphor by emphasising the invisible symbiotic relationship of fungi with the root system.

Mycorrhizae are difficult if not impossible to bound and close, yet not indefinite or elusive. They are very hard to kill, but also vulnerable. They may lie dormant for lengthy periods of drought or cold, then generate again vibrant visible mushrooms when the conditions are right. They are made up of heterogeneous participants working symbiotically, thriving on mutually beneficial or also exploitative partnerships with plants and other organisms. (Engeström 2007, p. 52)

While the term mycorrhizae and the organic metaphor are difficult concepts to use in practice, the idea has some interesting features, in particular the relationship between the impermanent knotworking and the more stable and permanent structures on which these unstable forms depend. The horizontal and invisible mycorrhizae depend on plants and they generate fruiting bodies that are visible, vertical, and more or less durable. The transitory network forms of knotworking in organisations similarly depend on institutional and relatively stable structures. As such they are not a replacement for more traditional forms of organisation, they supplement and potentially reinvigorate them.

The University and the Digital

The university remains a central element helping to determine the ways that technologies are deployed in higher education. This chapter explores the relationship between the university and digital and networked technology. It begins by drawing the reader back to the kind of societies in which universities developed and the contemporary society in which networked learning is developing, and the way these locations change the demands on education, the organisational form of the university, and the processes by which education is achieved and accredited.

While higher education has wider roots (Perkin 2007) the University in the organisational form we know it today, granting Bachelor, Masters and Doctoral qualifications, can date its origins back to the European middle ages (Collini 2012; Scott 2006). The corporate form that the university has taken is related to medieval guild traditions and it retains aspects of the self-governing bodies of teachers and scholars that grew up in early Europe. Universities preserve the right to award credentials, in the granting of degrees, and they also maintain a key liberty, academic freedom, intended to protect universities from power. Although early universities had their roots in the church, and they and were frequently established by Kings, the university retained an ability to self-govern, even as the nation state developed and it maintained quasi-independence from both secular and religious power.

Despite this lengthy history the university is also distinctly modern as an institution (modern in the historical sense of post-dating the premodern and medieval):

> The university may have a longer history than virtually any other macroinstitution of the present day, excepting the Church and perhaps one or two others. However, as an institution with research at its core, the university is distinctly modern and largely formed by developments of the last two centuries. (Wittrock 2012, p. 199)

The 'mission' of the university over this historical time period has been analysed by Scott (2006) and he concluded that despite historic transformations there remained a core feature to the university:

> From medieval to postmodern times, service is the keynote. All universities were and are social organizations designed to provide higher educational services such as teaching, research, and a host of other academic services to the church, governments, individuals, public, and in the future, perhaps, the world. (Scott 2006, p. 3)

The abstract and to some extent imagined continuity of the university's corporate form and mission of service masks periods of rapid and significant change. Wittrock (2012) for example argues that three major transformations can be identified, the late eighteenth and early nineteenth century in continental Europe, the late nineteenth and early twentieth century with the expansion of the research mission in universities and the second half of the twentieth century with the move from elite to mass higher education. The modern research intensive university emerges from periods of nation building, war and empire and from the late nineteenth century and an engagement with industrial development using science and technology. The move from elite to mass universities has taken place at different times and with somewhat different motivations in the twentieth century. However I would argue that the contemporary university is probably subject to its most significant period of change.

The university as an institution has extended rapidly across the globe and student numbers continue to increase. There are recurrent pressures for the university to become more relevant and for universities to engage in society and to have a measurable impact. The history of the university as an institution in society is a complex mixture of imagined stability and change, of relative academic freedom and requirements for public accountability. Within those changes, and intertwined with them, is the extensive institutional and societal deployment of digital and networked technologies. While in much public discourse the university retains its imagined continuity with the past it is well known that digital and networked technologies are being deployed in the wider society and for learning in universities. The nature of academic work is affected and arguably there is an emergence of digital scholarship and the digital scholar (see Chap. 7). The nature of the student intake is changing, in ways related to new technology, even if not in the dramatic and determinist way that the digital native thesis would suggest (see Chap. 8). New technologies are said to be changing fundamental aspects of university practices including what it means to learn, the practices of academic reading and the way scholarship is conducted. The digital university probably does not currently describe any real or existing university but its features are becoming more clearly defined and some universities are now consciously developing their profile using this term (Jones 2013). In the sections that follow some of the features that have become clear and are related to institutional provision are discussed. Firstly the impact of informating technology and the growth of learning analytics are assessed. Secondly the way that networked and digital technologies have influenced the notion of openness and open educational resources is considered and finally the recent development of MOOCs and the threat they are said to pose to the university as an institution is evaluated.

The University and Learning Analytics

One of the general issues identified with the changing nature of work was the way in which digital technologies 'informate' work (Zuboff 1988). By 'informate' Zuboff described a significant feature of the new technologies. Whereas automation increased and deepened the process that rationalised work and decreased dependency on human skills, the technologies that informate a process increase the explicit information content of tasks. Zuboff argued that the characteristics of technologies that informated were often unintended consequences of change. The capacity to informate was not the opposite of automation but 'hierarchically integrated. Informating derives from and builds upon automation' (Zuboff 1988, p. 11). It might be thought that this insight is now dated but Kallinikos noted that the central themes of the book remained relevant. Kallinikos noted that:

> Paper-based documents are by large mnemonic devices; the knowledge by which they are produced is to a large extent mobilized by sentient human beings, enacting rules of sense making and expertise gained through formal training and experience, that is, skill interiorization. Computer-based systems increasingly explicate these rules, embody them in programs, and automate their execution. (Kallinikos 2010, p. 1100)

This capacity of computers to externalise processes has also led to the generation, collection and storage of vast amounts of information as data. This has become known as 'big data' and it is more properly known as data-intensive science.

Data-intensive science makes it possible using the same computing power that enables collection to detect patterns in large data. This trend has been called the 'Fourth paradigm' (Hey et al. 2009) and located in the recent rise of computational science. It is claimed to be distinctly new because of the way data is collected, processed by software, stored in a computer and only at the latter stages of the process is it processed by scientists using data management and statistical techniques (Hey et al. 2009). The idea that the scale of the data is what sets it apart has been challenged by noting that it is often the relational and networked nature of the data that make it important. Boyd and Crawford argue that:

> There is little doubt that the quantities of data now available are often quite large, but that is not the defining characteristic of this new data ecosystem. In fact, some of the data encompassed by Big Data (e.g., all Twitter messages about a particular topic) are not nearly as large as earlier data sets that were not considered Big Data (e.g., census data). Big Data is less about data that is big than it is about a capacity to search, aggregate, and cross-reference large data sets. (Boyd and Crawford 2012, p. 663)

So the term 'big' data should be treated cautiously as it often signifies more about its source and the relations it has with other data than its scale.

Furthermore there are those that contend that paradigm questions the role and position of theory:

> This is a world where massive amounts of data and applied mathematics replace every other tool that might be brought to bear. Out with every theory of human behavior, from linguistics to sociology. Forget taxonomy, ontology, and psychology. Who knows why people do what they do? The point is they do it, and we can track and measure it with unprecedented fidelity. With enough data, the numbers speak for themselves. (Anderson 2008)

The idea that 'numbers speak for themselves' and that theory is, at best, irrelevant would be extremely dangerous if applied in universities and there are well-known weaknesses in a reliance on 'big data' as set out by Boyd and Crawford (2012). The term analytics has been applied to the use of big data but it does not have a consistent definition:

> A variety of terms for analytics also exist in the educational domain. Higher education's approach to defining analytics is particularly inconsistent. Some definitions are conceptual (what it is), while others were more functional (what it does). Analytics is the process of data assessment and analysis that enables us to measure, improve, and compare the performance of individuals, programs, departments, institutions or enterprises, groups of organizations and/or entire industries. (van Barneveld et al. 2012, p. 2).

Learning analytics are a focus for emerging debates because they follow a trend towards business analytics and they engage with powerful policy and market interests (Brown 2011). The term learning analytics has become popular in higher education, although it can be used to refer to somewhat different topics (Siemens 2013). Learning analytics can be focused most clearly on the student experience and data related to that topic. Learning analytics can equally be focused more widely to include the administration of the university and the data required for reporting to funders and governments. The range and extent of the data sources included in a broad view of learning analytics can be seen from the list provided by Norris and Baer investigating applications of analytics in the United States (2013, p. 9):

- ERP systems (student, finance, financial aid, human resources, advancement and other modules to be added over time)
- Third-party administrative systems (co-curricular systems, parking, residence hall, food service, bookstore, other auxiliary enterprises)
- Academic enterprise systems (LMS, other personalised learning systems, library, academic support services)
- Assessment (testing, student evaluation, course and faculty evaluation, NSSE/CSSE)
- Customer relationship management systems and/or CRM functionality in other systems
- Peer institution and benchmarking data
- Open educational resources and experiences, with associated learning analytics

The way that big data has become integrated in higher education in ways relevant to networked learning is explored below in relation firstly to what I am calling *learner* analytics and then in relation to institutional analytics through the lens of Enterprise Resource Planning (ERP).

Learner Analytics

I have chosen to use the term learner analytics to identify those aspects of learning analytics that focus on the learner or student as opposed to the institutional or business aspects of analytics. Siemens amongst others makes a similar distinction between a more business focused approach and a focus on learning but retains the term learning analytics for learner focused activity (Siemens 2013). The definition of learning analytics set out in the call for papers for the first international conference in this area was:

> Learning analytics is the measurement, collection, analysis and reporting of data about learners and their contexts, for purposes of understanding and optimising learning and the environments in which it occurs. (LAK 2011 as reported in Ferguson 2012)

This learner focused definition is rooted in earlier social science information system developments such as social network analysis and data mining but it is driven by more immediate institutional and political concerns and the increasing availability of machine readable data sets produced by digital technologies, including the learning management systems deployed in many universities (Ferguson 2012). Ferguson provides a useful overview of the state of the field and of the kinds of drivers that promote the development of analytics. When she considers the question of who benefits from learning analytics Ferguson considers three interest groups:

> … governments, educational institutions and teachers/learners. Although the interests of all three groups overlap, they require analytics work on different scales and at different granularities. The choice of target audience therefore affects how researchers conceptualise

problems, capture data, report findings, act on their findings and refine their models. As the
following sections show, the field of analytics changes and develops as the balance between
these three drivers and three interest groups shifts. (Ferguson 2012, p. 307)

What this quote amply illustrates is that the apparently technical exercise of data
collection and analysis involved in learner analytics is in fact a site of struggle
(Feenberg 1991). Like other technological developments the various interested parties have an influence on the functioning and basic structure of the technological
solutions that are developed and implemented.

Currently a number of universities are exploring how these large data sets can be
managed and analysed to provide meaningful information to institutional managers,
course teams, teachers and students (Norris and Baer 2013). The struggle over analytics in universities will be important not least because it will determine the ways
that institutions conceive of the student-academic-institution nexus. If a broad
administrative view of analytics is taken then analytics can be just another management and administrative tool that will shift the balance in institutions away from
academic and pedagogic concerns towards market and business concerns with measurable performance and value for money. Measurements of quality, progression and
dropout when seen in terms of students as units of resource are quite different from
measures of quality understood in terms of human development and citizenship.

Ferguson (2012) notes that analysis of data for educational purposes has a history that extends back into the late twentieth century and that early interest in analytics was focused largely on business process whereas earlier concerns with the use
of data to improve the effectiveness of learning and learning processes was initially
the province of educational data mining. She dates the early development of analytics focused on the learner and learning process to 2003 and work deriving from
Social Network Analysis and a networked learning perspective (Aviv et al. 2003; De
Laat et al. 2014). In Ferguson's view the development of the field leads in different
directions but what she identifies as learning analytics most closely matches the idea
of learner analytics used here: that is an educational focus on analytics optimising
the opportunities for learning. A current example of how learner data can be applied
comes from The Open University (Wolff and Zdrahal 2012) who use student data to
identify students 'at risk' using predictive models in order to help improve retention
rates and more broadly the 'student experience'. The practicality and robustness of
many of these kinds of approaches are still to be tested and the promise often
remains more than the current reality.

Learner analytics used in this sense has been applied beyond the university to
learners and learning in the workplace (De Laat and Schreurs 2013). In a similar
way to learner analytics in the university the application of analytics to learners in
the workplace aims to find methods to make informal and largely invisible processes explicit within the organisation. Their method detects and visualises informal
professional networks. The aim of these visualisations is to aid value creation by
connecting ideas often held in isolated networks within organisations. The aim of
the project was to generate real time, automated learning analytics in large-scale
systems to accomplish this task of making informal networks visible. The method
that they applied combined social network analysis (SNA) with content analysis
(CA) and context analysis (CxA) (see Fig. 5.1).

Fig. 5.1 Multimethod
research framework for
studying networked learning.
(De Laat 2006 p125)

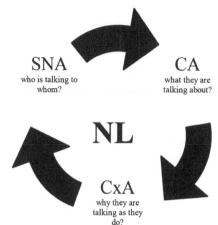

Using this approach De Laat and Schreurs developed a Network Analysis Tool
that could provide visualisations of personal networks and the place of the person in
wider networks automatically and immediately. This system relies on users describing
and tagging problems that are part of their learning and add people they collaborate
with. Users can also link themselves with problems others have already described.
Such a system is quite different in character to learner analytics that are part of a
top-down institutional process and the system relies on professional activity to
ensure the quality and availability of data.

Learner Analytics Raises a Large Number of Questions Including:

- Which interest group(s) will dominate in determining the developments that take
  place?
- Will development of analytics be a top-down or bottom-up process?
- What are the pedagogically useful indicators that can lead to robust
  recommendations?
- How can learner analytics be made accessible for non-specialist users?
- What are the ethical considerations that need to be included in using student and
  learner data?

To be useful the data has had to be managed, curated and presented in relevant
and usable forms. Learning analytics will require the application of a significant
effort to manage, curate and process the raw data derived from a variety of systems
that are not necessarily compatible or interoperable with each other. The settings
for data collection and the questions asked in survey data collection will have a
large influence on the quality of data included for analysis. Currently it is not clear
how systematic these processes will be or which groups in the university will carry
the responsibility to ensure a robust and coordinated process. The implementation
of learner analytics is a complex organisational as well as technical process.

Enterprise Resource Planning

Learning analytics has been used in ways that include organisational and adminis-trative data (Norris and Baer 2013). I have distinguished between learning analytics focused on the learner which I have called learner rather than learning analytics. The other aspect of learning analytics is institutional in focus and deals with the integration of IT systems across the university. For example in the United Kingdom the Joint Information Systems Committee (JISC) promotes Enterprise Architecture which they characterise as enabling organisations to adapt to change by defining how their business processes work in tandem with their Information and Communications Technology systems (JISC 2010). The need for an enterprise approach is clearly located in the pressure to change:

> Universities and colleges are increasingly complex sociotechnical organisations that are hard to change, and yet they face enormous pressures to increase operational efficiencies and adapt to new challenges. (JISC 2010 Online)

In this Sect. 5.1 have chosen to discuss one aspect of the organisational use of analytics in the deployment of Enterprise Resource Planning in universities. Enterprise used in this context is synonymous with institution, although it carries with it a business- and market-oriented notion of a 'bottom line' and a singular goal which is often absent from universities despite contemporary pressures to view uni-versities as businesses. There are other systems that are cross institutional, such as the student and academic facing Learning Management Systems (LMS), which feed into learner analytics, and library systems which also have a learner focus, and there are additional administrative and organisational systems, such as those dealing with customer relations, parking, residences, catering etc. The ERP is however the focus of administration and it is central to the rationalisation of the many dispersed and often bespoke systems found across universities. ERP in a university context has generated a literature dealing with specific case studies (see for example in the UK context JISC 2009) and it has been investigated by a significant number of research-ers with a more sector wide focus including Scott and Wagner (2003), Pollock and Cornford (2004), Lee and Myers (2004), Wagner and Newell (2005), Pollock et al. (2007), McCluskey and Winter (2012). ERP in this chapter is used broadly and it includes elements that would not normally be included under this term. This is because ERP is usually a single business management computer system and Enterprise Architecture as used in the JISC literature refers to a looser transitional process of integration that may include several systems. Enterprise Architecture also suggests a link to the current trend away from single systems towards a more flexible approach based on open standards similar to the discussion between single LMSs and an open systems- and service-oriented architecture (often characterised as Web 2.0) developed for similar purposes (Weller 2007).

The introduction of enterprise systems aims to transform the administration of the university and the discussion that follows focuses on two contrasting ways of under-standing that process. The first example is drawn from the writing of Pollock and Cornford (2004, 2005) and Pollock et al. (2007), and the second from McCluskey and Winter (2012). The provision of comprehensive enterprise systems suggests that there is a potential to move from an administrative culture to one in which there is a degree of academic self-management (Pollock and Cornford 2005). The self-management enabled by such systems is not of course unlimited, indeed it follows the New Public Sector management dictum of regulated autonomy or 'freedom within boundaries' (Hoggett 1991; Enders 2012) in that the academic self-manages but only within the confines of what is allowed by the system. The enterprise systems are engaged in a process of de-skilling some administrative staff while re-skilling others and academic staff are encouraged to take on new administrative roles as they 'self-manage' in active interaction with technical systems. Pollock and Cornford (2004) were also interested in the dynamics of ERP implementation in what some argue is a unique organisation. They suggest that the similarity or difference of the university, seen as an enterprise, and the business base from which ERP systems originate, sets up a tension which was exemplified the university that they studied:

> ...the construction of similarity/difference occurred not simply within the confines of the project team but was also the outcome of a set of relationships the university has with the system, its supplier, various internal departments, and other institutions involved in similar implementations. (Pollock and Cornford 2004, p. 32)

In this view the technology is part of a larger assemblage engaged with the implementation of a sociotechnical system. The technology is in a negotiation with a variety of other actors and the outcome is not predetermined but negotiated. Key figures, such as the university Vice Chancellor set the terms of these negotiations by setting goals that emphasised the similarities between the university and businesses with a pressure on staff to rethink processes and procedures in business terms using Enterprise language, even when this caused irritation and resistance (Pollock and Cornford 2004). The pressure for standard business solutions led to the creation of 'work-arounds' allowing users to find ways to resolve conflicts between business processes and the specific needs of the institution. A third feature of the process of implementing ERP in the university was that solutions were increasingly sectoral rather than institution-specific, that is university-specific demands could be accommodated in-so-far as they were variants of a sector-wide issue and the specific issue could be made generic and applicable beyond one institution.

The process of implantation showed how ERP systems built 'bridges' between diverse organisational users through a process of 'generification' (Pollock et al. 2007). The idea of generification is an important indication of the limits of viewing every instance as unique and of computer-based systems as being unable to travel or transition between contexts:

> Rather than focus on the collision between unique organizational practices and the generic solution we should also address how technologies are made (and continuously remade) to bridge these different locales, as part of our enquiry into the broader and longer-term co-evolution of artefacts and their social settings of use. We have argued that generic solutions do exist and that they do travel to many different places; though, of course, they don't go everywhere. (Pollock et al. 2007, p. 274)

While ERP systems standardised processes they did not do this as a crude invasion of the university by an external system, but through an interactive process in which generic processes were a 'precarious' achievement. The process of achieving this outcome also extended beyond single institutions:

> The universities, in other words, were increasingly forced to think as a "community" or "sector" when identifying their needs. This has obvious implications for organisational shaping... as well as future procurement strategies, where presumably the university will have to negotiate and struggle both with suppliers and other higher education institutions. (Pollock and Cornford 2004, pp. 47–48)

From a suppliers point of view the technology had to have a manageable level of diversity, while from the universities' point of view the relatively standardised processes needed to incorporate the local and particular practices of very different kinds of institutions and local contexts. The achievement of a managed process required the university to master a number of complex translation processes and highlighted and refashioned the boundaries between universities and other organisations. The process also challenges the unique identity that universities claim for themselves by the drift towards standardisation with business processes.

This account of ERP systems contrasts with McCluskey and Winter (2012) who, writing from a largely US position, argue that ERP systems make 'exceptions to rules all but impossible' (ibid, p. 13), control 'all aspects of college life' and 'dictate the pace of the modern university' (ibid, p. 14). The process of standardisation implicit in the deployment of ERP systems is claimed to have serious implications for academic life. However in this account the choices that are available are often ignored as they can be at the messy institutional level of negotiation and translation outlined above rather than at the individual scholar's level. When McCluskey and Winter do focus on the institutional level they propose a 'BLT' model in which there are three basic kinds of university governance, a Bureaucracy, a Learner, and a Teacher-centred model. The Bureaucratic Centred Model (B-governance) characterises many current university administrations and roughly equates to the model found in descriptions of New Public Management in universities (Lorenz 2012). The management and administration are professional and positions are largely appointed rather than elected. The Teacher-Centred Model (T-governance) will also be familiar because it is focused on the forms of faculty governance found in older collegiate systems of university governance. In this model many of the key managerial posts are elected positions and they are in some sense representative of the academic staff. This model has echoes of the early medieval model, especially that based on Paris, which embodied the university as a collective of academics (the Italian, Bologna model in contrast was a student collective). The final model is described as a Learner-Centred Model (L-governance) but it is based on Enterprise systems of data management. It may come as a surprise to find that being 'learner-centred' depends on a form of governance that has at its heart 'big data' and learning analytics. The argument made by McCluskey and Winter (2012) is a determinist argument that suggests that the old institutions need to be broken apart to allow the emergence of a data focused university.

McCluskey and Winter (2012) note that when ERP systems were adopted the universities involved began to link all the kinds of information that was collected by the institution. As a consequence the digital university they envisage is less a learner-centred model than it is data-centred. They argue that the new combined sources of data enabled by digital technologies provide new opportunities for governance based on data analysis but they largely ignore the ethical implications of this. They mention the ethics of software development as a subject to be taught but they do not discuss the ethical implications of an ERP and data-driven governance of the university. The ethical issues raised by learning analytics have recently been raised by the Director of Teaching and Learning at The Open University (Sclater 2014). Sclater argues that risks are a consequence of exploring the potentials of learning analytics:

> With these possibilities come dangers that the data could be used in ways undesirable to students. These include invading their privacy, exploiting them commercially by selling their data to third parties or targeted marketing of further educational products (Sclater 2014 Online)

These dangers of course also extend to staff and universities have clear legal responsibilities to comply with data protection legislation, restricting access by third parties to data collected about staff and students. Universities should also allow students and staff access to view data held about them and universities should also make them aware when data is being collected and what purposes it might be used for. Some data protection legislation, for example in the EU, also restricts where data can be stored raising questions about many cloud-based applications with US-based storage. Overall the ethics of data collection and management needs much closer scrutiny and the bland assumption that because data can be collected it should be collected needs to be challenged (Slade and Prinsloo 2013). Learning analytics at an institutional level could lead to a new form of university governance, but this requires an informed choice. The idea of a data-driven university points back to questions of surveillance and discipline as noted in relation to LMS/VLEs by Land and Bayne (2005). They concluded their work by suggesting that technology presented a range of choices, and a proper understanding of the technology could enhance provision, but that choices based on data alone, or based on power-driven approaches, threatened to be disempowering to those subject to it.

Openness, Open Educational Resources and the University

Digital and networked technologies have the potential to change the relationship between learners and the institutions of learning to their resources. Digital technologies can reduce to almost zero the costs associated with reproducing digital material and they can theoretically be copied many times and be circulated at almost no additional cost. The potential of these features of digital and network technologies depends on them being institutionally enacted for them to be realised as affordances for learners. A key element of the definition of networked learning that informs this book is the connection of learners with learning resources. Networked learning takes place between people but also between a learning community and their learning resources. The definition suggests that the use of online materials is a necessary but not a sufficient condition for networked learning because interaction needs to be both with the materials and with other people. In recent years there have been a number of developments beyond the purely technical that have impacted on the institutional provision of learning resources. Many of these developments are located in universities and other related institutions. These changes began with the idea of learning objects and more recently the concern has been with open educational resources (OER) (see for example Weller 2007; Pegler 2011 and Pegler 2013; Selwyn 2014). The simple idea behind OER is that universities and other institutions generating knowledge make their materials freely available online for anyone to use. Wiley et al (2014) state that OER are educational materials which use a Creative Commons license or which exist in the public domain and are free from copyright restrictions. This raises a raft of questions, some practical concerning how this change can be enabled but others are fundamental concerning for example who actually pays, because as is already well known nothing is absolutely free, even when it is free to use. The openness of OER is a also a concern for MOOCs, which are the subject of the next section of the chapter, but both OER and MOOCs are said to raise basic questions about the institutional form of the university, and perhaps about institutional forms per se (Selwyn 2014). The university is central to the development not just of open resources but of the organisational and institutional arrangements that can support and sustain open development, curation and re-use.

The key moment that raised the profile of open educational resources was the announcement by Massachusetts Institute of Technology (MIT) of the MIT Open Courseware (OCW) initiative.[1] The initiative continues and it has been a success in its own terms, sharing a large number of MIT resources and attracting large numbers of people to MIT online. As I write this chapter the MIT OCW web site shows figures of use ending in 2012 with 2150 published courses and 125 million views. The MIT initiative began using a grant from the Hewlett Foundation and they have continued to fund other large OER initiatives such as The Open University's Open Learn[2] which began in October 2006 and claims to have reached more than 23 million people. Despite the success of these university level initiatives the trend towards OER has its limits as Conole notes:

> However, despite the rhetoric about new social and participatory media generally and OER specifically, the reality is that their uptake and reuse in formal educational contexts has been disappointing. (Conole 2012, p. 131)

Although the OER movement is recent Pegler (2013) points out that the term open content was in use by 1998 and the idea of openness cuts across earlier initiatives such as The Open University and open source software (Selwyn 2014). The idea of openness as it is used in OER can include being free to the user, immediately accessible online and being available for further distribution and re-use with the author only retaining attribution rights (Sclater 2011). Sclater reports that the definition of OER developed by UNESCO at meetings in 2002 and 2004 included the following areas:

- Learning resources
- Courseware, content modules, learning objects, learner support and assessment tools, online learning communities

---

[1] MIT OCW: http://ocw.mit.edu/index.htm

[2] Open Learn: http://www.open.edu/openlearn/

- Resources to support teachers
- Tools for teachers and support materials to enable them to create, adapt and use OERs; as well as training materials for teachers; and other teaching tools
- Resources to assure the quality of education and educational practices

There is clearly a wide diversity of the kinds of OER that are being developed and the idea of OER is, perhaps necessarily, something of an umbrella term. In some ways open resources only make sense when they are seen as a contrast to the extensive attempts to restrict access to what is currently characterised as 'intellectual property'.

The early sociology of science[3] understood that 'communism' was a central norm for the development of science (Merton 1942). Communism was one of four institutional norms identified by Merton, sometimes summarised by the acronym CUDOS (Communism, Universalism, Disinterestedness and Organised Scepticism). By communism Merton meant that the outcomes of scientific research should be the common property of the scientific community. Merton recognised that reputation was an important aspect in the motivation of scientists and that they were interested in the attribution of originality and intellectual property in an honorific and reputational sense. However in contemporary conditions intellectual property is conceived of in more individualistic terms and in relation to criminal sanctions, commercial advantage and monetary value (Manta 2011). Because of this recent shift in intellectual property rights openness advocates have argued strongly against strong protection of intellectual property and for a variety of less restrictive licenses, most notably the Creative Commons licenses (Lessig 1996, 2004). In this the openness of OERs is part of a long historical argument about the place of intellectual property in the acquisition and circulation of knowledge and in the tension between social forms of production and the individual appropriation of rewards.

OER have a potential to support education when conceived of as a public rather than a private good. While higher education benefits the person, by way of their capacity and potential career trajectory, it is also a core component of civic life, a way to transmit culture and develop societies. As Sclater notes this gives OER an implicit if not explicit political agenda:

> While there are potential commercial motivations too… the desire to give something back to society is arguably the strongest driver for the organisations and individuals in the OER movement. An analysis of the open content phenomenon is therefore heavily influenced by the wider socio-political agenda, as defined by representatives of developing nations as well as the charitable foundations who have driven and provided much of the funding for OER projects. (Sclater 2011, p. 180)

The politics of OER is also explored by Selwyn (2014) and Phelan (2012). Selwyn notes that OER have their supporters among both left leaning advocates of collaboration, flat-hierarchies and worker/producer control and on the right by neoliberal influenced libertarians attracted by the possibility of reduced 'interference' by institutions and the state. Underpinning both approaches is a notion that OER

---

[3] This use of science should be understood as systematic knowledge, in a similar sense to the German word Wissenschaft.

lead to new learner-driven notions of learning which link OER to broader pedagogic notions of constructivism, constructionism and a sociocultural approach to knowledge building. In this way OER fit into a long line of educational debates in which shrill calls for change cloaking wider ideological agendas and as Selwyn notes:

> ...much of the current enthusiasm for openness is (un)consciously yoked to wider ideological motivations of re-engineering and reorientating the social relations of educational technologies and educational institutions. (Selwyn 2014, p. 75)

Phelan provides an apparently less radical critique but notes that:

> Open education historically and currently embodies a very clearly defined politics, centered strongly in a commitment to access and equity. In contrast, distance education programs may or may not be grounded in a commitment to access and equity...The politics of access and equity is even starker with regard to OER. Making learning materials freely available to all with adequate Internet access at least suggests a potentially radical broadening of access to learning. However, as with distance education, it may not necessarily be so. (Phelan 2012, p. 280)

Phelan goes on to make a case for autodidacticism, for a radical re-conceptualisation of the learner and by implication this would reconsider any requirement for the teacher and teaching in higher education. What is clear from both authors is that discussion of OER cannot be restricted to the practicalities of their production and use and that debate needs to extend to the way that OER are mobilised as part of an assault by both left and right on the university as an institution.

The potential benefits of OER may seem obvious and clear although there are many practical issues to surmount to make OER genuinely useful. The risks and dangers might not seem so apparent but OER can be a way of cheapening the production of courses in existing and developed core institutions. OER rather than expanding available resources can be used to replace the further production and refining of materials, enabling their replacement by freely available open resources. If this route were to be followed then the potential for OER could be self-defeating with the sources for such materials drying up. A further risk comes from the need for technical support staff who can convert materials into OER format and translators (for both language and cultural nuance) if the work is to transfer to a global user base. Currently Wiley et al (2014) note that re-use and translation of resources is still rare. For OER to work as they are intended to there are necessary costs in time and money to localise and re-use resources even if they are made available and free to use (Caswell et al 2008).

Both Knox (2013a) and Selwyn (2014) provide critical analysis of the current state of the OER movement and the openness agenda more generally. Knox argues that there has been an undertheorisation of openness and a simultaneous privileging and rejection of institutional authority. He suggests that OER diminish the role of pedagogy by emphasising a learner-centric model of education that rests on assumptions of an unproblematic self-direction and autonomy. Overall he suggests that OER are in alignment with the contemporary needs of capital in which the learner is enabled to continually seek new and relevant knowledge, to make themselves a more desirable educated and flexible labour commodity. In his critical analysis Selwyn identifies a set of five issues raised by the suggested benefits of OER. These issues include:

1. Tensions between individual competition and 'communal' production
2. Power imbalances within open processes of production
3. Mass consumption of openly produced products
4. The limited outcomes of open production processes
5. Open production as a site of exploitation and commodification

It can clearly be seen from this list that Selwyn's focus is largely on the processes of production. Ehlers (2011) in contrast argues that the second phase of OER development should move from the production of resources and providing access to them, to what he defines as open educational practices (OEP).

> OEP are defined as practices which support the (re)use and production of OER through institutional policies, promote innovative pedagogical models, and respect and empower learners as co-producers on their lifelong learning path. OEP address the whole OER governance community: policy makers, managers/administrators of organisations, educational professionals and learners. (Ehlers 2011, p. 3)

OEP change the focus from production to use and management including the institutional policies and pedagogic models that surround the resources (Andrade et al. 2011). Murphy (2013) takes this a step further by including formal recognition and assessment of OER learners beyond formal programmes:

> … open educational practices will therefore be considered as policies and practices implemented by higher education institutions that support the development, use and management of OERs, and the formal assessment and accreditation of informal learning undertaken using OERs. (Murphy 2013, p. 202).

The change of focus from resources to practices is a useful reminder of the institutional supports that are necessary for successful education to take place (Knox 2013). The question moves from the production of resources to the supports that might be required at an institutional level.

Institutional Supports for Openness

Openness is not new and a previous iteration of university development was initiated by the development of The Open University in the United Kingdom. An explicitly social-democratic and Labour Party initiative there was no attempt to disguise the political agenda of the early Open University. Although still political in nature it is clear that the politics of OER are less explicit and more diverse, finding support from both left and right. What unites both is a suspicion of the university and larger social institutions such as the state. However some of the well-known issues affecting OER are linked, at minimum, to institutional if not national and international solutions. The university can provide the basis for sustainable development, discovery, quality assurance and the contextualisation and localisation of OER. It is university practices that can make OER viable and provide them with a 'business' model.

There are two interrelated issues of sustainability of OER, the first is maintaining a base of users the second is financial (Wiley et al. 2014). Pegler notes that OER based on existing resources which are by-products of conventional educational practices require less resource (Pegler 2013). She also argues that by way of contrast new resources created purely for OER require 'an exceptional flow of funding or effort' (ibid, p. 149). Universities are central to the development of OER because they provide a sound and relatively permanent basis for organising the effort required to either repurpose existing resources or to develop new ones. They also have the potential to be beneficiaries to this development effort and can reward and incentivise staff to generate and support OER. The 'business model' for OER without institutional support from a university could be the kind of dystopia outlined by Selwyn (2014) in which OER lead to the 'corporate misappropriation' of free labour supplied for ethical and moral reasons. This criticism relates strongly to the issues raised in Chap. 2 about the contemporary phase of capitalism and the development of 'immaterial labour' (Hardt and Negri 2005).

Being able to find OER is not simply a technical question although it clearly involves the development of standards and specifications (Wiley et al. 2014). Work on learning objects led to a significant technical development of metadata standards and specifications intended to make learning objects easier to find. To be discoverable will require frameworks allowing major search engines to provide properly focused results. The technical question of discovery points to a displacement and repositioning at the heart of OER. OER are positioned as an outcome of co-production and voluntary effort but they may also require complex technical support such that rather than replacing resources controlled by publishers and institutions with cooperatively developed alternatives, OER replace one system of organisation and power with another. In this case one potentially dominated by technical experts and administrative requirements rather than publishers and university administration. The hope for OER is that they would translate the idea of the prosumer (Toffler 1980; Ritzer and Jurgenson 2010), someone who did more than simply consume into an educational context. The danger is that without universities and a coordinated university sector providing institutional supports OER will simply lead to a mass of consumers, control by a technological elite, a corporate takeover of the business, and a narrow band of activist producers organised around a complex technical infrastructure and corporate financial 'business' models.

A traditional area of university activity has been in the assurance of the quality of materials produced. One answer to why universities charge or cost the public purse for their services has been provided by Brown and Duguid who argued that the core function of a university was as a degree granting body. Their claim was that universities provided credentials to learners, allowing their prior learning to be acknowledged in the labour market. However in this context the credentials were valued in the market because the university and the procedures they followed in the production of knowledge, its circulation, assessment and validation provided a warrant (Brown and Duguid 2000). The university as an institution stands behind the materials and qualifications it produces. If discovery is a problem for OER this is compounded by a quality problem when there is an oversupply of material. If a search engine generates thousands of results for a topic how can the user decide between them, which are the high quality resources and which can be discarded?

The assessment of quality relies on a complex set of decisions that are not simply about the quality of the resource itself but on its appropriateness for the context it is intended to be integrated into. Resources are another example of the relational processes in learning in which a learning resource is only assessable for quality in a dynamic relationship between the features of the resource, the intentions of the user and the characteristics of its destination setting.

The need for contextualisation has been recognised as a challenge for OER (Wiley et al. 2014). Pegler (2013) argues that translation alone can lead to positive benefits including allowing users rather than suppliers to lead decisions and spread large quantities of resources. She also argues that this can lead to reciprocity with resources being shared back from what were originally 'read only' exchanges to examples of reciprocity. For these benefits to be achieved there is a considerable effort required not only to translate resources into different languages but to make them available in a new context. Resources made freely available by Ivy league universities in the United States might not be readily absorbed into linguistically, culturally and politically diverse contexts. It could be the eventual users who repurpose the resource but that then raises questions about how that effort in repurposing is going to be supported and sustained. It seems that OER do not remove the requirements for institutional frameworks for the work necessary for education even though they might displace them and generate new or reformed institutional approaches. One of the revised forms for the institutional use of OER has been the development of Massive Open Online Courses (MOOC) and the development of MOOCs is the subject of the next section of this chapter.

The University and the Challenge of MOOCs

The Massive Open Online Course is a current focus for debates about learning via digital and networked technologies. It has raised the visibility of issues that had previously only been discussed in academic circles and placed them into the public domain by way of media discussion (see for example BBC[4], The Guardian[5]). MOOCs have become the basis for another round of wild claims about the likelihood of radical change in universities (Barber et al. 2013). MOOCs have generated an atmosphere in which it is important for university and government policy makers to express clear ideas about how their ideas are connected to this new approach to teaching and learning. In this flurry of activity and overhyped claims it is difficult to remember the niche beginnings of the MOOC in Canada and its associations with the idea of networked learning (Daniel 2012)

> The first course carrying the name MOOC was offered in 2008, so this is a new phenomenon. Second, the pedagogical style of the early courses, which we shall call cMOOCs, was based on a philosophy of connectivism and networking. (Daniel 2012, p. 2)

---

[4] BBC Massive open online course- threat or opportunity 1st July 2013: http://www.bbc.co.uk/news/education-23069542

[5] The Guardian: Peter Scott. Moocs: if we're not careful so-called *open* courses will close minds 5th August 2013. http://www.theguardian.com/education/2013/aug/05/moocs-online-higher-education

The origins of the educational idea of the MOOC are still contested, although there is certainty about the role of connectivism in the process. Both Daniel (2012) and Clarà and Barberà (2013a, b) link connectivism with the ideas of Ivan Illich (1970), but this is contested by Downes (2013). Whatever the connection between connectivism and Illich there is, as Daniel noted a link between the aims of Illich and the aim of cMOOCs, which is:

> to provide all who want to learn with access to available resources… empower all who want to share what they know to find those who want to learn it from them (Daniel 2012, p. 3)

This early form of MOOC has not gone away and the term cMOOC has been used to distinguish the connectivist style of MOOCs from the new kinds of xMOOCS developed by elite universities and private corporate interests, largely in the United States (Siemens 2012). The aim of cMOOCs stands in sharp contrast to the xMOOCs which generally embody an instructivist approach to education, with video lectures, multiple choice assessment and limited peer-to-peer interaction. The cMOOCs were initially developed prior to and at the point of the global financial crisis, whereas the xMOOCs have gained prominence as the global financial crisis and austerity began to bite. In these changed economic conditions the utopian aims of cMOOCs gave way to a focus on the market and the need for a 'business model' for MOOCs (Barber et al. 2013). The emergence of xMOOCs is still very recent as Daniel records:

> Early in 2012 Stanford University offered a free, chunked course on Artificial Intelligence online and 58,000 people signed up. One of the faculty members involved, Sebastian Thrun, went on to found Udacity, a commercial start-up that helps other universities to offer xMOOCs (Meyer 2012). MIT (2011) announced MITx at the end of 2011 for a launch in spring 2012. MITx has now morphed into edX with the addition of Harvard and UC Berkeley (edX 2012). Since then similar initiatives from other well known US universities have come thick and fast. There seems to be a herd instinct at work as universities observe their peers joining the xMOOCs bandwagon and jump on for fear of being left behind. (Daniel 2012, pp. 3–4)

Coursera, a for-profit MOOC platform, has launched a range of courses mainly in the US but with examples in various countries including the United Kingdom (Moocs@Edinburgh Group 2013). It is this wave of activity that has given rise to the political, policy and public interest in the issue of MOOCs. It has also led to a renewed interest in the ways the introduction of new technologies presents a challenge to the university and its current institutional form.

In early 2013 the Institute for Public Policy Research, a UK think-tank produced an essay entitled: 'An avalanche is coming: Higher education and the revolution ahead' (Barber et al. 2013). The essay proposes an apocalyptic vision as outlined in the Forward by Lawrence Summers the President Emeritus of Harvard University:

> An Avalanche is Coming sets out vividly the challenges ahead for higher education, not just in the US or UK but around the world. Just as we've seen the forces of technology and globalisation transform sectors such as media and communications or banking and finance over the last two decades, these forces may now transform higher education. The solid classical buildings of great universities may look permanent but the storms of change now threaten them. (Barber, Donnelly, and Ritzvi 2013, p. 1)

The three fundamental challenges to the university that the authors identify are:

1. How can universities and new providers ensure education for employability? 'Given the rising cost of degrees, the threat to the market value of degrees and the sheer scale of both economic change and unemployment, this is a vital and immediate challenge'.
2. How can the link between cost and quality be broken? 'in the era of modern technology, when students can individually and collectively create knowledge themselves, outstanding quality without high fixed costs is both plausible and desirable'.
3. How does the entire learning ecosystem need to change to support alternative providers and the future of work? (Barber, Donnelly, and Ritzvi 2013, p. 6)

The style of the report can be seen in this example of a somewhat apocalyptic business style of language:

> the new student consumer is king and standing still is not an option (ibid, p. 6).

The report cannot be thought of in the same terms as research led commentary, rather it is an example of a call to action for policy makers across the higher education system couched in neoliberal business rhetoric.

The imperative for change although based on the availability of new technologies and the preexisting process of globalisation is the contemporary global financial crisis:

> the global economy is also dealing with a trauma of the worst crisis in modern times, as the consequences of two decades of irrational exuberance slowly unwind. (ibid, p. 11)

The financial crisis provides an incentive to examine the overall cost of universities and to argue that the costs of higher education are rising in an unsustainable way. MOOCs are presented in this essay as a tipping point, a cause of sudden and discontinuous change and a potential source of a solution to the problems arising from that change. The way MOOCs are presented is an example of the solutionism identified by Morozov (2013). Morozov argues that solutionism is the recasting of complex social situations as either:

> neatly defined problems with definite, computable solutions or as transparent and self-evident processes that can easily be optimised (Morozov 2013, p. 5).

Solutionism goes further than supplying technological fixes for difficult or 'wicked' problems by finding problems in areas that are not actually problematic at all. In the case of the argument for MOOCs it is the increasing cost of higher education. The European University Association showed a fall in the percentage of GDP spent on university funding between 2008 and 2013 in ten EU countries and an increase in eight (EUA 2013). In the United Kingdom (England and Wales) they found that university spending is falling as a proportion of GDP. After rising from 2008 to 2011, expenditure fell to 0.46 % of GDP, with only Hungary, Italy, Portugal and Greece having lower proportional expenditure. It would seem that in Europe the overall cost of higher education is hardly a problem requiring radical institutional change in universities. In fact there has been a nominal change in expenditure of −10 % between 2008 and 2012, increasing to −13 % if inflation is taken into account.[6] In the United States the debate has largely focused on the cost of higher education and the fees paid in relation to earnings (Table 5.1).

---

[6] Figures from: http://www.eua.be/publicfundingobservatory

Table. 5.1 Public and private spending as proportion of GDP on tertiary education (2009 data last updated 2012)

Source: OECD Stat Link: http://dx.doi.org/10.1787/888932662599

This debate disguises a process of privatisation in the US higher education sector that has led to increasing costs. Expenditure as a proportion of GDP is high in the United States at 2.6 % of GDP compared to an average in the OECD of 1.6 % (all figures 2009). However the US expenditure is skewed towards private sources. In the United States, 38 % of higher education expenditures come from public sources, and 62 % comes from private sources whereas cross all OECD countries, 70 % of expenditures on higher education come from public sources, and 30 % are from private sources. The high price of higher education to the student is based on the fact that 45 % of expenditures on higher education in the United States come from households.[7] The United States is not alone in higher education relying heavily on expenditures from households because it is even higher in Chile (68.1 %), Japan (50.7 %), Korea (49.2 %) and the United Kingdom (58.1 %). The crisis that MOOCs are said to provide a solution to is not a crisis caused by the overall cost of higher education, but the increasingly private nature of funding with the burden being shifted away from public sources to private households.

The drive to lower costs to the student has been picked up by bodies representing universities in the United Kingdom and linked directly to the potential of MOOCs.

MOOCs may also help to restructure and lower the costs of higher education in ways that might be attractive to learners looking for lower cost provision and which presents opportunities for new and existing providers (Universities UK 2013, p. 2)

It has also been picked up by senior ministers in the UK government responsible for universities, for example David Willetts:

Yes, I do think MOOCs are significant, there are people who have been around for a long time, who say that they aren't as new or as significant as the current flurry of excitement, but I first came across MOOCs in California in 2011 and my view is by and large, when the Tech Community in California put their ingenuity and their money behind what they see as

---

[7] All figures OECD from: http://www.oecd.org/unitedstates/CN%20-%20United%20States.pdf

the next "big thing," in the web and the social media by and large, they know what they are doing. And there is a real buzz there and when Goldman Sachs are investing and Stanford say it is significant and big players are coming in, my view is, this is a significant moment in the spread of education, notably, but not only higher education (Willetts 2013)

The remarks made by Willetts illustrate the way that MOOCs mix together a US centric mix of Silicon valley with large banking capital and Ivy League endorsement. MOOCs are identified by Willetts as having the potential to increase international recruitment, apply data analytics to large student numbers and develop employment skills, specifically IT skills for large corporations e.g. Microsoft. Although MOOCs may represent a further iteration in the technological platform available for networked learning they are not really novel in either educational or business terms. Daniel for example notes how little attention seems to have been paid by those commenting on the MOOC phenomena to previous experiences, either in the university expansion online in the dot com boom or in the open university movement (Daniel 2012, p. 9). A question for networked learning will be to what degree the principles that inform MOOCs will be drawn from the longer tradition of Open and Distance learning, including networked learning, and to what degree they will represent a degradation of these principles and a replication of an instructivist model in xMOOCs.

The rise of MOOCs in terms of public attention and large-scale implementation coincided with the adoption of austerity policies in advanced industrial countries following the financial crash of 2008. This coincidence has meant that MOOCs have been incorporated in agendas that are focused on the reduction of cost, both to the prospective student and to the public purse. In pedagogic terms this has been marked by a move away from a pedagogy informed by a notion of networked learning with an emphasis on dialogue, which informed cMOOCs, to a more classically instructivist model based in the transmission of knowledge in xMOOCs. The MOOC moment fitted into a more general debate amongst policy makers that advocated a particular kind of educational reform based on the identification of new technology as a source of 'disruptive innovation' that could lead to 'unbundling' the university. These ideas are not exclusively linked to the rise of MOOCs and OER were also discussed in these terms. This approach to change in universities will also be taken up in Chap. 8 when the source of disruption is supposed to be a new generation of digital native students. The relationship of MOOCs to the university may not be as disruptive as many have thought and Brady writing in the New Inquiry argued that:

These MOOCs [xMOOCs] are just a new way of maintaining the status quo, of re-institutionalizing higher education in an era of budget cuts, sky-rocketing tuition, and unemployed college graduates burdened by student debt. If the MOOC began in the classroom as an experimental pedagogy, it has swiftly morphed into a process driven from the top down, imposed on faculty by university administrators, or even imposed on administrators by university boards of trustees and regents. From within academia, the MOOC phenomenon is all about dollars and cents, about doing more of the same with less funding. (Brady 2013)

The idea of a MOOC began with a notion of educational reform based on principles familiar to those involved in the study of networked learning. Personally I have always been somewhat sceptical and I am cautious about the kinds of radical individualism that MOOCs seem to embody and I am equally sceptical about the dismissiveness found in relation to MOOCs concerning the institutional form of the university. The re-invention of the MOOC in the United States as the xMOOC has been accompanied by a re-hashing of familiar and stale agendas based on a largely transmissive pedagogy and private interests have reinforced a rhetoric that diminishes choice and emphasises a determinist account of change. To highlight the significance of choice in relation to MOOCs it is instructive to see what can still be done within the confines of an xMOOC platform. The Edinburgh MOOC 'E-learning and Digital Cultures', although based on the Coursera platform applied a pedagogy more usually associated with cMOOCs (Knox et al. 2012; Knox 2014). The new xMOOC platforms are no more determinist than any other technology and those interested in networked learning should experiment and explore the limits that xMOOC platforms will allow.

Conclusions

The university is changing but the claims that disruptive technologies will sweep it away are not just premature they are wrong because they ignore the strength of the forces (assemblages of people and things) that will re-order, stabilise and renew universities as institutions (see Chap. 6 for further development of this point). The MOOC is the current favourite technological disruptor, but the MOOC is not really a technological phenomenon, although it relies on a number of technological features. MOOCs represent a certain kind of mobilisation of aspects of the new technologies, but they are being mobilised by different groups for different purposes, even within a single institution. Similarly big data and analytics are enabled by the capacity of new technologies to track and trace their users, but the technology does not determine the decisions that institutions have made and those they will make about which data to capture and what uses it will be put to. The public nature of universities is highlighted by the use of open educational resources because they embody a notion of sharing that is distinctly different to market-driven notions of intellectual property. The university is under pressure and that pressure comes from political choices as much as it does from technological innovation. The decision in England to introduce fees was justified by austerity and the financial crisis, even though the changes may not save any money. The rhetoric that reduces universities complex duties to businesses and students to consumers has little to do with technology, but it has a great deal to do with political choices about the kinds of economic and educational systems that are preferred.

The university is a good illustration of the importance of levels and the need to avoid a binary between universal structures and individual agency. Universities are organisational points in which persons act in their organisational roles and not just as individuals. Institutions are sites for action in which people acting collectively and recursively can alter the conditions in which they find themselves. The organisational actors take situated decisions in technological contexts, some of which are locally determined and some of which are outside institutional control. These decisions are also more than simply technical decisions and the technology is a point of contestation between different visions of the university. Networked learning has a strong view about what 'good' learning might entail. Good learning involves discourse, mediation and interaction between people and their learning resources. As a consequence networked learning has a view about the university as a public institution. This view of networked learning supports strong institutional public provision, even though it may oppose particular institutional policies. This separates this version of networked learning from those who see institutions as barriers to good learning and technology as a means to undermine current institutional provision (See Downes 2006, 2007a) and to a lesser degree Siemens (2005) for an alternative view of networked learning as personal and de-institutionalised).

Institutions are intertwined with infrastructures which are the subject of the next chapter. Levels and the intermediate mesolevel is one of the key ideas that can be found in various chapters of this book, but they are a particular focus of the next chapter. In terms of institutions levels are important in relation to the disciplinary differences and research cultures that form the basis for academic tribes and territories (Becher and Trowler 2001 see also Chap. 7). Institutions do not form single homogenous entities and they are better described in terms of an assemblage, a sociomaterial complex with more than one centre. Discipline and subject area, provide opportunities for self-organisation within and beyond institutions and the functional units for technical support and administration act as separable elements within the university. Faculties, departments and schools all sit at mesolevels within institutions but they vary considerably in terms of their structure. In some universities collegial forms of self-organisation remain, in others it is truncated or replaced by a purely managerial hierarchy unanswerable to the academic community. The use of learning analytics is another area in which institutional concerns are intertwined with infrastructure and where the issues can be viewed at various levels. Buckingham Shum (2012), for example has discussed making use of the idea of micro-, meso-, and macrolevels in terms of understanding the various uses of learning analytics. The institution in all its complexity is enmeshed with a set of infrastructures. Some of these are largely external to the institution and beyond institutional control. Other aspects of infrastructure are closely aligned with institutional structures and increasingly there are new hybrid forms, such as cloud computing, that combine an institutional aspect with a universal service. It is this complex set of relationships that forms the basis of the next chapter.

References

Anderson, C. (2008). The end of theory, will the data deluge make the scientific method obsolete? *Edge*. Retrieved from http://www.edge.org/3rd_culture/anderson08/anderson08_index.html

Andrade, A., Ehlers, U. D., Caine, A., Carneiro, R., Conole, G., Kairamo, A. K., Holmberg, C. (2011). *Beyond OER: Shifting focus to open educational practices*. Open Educational Quality Initiative. Retrieved from https://oerknowledgecloud.org/sites/oerknowledgecloud.org/files/OPAL2011.pdf

Aviv, R., Erlich, Z., Ravid, G., & Geva, A. (2003). Network analysis of knowledge construction in asynchronous learning networks. *Journal of Asynchronous Learning Networks, 7*(3), 1–23.

Barber, M., Donnelly, K., and Ritzvi, S. (2013). An avalanche is coming: Higher education and the revolution ahead. London: IPPR. Retrieved from http://www.ippr.org/publication/55/10432/an-avalanche-is-coming-higher-education-and-the-revolution-ahead

Becher, T., & Trowler, P. (2001). *Academic tribes and territories* (2nd ed.). Buckingham, England: SRHE and Open University Press.

Boyd, D., & Crawford, K. (2012). Critical questions for big data. *Information, Communication & Society, 15*(5), 662–679.

Brady, A. (2013). The MOOC moment and the end of reform. *The New Inquiry.* Retrieved from http://thenewinquiry.com/blogs/zunguzungu/the-mooc-moment-and-the-end-of-reform/

Braverman, H. (1974). *Monopoly capitalism.* New York: Monthly Review Press.

Brown, M. (2011). Learner analytics: The coming third wave. Educause Learning Initiative brief. Retrieved from Apr, 2011, http://www.educause.edu/Resources/LearningAnalyticsTheComingThir/227287

Brown, J. S., & Duguid, P. (2000). *The social life of information.* Boston: Harvard Business School.

Buckingham Shum, S. (2012). *Learning analytics.* UNESCO Institute for Information Technologies in Education (ITTE), Policy Brief. Moscow: UNESCO ITTE. Retrieved from http://iite.unesco.org/pics/publications/en/files/3214711.pdf

Caswell, T., Henson, S., Jensen, M., & Wiley, D. (2008). Open content and open educational resources: Enabling universal education. *The International Review of Research in Open and Distance Learning, 9*(1). Retrieved from http://www.irrodl.org/index.php/irrodl/article/view/469

Clarà, M., & Barberà, B. (2013a). Learning online: massive open online courses (MOOCs), connectivism, and cultural psychology. *Distance Education, 34*(1), 129–136.

Clarà, M., & Barberà, B. (2013b). Three problems with the connectivist conception of learning. *Journal of Computer Assisted Learning, 30*, 197–206. doi:10.1111/jcal.12040.

Collini, S. (2012). *What are universities for?* London: Penguin Press.

Conole, G. (2012). Fostering social inclusion through open educational resources (OER). *Distance Education, 33*(2), 131–134.

Daniel, J. (2012). Making Sense of MOOCs: Musings in a Maze of Myth, Paradox and Possibility. *Journal of Interactive Media in Education.* Retrieved from http://jime.open.ac.uk/2012/18

De Laat, M., & Schreurs, B. (2013). Visualizing informal professional development networks: Building a case for learning analytics in the workplace. *American Behavioral Scientist, 57*(10), 1421–1438.

De Laat, M. F., Schreurs, B., & Nijland, F. (2014). Communities of practice: Balancing openness, networking and value creation. In R. F. Poell, T. S. Rocco, & G. L. Roth (Eds.), *The Routledge companion to human resource development.* London: Routledge.

Deleuze, G., & Guatarri, F. (1987). *A thousand plateaus: Capitalism and schizophrenia.* London: University of Minnesota Press.

Downes, S. (2006). Learning networks and connective knowledge. *Instructional Technology Forum: Paper 92.* Retrieved from http://it.coe.uga.edu/itforum/paper92/paper92.html

Downes, S. (2007a). Learning networks in practice. In: Ley, D., (ed.) *Emerging technologies for learning.* London: BECTA. Retrieved from http://nparc.cisti-icist.nrc-cnrc.gc.ca/npsi/ctrl?action=rtdoc&an=8913424&lang=en

Downes, S. (2013). On the three or four problems of Connectivism. Retrieved from http://halfan-hour.blogspot.ca/2013/10/on-three-or-four-problems-of.html

edX (2012). *UC Berkeley joins edX.* Retrieved from https://www.edx.org/press/uc-berkeley-joins-edx

Ehlers, U. D. (2011). From open educational resources to open educational practices. *Elearning Papers, 23*, 1–8. Retrieved from http://openeducationeuropa.eu/en/paper/open-education-changing-educational-practices

Enders, J. (2012). The university and the public and private good. In C. Teelken, G. Ferlie, & M. Dent (Eds.), *Leadership in the public sector: Promises and pitfalls* (pp. 195–213). Abingdon, England: Routledge.

Engeström, Y. (2005). *Developmental work research: Expanding activity theory in practice.* Berlin, Germany: Lehmanns Media.

Engeström, Y. (2007). From communities of practice to mycorrhizae. In J. Hughes, N. Jewson, & L. Unwin (Eds.), *Communities of practice: Critical perspectives* (pp. 41–54). Abingdon: Routledge.

Engeström, Y. (2008). *From teams to knots: Activity-theoretical studies of collaboration and learning at work*. Cambridge: Cambridge University Press.

Engeström, Y., Engeström, R., & Vähäaho, T. (1999). When the center does not hold: The importance of knotworking. In S. Chaiklin, M. Hedegaard, & U. J. Jensen (Eds.), *Activity theory and social practice* (pp. 326–374). Aarhus, Denmark: Aarhus University Press.

Feenberg, A. (1991). *Critical theory of technology*. New York: Oxford University Press.

Ferguson, R. (2012). Learning analytics: Drivers, developments and challenges. *International Journal of Technology Enhanced Learning, 4*(5–6), 304–317.

Fuchs, C. (2008). *Internet and society; social theory in the information age*. New York: Routledge.

Fuller, S. (2009). *The sociology of intellectual life: The career of the mind in and around the academy*. London: Sage.

Hardt, M., & Negri, A. (2005). *Multitude: War and democracy in the age of empire*. London: Hamish Hamilton.

Harvey, D. (2005). *A brief history of neoliberalism*. Oxford: Oxford University Press.

Hey, T., Tansley, S. and Tolle, K. (eds) (2009) *The fourth paradigm data-intensive scientific discovery*. Redmond, WA: Microsoft Research. Retrieved from http://research.microsoft.com/en-us/collaboration/fourthparadigm/

Hoggett, P. (1991). A new management in the public sector? *Policy & Politics, 19*(4), 243–256.

Ilich, I. (1970). *Deschooling society*. New York: Harper and Row. Retrieved from http://www.preservenet.com/theory/Illich/Deschooling/intro.html

JISC (2009). Doing enterprise architecture: Enabling the agile institution. Joint Information Systems Committee, Technology and Standards Watch Early Adopter Study, Document No 533. Retrieved from http://www.jisc.ac.uk/media/documents/techwatch/jisc_ea_pilot_study.pdf

JISC (2010). Enterprise architecture, version 2. Joint Information Systems Committee, Document No 700. Retrieved from http://www.jisc.ac.uk/media/documents/publications/briefingpaper/2010/bpeav2.pdf

Jones, C. (2013). The digital university: A concept in need of a definition. In R. Goodfellow & M. Lea (Eds.), *Literacy in the digital university—Critical perspectives on learning, scholarship, and technology* (pp. 162–172). London: Routledge.

Kallinikos, J. (2010). The "Age of Smart Machine": A 21st century view. In P. A. Laplante (Ed.), *Encyclopedia of software engineering, 1:1* (pp. 1097–1103). London: Taylor & Francis.

Knox, J. (2013). Five critiques of the open educational resources movement. *Teaching in Higher Education, 18*(8), 821–832.

Knox, J. (2014). Digital culture clash: 'massive' education in the E-learning and digital cultures MOOC. *Distance Education (Special Issue on Massively Open Online Courses), 35*(2), 164–177.

Knox, J., Bayne, S., Macleod, H., Ross, J. & Sinclair, C. (2012). MOOC pedagogy: the challenges of developing for Coursera. Retrieved from http://newsletter.alt.ac.uk/2012/08/mooc-pedagogy-the-challenges-of-developing-for-coursera/

Land, R., & Bayne, S. (2005). Screen or monitor: Issues of surveillance and disciplinary power in online learning environments. In R. Land & S. Bayne (Eds.), *Education in cyberspace* (pp. 165–178). Abingdon, England: Routledge Falmer.

Lane, J.-E. (2002). *The new public management: An introduction*. London: Routledge.

Lash, S., & Urry, J. (1987). *The end of organized capitalism*. Cambridge: Polity Press.

Lee, J., & Myers, M. (2004). Dominant actors, political agendas, and strategic shifts over time: A critical ethnography of an enterprise systems implementation. *Journal of Strategic Information Systems, 13*, 355–374.

Lessig, L. (1996). Intellectual property and code. *Journal of Civil Rights and Economic Development. 11*, 3, Article 6. Retrieved from http://scholarship.law.stjohns.edu/jcred/vol11/iss3/6

Lessig, L. (2004). *Free culture: The nature and future of creativity*. London: Penguin Press.

Lorenz, C. (2012). If you're so smart, why are you under surveillance? Universities, neoliberalism, and new public management. *Critical Inquiry, 38*(3), 599–629.

Manta, I. D. (2011). The puzzle of criminal sanctions for intellectual property infringement. *Harvard Journal of Law & Technology, 24*(2), 469–518.

McCluskey, F., & Winter, M. (2012). *The idea of the digital university: Ancient traditions, disruptive technologies and the battle for the soul of higher education.* Washington, DC: Policy Studies Organisation/Westphalia Press.

Merton, R. K. (1942). The normative structure of science. In N. Storer (Ed.), *The sociology of science: Theoretical and empirical investigations* (pp. 267–278). Chicago: The University of Chicago Press.

Meyer, R. (2012). *What it's like to teach a MOOC (and what the heck's a MOOC?).* Retrieved from http://www.theatlantic.com/technology/archive/2012/07/what-its-like-to-teach-a-mooc-andwhat-the-hecks-a-mooc/260000/.

Miles, E., & Trott, W. (2011). *Collaborative working.* London: Institute for Government.

MIT (Massachusetts Institute of Technology). (2011). *MIT announces online learning initiative.* Retrieved from http://web.mit.edu/newsoffice/2011/mitx-education-initiative-1219.html.

Moocs@Edinburgh Group (2013). Moocs@Edinburgh Report #1. Retrieved from http://hdl.handle.net/1842/6683

Morozov, E. (2013). *To save everything click here: Technology, solutionism and the urge to fix problems that don't exist.* London: Allen Lane.

Murphy, A. (2013). Open educational practices in higher education: Institutional adoption and challenges. *Distance Education, 34*(2), 201–217.

Neilson, J., Pritchard, B., & Yeung, H. W. (2014). Global value chains and global production networks in the changing international political economy: An introduction. *Review of International Political Economy, 21*(1), 1–8.

Norris, D.M., and Baer, L.L. (2013). Building organisational capacity for analytics. Boulder, CO: Educause. Retrieved from http://www.educause.edu/library/resources/building-organizational-capacity-analytics

O'Connor, J. R. (1973). *The fiscal crisis of the state.* New York: St Martins Press.

Pegler, C. (2011). Reuse and repurposing of online digital learning resources within UK higher education: 2003–2010. Ph.D. thesis, The Open University. Retrieved from http://oro.open.ac.uk/32317/

Pegler, C. (2013). The influence of open resources on design practice. In H. Beetham & R. Sharpe (Eds.), *Rethinking pedagogy for a digital age: Designing for 21st century learning* (2nd ed., pp. 145–161). London: Routledge.

Perkin, H. (2007). History of universities. In J. Forest & P. Altbach (Eds.), *International handbook of higher education* (pp. 159–205). Dordrecht, The Netherlands: Springer.

Phelan, L. (2012). Politics, practices, and possibilities of open educational resources. *Distance Education, 33*(2), 279–282.

Piore, M. J., & Sabel, C. F. (1984). *The second industrial divide: Possibilities for prosperity.* New York: Basic Books.

Pollock, N., & Cornford, J. (2004). ERP systems and the university as a "unique" organisation. *Information Technology & People, 17*(1), 31–52.

Pollock, N., & Cornford, J. (2005). *Implications of enterprise resource planning systems for universities: An analysis of benefits and risks.* London: The Observatory on borderless education.

Pollock, N., Williams, R., & D'Adderio, L. (2007). Global software and its provenance: Generification work in the production of organizational software packages. *Social Studies of Science, 37*(2), 254–280.

Ritzer, G. (1993). *The MacDonaldization of society.* London: Sage.

Ritzer, G., & Jurgenson N. (2010). Production, consumption, prosumption: The nature of capitalism in the age of the digital 'prosumer'. *Journal of Consumer Culture, 10*(1), 13–36.

Sclater, N. (2011). Open educational resources: Motivations, logistics and sustainability. In N. F. Ferrer & J. M. Alonso (Eds.), *Content management for E-learning* (pp. 179–193). London: Springer.

Sclater, N. (2014). Snooping professor or friendly don? The ethics of university learning analytics. *Conversation*. Retrieved from 26 Feb, 2014, https://theconversation.com/snooping-professor-or-friendly-don-the-ethics-of-university-learning-analytics-23636

Scott, J. C. (2006). The mission of the university: Medieval to postmodern transformations. *The Journal of Higher Education, 77*(1), 1–39.

Scott, S. V., & Wagner, E. L. (2003). Networks, negotiations, and new times: The implementation of enterprise resource planning into an academic administration. *Information and Organization, 13*(4), 285–313.

Selwyn, N. (2014). *Distrusting educational technology: Critical questions for changing times*. London: Routledge.

Shattock, M. (2010). Managing mass higher education in a period of austerity. *Arts and Humanities in Higher Education, 9*(1), 22–30.

Siemens, G. (2005). Connectivism: a theory of learning for the digital age. *International Journal of Instructional Technology and Distance Learning, 2*(1), Retrieved from http://www.itdl.org/Journal/Jan_05/article01.htm

Siemens, G. (2012). What is the theory that underpins our MOOCs? Elearnspace [blog]. Retrieved from http://www.elearnspace.org/blog/2012/06/03/what-is-the-theory-that-underpins-our-moocs/

Siemens, G. (2013). Learning analytics: The emergence of a discipline. *American Behavioral Scientist, 57*(10), 1380–1400.

Slade, S., & Prinsloo, P. (2013). Learning analytics: Ethical issues and dilemmas. *American Behavioral Scientist, 57*(10), 1510–1529.

Stuart, M., Grugulis, I., Tomlinson, J., Forde, C., & MacKenzie, R. (2013). Reflections on work and employment into the 21st century: Between equal rights, force decides. *Work Employment Society, 27*, 379–395.

Tapscott, D., & Williams, A. (2010). Innovating the 21st century university: It's time. *Educause Review, 45*(1), 17–29.

Toffler, A. (1980). *The third wave*. New York: William Morrow.

Universities UK (2013). Massive open online courses: Higher education's digital moment? Retrieved from http://www.universitiesuk.ac.uk/highereducation/Documents/2013/MassiveOpenOnlineCourses.pdf

EUA (European Universities Association) (2013). EUA's Public Funding Observatory Report Spring 2013. Retrieved from http://www.eua.be/Libraries/Governance_Autonomy_Funding/EUA_PFO_report_2013.sflb.ashx

van Barneveld, A., Arnold, K.E., & Campbell, J.P. (2012). Analytics in higher education: Establishing a common language. ELI Paper 1. Boulder, CO: EDUCAUSE. Retrieved from http://net.educause.edu/ir/library/pdf/ELI3026.pdf

Wagner, E., & Newell, S. (2005). Making software work: Producing social order via problem solving in a troubled ERP implementation. ICIS 2005 Proceedings. Paper 37. Retrieved from http://aisel.aisnet.org/icis2005/37

Weller, M. (2007). *Virtual learning environments: Using, choosing and developing your VLE*. Abingdon, England: Routledge.

Wiley, D., Bliss, T. J., & McEwan, M. (2014). Open educational resources: A review of the literature. In J. M. Spector, M. D. Merrill, J. Elen, & M. J. Bishop (Eds.), *Handbook of research on educational communications and technology* (4th ed., pp. 781–789). New York: Springer.

Willetts, D. (2013). Address to QAA "We need to talk about quality: MOOCs," 8th July 2013. QAA podcast. Retrieved from http://www.qaa.ac.uk/Publications/Podcasts/Transcripts/Pages/David_Willetts_MOOCS_speech_8July2013.aspx

Wittrock, B. (2012). The modern university in its historical contexts: Rethinking three transformations. In M. Feingold (Ed.), *History of universities* (pp. 199–226). Oxford: Oxford University Press.

Wolff, A., and Zdrahal, Z. (2012). Improving retention by identifying and supporting "at-risk" students. *EDUCAUSE Review Online*. Retrieved from http://www.educause.edu/ero/article/improving-retention-identifying-and-supporting-risk-students

Zuboff, S. (1988). *In the age of the smart machine: The future of work and power*. New York: Basic Books.

Chapter 6
The Infrastructures

Networked learning depends on the existence of a variety of infrastructures and in particular the digital and networked technologies that support education. Some of these are supplied by universities and depend on the kinds of institutional processes that were discussed in the previous chapter, but some are not institutionally bounded and they can be incidental to formal learning but important to the informal processes surrounding it. I have been part of two institution wide change processes which involved significant modifications to the university's infrastructures for learning. Both have involved dispersed decision making in which 'the' university has proved to be a black box, assembled out of a variety of competing interests, material and social constraints and an array of loosely coupled technological systems. Some of the infrastructures involved in the changes were institutional in scale, but others involved external actors and their integration into university processes. If networked learning is to be an effective approach it has to take into consideration those assemblages that are brought together in infrastructures because the interactions and connections that networked learning requires depend on the continuing construction and maintenance of an often invisible substrate of infrastructural activity. My argument is that infrastructures are important for networked learning but more than that I argue that digital and network infrastructures, and an understanding of the issues they raise, are fundamental to understanding contemporary society and the world in which networked learning takes place.

The view that infrastructures are fundamental has been explored in a number of contexts and it is neatly summarised by Edwards:

> To be modern is to live within and by means of infrastructures: basic systems and services that are reliable, standardized, and widely accessible, at least within a community. For us, infrastructures reside in a naturalized background, as ordinary and unremarkable as trees, daylight, and dirt. Our civilizations fundamentally depend on them, yet we notice them mainly when they fail. They are the connective tissues and the circulatory systems of modernity. (Edwards 2010, p. 8)

This quote outlines a standard view of infrastructure as something that is already in place, ready-to-use, completely transparent and not requiring consideration.

© Springer International Publishing Switzerland 2015
C. Jones, *Networked Learning*, Research in Networked Learning,
DOI 10.1007/978-3-319-01934-5_6

The most recent infrastructure understood in this way, and most relevant to networked learning is the infrastructure that supports the Internet and the Web. As Edwards notes infrastructures though generally unnoticed come into sharp focus when they fail. This way of thinking can lead to infrastructure being thought of as an object, a set of artefacts that are built and maintained that usually remain relatively unscrutinised and simply provide the background to everyday life. In Chap. 4 I introduced the idea of sociomateriality and the way the material and the social were intertwined and imbricated with each other. Infrastructure in my view is a strong example of an aspect of contemporary life that is best understood in these terms. For example the practices of academic staff and students in relation to their personal mobile devices are conditioned by the infrastructural provision of institutions and service providers. If a networked learning pedagogy envisages the incorporation of mobile devices then the provision of a robust wireless infrastructure is a necessary precondition for such an approach to be successful.

Infrastructure also raises questions concerning *levels* of activity. Infrastructures are beyond local, small-scale and short-term interactions at a microlevel and they involve activity at scale and with a significant duration at either meso- or macrolevels. Strong conceptions of actor-network theory have been used to inform understandings of sociomateriality and these are resistant to accepting the idea of levels (Latour 2005). I make the case later in this chapter for a relational understanding of levels, which I contend is compatible with a sociomaterialist outlook. In the view I outline meso- and macrolevels of activity are central to thinking about infrastructure concerning networked learning. In educational settings it is common for local and small-scale interaction to be dependent on decisions about the infrastructural provision for connectivity and network access made beyond individual classes in departments, faculties, universities and beyond. Increasingly networked learning is less reliant on single 'lone ranger' innovators and it has become more dependent on collective actors, universities, governmental institutions and the corporate sector. The first university course I researched in terms of networked learning the mid-1990s was the initiative of a sole academic and it ran on a single basic Apple desktop PC running First Class computer conferencing (Jones and Cawood 1998; Jones 1998). The course relied on several infrastructural provisions, including computer labs and the university's dial in network for remote access, however it was very much a personal innovation. Currently many academics still experiment with novel and innovative ways of providing networked learning. However in contemporary conditions there is an increased dependency on a range of infrastructural provisions, from wireless connectivity to single sign on to a variety of university services including remote access to resources via libraries to e-journals and books. Even the selection of essential collaborative software has become centralised such that courses designed with the features of one LMS in mind can be significantly altered by a university level decision to move from one LMS provider to another. The infrastructure in education has both a technical and a social character and the activity of individual academic innovators is conditioned by the kinds of infrastructures for learning that are provided for them.

Infrastructure

Star and Ruhleder (1996) argue that infrastructure is something that emerges for people in practice, and it is connected to activities and structures. This suggests a relational understanding of infrastructure and one that is similar to the argument presented in Chap. 2 about affordances. An infrastructure only emerges in relation to those who use it and their purposes in the context of organised practices. Star and Ruhleder:

> …hold that infrastructure is a fundamentally relational concept. It becomes infrastructure in relation to organized practices. Within a given cultural context, the cook considers the water system a piece of working infrastructure integral to making dinner; for the city planner, it becomes a variable in a complex equation. Thus we ask, when—not what—is an infrastructure. (Star and Ruhleder 1996, p. 113)

To characterise the relational nature of infrastructure Star & Ruhleder suggest eight dimensions:

1. *Embeddedness* (integrated in social structures and practices)
2. *Transparency* (can be used without removing focus from the task)
3. *Reach or scope* (goes beyond individual tasks or processes, either temporal or spatial)
4. *Learned as part of membership* (an inherent part of an organisation)
5. *Links with conventions of practice* (shapes and is shaped by a community of practice)
6. *Embodiment of standards* (builds on standards and conventions, able to plug into other infrastructures)
7. *Built on an installed base* (is not de novo and wrestles with existing technologies)
8. *Visible upon breakdown* (loses transparency and is drawn into focus when it breaks down) (adapted from Star and Ruhleder 1996, p. 113).

To these Edwards adds a ninth dimension:

9. *Is fixed in modular increments, not all at once or globally.* Because infrastructure is big, layered, and complex, and because it means different things locally, it is never changed from above. Changes require time, negotiation, and adjustment with other aspects of the systems involved. (Edwards 2010, p. 9)

Edwards argues that most of the entities commonly classified as infrastructures are network structures, but it should be noted that his focus is on large-scale socio-technical structures that can be global in extent. He also notes that infrastructures often gain their network structures via gateway technologies and standards that can bring together otherwise incompatible local systems. Infrastructures are reliant on standards and protocols to link together heterogeneous local systems by way of a distributed coordination processes (Hanseth and Lundberg 2001). This interaction between global and locally bounded aspects of infrastructure will be examined in terms of the infrastructures associated with institutions and in relation to infrastructures for learning later in the chapter. In the case of an institutional infrastructure they are generally more limited in scale and circumscribed in terms of social and organisational practices. Star and Ruhleder (1996) argued that an infrastructure occurred when the tension between local and global is resolved so it is the connection between local practices and large-scale sociotechnical systems that will be the focus of attention in the interactions between institutions, infrastructures and learning. Because infrastructures are sociotechnical systems they are always reliant on complex organisational practices for maintenance and development and they also rely on the integration of heterogeneous artefacts at various levels of scale in a dialectical process with the social aspects of the system. Finally it is worth reinforcing the definitional feature of an infrastructure, which is that it resides naturalised in the background and is only brought into view at points of breakdown when it fails in its typical functions.

Information Infrastructures

I have been writing about infrastructure generally, in ways that include the electricity supply, road and rail systems and a variety of other physical systems. In this section I want to develop a little further the idea of infrastructure that is of greater relevance to networked learning, the infrastructure based on digital and networked technologies. The most commonly used term for this kind of infrastructure is an information infrastructure:

> Superadded to the term 'information,' infrastructure refers loosely to digital facilities and services usually associated with the internet: computational services, help desks, and data repositories to name a few. In the same vein but in a broader sweep, the Global Information Infrastructure (GII) refers to worldwide information and communication systems that process and transport data inside and outside national boundaries. (Bowker et al. 2010, p. 98)

An early articulation of this linkage between information and infrastructure can be found in Bowker (1996) in which he argues for an 'infrastructural inversion' in which the infrastructural background is made visible and contingent. The view of infrastructure captured by the term information infrastructures highlights the need for standardisation across the variety of complex systems and organisational practices that underpin modern knowledge and educational practices (Hanseth et al. 1996). These include but are not confined to large-scale e-research, library systems, databases, search engines, co-laboratories, museums, publishers, funding agencies and review systems. Information infrastructures also point to the need to think in terms of relatively longer time scales:

> An alternative vision of infrastructure may better take into account the social and organizational dimensions of infrastructure. This vision requires adopting a long term rather than immediate timeframe and thinking about infrastructure not only in terms of human versus technological components but in terms of a set of interrelated social, organizational, and technical components or systems (whether the data will be shared, systems interoperable, standards proprietary, or maintenance and redesign factored in). (Bowker et al 2010, p. 99)

Edwards argues that knowledge is itself an enduring, widely shared sociotechnical system and he defines knowledge infrastructures as comprising robust networks of people, artefacts, and institutions that generate, share, and maintain specific knowledge about the human and natural worlds (Edwards 2010).

Digital and network infrastructures in many ways have a standard physical form because they rely on servers, cables, routers and all the physical elements that provide the backbone on which digital interactions take place. They differ however in the way in which they also constitute 'virtual' worlds, code spaces (Kitchen and Dodge 2011) which have their own geography and rely on lines of code to control physical hardware.

> Software, like steam once did, is shaping our world—from the launch of billion-dollar spacecraft to more mundane work such as measuring and displaying time, controlling traffic lights, and monitoring the washing of clothes. Indeed, whatever the task—domestic chores, paid work, shopping, traveling, communicating, governing, playing—software increasingly makes a difference to how social and economic life takes place. In short, software matters … (Kitchen and Dodge 2011, p. 3)

In this way digital infrastructures are different because they are material but in addition they rely on code, the lines of instructions and algorithms that combine and once activated by suitable inputs generate complex digital functions which produce real and tangible effects. Code is the 'governing power' of digital and network infrastructures because it makes things happen and shapes future actions through self-governing feedback loops (Williamson 2015). Digital and network infrastructures are twice invisible, firstly being hidden in the background and secondly by being dependent on relatively invisible code. Kitchen and Dodge argue that coded software is embedded at four different levels in coded objects, coded infrastructures, coded processes, and coded assemblages. They define the infrastructural level in this way:

> Coded infrastructures are both networks that link coded objects together and infrastructures that are monitored and regulated, fully or in part, by software. (Kitchen and Dodge 2011, p. 6)

It is this self-governing capacity to monitor and regulate that gives software its governing power and suggests that code not only reflects the world but shapes it. Relevant to the use of infrastructure in this chapter is the level Kitchen and Dodge identify as the coded assemblage, which comprises more than one infrastructure and includes both those elements that use coded process and those that do not.

> Coded assemblages occur where several different coded infrastructures converge, working together—in nested systems or in parallel, some using coded processes and others not—and become integral to one another over time in producing particular environments, such as automated warehouses, hospitals, transport systems, and supermarkets. For example, the combined coded infrastructures and coded processes of billing, ticketing, check-in, baggage routing, security screening, customs, immigration, air traffic control, airplane instruments, and so on work together to create a coded assemblage that defines and produces airports and passenger air travel (Kitchen and Dodge 2011, p. 7).

Digital and network infrastructures in the context of networked learning are likely to include both the level they identify as infrastructure and the additional level of assemblages described by Kitchen and Dodge.

The initial concept of an infrastructure that I have introduced has now been extended into the digital and network domain and to both information and knowledge. It points towards the out-of-sight, naturalised elements that allow the normal practices of learning and education to take place. It suggests that to research networked learning an infrastructural inversion is necessary—to make visible that which usually resides in the background. It also suggests an evolutionary parallel with the development of technology because infrastructure also has a modular and evolutionary pattern of development (Arthur 2009). An evolutionary perspective, allows for change to take place in modular elements within an infrastructure in a gradual way that can occasionally lead to rapid change in a form of punctuated equilibrium (Eldridge and Gould 1972; Gould 2007). There are some additional key ideas that arise from research arising from this conception of infrastructure that are especially relevant to networked learning. At a general level infrastructures are emergent systems that rely on: (a) scale, (b) transfer and translation from one time or place to another (c) standards and protocols to provide gateways forming networks, internetworks and Webs between heterogeneous systems (Jackson et al. 2007).

This view of infrastructure as having a long duration stands in contrast to the revolutionary rhetoric that often surrounds new technologies (see for example Barber et al. 2013; Tapscott and Williams 2010). A key issue identified by examining sociotechnical systems as infrastructures is the question of time. Infrastructures are often modular and develop incrementally (in their parts and sub-systems) as much as they do by way of sharp periods of change. As infrastructures develop they can face points at which significant choices have to be made that depend on prior decisions and historical inheritances. Once the choice has been taken the effects are then evident as the infrastructure develops further.

> …one needs to elaborate more of a theory of path-dependency in higher education institutions. With this, one might reach a new understanding about the extent to which learning the 'new, new thing' necessarily borrows from the past. This would engender an appreciation of the continuity of adaptation processes, to complement the one-sided emphasis on discontinuity and change that now prevails in the literature. (Krücken 2003, p. 334)

The final linked point is about the importance of lock-in, the kind of inertia that affects infrastructure once a technology has been adopted. Such an approach does not dismiss occasional radical change, but as with natural evolution infrastructural change has a pattern of punctuated equilibrium (Eldridge and Gould 1972; Gould 2007). Edwards et al. (2013) summarised the evolutionary nature of infrastructural change:

> Key to the infrastructure perspective is their modular, multilayered, rough-cut character. Infrastructures are not systems, in the sense of fully coherent, deliberately engineered, end-to-end processes. Rather, infrastructures are ecologies or complex adaptive systems; they consist of numerous systems, each with unique origins and goals, which are made to interoperate by means of standards, socket layers, social practices, norms, and individual behaviors that smooth out the connections among them. This adaptive process is continuous, as individual elements change and new ones are introduced—and it is not necessarily always successful. (Edwards et al. 2013, p. 5)

Punctuated equilibrium allows for periods of rapid change in this kind of evolutionary process and as such it provides a distinctly different view of change to claims of radical or revolutionary ruptures determined by technological change.

Because these systems are emergent their histories are critical to their development and the way change happens in infrastructures can be described in terms of (a) starting conditions, (b) path dependency and (c) lock-in. These ideas suggest that very minor differences in the start conditions for a process can lead to significant differences in outcomes. If I take an example from one of the change processes I was involved in at The Open University I can illustrate some of these points. The university began a process of change under the banner of the OU VLE (The Open University Virtual Learning Environment) in 2004. A report was published and a change manager appointed in 2005 at the same time that I began my appointment at the university (Sclater 2008a). The OU VLE was a large-scale institutional change that aimed to deploy new tools and technologies (e.g. blogs, wikis and e-portfolio tools) and the integration of a range of existing tools and technologies into a recognisable and unified whole. The start conditions were important because the initial report that sets the projects start conditions envisaged an open, service-oriented architecture based around web services however this was amended after the Phase 1 project setting out the aims was concluded to focus on providing the backbone of the new OU VLE using the open source Moodle LMS. This decision was then ratified when the new Director of the OU VLE project was appointed. The process was path dependent and the decision to adopt Moodle then had a series of knock-on consequences. Path dependency is the condition in which what happens next is related to what happened previously. These may not be start conditions but also include events that take place at various points over an infrastructure's history. I noted in an evaluation report on the process that the Moodle platform was a course-based system and in many ways it was based on the metaphor of the lone academic, or a small course team producing and presenting courses to a cohort of students in a relatively simple and small-scale process. This was of course radically different to the large-scale distance processes embedded in The Open University and it required the OU to revise and customise Moodle and for the university to amend procedures when Moodle couldn't cheaply or efficiently be amended.

> Where Moodle was deficient was in the actual tools within it, as the functionalities of the tools were very basic. It was also very much designed for—in effect—classroom online. It's a single academic teaching to a cohort of students. Everything's based around the course rather than the individual student. So it's teaching to a cohort rather than to an individual, so a lot of the work has gone in developing, for example, a much more sophisticated roles and permissions capability. There really are only three roles administrator, instructor, and student, but we have multiple roles and we want people to play the way we've used conferencing. For example, the First Class system where a tutor might want to group a number of students together, multiple ways of aligning students together, and we have got eight different models that the conference infrastructures within First Class [allow], that course teams part pay for and get set up, so it was really extending that—which allowed it to fit better to our other teaching model. (Open University Senior Manager)

The process also illustrated the lock-in effect of previous systems. The FirstClass computer conferencing system was replaced on courses by Moodle, but FirstClass was also the system that was used for student email for over 200,000 students. It took several years to migrate student email out of FirstClass, which was eventually achieved by adopting a Google mail solution. The OU example illustrates how large-scale institutional processes concerning infrastructure impact on the boundaries within which courses are planned and designed and they also impacted on the possibilities for the interpersonal engagement and connections necessary for networked learning.

There are numerous examples of lock-in in education in the Learning Management Systems, library systems and administrative systems that have been adopted by a university at one point in time that remain in place, not because they are the best available option, but because the costs in effort and resources involved in exiting the system is too much to contemplate. Lock-in can involve the economic costs in terms of vendor lock-in, but it can also involve network effects such as the lock-in involved in the widespread use of the QWERTY keyboard (David 1985). The QWERTY keyboard illustrates most of the issues of lock-in. Although not universal because it is transferred and translated into a variety of national (e.g. AZERTY, QWERTZ) and technological contexts (Computer keyboard), the open standard remains prevalent. The start condition was ensuring that the most used keys did not lock up a manual typewriter, but once set out these start conditions led to infrastructural outcomes involving both technologies and practices that make the replacement of the standard keyboard impractical, despite better keyboards having been designed and marketed. Infrastructures are in these ways historical phenomena that need to be understood using concepts that capture these large-scale processes.

Infrastructures for Learning

Networked learning depends on infrastructures to enable learning and as noted above digital and network infrastructures have a capacity to act. Digital and network infrastructures enable learning analytics, as discussed in the previous chapter, and Williams (2015) makes the point that in education the data collected from networks and digital devices is being used to interpret learner's activity and to provide real-time feedback, which can be used to adapt and adjust the learner's future behaviour. As a consequence digital infrastructure plays an active part in constituting the type of learner that educational processes develop over time. These actions take place in different kinds of infrastructure and Hanseth and Lundberg (2001) distinguish between what they call universal service infrastructure and work-oriented infrastructures. Universal service infrastructures are the kinds of infrastructures that much of the preceding discussion has been concerned with and in principle they are open to, and provide services for all. Working from an ethnographic study of information technology within hospitals Hanseth & Lundberg drew out some general experiences of another more restricted class of infrastructure:

> A careful analysis of the infrastructures used within hospitals will teach us, we believe, lessons which will be useful in the development and deployment of such IT solutions. We also believe that these lessons will be helpful in the development of a larger class of infrastructures. We call this class work oriented infrastructures. This term draws our attention to the fact that such infrastructures are developed to support specific work tasks and practices as opposed to the simple and universal services provided by traditional infrastructures

like those mentioned above (i.e. electric power at a certain voltage, access to telephone networks, water in a pipe, etc.) (Hanseth and Lundberg 2001, p. 348)

Hanseth and Lundberg argued that universal service infrastructures could be designed by engineers whereas work-oriented infrastructures with their more specialised locations should be designed by their users (Hanseth and Lundberg 2001). This distinction is useful and it has relevance for infrastructures in educational contexts.

Education is in one sense a work setting, although it has many special characteristics, and Guryibe and Lindström (2009) have extended the idea of work-oriented infrastructure to identify *infrastructures for learning*:

An infrastructure for learning is a set of resources and arrangements—social, institutional, technical—that are designed to and/or assigned to support a learning practice. (Guribye and Lindström 2009, p. 105)

This usage of the term infrastructures for learning has similar characteristics to the discussion of infrastructures in general, but it has a specific relationship to the practices of education, learning and the development of knowledge. Guribye has argued that infrastructures for learning, unlike either universal service infrastructures or work oriented infrastructures, are commonly designed by a variety of actors and not simply engineers or their users (Guribye 2005). To add to this complexity I have previously argued that infrastructures for learning are becoming increasingly intertwined with universal service architectures (Jones and Dirckinck-Holmfeld 2009). The experience I had of moving student email at The Open University from local provision using FirstClass to a Gmail service provided a strong example of this. At one level this intertwining of universal infrastructures with learning is beyond the scope of the institution and it concerns the use of search engines, social networks and some more closely aligned universal services such as Google Scholar. At another level there are now universal services that have been incorporated in institutional settings such as in the institutional adoption and often branding of services. These developments are blurring the lines between institutional infrastructures in the form of 'walled gardens' and the universal provision of infrastructure that characterises social life in general.

It should be noted that the term infrastructure has been used by other authors in relation to learning but in significantly different ways (Bielaczyc 2001, 2006; Lakkala et al. 2008, 2010). Lakkala et al. make an explicit reference to the notion of infrastructure in the way it has been developed in this chapter, but they locate the level of activity quite differently because they do not consider infrastructure to be a matter of scale.

In a complex learning setting, the elements that build affordances for students' actions, designed by the teacher or based on the conventions of the educational institution, can similarly be said to consist of components that form a pedagogical infrastructure to afford and facilitate certain types of learning activity. Pedagogical infrastructure mediates cultural practices and directs students' activity both explicitly and implicitly... (Lakkala et al 2008, p. 37)

These authors use infrastructure mainly to indicate the way aspects of the setting fade into the background and they offer frameworks for the use of design features to increase the visibility of these factors. Bielaczyc (2001, 2006) concentrates on four dimensions of social infrastructure in the classroom including cultural beliefs, practices, socio-techno-spatial relations and interaction with the outside world. Lakkala et al. (2008) expand on this by introducing further components including a cognitive infrastructure. Infrastructure in both of these accounts is at a local classroom or course level of design. This use of infrastructure in the context of learning does not engage with the idea that infrastructures bridge between the local and global. Nor do these authors consider infrastructure as consisting of large historical systems set at a different levels of scale to local micro interactions. The differences between this microlevel of pedagogic design in the classroom and the concept of infrastructure used in this chapter are explored below in relation to the idea of scale and the terms micro, meso and macro applied to different levels (Jones et al. 2006; Jones and Dirckinck-Holmfeld 2009).

Infrastructure and Levels

I have argued previously that networked learning needs to attend to the different levels of sociomaterial organisation that can be described using the terms micro-meso-macro (Jones et al. 2006; Jones and Dirckinck-Holmfeld 2009). The meso-level is of particular interest in the context of this chapter because it is institutions and infrastructures that are most commonly identified as being at the meso- or macrolevel of organisations and the mesolevel is the one which is most open to routine collective action. Often research in distance learning and educational technology has focused on the learning that takes place in the classroom and at the level of small groups, courses and modules, with limited attention being placed on macro- and mesolevel issues (Zawacki-Richter 2009). A similar limitation can be seen in those fields of research that are most closely related to networked learning such as Computer-Supported Collaborative Learning in which the focus has often been on collaboration in small groups (Stahl 2006). Overall this primary focus on the local and micro is not a universal pattern and there are good examples of approaches which link different levels of analysis. For example in CSCL:

> The understanding of collaborative learning requires both a microanalysis of group interactions and a macro analysis with regard to the socio-cultural context in which learning occurs. (Dillenbourg in Strijbos et al. 2004, p. xvii)

While attention is drawn to the sociocultural in this quotation it should be noted that the sociocultural is viewed as a context within which learning takes place. A sociomaterial approach sees learning as distributed across a variety of entities both human and material and learning from this perspective is not contained in a context of whatever kind. My own view is that learning is not a microlevel activity located in a meso- or macro- context and learning can be thought of as distributed across the various levels.

   In Chap. 3 the discussion of Activity Theory derived from the early Soviet tradition of Vygotsky noted its ability to deal with issues at different levels of granularity.

The tradition of Cultural Historical Activity Theory developed by Engeström and others has been notable for its ability to locate activity systems at various levels in any given social system, including whole institutions. Activity systems are not restricted to the level of single small groups and activity theory has been applied to various levels of analysis (Engeström 1987, 2005, 2007, 2008, 2009). Beyond Activity Theory and its distinct forms of analysis there have been a number of authors who have begun to analyse educational technology using the terms micro-meso-macro. Some use the terms more or less systematically (Dysthe and Engelsen 2011; Hannon 2013), but many remain theoretically underdeveloped and simply associate the mesolevel with institutions and infrastructures and provide little further development of the idea of levels (Selwyn 2010, 2011). There are others who apply meso simply to indicate a middle ground between two ends of an arbitrary scale, for example using micro to indicate student activity, meso for curricular activity and macro for organisational activity (Barbera et al. 2014; Collis 2002). In this section of the chapter I will try to amplify the meaning of these terms and to engage with some of the criticisms that have been applied to the use of levels and scalar thinking in the way I propose.

At its most simple the mesolevel can be thought of as the level of interaction that is intermediate between small scale, local interaction and large-scale (global) processes. The idea of a tripartite division into macro-, meso- and microlevels has been applied in various academic areas for example in the study of complex systems and evolutionary economics (Liljenström and Svedin 2005; Dopfer et al. 2004). Complex systems are characterised by non-linear interrelationships between variables, including thresholds, lags and discontinuities, features that are also appropriate for the investigation of infrastructures in the context of networked learning. Thresholds mark qualitative changes in system characteristics, and an example in terms of an infrastructure in education might be a support for mobile technologies and smart phones. Once the usage of smart phones reaches a certain threshold level amongst students there is an incentive for the provision of an infrastructure to support educational smart phone use. If the infrastructure is deployed to support mobility and smart phone use those students who still have simpler feature phones have an additional incentive to upgrade their phone, solidifying the infrastructural shift. Infrastructures like other complex systems are not planned in a formal top-down manner, even though they are patterned and have regularities which allow them to be open to interventions including design. Perhaps most importantly complex social systems include human agents and as a consequence they are prone to both feedback and feed-forward loops and radical indeterminacy. These aspects of complex systems are relevant to the earlier discussion of networks in Chap. 4 and in particular to the idea of emergence. The mesolevel from this point of view is:

> ...the level in between the micro and the macro, as that is the domain where bottom-up meets top-down. (Liljenström and Svedin 2005, p. 5).

The mesolevel helps to differentiate between the actions of persons and the activity of organisations, institutions and infrastructures and large-scale and at times global processes that extend over significant distances and times. This analytic focus can help in identifying critical details in what otherwise could appear to be a simple or monolithic social system.

Often the temporal and the spatial are interlinked and micro process, such as classroom interactions are both local and short in duration. For networked learning the term micro then identifies contingent, small group interaction with a highly local (not only spatially local) setting occurring over short time periods. Meso identifies those interactions beyond the small group. These may still have a localised focus and a limited duration but the localisation is such that interactions are beyond immediate control, but they are likely to be open to routine control and intervention over moderate time spans. This might be at the level of a school, faculty or department in a university or a functional unit in a large corporation. Macro in this interconnected set of relationships identifies the level of interaction beyond meso that has a general or global character (even if it is represented locally) and the macrolevel is not usually open to routine control within moderate or short time spans. An exception to this would be occasions involving revolutionary change, in evolutionary terms the periods of punctuation—when as Marx put it in the Communist Manifesto 'all that is solid melts into air'. In this nested set of relationships while the micro is highly contingent the macrolevel can usually be treated as a given.

Monteiro et al. (2013) noted a skew in CSCW research towards the local and in my terms the microlevel:

> The field appears to privilege particular forms of cooperative work. We find many examples of what could be described as 'localist studies', restricted to particular settings and time-frames. This focus on the 'here and now' is particularly problematic when one considers the kinds of large-scale, integrated and interconnected workplace information technologies—or what we are calling Information Infrastructures—increasingly found within and across organisations today. (Monteiro et al. 2013, p. 575)

Although they do not use the term mesolevel I think their reflections on CSCW research are relevant to both networked learning and CSCL. The focus of their paper is on the conception of Information Infrastructures which was introduced earlier in this chapter (Hanseth et al 1996; Bowker 1996; Bowker et al. 2010). They argue that when research focuses on a single locale or a specific time period important influences from other levels and other moments in time during the design and evolutionary processes may be lost. To counter this restricted research focus they suggest supplementing the local view with what they describe as an extended design perspective. The idea of extended design is intended to examine how technologies are shaped across multiple contexts and over extended periods of time. The conclusions they draw from their review are as applicable to networked learning and CSCL as they are to CSCW. They suggest that CSCW would benefit from being moved away from restricted and specialised forms of cooperation to a more open agenda with a new research emphasis on infrastructural problems. Early CSCW research drew attention to the gap between formalised representations of organisational processes and the actual diversity of circumstances. They also drew attention to the difficulties of formalising the heterogeneity in organisational practices, which were so serious that in some cases systems had to be built around the unique circumstances of particular organisations (Monteiro et al. 2013). Their proposal is that greater attention needs to be paid to the changes in information systems and in particular to the array of increasingly integrated intra-organisational, and inter-organisational systems. The changes they identified that required attention were:

- New models for provision of computer services—Software as a Service (SaaS) and 'cloud computing'
- Web 2.0-based approaches
- Ubiquitous and ambient computing
- Ideas about 'social computing' that integrate several trends into a vision of hybrid-human computer information systems
- Establishment of platforms for ecosystems/ecologies (e.g. Apple App Store/ iTunes etc.) (Adapted from Monteiro et al 2013)

The list illustrates how many of the issues identified in terms of cooperation at work apply equally to networked and collaborative learning. In particular I want to draw attention to the two issues of scale raised above. Research that takes account of an infrastructural perspective needs to be concerned with multiple contexts and studies across locations and it also needs to be focused on types of analysis that have a longer temporal duration.

My aim is to use levels and the distinctions between macro, meso and micro in an analytic way. The mesolevel understood from this perspective can be related to the place of social practice as the locus in which broader social processes are located in small, local group activity (Schatzki 1996; Schatzki et al. 2001). It is at the meso-level that much of the work is done that links together microlevel interactions with macrolevel processes. In this analytic form meso is an element of the *relational* perspective which is advocated throughout this volume. Levels are seen as descriptive of analytically separable elements in a setting and they are not conceived of as abstract universal properties of things. A particular organisational arrangement or a technological system is not meso in its essential form; it only becomes a mesolevel process or system in relation to other aspects of the setting. Furthermore meso is not a characteristic that adheres to any particular set of arrangements and it only arises in the processes of relating these arrangements upward towards macro processes and downward into micro processes. The elements in these relationships between micro-meso-macro can be separated over both space (in terms of localisation) and time (in terms of duration).

From the previous discussion of infrastructure it should be clear that infrastructure is largely a macro or mesolevel phenomenon. Infrastructures occur at scale however infrastructures are not always macrolevel features and it is possible to think in terms of work-oriented infrastructures (Hanseth and Lundberg 2001) which can be institutionally, professionally or sectorally bounded. It is this level of infrastructure that might be most interesting for networked learning because it is related to the idea of infrastructures for learning (Guribye and Lindström 2009). An infrastructure for learning is most likely to be found at a mesolevel, either within an institution or beyond a single institution and provided by a layer of government or a large corporate provider. The meso nature of infrastructures for learning arises from their activity in bridging between educational and technical requirements which are often set at a national or global level and the day-to-day operations of educational activity, taking place in classrooms, Learning Management Systems and libraries. It is the relational position of infrastructures at points of negotiation that have a potential for design that makes them so important for networked learning.

Institutional Infrastructures

Institutional infrastructures were touched upon in the previous chapter in relation to learning analytics and the use of Enterprise Resource Planning in universities. The focus here is more sharply on infrastructures for learning as defined by Guribye and Lindström (2009). Institutional infrastructures are of course much more than systems intended to support learning and even when the systems have that intention they are often infrastructural assemblages of various systems using the kinds of gateways discussed earlier that allow heterogeneous entities come together in a single interface. For example many universities now want to present their students with dynamic calendars presented on a variety of devices, especially mobile devices. To do this is not entirely a technical task and it involves questions about the way that data is collected about class times. Sometimes lecture classes are well documented but seminar, lab and workshop sessions are not. Often this concerns institutional issues concerning where the data is held and at times this data is held at faculty or school level rather than at the university level. The data that is held may not be reliable or up-to-date and frequently the data held on sessions that are not timetabled centrally relies on informal and irregular procedures reliant on staff goodwill and compliance. In short the apparently technical task of presenting students with a dynamically updated calendar, including all their different class types, is a procedural, process-driven sociotechnical problem that involves organisational structures and practices as much as it does the technology involved in the infrastructure. The technology relies on standards and protocols to bring together the various systems so there are serious technical questions about the integration of data, but they are never divorced from the issues of organisational practice. Institutional infrastructure is a clear example of the importance of sociomaterial factors in even the more mundane aspects of learning.

Infrastructures for learning concern the provision of technologies such as Learning Management Systems (LMS or VLE in the UK), for example Blackboard and Moodle deployed within institutional boundaries. These systems often replaced earlier computer conferencing systems such as FirstClass and they integrated computer-mediated communications with the delivery of course materials and a range of administrative functions. Integrated into learning at an institutional level an LMS/VLE is neither simply a virtual classroom nor does it encompass the totality of resources that both students and educators call on, for example Google Scholar, iTunesU and YouTube. As LMS/VLEs have developed these systems have added a variety of additional administrative and organisational features and the contemporary LMS/VLE can be seen to be at the heart of a complex process of change:

> ...underlying all of these activities is the environment in which e-learning takes place, the VLE or LMS... The pedagogical, political, technical and economic arguments that pervade e-learning are reflected in the choice, deployment and development of a VLE in an organization. (Weller 2007, p. 1)

Weller defines an LMS/ VLE as a software system that combines aspects of the delivery of materials and of communication with the latter being clearly identified as enabling facilitation of learning around content. Weller describes the tensions between these aspects of delivery and communication in the LMS/VLE as being between the broadcast and discussion viewpoints (Weller 2007). In this way the technological features of the LMS/VLE mirror the broader debate between transmission models of learning and participative models. Sfard (1998) for example has discussed these issues in terms of two metaphors for learning and argued that there is a danger in just choosing one. The contrast Sfard makes is between what she calls an 'acquisition' metaphor and a 'participation' metaphor, but like Weller she argues that the metaphors are not mutually exclusive and that real strength lies in combining the two perspectives rather than relying on one.

Weller (2010) has also argued that there is a cyclical trend in the organisational adoption of LMS/VLE with the cycle moving between centralisation and decentralisation in institutional systems. From the early decentralised 'Lone Ranger' and 'Boutique' approaches to innovation (Bates 1995; Taylor 1999) the cycle moved on to greater centralisation and institutional provision of the LMS/VLE. The context for Weller's article was the challenge to these centralised systems by Web 2.0 technologies and services (Sclater 2008b). Web 2.0 environments seemed to offer greater choice and the possibility of personalisation in learning and Web 2.0 provided a contrast to the institutional and centralised approach embedded in the LMS/VLE systems provided by most universities. Sclater noted that Weller had argued that the LMS/VLE as a large application was unsustainable and that the future provision of services by universities was likely to be an assemblage of a range of components built by different companies or projects which interacted with each other over the Internet (or an intranet) via web services in the form of a distributed learning environment (Sclater 2008b).

Weller (2010) usefully summarised the choices that arise between the centralised LMS/VLE and more personalised systems in terms of a cyclical process moving between centralisation and decentralisation. Weller himself is personally identified with the advocacy of decentralised and personalised systems but he concludes that a fully individualised personal learning environment (PLE) may not be either possible or desirable in higher education. The fundamental issue identified by Weller as placing a systemic restriction on the full development of personalisation and decentralisation is the need for institutional control in higher education. Previously Brown and Duguid (2000) had identified what they considered to be the core functions of universities as 'Degree Granting Bodies'. They argued that it is because universities need to maintain this core function (by providing credentials, such as degrees and certificates, and standing behind these awards by warranting the procedures) that centralised control is maintained and essential to the university's mission. The cyclical movement between centralisation and decentralisation described by Weller is related to both technological change and the political and institutional choices made in relation to this core social function of the university.

Weller also noted some of the disadvantages of assembling a learning environment from many sources noting student confusion with multiple systems and log-ins and the concerns of teaching staff that the system was an unstable assembly of components only loosely aggregated together. He concluded that:

> There is clearly a balance to be struck between using pedagogically appropriate tools, giving students experience of a range of tools while also ensuring the proliferation of technologies do not become a barrier to learning. (Weller 2010, p. 5)

One of the quality issues identified by Weller as a justification of more central-ised provision of an LMS/VLE is the need to provide quality assurance and access of a roughly uniform nature for all students. In terms of students with various forms of disability this provision is highly reliant on the university infrastructures as Lewthwaite points out:

> In terms of disability however, for students using specialised and generalised technologies for assistance, disruption to home internet infrastructure meant disruption to many of the 'reasonable adjustments' that constituted an equitable student experience. This was particu-larly true for students with mobility and visual impairments, for whom physical barriers in the university's built environment precluded easy travel and/or transport of personal tech-nologies around a campus over the course of a day (Lewthwaite 2011, p. 253)

In the footnote that accompanies this quote Lewthwaite noted that many of the students she studied used communal computing facilities but that for students using assistive technologies, especially those requiring privacy such as voice recognition, assistive technology was provided in specialised suites that required advance book-ing or face-to-face contact to collect a key. Other students when they were doing serious work relied on a specialised screen in their residence even when they had a portable device. These issues when taken together make disabled students particu-larly reliant on a stable university infrastructure both on campus and in university residences. The issues raised by the institutional need for rough equality of experi-ence between students will be taken up again in the following section in relation to universal service infrastructures.

Universal Service Infrastructures

The idea of a personal learning environment rests on assembling together for insti-tutional purposes services that are available generally to the public outside of the institutional boundaries. The kinds of services that are (at least in principle) avail-able to all have been described as universal service infrastructures by Hanseth and Lundberg (2001). At a fundamental level networked learning is based on the avail-ability of a universal infrastructure provided by the Internet and the Web. When Hiltz and Turoff wrote Network Nation in 1978 their work was prescient because it was written in a world in which computers were not on the desktop and networks were mainly separated from each other not interconnected into an Internet (Hiltz and Turoff 1978). Indeed the revised edition in 1993 only contains five references to the Internet and only two in the main body of the text. Both of these references mention events following the first edition. The infrastructure they refer to in this early book is based on computer conferencing systems, some of which were designed by Turoff himself, and the social forms that were enabled by them, which were envisaged in terms of online community. Hiltz and Turoff (1978), even at this early stage argued that:

> ...to understand computer mediated communications at all, you must see them as a social process. (Hiltz and Turoff 1978, p. 27)

The infrastructure for networked learning originates in the capacity of computers to afford communication and the social processes this capacity to communicate enables. The extension of this network capacity from islands of connectivity, often primarily located in institutions and circumscribed by their boundaries, into the Internet, a universal service infrastructure was a major catalyst in the conception of networked learning (see Chap. 2 and Harasim 2012).

In the early stages of the Internet, text-based resources became accessible but multimedia resources were still largely accessed via standalone devices. At this stage Internet-based systems did not rely on hypertext transfer protocol (http) for their operation and were more likely to use remote log-in (Telnet) and file transfer (FTP) (Harasim et al 1995). A second major infrastructural shift came with the development of the Web and the services that it enabled. A sense of the shift that took place as this new Internet-based service was developed can be gauged from the afterword in Rheingold's book Virtual Community (1993). The original text had been written about bulletin boards such as the WELL (Whole Earth 'Lectronic Link), but the book was published just at the point when access via the Internet began to move to the Web. Looking at the Web through the Mosaic interface on a trip to Japan Rheingold records that:

> I knew I was looking at a new world. I literally jumped, the first time Joi pointed at the picture of a pop group and music came out of the speakers. (Rheingold 2000, p. 401)

The Web changed the possibilities available via the Internet by the inclusion of simple access to multimedia resources. However the Web developed some other ways that can be seen as negative and Manovich (2001) for example drew attention to the preprogrammed nature of the software which prompted the user to select from predefined options which could restrict choices and interactions with media form and content. The infrastructure of the Internet prior to the Web was seen in terms of a communication network and the educational applications focused on communication, collaboration and community. In contrast the Web had been designed as a means to access resources (Berners-Lee and Fischetti 1999). Commenting on its original design Berners Lee reported that it was originally called Enquire, derived from *Enquire within Upon Everything*, a Victorian book his parents had kept at home. It led to his notion for a portal to a world of information:

> The vision I have for the Web is about anything being potentially connected to anything (Berners-Lee and Fischetti 1999, p. 1)

Berners-Lee's concept is clearly a network vision but it is not necessarily a communicative vision. A singular change in the existing infrastructure brought about by the development of the Web altered the kinds of possibilities available for networked learning. Connection in this case is not always communication and the Web emphasised the possibility of providing access to resources rather communication.

The Web has developed since the early 1990s and more recently discussion has focused on Web 2.0 which involves large-scale network effects and the ability to interact in, and contribute to, large groups (Kafai and Peppler 2011; Goodyear et al. 2014 see also Chapter 3). The development of Social Media use in education and the development of MOOCs illustrate this kind of development. The term Web 2.0 is not precise and a large number of definitions of Web 2.0 can be found. However for the purposes of this chapter I will focus on Dohn's (2009) practice perspective on Web 2.0:

- Collaboration and/or distributed authorship
- Active, open-access, 'bottom-up' participation and interactive multi-way communication
- Continuous production, reproduction and transformation of material in use and reuse across contexts
- Openness of content, renunciation of copyright, distributed ownership
- Lack of finality, 'awareness-in-practice' of the 'open-endedness' of the activity
- Taking place on the WWW, or to a large extent utilising Web-mediated resources and activities

Many of the Web 2.0 technologies have blurred the distinction, commonly made since the earliest computer conferencing, between synchronous and asynchronous communications by incorporating both features in a single interface. However Web 2.0 is primarily an asynchronous medium because for a variety of reasons, such as differing time zones, asynchronous communication is the most amenable to scale. Web 2.0 places emphasis on user-generated content and participation, focused on the generation, manipulation and sharing of content. Web 2.0 applications in education have taken a variety of forms (Dohn 2010) and empirical studies have reported on the collaborative use of blogs (Ducate and Lomicka 2008; Farmer et al. 2008), wikis (Minocha and Thomas 2007), Virtual Worlds (Konstantinidis et al 2010) and mobile social media (Lewis et al. 2010).

The interface has become an important site for the aggregation of Web 2.0 services because of the way in which digital and networked infrastructures are represented via the interface (Manovich 2001; Galloway 2012). Manovitch argues that interfaces, which he does not restrict to the computer interface, have become a dominant filter for contemporary culture providing users with distinct 'models of the world'. He argues that the user-interface provides a cultural wrapper which (re-) presents technological features, a codified access point for understanding mediated forms of social practice in which features of the technology can become affordances for the user. The interface in this view becomes the access point to the infrastructure and the place in which machine-readable digital code is transformed into the 'cultural codes' that are accessible to everyday users (Manovich 2001). In education the cultural codes of the new Social Media are not necessarily conducive to education as Friesen and Lowe note:

> These services [Twitter and Facebook], by design, clearly serve interests and priorities other than (and in many cases opposed to) those of learning. If anything, they represent a new way of selling viewers to advertisers, rather than a '2.0' version of social or connective learning or education. (Friesen and Lowe 2012, p. 193)

The cultural codes framing interaction in Social Media are not educational in origin and set priorities that might even threaten the forms of dialogue central to the idea and practice of networked learning.

One of the key claims in educational literature concerning Web 2.0 has been the potential for participation and the development of a participatory culture in Web 2.0 environments (Jenkins 2009). The participatory aspects of Web 2.0 technologies are seen as having a connection to the participation metaphor of Sfard (1998) and the knowledge building approaches of Scardamalia and Bereiter (2006), and knowledge construction of Paavola and Hakkarainen (2005). Lewis et al. (2010) argue that social media in learning may offer the potential to foster collaborations at scale and in tighter time cycles. However these potentials rely on the capacity of commercial social networks to be supportive of educational priorities and aims because as Friesen and Lowe noted the participatory metaphor may sometimes obscure the commercial interests of the service suppliers, who are more interested in users data than in genuine participation. Furthermore Web 2.0 and educational practices may implicitly represent divergent understandings of knowledge and learning because education implicitly embodies the acquisition metaphor of learning whereas Web 2.0 embodies the participation metaphor (Dohn 2009). Participation may also be something of a minority activity as the long tail characteristic of scale-free networks implies that only a small number of active users will participate fully whereas a large number of other users will participate at very low levels (see Chap. 4). Personally I tend to agree with Goodyear et al (2014) who argue that the opposition drawn by Dohn between Web 2.0 and education is excessive and binary and following Sfard they argue that education requires the use of both participation and acquisition metaphors (Sfard 1998). Web 2.0 can be seen as tilting the balance towards participation but in a way that is not in contradiction with educational practice, even though it embodies commercial rather than educational priorities. The architecture of participation is an architecture of scale and Web 2.0 suggests that the value of a service increases with the number of users that share that service. As a consequence design in Web 2.0 may need to take place at the level of the social and technical infrastructures in which participatory cultures and new forms of collaboration take place (Fischer and Giaccardi 2006).

The specific design of sites and digital architectures are recognised as increasingly important in understanding social practice in Web 2.0 environments. Design has become a focus of attention in cultural studies of Social Media (Boyd 2011; Papacharissi 2009, 2011; Zhang and Wang 2010 and Langlois et al. 2009; Langlios 2011). These authors draw attention to the infrastructure of communication and how Social Media are configured by the wider technological infrastructure, software engineers and Web designers and that Social Media are part of a wider network ecology in which their designs embody a politics reflecting the strategic decision making of particular interests (Jones 2013). Boyd (2011) examined the intermeshing of digital network infrastructures and contemporary networked social forms and argued that the emergence of networked publics is related to the architectural features and potential affordances of digitally networked media. Papacharissi (2011) suggests that these digital architectures provide a conceptual lens to explore structural differences in the ways digital technologies relate to practice. She defines the architecture of virtual spaces as the 'composite result of structure, design and organisation' (Papacharissi 2009, p. 205). Langlois argues that:

> ...we should not focus on the content of what users are saying online, but rather on the conditions within which such a thing as user expression is possible in the first place. That is, this article argues that we should focus less on signification, and more on the question of regimes of the production and circulation of meaning. (Langlios 2011, p. 1)

The implication of this approach is that users of Social Media have to learn to work within the constraints and possibilities of the designed media infrastructure (Boyd 2011).

Zhang and Wang (2010) illustrate the ways variations in the features found on various sites interweave with practice. Zhang and Wang (2010) analysed two different Chinese Social Network Sites (SNS) (Douban.com and Xianonei.com) and considered the implications specific design features had for different types of networking activity, in particular forms of collective action. Zhang and Wang argued that collective action was related to the crossing of public and private boundaries and that the two sites provided users with different means for privacy control with important implications for the nature of the networked connections that were forged. Zhang and Wang compared Douban, which took the form of an interest-orientated SNS and encouraged new ties amongst strangers with Xiaonei, which had a relationship-orientated form which supported the formation of strong ties. Zhang and Wang's analysis of the technical design of the sites showed that there was an interactive process between the actual use of the two sites and their structures. Structural features encouraged certain patterns of practice, but active users interpreted and interacted with the site structures in ways that reflected both individual differences and organisational and collective purposes and processes.

The comments about the technical design of SNS may remind readers of the discussion of technological features and affordances (Chap. 2) and the importance of indirect design in networked learning (Chap. 3). The relationship between patterns of interaction and the structural features of a designed infrastructure for learning are areas that are beginning to receive some attention. Williamson (2015) argued that there were two emerging developments in educational governance requiring empirical documentation and analysis. The first of these were the network structures that criss-crossed borders and boundaries between education, politics and digital R&D. Secondly he drew attention to the way this system of dispersed governance was related to the delegated forms of 'socio-algorithmic' and 'zero-touch' procedures that involve massive data collection and machine learning in the anticipation and formation of future subjectivities. Networked learning needs to describe and understand these kinds of infrastructural processes that influence the forms of practice that are available and attainable in designed systems. Edwards and Carmichael (2012) argued that information technologies and semantic technologies in particular embedded a hidden curriculum and that the code became an actor enabling and constraining knowledge, reasoning, representation and students. They argue that the code hides the work it is doing in making some readings possible and privileging some reasoning and representations above others. Appearing to simply represent data such systems are selective and give credibility to the selected versions. Williamson (2015) reinforces the arguments I have made about the politics of technology and the importance of choice while Edwards and Carmichael (2012) draw our attention to the need to understand technologies and code as active agents in education.

One of the critical aspects of universal service infrastructures is the way they may not instantiate the necessary uniform quality required for educational purposes. For example SNS have been shown to be poor in terms of accessibility for disabled users, both for access to the sites themselves and in terms of their navigability and usability (Lewthwaite 2011). More generally there are few research studies considering disabled students' uses of technology in higher education (Seale et al. 2010). If universal service infrastructures and Social Media enabled by these are to be used in education then their suitability for disabled students is a necessary consideration. Disabled students like all students need to make judgements about priorities but because of the difficulties that can be associated with accessing social network sites some disabled students view them as a distraction (Seale et al. 2010). There are also ethical issues about whether it is justifiable to make use of scarce equipment in assistive technology suites for what could be considered leisure. These are social features rather than technical constraints but Lewthwaite makes the point that difficulties also arise from the technical architecture of SNS:

> At the technical level, student experiences of Facebook's inaccessibility to specialised assistive technologies and a design predicated upon inflexible cognitive and embodied norms meant the SNS creates disability by presenting barriers to particular user groups. (Lewthwaite 2011, p. 344)

The key in relation to this chapter is that the use of universal service infrastructures carries risks for educational provision in general and the development of networked learning in particular. Although social networks are becoming essential to student life (See Chap. 8) not all students have the same access to them. The danger of infrastructures developed outside education being used widely within an educational context is that they introduce an unnecessary digital divide. Lewthwaite also points out that social networks redefine some divides:

> …the networks represent a redefinition of dis/ability, where some students with impairments experience non-disabled subjectivities, or may adopt non-disabled interactions. As a result, however, diversity remains suppressed, arguably leading to a situation where an exclusionary divide is maintained and those who are unable or unwilling to access the networked public are further marginalised. In this respect, students disabled by the network are doubly disadvantaged as disability is rendered invisible and the digital and social divide of the network is reinforced. (Lewthwaite 2011, p. 346)

One of the ways the distinction between the kinds of universal service infrastructures represented by Social Media is being blurred is in the institutional adoption of infrastructures. Not in the way discussed above, in which educational practice includes technologies universally available but by an active organisational adoption of institutional variants of what otherwise might be universal. These hybrids of institutional and universal services can make provision for some of the deficiencies identified in universal provision, but they also present a danger because they can act as a Trojan horse introducing external commercial interests and objectives into educational institutions.

Hybrid Infrastructures

The rather crude distinction between institutional infrastructures, bounded by organisational borders and forming a 'walled garden' has been contrasted with universal service infrastructures which are at least potentially accessible by all. This binary division, while analytically robust is blurred in practice. Hybrid infrastructure is used in this book to identify those infrastructural elements that are combinations of institutional and universal elements and the hybridity is between these two potentially conflicting elements. The PLE mentioned in terms of institutional infrastructure relies on universal services, while the use of social media in education is often integrated with institutional provision, for example with Facebook groups mirroring university courses and modules. A major concern of the Joint Information Systems Committee initiative the Distribute National Electronic Resource (DNER), later rebranded as the Information Environment (IE) was developing a single log-in for staff and students. The task was to integrate heterogeneous services at an institutional level so that there could be a relatively seamless integration of services, some of which were external to the institution. Today this kind of experience is commonplace, but it relied on systematic effort taking place at a national (UK) and institutional level over a considerable period of time.

The DNER was informed by both explicit and implicit theories of change in education (Goodyear and Jones 2003). The initial educational aim of the DNER was set out in the call for the development:

> There is a strong requirement to improve the interaction between the people who are involved in the development of new learning environments and the national information systems and services being developed by the JISC. It is therefore proposed that an initiative be funded to integrate learning environments with the wider information landscape aimed at increasing the use of on-line electronic information and research datasets in the learning and teaching process.' (JISC 1999, para 8).

The kind of change that took place with the introduction of the DNER/IE was described by the evaluation team as a kind of punctuated equilibrium with discontinuous change that would be difficult in terms of staff development and organisational planning. This was because the patterns of change varied in different disciplines and with the different technologies, because adoption or enthusiasm for one technology did not automatically transfer to another (Kemp and Jones 2007). The DNER/IE was an example of a large-scale infrastructural development at a national scale involving both institutional and universal service infrastructures.

A second example of these developments of hybrid infrastructures is in the spread of national and international academic networks. Often led by research concerns the backbone infrastructures that universities rely on are now supplied by a mixture of government initiatives and corporate sector developments (Abbate 2010). This was the outcome of a choice between a government sponsored system and a privatised Internet which led to a set of unintended consequences because the Internet itself had to be privatised prior to a process of re-regulation:

> Perhaps the most important historical lesson is that virtually all the visions cherished by participants were abandoned or transformed. Scientists did not get a special-purpose, integrated computing system. Commercialization did not solve the congestion problem that had been a major rationale for privatization. (Abbate 2010, p. 19)

National and international bodies have developed to manage the common research and educational infrastructure. In the UK, universities and colleges rely on the Janet network, an exceptionally early National Research and Education Network (NREN) starting in 1984, which is part of the JISC infrastructure. It is linked to the European research area (EU plus additional countries) NREN which are coordinated in (GÉANT) (GÉANT Expert group 2011). The backbone for GÉANT is provided by DANTE a non-profit corporation and TERENA the Trans-European Research and Education Networking Association provides a supporting network for collaboration and development. These kinds of non-governmental agencies cooperating with non-profit and commercial interests are found elsewhere in the cyberinfrastructure of the United States (Atkins et al. 2003) and various NREN found in developed and developing countries (see for example Mbale et al. 2012). The tradition of NREN is very much based on a public sector provision model, but as noted in relation to the United States and the privatisation of the Internet there is a constant tension between government sponsored development and relinquishing control of the education and research infrastructure to private sector and universal service providers. The question that spans both forms of provision is the separateness of educational provision and the need for specialised regulation in this sector. Because of these requirements research and education networks are likely to remain hybrid, neither universal service infrastructures nor confined to either institutional or national boundaries, but always constrained by the needs of the educational walled garden.

Cloud Computing and Hybrid Infrastructures

Some of the large corporations involved in Web-based services, notable Google, Microsoft and Amazon developed large, high speed distributed networks of computers which they could open up to other organisations. These large-scale distributed networks provide a high degree of resilience and flexibility, being able to respond to fluctuations in demand and enabling modular updating of equipment without any disruption to the services they enabled. Both Google and Microsoft have begun to offer services which can be integrated with institutional provision, sometimes even replacing institutional provision. Google Apps for Education and Microsoft 365 (previously Live@edu) package tools which can be branded and customised but are often hosted on external servers in the 'cloud' (Sclater 2010).

The possibilities of cloud computing also challenge the provision of network access by NREN. Demchenko et al. (2013) argue that there is a need to address performance and manageability issues in combined cloud and service delivery infrastructure. They propose an Open Cloud eXchange (OCX) which is intended to bridge the gap between two aspects of the cloud services infrastructure:

1. *Cloud Service Provider (CSP) infrastructure that typically has a global footprint and is intended to serve the global customer community; and*
2. *cloud services delivery infrastructure which in many cases requires dedicated local infrastructure and quality of services that cannot be delivered by the public Internet infrastructure. (Demchenko et al. 2013, p. 82)*

They go on to argue that there is a need to join or combine CSP infrastructure and local access network infrastructure to solve the 'last mile' problem of delivering cloud services. In this way the development of cloud computing is an example of the ways in which institutional infrastructures are being merged in complex ways with universal service infrastructures.

Cloud computing has various definitions and Vaquero et al. (2009) propose the following:

> Clouds are a large pool of easily usable and accessible virtualized resources (such as hardware, development platforms and/or services). These resources can be dynamically reconfigured to adjust to a variable load (scale), allowing also for an optimum resource utilization. This pool of resources is typically exploited by a pay-per-use model in which guarantees are offered by the Infrastructure Provider by means of customized SLAs. (Vaquero et al. 2009 p. 51)

Another way of thinking about Cloud computing is as a form of utility, a separation of the service from the supplier. The key advantage is that cloud computing is supplied on demand, by the minute or the hour so that the consumer pays for the level of use. This kind of supply means that there are potentially significant cost advantages and a range of options available, from simple data storage to client–server arrangements where the application is also stored and maintained by the cloud supplier (Sclater 2010). Cloud services can allow for spikes in use and they are, at least in principle, infinitely scalable. In higher education there has been a significant take up of Google Apps, Office 365-Education (Live@edu) and Apple apps for education. There are many serious issues for universities that arise as a consequence of the use of cloud computing and these include the admission that Google has data-mined hosted email (as its terms of service now make clear) and educational apps (Hern 2014). Sclater (2010) has argued that the 'Googlisation' of university services could lead to a backlash if Google becomes too closely associated with the university.

There are also concerns about the storage of sensitive staff and student data and to deal with this issue some universities have resorted to blanket bans on the use of cloud services. The concerns about data storage are of particular concern where there are different legal regimes in place where the service is accessed and where the data is stored, for example if storage is located in the United States and the service is accessed within the EU with its own strict data protection laws. Such concerns have of course recently been exacerbated by the Snowden revelations about government surveillance by the NSA in the United States and GCHQ in the United Kingdom. Cloud service providers are of course keen to claim that student data will be held in compliance with local laws, and generally companies have privacy policies which restrict or prohibit data sharing with third parties and data mining of individuals' information, but as the Google data mining case shows, such assurances cannot be taken at face value (Hern 2014). Furthermore large corporate suppliers of cloud services are not immune from service disruptions and a single cloud supplier is potentially a single point of failure, even if the data centres themselves are distributed (Sclater 2010). Importantly there are still accessibility issues for disabled users, demonstrated by tests at the OU (UK) particularly with regard to screen readers, and in addition both Google and Microsoft systems do not function equally well on all Web browsers (Sclater 2010). There are also lingering usability issues that may be addressed in later versions of HTML, such as the ability to drag a document from the desktop to a Web browser window.

Cloud computing when incorporated with university systems in a hybrid infrastructure can offer some significant advantages in terms of cost, dealing with uneven demand, and the potential for scalability. However for institutional reasons the technical availability of cloud computing has to be balanced against the needs of the university in providing services to all potential students regardless of variations in ability and the need to provide secure data storage that respects staff and student requirements for confidentiality. These university requirements are not necessarily at the forefront of the issues that suppliers and designers confront when developing commercial services and universities have a number of significant choices to make if they wish to make use of the commercial benefits of cloud computing.

Conclusions

Digital and network infrastructures pervade educational institutions and learning practices. They reside in the background in the way that other physical infrastructures do, becoming visible when things go wrong, when the normal functioning of the infrastructure breaks down. In these ways the network and digital infrastructures are similar to the many other infrastructures that define modern life. Digital and network infrastructures have a standard physical form because they rely on servers, cables, routers and all the physical elements that provide the backbone on which digital interactions take place. They differ because they are both material and also dependent on code which once activated by appropriate inputs can produce real and tangible effects. Digital and network infrastructures are in this way twice invisible being both hidden in the background and dependent on relatively invisible code. Digital and network infrastructures have an historical dimension because infrastructures are emergent and evolve over time. In particular infrastructures display characteristics that can be described as path dependency and lock-in. That is small differences in the start conditions of an infrastructure can lead to large divergences in terms of outcomes and the features that are highly contingent in their origins can become fixed and very difficult to change once the infrastructure is established. Infrastructures also require standards and processes of standardisation to allow for extension and interconnectivity of infrastructural elements. The demands for standardisation can be implicated in an organisational pressure to centralise and a dialectical tension between centralisation and decentralisation rooted both in technological requirements and separately in New Public Management strategies promoting the idea of 'freedom within boundaries' (Hoggett 1991).

The complex nature of infrastructures and their emergent properties imply the need to examine infrastructures in terms of time and scale. This chapter has argued that the mesolevel, sitting between top-down and bottom-up is the most productive location for future analysis and research and I have argued that research on infrastructure needs to be focused on multiple contexts and research studies that take place across locations and involve analyses that have a longer temporal duration. Discriminating between different levels of scale involves qualitative differences between levels and the adoption of a relational standpoint because levels do not exist alone but only in relation to each other. The chapter has identified areas key for research in CSCW that are also relevant to networked learning from the work of Monteiro et al (2013). These include aspects of cloud computing and the provision of Software as a Service (SaaS), ideas about social computing that integrate hybrid-human computer information systems, and the establishment of platforms for ecosystems/ecologies (e.g. Apple App Store, iTunes etc). Infrastructures generally occur at meso- and macrolevels and they are concerned with more complex systems than artefacts, tools and devices. However in the context of networked learning it is mesolevel systems that are institutionally, professionally or sectorally bounded which are the primary focus. Infrastructures for learning are most likely to be found at a mesolevel, bridging between educational and technical requirements which are often set at a national or global level and day-to-day educational activity. It is the mesolevel relationships of infrastructures for learning that make them so important for networked learning and the design of networked learning settings.

The relationships between infrastructures for learning and institutions are becoming more complex. Universities have incorporated open source and commercially provided systems to manage various key functions and some of these are more or less institutionally bounded, even when they have a more or less global reach. The current dominance of Learning Management Systems such as Blackboard and Moodle are examples of these kinds of institutional infrastructures. Some universal services have also been incorporated into the institutional practices of educational institutions and the use of search engines such as Google and the more specific searches via Google Scholar are examples of this kind of integration. There are also widespread examples of the use of some universal service infrastructures such as Facebook in the provision of core educational services and contexts. The use of such services can be presented as liberating, allowing more flexible learning than provided for by institutional provision and enabling personally constituted services in Personal Learning Environments (PLE). It is in this context that I have proposed the idea of *Hybrid Infrastructures* to encompass the emerging space of managed relationships between institutions and partly sequestered versions of universal services. The idea of hybrid infrastructure builds on the current use of the term hybrid to describe forms of cloud computing reliant on both public and private services. Currently hybrid infrastructures are being used in education to provide student email, additional student services beyond core institutional provision and to provide locally hosted versions of cloud computing in ways that at least attempt to include and incorporate essential institutional requirements such as a rough equivalence in student experience and basic (legally required) levels of data protection.

The following two chapters explore the ways in which academics and students interact using the infrastructures and institutions outlined in the previous chapters. Networked learning is always fundamentally concerned with human–human interaction, even though that interaction is necessarily sociomaterial in character and mediated by the organisations, technologies and infrastructures that define the contemporary network society.

References

Abbate, J. (2010). Privatizing the internet: Competing visions and chaotic events, 1987–1995. *IEEE Annals of the History of Computing, 32*(1), 10–23.

Arthur, W. B. (2009). *The nature of technology: What it is and how it evolves*. London: Allen Lane.

Atkins, D. E., Droegemeier, K. K., Feldman, S. I., Garcia-Molina, H., Klein, M. L., & Messerschmitt, D. G., et al. (2003). *Revolutionizing science and engineering through Cyberinfrastructure: Report of the National Science Foundation Blue-Ribbon Advisory Panel on Cyberinfrastructure*. NSF. Retrieved from http://hdl.handle.net/10150/106224

Barber, M., Donnelly, K., & Ritzvi, S. (2013). *An avalanche is coming: Higher education and the revolution ahead*. London: IPPR. Retrieved from http://www.ippr.org/publication/55/10432/an-avalanche-is-coming-higher-education-and-the-revolution-ahead

Barbera, E., Gros, B., & Kirschner, P. (2014). Paradox of time in research on educational technology. *Time and Society*. Retrieved from Mar 2014, 10.1177/0961463X14522178

Bates, A. W. (1995). *Technology, open learning and distance education*. London: Routledge.

Berners-Lee, T., & Fischetti, M. (1999). *Weaving the web: The original design and ultimate destiny of the world wide Web, by its inventor*. New York: Harper Collins.

Bielaczyc, K. (2001). Designing social infrastructure: The challenge of building computer-supported learning communities. In P. Dillenbourg, A. Eurelings, & K. Hakkarainen (Eds.), *European perspectives on computer-supported collaborative learning* (pp. 106–114). The Proceedings of the First European Conference on Computer-Supported Collaborative Learning, University of Maastricht, Maastricht, The Netherlands.

Bielaczyc, K. (2006). Designing social infrastructure: Critical issues in creating learning environments with technology. *The Journal of the Learning Sciences, 15*(3), 301–329.

Bowker, G. C. (1996). The history of information infrastructures: The case of the international classification of disease. *Information Processing & Management, 32*(1), 39–61.

Bowker, G. C., Baker, K., Millerand, F., & Ribes, D. (2010). Toward information infrastructure studies: Ways of knowing in a networked environment. In J. Hunsinger, L. Klastrup, & M. Allen (Eds.), *International handbook of internet research* (pp. 97–117). Dordrecht, The Netherlands: Springer.

boyd, D. (2011). Social network sites as networked publics: Affordances, dynamics, and implications. In Z. Papacharissi (Ed.), *A networked self: Identity, community, and culture on social network sites* (pp. 39–58). London: Routledge.

Brown, J. S., & Duguid, P. (2000). *The social life of information.* Boston: Harvard Business School.

Collis, B. (2002). Information technology for education and training. In H. H. Adelsberger, B. Collis, & J. M. Pawlowski (Eds.), *Handbook on information technologies for education and training* (pp. 1–20). New York: Springer.

David, P. A. (1985). Clio and the economics of QWERTY. *American Economic Review, 75*(2), 332–337.

Demchenko, Y., van der Ham, J., Ngo, C., De Laat, C., Matselyukh, T., & Escalona, E., et al. (2013). Open cloud exchange (OCX): Architecture and functional components. *IEEE International Conference on Cloud Computing Technology and Science.* Retrieved from http://ieeexplore.ieee.org/Xplore/home.jsp

Dohn, N. (2009). Web 2.0: Inherent tensions and evident challenges for education. *International Journal of Computer-Supported Collaborative Learning, 4*(3), 343–363.

Dohn, N. (2010). Teaching with wikis and blogs: Potentials and pitfalls. In L. Dirckinck-Holmfeld, V. Hodgson, C. Jones, D. McConnell, & T. Ryberg (Eds.), *Proceedings of the 7th International Conference on Networked Learning,* (pp. 142–150), Aalborg, Denmark, 3–4 May 2010. Lancaster, England: Lancaster University.

Dopfer, K., Foster, J., & Potts, J. (2004). Micro meso macro. *Journal of Evolutionary Economics, 14,* 263–279.

Ducate, L., & Lomicka, L. (2008). Adventures in the blogosphere: From blog readers to blog writers. *Computer Assisted Language Learning, 21*(1), 9–28.

Dysthe, O., & Engelsen, K. S. (2011). Portfolio practices in higher education in Norway in an international perspective: Macro-, meso- and micro-level influences. *Assessment & Evaluation in Higher Education, 36*(1), 63–79.

Edwards, P. N. (2010). *A vast machine: Computer models, climate data, and the politics of global warming.* Cambridge, MA: MIT Press.

Edwards, R., & Carmichael, P. (2012). Secret codes: The hidden curriculum of semantic web technologies. *Discourse, 33*(4), 575–590.

Edwards, P. N., Jackson, S. J., Chalmers, M. K., Bowker, G. C., Borgman, C. L., & Ribes, D. et al. (2013). *Knowledge infrastructures: Intellectual frameworks and research challenges.* Ann Arbor, MI: Deep Blue. Retrieved from http://hdl.handle.net/2027.42/97552

Eldridge, N., & Gould, S. (1972). Punctuated equilbria: An alternative to phyletic gradualism in models of paleobiology. In T. J. M. Schopf (Ed.), *Models in paleobiology* (pp. 82–115). San Fransisco: Freeman, Cooper.

Engeström, Y. (1987). *Learning by expanding: An activity theoretical approach to developmental research.* Helsinki, Finland: Orienta-Konsultit Oy. Retrieved from http://lchc.ucsd.edu/mca/Paper/Engestrom/expanding/toc.htm

Engeström, Y. (2005). *Developmental work research: Expanding activity theory in practice.* Berlin, Germany: Lehmanns Media.

Engeström, Y. (2007). From communities of practice to mycorrhizae. In J. Hughes, N. Jewson, & L. Unwin (Eds.), *Communities of practice: Critical perspectives* (pp. 41–54). Abingdon, England: Routledge.

Engeström, Y. (2008). *From teams to knots: Activity-theoretical studies of collaboration and learning at work.* Cambridge, England: Cambridge University Press.

Engeström, Y. (2009). Expansive learning: Toward an activity-theoretical reconceptualization. In K. Illeris (Ed.), *Contemporary theories of learning: Learning theorists… in their own words* (pp. 59–73). London: Routledge.

Farmer, B., Yue, A., & Brooks, C. (2008). Using blogging for higher order learning in large cohort university teaching: A case study. *Australasian Journal of Educational Technology, 24*(2), 123–136.

Fischer, G., & Giaccardi, E. (2006). Meta-design: A framework for the future of end user development. In H. Lieberman, F. Paternò, & V. Wulf (Eds.), *End user development: Empowering people to flexibly employ advanced information and communication technology* (pp. 427–457). Dordrecht, The Netherlands: Kluwer Academic.

Friesen, N., & Lowe, S. (2012). The questionable promise of social media for education: Connective learning and the commercial imperative. *Journal of Computer Assisted Learning, 28*(3), 183–194.

Galloway, A. R. (2012). *The interface effect.* Cambridge, England: Polity Press.

GÉANT Expert Group (2011). *Knowledge without borders: GÉANT 2020 as the European communication commons.* Report of the GÉANT Expert Group October 2011. Brussels. Belgium: European Commission. Retrieved from http://cordis.europa.eu/fp7/ict/e-infrastructure/docs/geg-report.pdf

Goodyear, P., & Jones, C. (2003). Implicit theories of learning and change: Their role in the development of e-learning environments for higher education. In S. Naidu (Ed.), *Learning and teaching with technology: Principles and practices* (pp. 25–37). London: Routledge.

Goodyear, P., Jones, C., & Thompson, K. (2014). Computer-supported collaborative learning: Instructional approaches, group processes and educational designs. In J. M. Spector, M. D. Merrill, J. Elen, & M. J. Bishop (Eds.), *Handbook of research on educational communications and technology* (4th ed., pp. 439–451). New York: Springer.

Gould, S. J. (2007). *Punctuated equilibrium.* Cambridge, MA: Belnap Press of Harvard University Press.

Guribye, F. (2005). *Infrastructures for learning—Ethnographic inquiries into the social and technical conditions of education and training.* Doctoral thesis, University of Bergen, Bergen, Norway.

Guribye, F., & Lindström, B. (2009). Infrastructures for learning and networked tools: The introduction of a new tool in an inter-organisational network. In L. Dirckinck-Holmfeld, C. Jones, & B. Lindström (Eds.), *Analysing networked learning practices in higher education and continuing professional development* (pp. 103–116). Rotterdam, The Netherlands: Sense Publishers, BV.

Hannon, J. (2013). Incommensurate practices: Sociomaterial entanglements of learning technology implementation. *Journal of Computer Assisted Learning, 29*(2), 168–178.

Hanseth, O., & Lundberg, N. (2001). Designing work oriented infrastructures. *Computer Supported Cooperative Work, 10,* 347–372.

Hanseth, O., Monteiro, E., & Hatling, M. (1996). Developing information infrastructure: The tension between standardization and flexibility. *Science, Technology and Human Values, 21*(4), 407–426.

Harasim, L. (2012). *Learning theory and online technologies.* New York: Routledge.

Harasim, L., Hiltz, S. R., Teles, L., & Turoff, M. (1995). *Learning networks: A field guide to teaching and learning online.* Cambridge, MA: MIT Press.

Hern, A. (2014). *Google faces lawsuit over email scanning and student data.* The Guardian 19 March 2014. Retrieved from http://www.theguardian.com/technology/2014/mar/19/google-lawsuit-email-scanning-student-data-apps-education

Hiltz, S. R., & Turoff, M. (1978). *The network nation: Human communication via computer* (1st ed.). Reading, MA: Addison-Wesley [Revised Edition. Cambridge, MA: MIT Press, 1993.].

Hoggett, P. (1991). A new management in the public sector? *Policy & Politics, 19*(4), 243–256.

Jackson, S. J., Edwards, P. N., Bowker, G. C., & Knobel, C. P. (2007). Understanding infrastructure: History, heuristics, and cyberinfrastructure policy. *First Monday, 12*(6). Retrieved from http://firstmonday.org/issues/issue12_6/jackson/index.html

Jenkins, H. (2009). *Confronting the challenges of participatory culture: Media education for the 21st century.* Cambridge, MA: MIT Press.

JISC (1999). *Developing the DNER for learning and teaching,* JISC Circular 5/99. Retrieved from http://www.jisc.ac.uk/fundingopportunities/funding_calls/2000/01/circular_5_99.aspx

Jones, C. (1998). Evaluating a collaborative online learning environment. *Active Learning, 9*, 31–35.
Jones, C. (2013). Designing for practice: A view from the social sciences. In H. Beetham & R. Sharpe (Eds.), *Rethinking pedagogy for a digital age: Designing for 21st century learning* (2nd ed., pp. 204–217). London: Routledge.
Jones, C., & Cawood, J. (1998). The unreliable transcript: Contingent technology and informal practice in asynchronous learning networks. In *Networked lifelong learning; innovative approaches to education and training through the Internet. Proceedings of the 1998 International Conference*, (pp. 1.9–1.14). Sheffield, England: University of Sheffield. Retrieved from http://www.networkedlearningconference.org.uk/past/nlc1998/Proceedings/Jones-1.9-1.14.pdf
Jones, C., & Dirckinck-Holmfeld, L. (2009). Analysing networked learning practices: An introduction. In L. Dirckinck-Holmfeld, C. Jones, & B. Lindström (Eds.), *Analysing networked learning practices in higher education and continuing professional development* (pp. 1–27). Rotterdam, The Netherlands: Sense Publishers, BV.
Jones, C., Dirckinck-Holmfeld, L., & Lindström, B. (2006). A relational, indirect, meso-level approach to CSCL design in the next decade. *International Journal of Computer Supported Collaborative Learning, 1*(1), 35–56.
Kafai, Y. B., & Peppler, K. A. (2011). Beyond small groups: New opportunities for research in computer-supported collective learning. In H. Spada, G. Stahl, N. Miyake, & N. Law (Eds.), *Connecting computer-supported collaborative learning to policy and practice: CSCL2011 Conference Proceedings: Vol. I—Long papers.* (pp. 17–24). Hong Kong, China: The University of Hong Kong.
Kemp, B., & Jones, C. (2007). Academic use of digital resources: Disciplinary differences and the issue of progression revisited. *Educational Technology & Society, 10*(1), 52–60.
Kitchen, R., & Dodge, M. (2011). *Code/space: Software and everyday life.* Cambridge, MA: MIT Press.
Konstantinidis, A., Tsiatsos, T., Terzidou, T., & Pomportsis, A. S. (2010). Fostering collaborative learning in second life: Metaphors and affordances. *Computers & Education, 55*(2), 603–615.
Krücken, G. (2003). Learning the 'New, New Thing': On the role of path dependency in university structures. *Higher Education, 46*, 315–339.
Lakkala, M., Ilomäki, L., & Kosonen, K. (2010). From instructional design to setting up pedagogical infrastructures: Designing technology-enhanced knowledge creation. In B. Ertl (Ed.), *Technologies and practices for constructing knowledge in online environments: Advancements in learning* (pp. 169–185). New York: Information Science Reference.
Lakkala, M., Paavola, S., & Hakkarainen, K. (2008). Designing pedagogical infrastructures in university courses for technology-enhanced collaborative inquiry. *Research and Practice in Technology Enhanced Learning, 3*(1), 33–64.
Langlios, G. (2011). Meanings, semiotechnologies and participatory media. *Culture Machine, 12.* Retrieved from www.culturemachine.net
Langlois, G., Elmer, G., McKelvey, F., & Deveroux, Z. (2009). Networked publics, the double articulation of code and politics on facebook. *Canadian Journal of Communication, 34*, 415–434.
Latour, B. (2005). *Reassembling the social. An introduction to actor-network theory.* London: Routledge.
Lewis, S., Pea, R., & Rosen, J. (2010). Beyond participation to co-creation of meaning: Mobile social media in generative learning communities. *Social Science Information, 49*(3), 351–369.
Lewthwaite, S. (2011). *Disability 2.0: Student dis/connections: A study of student experiences of disability and social networks on campus in higher education.* Ph.D. Thesis, University of Nottingham, Nottingham, England. Retrieved from http://etheses.nottingham.ac.uk/2406/
Liljenström, H., & Svedin, U. (Eds.). (2005). *Micro, meso, macro: Addressing complex systems.* London: World Scientific.
Manovich, L. (2001). *The language of new media.* Cambridge, MA: MIT Press.
Mbale, J., Kadzamina Z. D., Martin, D., & Kyalo, V. (2012). Ubuntunet alliance: A Collaborative Research Platform for sharing of technological tools for eradication of brain drain. *International*

Journal of Emerging Technologies in Learning, iJET, 7(4), 65–74. Retrieved from http://online-journals.org/i-jet/article/view/2285

Minocha, S., & Thomas, P. G. (2007). Collaborative learning in a wiki environment: Experiences from a software engineering course. *New Review of Hypermedia and Multimedia, 13*(2), 187–209.

Monteiro, E., Pollock, N., Hanseth, O., & Williams, R. (2013). From artefacts to infrastructures. *Computer Supported Cooperative Work (CSCW), 22*(4–6), 575–607.

Paavola, S., & Hakkarainen, K. (2005). The knowledge creation metaphor: An emergent epistemological approach to learning. *Science and Education, 14*(6), 535–557.

Papacharissi, Z. (2009). The virtual geographies of social networks: A comparative analysis of facebook, LinkedIn and a small world. *New Media & Society, 11*, 199–220.

Papacharissi, Z. (2011). Conclusion: A networked self. In Z. Papacharissi (Ed.), *A networked self: Identity, community, and culture on social network sites* (pp. 304–318). London: Routledge.

Rheingold, H. (1993). *The virtual community: Homesteading on the electronic frontier*. Reading, MA: Addison-Wesley.

Rheingold, H. (2000). *The virtual community: Homesteading on the electronic frontier* (2nd ed.). Cambridge, MA: MIT Press.

Scardamalia, M., & Bereiter, C. (2006). Knowledge building: Theory, pedagogy and technology. In K. Sawyer (Ed.), *Cambridge handbook of the learning sciences* (pp. 97–115). Cambridge, England: Cambridge University Press.

Schatzki, T. R. (1996). *Social practices: A Wittgensteinian approach to human activity and the social*. Cambridge, England: Cambridge University Press.

Schatzki, T., Knorr-Cetina, K., & von Savigny, E. (Eds.). (2001). *The practice turn in contemporary theory*. London: Routledge.

Sclater, N. (2008a) *Large-scale open source E-learning systems at the Open University (UK)*. (Research Bulletin Issue 12). Boulder, CO: EDUCAUSE Center for Applied Research. Retrieved from http://www.educause.edu/ecar

Sclater, N. (2008b). *Web 2.0, personal learning environments and the future of learning management systems*. Educause (Research Bulletin Issue 13). Boulder, CO: EDUCAUSE Center for Applied Research, 2009. Retrieved from http://www.educause.edu/ecar

Sclater, N. (2010). e-learning in the cloud. *International Journal of Virtual and Personal Learning Environments, 1*(1), 10–19.

Seale, J., Draffan, E. A., & Wald, M. (2010). Digital agility and digital decision-making: Conceptualising digital inclusion in the context of disabled learners in higher education. *Studies in Higher Education, 35*(4), 445–461.

Selwyn, N. (2010). *Education and technology: Key issues and debates*. London: Continuum.

Selwyn, N. (2011). *Schools and schooling in the digital age: A critical analysis*. London: Routledge.

Sfard, A. (1998). On two metaphors for learning and the dangers of choosing just one. *Educational Researcher, 27*(2), 4–13.

Stahl, G. (2006). *Group cognition: Computer support for building collaborative knowledge*. Cambridge, MA: MIT Press.

Star, S. L., & Ruhleder, K. (1996). Steps toward an ecology of infrastructure: Design and access for large information spaces information systems research. *Information Systems Research, 7*(1), 111–134.

Strijbos, J.-W., Kirschner, P., & Martens, R. (Eds.). (2004). *What we know about CSCL: and implementing it in higher education*. Boston: Kluwer.

Tapscott, D., & Williams, A. (2010). Innovating the 21st century university: It's time. *Educause Review, 45*(1), 17–29.

Taylor, P. G. (1999). *Making sense of academic life: Academics, universities and change*. Buckingham, England: SRHE/Open University Press.

Vaquero, L., Rodero-Merino, L., Caceres, J., & Lindner, M. (2009). A break in the clouds: Towards a cloud definition. *Computer Communication Review, 39*(1), 50–55.

Weller, M. (2007). *Virtual learning environments: Using, choosing and developing your VLE*. Abingdon, England: Routledge.

Weller, M. (2010). The centralisation dilemma in educational IT. *International Journal of Virtual and Personal Learning Environments, 1*(1), 1–9.

Williamson, B. (2015). Governing software: Networks, databases and algorithmic power in the digital governance of public education. *Learning Media and Technology, 40*(1), 83–105. doi:10.1080/17439884.2014.924527.

Zawacki-Richter, O. (2009). Research areas in distance education: A Delphi study. *The International Review of Research in Open and Distance Learning, 10*, 3. Retrieved from http://www.irrodl.org/index.php/irrodl/article/view/674

Zhang, W., & Wang, R. (2010). Interest-oriented versus relationship-oriented SNSs in China. *First Monday. 15*, 8. Retrieved from http://firstmonday.org

Chapter 7
Academics and Digital Networks

The previous chapters in this section have dealt with the sociomaterial contexts within which people interact and co-constitute their contexts. In this chapter and the next the focus shifts towards the people, the human elements in these sociomaterial assemblages. This shift is of course only one of emphasis, human actors remain component parts of sociomaterial assemblages and the individual human is just as importantly always a social actor. We are dealing with persons in positions, and roles in sociotechnical systems, not simply individual actors. Furthermore learning includes the biological and material person and when we are dealing with knowledge and learning something, as Ellis and Goodyear note, happens 'between the ears' (Ellis and Goodyear 2010, p. 6). The brain between the ears is embodied and the whole person is imbricated with the external material world of objects, artefacts and technologies and with other people via discourses, emotions, organisations and cultures. This chapter examines the position of the academic in networked learning. It begins from the premise that the academic role is broader than either a single or a combined focus on teaching or research would imply. Secondly this chapter is interested in the interactions between academics and academic work, and the emergent practices that are co-configured by academic actors and those material and technological features enabled by digital and network technologies. In order to do this the chapter begins by examining the pressures on academic work and it explores a number of different approaches that have developed to explain the changing role of the academic.

There has been considerable research conducted examining the changing academic profession (Altbach 2000; Altbach, Reisberg, and Pacheco 2013b; Altbach, Reisberg, Yudkevich, Androushchak, and Kuzminov 2013a; Enders 2012; Locke and Teichler 2007). This body of research has focused on a number of significant drivers of change:

> ...the academic profession now faces enormous challenges, including 'massification' unprecedented growth), increased student diversity, privatization, pressures for accountability, global competition for talent, and the economic downturn. (Altbach, Reisberg, and Pacheco 2013b, p. 89)

© Springer International Publishing Switzerland 2015
C. Jones, *Networked Learning*, Research in Networked Learning,
DOI 10.1007/978-3-319-01934-5_7

A summary including these same factors can be found in many other policy documents and research-based publications over a number of years. Perhaps the one new factor to be added to these factors is the economic downturn following the 2008 financial crisis. There has also been work focused on the changes in the academic workforce (Musselin 2011; Rhoades 2005; Mills and Rath 2012). From a somewhat different perspective similar issues have been approached from a policy standpoint because the academic workforce is acknowledged to be in transition for the purposes of planning for the future workforce in higher education (Bexley et al. 2011; Blass et al. 2010; Locke and Bennion 2010). A particular concern in this regard has been the preparation and development of early career academics and the problems that can arise for the development of an academic identity as a consequence of the growth of precarious part-time employment and the decline of tenure track and equivalent career paths into the academic profession (Sutherland and Taylor 2011). The formation of identity in early career academics emphasises the social and situated nature of their role:

> Across disciplines, institutions, and national boundaries, the formation of an academic identity, and the sense of agency that motivates academics to live and develop that identity were mediated by the departmental and institutional cultures in which they pursued their work. (Sutherland and Taylor 2011, p. 185)

In these ways change in the academic profession is closely related to the changes taking place in the university and the institutions and infrastructures involved in networked learning. Notably absent from this synopsis is the rapid technological change that has happened over the past 40 years, affecting both academic work practices and the world which the academic world interacts with (for an exception see Rhoades 2011).

The academic profession includes teaching and the mentoring and supervision of post-graduate students and post-doctoral early career academics. Depending on the higher educational system some aspects of this work are treated as teaching, others (e.g. doctoral supervision) are treated as research, whilst further aspects (such as the mentoring of early career academics) can be treated as an aspect of management or administration. Perhaps the most discussed division in academic life is that between teaching and research (Boyer 1990). Within the academic profession it is regularly argued that research is the most important indicator of status and position and that teaching has a subsidiary place (e.g. Boyer 1990; Locke and Bennion 2009). The proportion of academic work dedicated to research varies between different national systems of higher education and between the diverse kinds of institution within various national systems. In some higher education systems there are an increasing number of 'teaching only' or primarily teaching institutions (Locke and Bennion 2009). In addition to teaching and research, and to varying degrees, most higher education systems recognise a varied collection of activities as forming a third aspect of an academic career.

> Almost all colleges pay lip service to the trilogy, teaching research and service, but when it comes to making judgments about professional performance, the three rarely are assigned equal merit. (Boyer 1990, p. 15)

'Service' can include the functions of the invisible college, such as reviewing for conferences and journals, external examining, and acting as external referees on appointment panels (Wagner 2008). Some aspects of a traditional service role would be playing an active role in collegial management, for example acting as a head of department and sitting on various university committees, although increasingly such positions are filled by management appointment rather than collegial election (Altbach 2000). Service also included leadership in research and teaching, for example by work in the organisation of inter-institutional professional societies, academic conferences, symposia and workshops. Many higher education institutions also included civic or community missions and academic work has been expected to include (often voluntary) work in wider society at local, regional and national levels.

Most recently there has been an increased requirement to be relevant and have impact, often tied to notions of entrepreneurialism (Slaughter and Leslie 1997; Clark 1998; Bok 2004). The three more traditional aspects of academic work, research, teaching and service have been expanded to include what is often confusingly termed a 'third mission' (Molas-Gallart et al. 2002). It is confusing because the third mission is not synonymous with service, but it includes some areas of activity that are close to or overlap with traditional service work, for example community engagement. The third mission differs from service in so far as it is explicitly and centrally concerned with entrepreneurship and business related activity (Laredo 2007; Zawdie 2010). The third mission began with a strong focus on the relationship with research activities in universities, largely in the natural sciences. A further issue related to the contemporary emphasis on an entrepreneurial third mission is the connection to open access, especially open access to data originating in universities (Vendetti et al. 2013). For certain parts of the commercial world universities hold extensive resources that open access can make freely available to business.

This brief summary shows that work in the academic profession contains a variety of roles and these roles are unevenly distributed between individual post holders, disciplines and institutions. There is no singe or universal academic role, although there are regular and recognizable patterns within a diverse profession, nor is there a standard template for academic life. The academic profession is subject to many pressures from a variety of directions and it is currently undergoing a process of change that has no clearly defined endpoint. The future for the academic profession is another site of struggle in which digital and networked technologies play various parts but they do not determine any particular outcome.

Disciplines, Scholarship and Digital Technology

The academic workforce do not necessarily view themselves as part of academia, although some do identify themselves with a common academic status or with the university as an institution. The work activity most academics are organised around and identify with usually takes place in faculties, schools and departments or their sub-units (Trowler and Knight 2000). However beyond the day-to-day activities of work many academics identify with their discipline or subject area (Becher and Trowler 2001). Research concerning disciplinary differences takes place at the mesolevel:

> Intermediate between these two categories—enquiries that concentrate on global issues and those which direct themselves to individual concerns—lies a further group of studies located at what may be termed the meso level. These embody a distinctive set of social and cognitive considerations relating to academic communities clustered around common intellectual interests. (Becher and Trowler 2001, p. 21)

Becher and Trowler argue that it is necessary to distinguish between disciplinary and in some cases sub-disciplinary groups because the diversity between groups makes them different in terms of both theoretical understanding and practical policy. They point to divergences in undergraduate teaching and learning, post-graduate education and training, the relationships between teaching and research, academic standards, perceptions of quality issues and approaches to departmental management and administration (Becher and Trowler 2001). Becher and Trowler continue by pointing out that one consequence of setting out undifferentiated policy requirements can be their tacit or overt rejection by those subject to them. These disciplinary differences also play out in terms of digital and network technologies. The natural sciences have often concentrated on digital infrastructure to enable big science, whereas the growing interest in digital humanities shows a different set of concerns. These disciplinary differences will be explored in following sections both in terms of teaching and learning and in relation to research.

A line of discussion, begun by Boyer (1990) places an inclusive notion of scholarship as being central to the academic profession and this way of thinking has led on to the development of ideas about how scholarship might be changing in relation to digital and network technologies (Borgman 2007; Weller 2011). Apart from the discussion about digital scholarship little of the general research which focuses on the academic profession has identified digital and network technologies as significant factors in the major changes taking place in the profession (Altbach 2000; Altbach, Reisberg, and Pacheco 2013b; Altbach, Reisberg, Yudkevich, Androushchak, and Kuzminov 2013a; Enders 2006, 2012; Locke and Teichler 2007). Research which examined the changing academic workforce (e.g. Bexley et al. 2011; PA Consulting Group 2010) acknowledged the influence of technology but paid little attention to the ways in which digital and networked technology affected academic practices and the academic profession. However the changes in the academic profession have taken place at the same time as significant changes in technology which are known to be associated with rapid transformations in aspects of academic work (Beetham and Sharpe 2013; Borgman 2007; Wagner 2008; Weller 2011).

As noted in Chap. 2 Säljö (2010) argues that digital technologies may be changing the nature of what it means to know something. Säljö argues that it is the capacity of digital technologies to store, access and manipulate information that can transform how knowledge is understood and that digital technologies should be considered in relation to social memory. His definition of social memory as: 'the pool of insights and experiences that people are expected to know about and to make use of' (Säljö 2010, p. 56) leads onto three issues relevant to academic practice:

1. The role of the technology as a tool for storing information and building up a social memory;
2. The consequences of the recent developments in our abilities to have access to social memory; and
3. The increasing capacity of technologies to perform analytical, cognitive-like operations that were previously made by people. (Säljö 2010, p. 56)

These consequences are not at the periphery of academic practice, they are central to the core activities of academic work. The sections that follow examine the ways in which digital technologies open up new possibilities and the ways that digital scholarship, however defined, remains an area of struggle and choice. Academic engagement with the kinds of open practices that digital technologies are said to enable are subject to choices made at various levels including the university, the state and the market. Currently it is not clear what kinds of practice are emerging from this complex of interacting influences on new academics but the outlines of what is currently known are set out below in sections dealing with pedagogy and teaching, e-research and digital disciplinarity, digital scholarship and the claim that we are witnessing the emergence of a new invisible college.

Also in Chap. 2 I noted how the expansion of higher education (HE) and the emergence of 'knowledge societies' have seen the perceived economic importance of HE grow because the university is seen as a site for the creation, dissemination and accreditation of knowledge. At the same time the academic profession has often experienced a reduction in social status, an increase in workload and a loss of autonomy (Enders 2006). The place of autonomy, academic freedom and the growing role of accountability and managerialism in HE are issues that have a degree of independence from the changes taking place in relation to new technology but at times they are also intertwined with these changes through issues such as the growth of Enterprise Resource Management (ERP) systems (see Chap. 5) and the audit and accountability culture in contemporary universities which are enabled and enhanced by the development of forms of data analytics applied to university systems (McCluskey and Winter 2012). In this way core academic values are brought into tension with large-scale social processes which involve, to varying degrees, the deployment of digital and network technologies. Take the current example of learning analytics, a broad movement which is currently stabilising as an academic field with a conference series and a journal dedicated to the emergent domain. Learning analytics as I argued in Chap. 5 involves different social actors and the particular versions of learning analytics that are developed and deployed will reflect the choices of the dominant social actors or alliances between a number of key actors. These actors can choose what will be measured and what will be rendered invisible or insignificant in the new analytic systems. Once deployed analytic systems will empower some and displace decisions from others. What are now academic decisions about student progress may become administrative decisions informed by analytics dashboards. A question this raises is—'How free is the academic to pursue their academic judgment when an administrator can judge the academic for the judgments they make using metrics and an analytics framework?' Annual academic appraisals and review processes can be transferred from personal and qualitative evaluations to impersonal numeric and outcome-based measurements.

Simultaneously new emergent professions are developing that are not fully academic but retain certain academic features. These new para-academics are sometimes employed in technical positions e.g. learning technologists, but they also include academic developers and enhanced forms of librarians dealing with digital and network technologies (Sutherland and Taylor 2011; Hudson 2009, Conole et al. 2007). In the UK the Dearing Report (Dearing 1997) a study of administrative and support staff (Report 4) identified a group of jobs with some common characteristics. The characteristics included being held typically by younger staff (under 35) with five or less years of experience with qualifications often unrelated to the posts they held and with roles that were generally ill-defined (See Oliver 2002). Oliver suggests that learning technologists are just one group of 'new professionals' emerging at the turn of the century in academic work. Para-academics are not assumed to have the same position with regard to academic freedom or autonomy as traditional academics and they are often hired on administrative rather than academic contracts of employment. The idea of a profession and even more so 'new' professions is a contested area and professionalisation of a group or of a job role can be seen as a dynamic social process in which the claim to be a professional can be a political act by those working in the job role or by others seeking to manage or control that group (for a fuller discussion of the contested nature of professions in this context see Hudson 2009). An early study of the career paths of learning technologists found that the group was engaged in ten central activities of which the most important was to keep up to date with developments in learning technology (Beetham 2000). Perhaps surprisingly the other nine were related to educational development and communication but they were not technical in character (Oliver 2002). At that time it was not clear if the development of the new professions was an international phenomenon or restricted to the United Kingdom. In the years that followed the growth of organisations supporting and representing the new professions has made it clear that this is a global development and the current nature and development of the new professions will be developed more fully later in this chapter. At this point is important to note that the new professions have a distinct relationship to disciplines and often form part of an institutional core of central services and they also have a distinct relationship to knowledge because they resemble technical workforces which make use of scientific knowledge but are less concerned with its generation (Barley and Orr 1997).

Digital Scholarship

Digital scholarship has a number of different definitions and I agree with Weller who argues that a simple definition of digital scholarship should probably be resisted (Weller 2011). Instead Weller notes that due to the ubiquitous availability of new technologies all scholars are digital now and the digital had affected his personal academic practice in three ways which were:

- The quantity of digital content
- The role of the social network,
- The types of information sources

These three issues affect academic practice generally and they suggest that while the practices of digital scholarship are currently a minority concern, the issues affect scholarship more broadly. Digital scholarship in all its various forms points towards the historic term 'scholarship' which locates the practices of scholarship largely, if not exclusively, in the university or other academic institutions (Boyer 1990). Scholarship connects to the employment relations of the academic workforce and scholarly behaviour, including public engagement, is enforced by institutional policies with regard to permanent employment and tenure, promotion and recognition (Ellison and Eatman 2008). Scholarship is also defined by a set of values and moral claims that set out how proper academic work should be carried out and that separate academic knowledge from other kinds of knowledge claims. Academic knowledge is based on specific work practices, such as peer review, which separate academic output from policy documentation (which may be written by the same people). Goodfellow (2013) summarises the relationship of scholarship to academic work in this way:

> This orientation [scholarship] values critical reflection, the cumulative aggregation of knowledge and understanding, distinct modes of operation relating to evidence and the warranting of its reliability, and the ethic of enquiry as a primary motivation (Andresen 2000; Cowan et al. 2008; Courant 2008). The combination of these characteristics is what distinguishes the construction of academic scholarly knowledge from other kinds of knowledge production (factual knowledge, practical knowledge, common-sense, morality, the 'wisdom of crowds', etc.). The existence of communities dedicated to these values in a general sense also distinguishes the sites of production of academic scholarly knowledge (universities, research institutes, museums) from most other arenas of social knowledge practice. (Goodfellow 2013, p. 69)

Scholarship as an ethical stance and a set of work practices is deeply embedded in the academic culture and organisational practices of academic institutions and in some ways it is emblematic of the values that underpin their core functions, such as the warranting and credentialing of knowledge and of the students who gain qualifications from them (Brown and Duguid 2000).

Digital scholarship derives from this definition of scholarship and it focuses attention on the introduction of the full range of digital technologies (Weller 2011; Pearce et al. 2010; Borgman 2007). The technologies are quite diverse and are at different levels of scale. As a result there are discussions about the personal use of blogs (Ferguson et al. 2010) or micro-blogging alongside considerations about institutional infrastructures and the global impact of the Web and Internet (Borgman 2003). Digital scholarship can as a consequence be an individually focused concern with the digital scholar and their personal practices, and/or a concern with digital scholarship considered as a broad social change affecting wider institutional and societal arrangements and the place of the scholar within them (Weller 2011).

Borgman (2009) uses digital scholarship as a broad term covering a range of disciplines, reserving digital humanities for the practices of digital scholarship in that particular disciplinary domain. Borgman's (2007) focus is at scale and even when concerned with the practices of individual digital scholars she is concerned with their activity in the context of institutions and infrastructures. It is in this broad sense of digital scholarship that the term is used here, rather than alternative uses which may refer more narrowly to either the practices of individuals or the curation and collection of digital resources.

Borgman's (2007) focus on infrastructural questions includes the design, development and use of digital repositories and archives and various digital media enabled by the Internet as a means for scholarly communication and the sharing of data. Borgman's work focuses on digital scholarship in the context of large distributed teams and large-scale infrastructure rather than individual or 'lone ranger' adoption of specific digital tools.

'The internet lies at the core of an advanced scholarly information infrastructure to facilitate distributed, data and information-intensive collaborative research.' (Borgman 2007, p. xvii)

This emphasis places the academic in an infrastructural and institutional system which accords with ideas such as networked individualism, and which also relies on large-scale infrastructure to enable personalisation and the flow of information across a network.

When viewed in terms of broad social change the idea of the digital scholar can be associated with the kinds of determinist arguments usually associated with the idea of digital native students or the net generation, for example:

New digital and web-based technologies are spurring rapid and radical changes across all media industries. These newer models take advantage of the infinite reproducibility of digital media at zero marginal cost. There is an argument to be made that the sort of changes we have seen in other industries will be forced upon higher education, either as the result of external economic factors (the need to be more efficient, responsive, etc.) or by a need to stay relevant to the so called 'net generation' of students… (Pearce et al. 2010, p. 33)

Others are more circumspect about committing themselves to the full implications of the argument (for example Weller 2011), but they are often still entranced by the possibility that there is a significant change in academic practice brought about by digital and network technologies:

In conclusion, then, there is some moderate evidence that there are some differences in the expectations of net generation learners and possibly an increase in dissatisfaction with education. (Weller 2011, p. 17)

Weller goes on to argue that it is less important whether there is a generational change if it can be shown that all of society is changing. The evidence he deploys to support this case is evidence of widespread use of the Internet, and various services such as Google and Facebook. While Weller admits that the evidence for a 'revolution in higher education' may not be as strong as he first thought he does argue that engagement with new technologies is a core practice and that while there is no 'absolute necessity' for using technology, there are 'unprecedented opportunities' and academic professionals shouldn't wait to seize these 'until the case has been proven' (Weller 2011, p. 28). Weller's argument is a classic form of soft technological determinism in that it argues scholars are not forced to change by the technology, but that in order to do things well they ought to do them using the new technologies. I have argued elsewhere (Jones 2011, 2012) that the net generation and digital native arguments do not stand up to empirical scrutiny and that the determinist logic that sits behind them is fundamentally flawed. This same argument applies to the soft determinism and the broad generalisations about technology that Weller uses to support his argument. Simply because technologies change and these technologies are in widespread use does not translate into specified or necessary changes in practice. Indeed I would argue that the idea that we don't have to wait for the case to be proven is an argument which is in itself antithetical to scholarly practices.

Goodfellow (2013) compared the approaches to digital scholarship taken by Borgman and Weller using a discourse analytic approach. He argues that both Borgman and Weller are engaged in a rhetorical project that aims to persuade as well as inform and that despite their shared object of study, and an apparent agreement on many of the facts, they construct the central 'issues' of digital scholarship differently (Goodfellow 2013). In particular he concludes that Borgman is trying to make scholarship more scholarly whilst Weller is trying to make it more digital. The idea of digital scholarship as Weller construes it is closely related to the development of 'openness' and Goodfellow (2013) contrasts their approaches.

> At some points in the texts the motivations of the authors do converge, on the importance of peer review, the efficiency of self-archiving, the need to widen access, etc., but at other points we can see real and divergent foci of concern: the responsibility of 'the digital' towards the accuracy of the scholarly record (Borgman) versus the responsibility of 'the scholarly' towards the media creativity of the digital academic (Weller). (Goodfellow 2013, p. 75)

Goodfellow's argument points to a real dichotomy and the values and assumptions informing that division concern a) the establishment of new kinds of 'truth values' for academic knowledge disrupted by new technologies and alternatively b) new 'use values' for academic knowledge involving new means of communication, new ways of participation and new media in the process of production and distribution of the final outputs of scholarly activity. The first outlook concerning truth values is explored below in relation to the 'new invisible college'. The second outlook which Goodfellow associates with Weller is linked to the idea of openness. In this case an openness of scholars to:

- New sites of production of academic knowledge (for example in citizen science)
- New ways to interact with audiences
- New ways to produce academic outputs including outputs in new formats and new media
- New low or zero cost ways of reproducing both academic outputs and the data from which those outputs are produced

In Weller's (2011) view it is the affordance of easy replication of a variety of media which particularly enables new forms of scholarly practice and these can affect significant debates regarding controversial issues such as climate change and genetic research. Disputes in these areas demonstrate the ways that the inclusion of new forms of debate, and new kinds of engagement enabled by digital and network technology, allow sections of the public to become involved in discussions about these important areas of scientific research and public policy (Holliman 2012). The argument that digital and network technologies afford new ways of working is reinforced in Weller's approach by an advocacy of new ways of structuring reward schemes and regimes of accountability to recognise digital scholarship and promote the new ways of working (Weller 2011). He argues that increasing the recognition of digital scholars would act as in indication of the value that the institution placed on these new ways of working. Such recognition would act as a spur to other academics and it would help to encourage institutional innovation. It also provides a link between digital scholarship and the regime of accountability and new managerialism found in many universities.

Weller's approach illustrates two features of the digital scholarship debate. While digital technologies open up new possibilities they also constrain other, perhaps older and more established practices. This tension is one of the reasons I reject the idea that academic change should proceed before a case has been proven. Digital scholarship remains subject to choices and in Weller's view the reluctance of academics to engage fully with the open practices that digital technologies enable is seen as a barrier and he argues for the use of rewards and recognition to support his preferred academic work practices. I argue that such an approach involves political and policy choices which have the potential to be used by governments and managements to apply undue pressure on staff to adopt one academic practice above others. It may still be important to ensure that a place remains in digital scholarship for a lone academic to cut away from current trends, to pursue academic paths that are currently out of fashion. Perhaps this would involve some academics in a sequestered, more monastic working life and a refusal to engage closely and routinely with the public. Some of the digital scholar's ways of working fit some forms of academic practice more than others, and they may prove to be a threat to the idea of academic freedom. Public pressure in socially and politically sensitive areas can lead to a narrowing of intellectual debate, to a playing down of academic and scientific criteria for judgment and to the introduction of populist, religious or overtly political standards into academic work. In line with the arguments made throughout this book, academic practices are not a determined outcome of technological change, nor are there specific ways of working that are the best or better suited to using new technology. Rather I think the future of scholarship should be open to the choice. Choices are made at various levels of organised social life, including the university, civil society, the market and the state as well as the individual scholar. Choice has also got to be exercised by academics collectively through their professional self-organisation in conferences and associations, in trade unions and in the democratic and accountable bodies found in some universities.

A 'New' Invisible College?

In Goodfellow's (2013) view there are two underlying approaches to digital scholarship found in the work of Borgman (2007) and Weller (2011). Borgman's approach is to make scholarship more scholarly using digital and network technologies and to establish new truth values to fit the changed conditions for academic work. Related to this search for revised ways of working that reinforce scholarly values while incorporating the affordances of new technologies Wagner (2008) has argued that the networked nature of modern science could lead to the emergence of a 'new' invisible college (Wagner 2008). Wagner (2008) drew on the history of the emergence of scientific disciplines and peer review procedures in the seventeenth century to suggest that digital technologies may have a similar profound effect on contemporary academic practices. Her point of departure is somewhat different to the arguments about digital scholarship because she really begins from the standpoint of globalisation and her concerns are with the way science has moved beyond the nation-state to take on an internationalised network structure. The reference back to the seventeenth century is intended to evoke the elusive network of people who were largely outside of academic institutions and hence developed their own 'invisible' college. In the twenty-first century the change is one that moves away from a professionalised science captured by the nation-state and looked on it as a national asset and a means to national development.

The new global network is described by Wagner as a complex adaptive system. That is there are many different interacting parts and each of these is capable of adapting to its context, even if that component part is not itself conscious. The system contains multiple levels and although not entirely predictable it can be described in terms of probability, regulation and rules. This description is very close to the emergent properties of networks discussed in Chap. 4 and the suggestion that such systems while not open to absolute control are open to regulation and design in ways that encourage some kinds of developments over others. Like scale-free networks these are open systems in the sense that they are extensible and new actors can join, but they are not flat and there is structure and there are centres of influence and power built into the network structure. This is the point of the 'new' invisible college, it is invisible because these structures and power relations while obvious to those active in the network can remain invisible to those outside and Wagner stresses this aspect specifically in relation to developing countries (Czerniewicz and Wiens 2013). One of the problems with this relative invisibility is that excellent work can be conducted in developing economies but the flow of the network means that the benefits are likely to flow out externally to the established nodes in the network, those largely in advanced industrial countries. To correct these imbalances national governments in developing countries need to do more than support science, they need to develop the infrastructure that supports science.

> They must broaden their focus to encompass the infrastructure that supports scientific capacity. Without this basic scaffolding, attempts to build science capacity by focusing on research and development are doomed to crumble—knowledge creating activities cannot be sustained without the services and functions of related science and technology services such as metrology or extension. (Wagner 2008, p. 94)

The elements of a scientific infrastructure identified by Wagner are:

1. Laboratories and equipment;
2. Standards, testing, and metrology services, including regulatory and compliance services;

3. Extension, technology transfer, an information collection services;
4. Intellectual property protection

Interestingly Wagner sees the final point, intellectual property protection as a temporary feature because she also argues for a more open system and claims that technological changes undermine current intellectual property laws.

Wagner's approach moves away from each nation-state trying to mirror each other with a common basic framework of services, and suggests that national science policies can focus on specialist areas and rely on standards and basic components of an infrastructure sourced from elsewhere. The example Wagner draws upon is Vietnam, a state born out of years of nationalist resistance and led by a communist party. That a regime with this history can see the benefits of international networks for science development is a significantly positive sign. However there are clear challenges that face Wagner's approach, as she herself recognises. The nation-state systems of funding allow for some degree of public accountability, the new invisible college and the forms of open funding that she recommends would disrupt and contest this form of necessary accountability. Wagner's approach reminds the reader that network society affects essential flows of ideas and knowledge and that the nation-state is reconfigured in this process. It also places emphasis on some of the basic arguments in this book—the centrality of network structures, the need to analyse in terms of levels, and the importance of sociotechnical infrastructure in supporting human activities.

Pedagogy and the Scholarship of Teaching and Learning

The development of networked and digital technologies has influenced academic practice in relation to teaching and learning for several decades. The concept of learning networks dates back to the late 1980s and early 1990s (Harasim et al 1995; Mason and Kaye 1990) and, prior to this period, the relationships between computers and education were already an established area of research (Cuban 1986). With the development of web technologies in the mid-1990s, the idea of e-learning became a commonplace and, since the beginning of the millennium, this has developed further with the deployment of what have become known as Web 2.0 technologies. Overall, the relationship between digital and network technologies and teaching and learning is the most developed area of research concerning academic work and technology (see Chap. 5 for discussion of learning analytics, OER and MOOCs).

The kinds of change that are associated with new technologies occur at several different levels. Academic work practices have been altered to include increasing levels of technology in the classroom and lecture theatre. Forms and methods of assessment have been affected both by the ability of students to access information and to duplicate it via new technology, and by reactive measures using new technology at institutional level (e.g. Turnitin). As noted in Chap. 5 these changes affect the relationships between the institution and the workforce and the balance between different sections of the workforce, specifically the relationships between management and administration and the academics organised collectively in the college. The academic role of the teacher has been affected by:

- Changes to student access to resources
- The inclusion of new media in teaching resources
- The development of institutional infrastructures and virtual learning environments
- Pressures to include more cooperative and collaborative methods
- The introduction of social media and mobile technologies
- Innovative and disruptive technologies (e.g. Massive Open Online Courses/ MOOCs)

Taken together, the pressures set out above the amount to a restructuring of the academic role in teaching (Beetham and Sharpe 2013).

There are two key aspects that I will deal with here, the changing organisational role of the academic as teacher and secondly the shift in pedagogy and the pressures that influence the direction of the changes in pedagogy. The role of the teacher and the teaching function associated with networked and digital technology is an issue as old as educational technology itself. From Skinner's teaching machines (Skinner 1958) to Sugata Mitra's minimally invasive education (Mitra 2000) and MOOCs (Daniel 2012), various forms of technology have held out the prospect of being able to advance learning without a) the skill and craft of the embodied teacher and b) the numbers of teachers previously required. In some cases instructional technologies and the promise of Artificial Intelligence suggested that 'teaching' could be programmed and the machine could replace aspects of direct human labour, for example by acting as a learning guide or explainer (Holmes 2005). Mass communications and later the Internet and Web suggested that a star professor located somewhere else, possibly anywhere, could engage many students at a distance, thus reducing the demand for professors and increasing the excellence of the teacher in a single move (Harasim et al 1995; Daniel 2012). The teaching function in these approaches is one that differs sharply from the idea contained in the seminal definition of networked learning. Networked learning is concerned with connections and it is less concerned with the medium through which these connections are maintained. Professors can be at a distance, mediated by way of a range of technologies, but a key to their role is having the time and organisational and technical capacity to make a variety of connections with their students. To do this involves the design of tasks and environments which can encourage students to engage in productive activities and develop congenial locales. The idea that teaching could be replaced either by a machine or by a distant professor dealing with large numbers of students does not make good sense in terms of networked learning or when designing networks for learning (Carvalho and Goodyear 2014).

One of the most persistent slogans that has emerged to characterise the changing role of the teacher in relation to network and digital technology is that the teacher must move 'from the sage on the stage to the guide on the side' (King 1993). Although the origin of the phrase is disputed it has had an extensive life and it is still used in current conditions to characterise changes associated with the newer technological developments. For example in a systematic review of literature related to the use of iPads in higher education Nguyen et al. noted that:

> Academics were found to be more sceptical about their changing role from the 'sage on the stage' to the 'guide on the side' (Nguyen, Barton, and Nguyen 2014, p. 9)

Critiques of the use of these phrases are long-standing (Jones 1999) but the case continues to have to be made. In the context of CSCL and TEL Dillenbourg argued against their use to dismiss or downgrade the role of the teacher:

> In technology-enhanced learning, the slogan 'from the sage on the stage to the guide on the side' became a commonplace to stress the evolution of the teacher's role. This vision was even stronger in CSCL because the idea that students learn from each other in some way weakens the teacher's role as knowledge provider. However, most CSCL scholars would agree that socio-constructivism does not mean 'teacherless' learning, but changes the role of the teacher to be less of a knowledge provider and more of a 'conductor' orchestrating a broad range of activities; this role is becoming a central concern in CSCL. (Dillenbourg et al. 2009, pp. 16–17)

The connection between collaboration and cooperation and the early development of networked learning is acknowledged to be strong (Goodyear 2014;

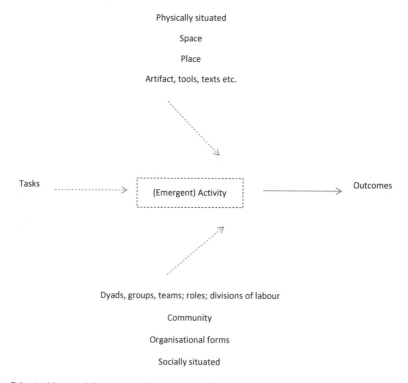

Fig. 7.1 Architectural framework (Carvalho and Goodyear 2014, p. 59)

McConnell et al. 2012 and Chap. 2 this volume) and the issue of the changed role of the teacher is in many ways common to both traditions. The advice from Dillenbourg et al (2009) and from Carvalho and Goodyear (2014) set out some of the ways that design and 'orchestration' of teacher like activities can take place. The design, experience and practice of the teaching function in networked learning are also addressed in Hodgson et al. (2014). Carvalho and Goodyear (2014) set out an analytic framework and in their conclusions they emphasise two areas of importance in the connection between design elements, firstly between set design and activity and secondly between epistemic design, tasks and activity Fig. 7.1.

The academic role in this framework conforms to the idea of indirect design introduced in Chap. 3. Importantly for the discussion of academic work the idea of the designer does not map directly on to the traditional academic and a learning designer might be drawn from the new professions of learning technologist or educational developer.

The distance universities that have fully engaged with new technologies, such as The Open University in the UK (OU UK) and the Open Universiteit in the Netherlands (OU NL) organise their workforces in a non-standard division of labour (Jones, Aoki, Rusman, and Schlusmans 2009). The OU (UK) has course teams which include representatives of Learning Teaching Solutions[1] a large internal unit that is separate from the academic departments and states its aim on the University web site in the following way:

> LTS is a modern centre for the development, production and delivery of creative and cost effective distance learning materials. It employs highly skilled teams who provide the expertise and experience to ensure that OU learning materials are delivered to the appropriate standards. (http://www.open.ac.uk/about/open-educational-resources/what-we-do/learning-and-teaching-solutions)

The position of LTS is at the border of academic content, quality control and university publication. The centralisation and standardisation implicit in this model is not a prerequisite of distance education and other models co-exist with the course teams models found in both the OU (UK) and the OU (NL), for example in the Open University (Japan) and Athabasca University in Canada, which have very different backgrounds but both have a greater focus on the individual academic in course delivery and development. The division of labour in distance education accentuates a tendency apparent across most of the sectors because new media increases the role of groups and teams in teaching and learning practices. Teaching which in a traditional form often involved a single academic as the creative force in lecturing, assessing and organising the work of teaching is now more likely to be part of a course/module team who develop their courses with the support of a technical team and educational development advisers (This is not universally the case and in Australia 'flexible learning' is more reliant on individual lecturers rather than

---

[1]The History timeline records the origins of LTS in this way: *2000*: Learning and Teaching Services (LTS) is created through the merger of Operations and part of the Academic Computing Service. The new unit is created to be the University's learning media development, production and delivery centre. http://www.open.ac.uk/researchprojects/historyofou/story/the-early-21st-century-the-ou-brief-history

course teams see Tynan et al. 2013). The academic is also likely to have absorbed administrative functions that were once separate, such as collecting work for assessment and making announcements to the cohort of students. These functions are now part of the LMS/VLE and attended to by academic staff. The introduction of new technology has in this way assisted in the decomposition of the traditional academic's practice and helped to recompose it in a new and more collective enterprise (Sappey and Relf 2010). One conclusion is that a persistent feature accompanying the introduction of network and digital technologies has been a tendency towards the disaggregation and re-composition of the teaching function.

The emphasis on moderation rather than content presentation has been accompanied in some national systems by the growth of adjunct or sessional staff who are contracted in precarious ways, often by more than one institution (Altbach, Reisberg, and Pacheco 2013b). The idea behind moderation was not to downgrade or deskill academic staff, but it is one factor that has given the opportunity to university managers to turn away from fully staffed courses and modules to modules designed by experienced and permanent staff which are then delivered by staff on a variety of inferior contracts (zero hours, temporary, part-time etc.). In this way place-based universities are beginning to mirror the core-periphery workforce already developed in the OU (UK) with a core of whole time professional staff and a periphery of part-time associates who conduct the day-to-day contact with students. Altbach comments on this worldwide phenomenon of the growth in adjunct and sessional staff in this way:

> The professoriate is changing in many parts of the world, and developing countries are not free from these changes. In developing countries, a higher proportion of academics work on part-time contracts or are subject to irregular hiring practices. In many developing countries, a large part of the profession is composed of part-time staff who teach a few courses and do not have regular academic appointments or real links to the university… In many countries, tenure is not guaranteed, and even full-time academics have little formal job protection, although, in fact, relatively few are actually fired. Clear guarantees of academic freedom or the assurance of a stable career are often missing. (Altbach 2011, p. 213)

Such developments raise serious questions about academic identity and the possibility of academic freedom. They are also changes that while they are loosely coupled to the deployment of new technologies they are not dependent on them and show a strong link to the general development of a casual and precarious workforce and the dominance of neoliberal economic models (Fuchs 2008).

As noted above an aspect of the changing teaching role has been an increased emphasis on cooperative and collaborative approaches to teaching. These approaches have had to contend with the actual provision of technologies within universities and the corporate sector. The dominance initially of computer conferencing systems and business inclined groupware in education was followed by a concentration on the development of Learning Management Systems (LMS/VLE) (see Chap. 6). The introduction of LMS/VLEs by institutions has led to a changed role for academic staff, but one that does not obviously assist the development of collaborative or cooperative forms of teaching. The design of LMS/VLEs varies and Moodle for example claims to be informed by constructivist thinking (Dougiamas and Taylor 2002) although some managers and developers have claimed that the design of Moodle and other LMS/VLEs are pedagogically neutral (Sclater 2008a). The design of the LMS/VLE is only one aspect of the sociomaterial assemblage that academic staff engage with. Much of the use of LMS/VLE has been institutionally guided, if not directly enforced as an institutional policy requiring academic staff to engage with the LMS/VLE. This has often led to a very basic use of the systems by academic staff, and the LMS/VLE is frequently used as a simple repository for content e.g. lecture slides, lecture notes and essential course materials. The discursive capabilities of the LMS/VLE are generally underused. In the dialectic between the broadcast (acquisition) or discussion (participation) models of the LMS/VLE the broadcast or acquisition metaphor has largely won out (Weller 2007; Sfard 1998). The institutional push to ensure that staff engage with the LMS/VLE has, as a consequence, led to a wide but shallow take-up of the technology and the possibilities latent within it (Selwyn 2007).

Furthermore the shift to the use of digital and network technologies has meant that much of the work currently undertaken by academics sits outside of dated workload allocation models (Tynan et al. 2013). Many teaching academics will recognise this conclusion:

> For the staff in this study, the struggle to accommodate new technologies and pedagogies in anachronistic workload models has proved nigh impossible; their determination to provide 'quality teaching' for their students means they are driven to work 'out of hours.' (Tynan et al. 2013, p. 9)

For networked learning to take root in such circumstances it will require intervention not at an individual staff level, but at a departmental or institutional level in ways that will alter the incentives, constraints and drivers of academic activity. The institutional policies that are intended to increase the use of the LMS/VLE and to develop the quality of academic interactions with students depend to a large extent on changes in the structure of the workforce and the introduction of new professionals and of learning technologists and academic/educational developers in particular.

Para-Academics and the Emergence of the New Professionals

The rise of the new professionals, the para-academics, is related to a number of factors but in teaching and learning it is focused on the twin dynamic of the introduction of new technology and the effects of neoliberalism in the form of the managed entrepreneurial university. In this process the new professionals are themselves an active component because they are both brought into being to advance the new agendas and in that process they advance themselves. The new functional units they belong to frequently cut across traditional disciplinary boundaries and blur the boundaries between management and administration. The very precariousness of their position in new areas of work and unstable organisational units make them more susceptible to management pressure and the demands of those holding power and influence in the university. Hudson in her exploration of learning technologists and educational developers concluded that:

> Both groups primarily aim to bring about change and support professional development. Accordingly, both groups aim to support teaching and learning, the use of learning technologies, research and the application and integration of new knowledge and skills. They also share principles and values that emphasise innovation. Both groups work in complex and uncertain workplace settings and struggle over their position, professional identity and symbolic capital. (Hudson 2009, pp. 218–219)

It is their focus on change and innovation that links the two groups and it is also linked to funding because both areas of work are either dependent on external funding or top sliced academic funding within the institution. This separation from core funding separates these groups from traditional academic staff (Hudson 2009). The vulnerability of their funding is not reflected in the influence that both groups can have on institutional strategy, particularly in helping to determine strategies for teaching and learning and the role of technology.

> In addition their often, central physical location in the university has placed them at the interface of management, faculty and departments. However, long-standing tensions for both groups concern their positioning between management and university teachers, and their increasingly politicised role which may, in the future, lead either to an increase in power or a reduction in influence and agency for one or other groups. (Hudson 2009, p. 222)

They can also exert external influence in the sector beyond individual universities via emergent professional bodies that can lobby independently. These new professional groups are one of the key reference groups for networked learning. The new professionals often provide the recruits to Masters and Doctoral programmes in which academics associated with networked learning work. While networked learning is conceived of as a critical and research led field it relies on the indirect support of this layer of new professionals in the academy. As a consequence it is critically important for networked learning to understand the intertwined relationship between the research field and the practice of the new professionals who are often driven by concerns and motivations that are distinct from the traditional academic.

E-Research and the Digital Humanities

The language used to describe the issues raised in the following sections is still immature so each section will take a slightly different slice from a topic which in many ways covers similar ground. Unlike the relationships between teaching and learning and digital and network technologies the relationships between academic work in research and service have not generated a single vocabulary and a wide range of terms are currently in use. Some of these are more aligned with the natural sciences such as Cyberinfrastructure, e-infrastructure and Grid technology. Ribes and Lee noted the early bias towards the natural sciences in this field in the introduction to a special edition of CSCW:

> Cyberinfrastructure (CI), eScience and eInfrastructure are the current terms of art for the networked information technologies supporting scientific research activities such as

collaboration, data sharing and dissemination of findings. These are the computational infrastructures that enable, for instance, global climate modelers to compile heterogeneous information sources in order to understand environmental change or the tools that make the massive quantitative data emerging from the Large Hadron Collider into tractable scientific visualizations. Within the US and Europe these ventures have garnered significant momentum in terms of funding and technological development. The greater funding of CI for the physical and biological sciences has led to a proliferation of CI studies in those areas (a bias reflected in our own special issue) with CI studies of humanities, arts, and social sciences growing more slowly. (Ribes and Lee 2010, p. 231)

Since that time other terms have grown up that focus more closely on the humanities and social sciences such as digital humanities and digital scholarship, and e-research itself has shifted from a concern of the natural sciences to a concern for all academic disciplines (Jankowski 2009; Meyer and Schroeder 2009). The general phenomenon that these terms point to is the way in which digital and networked technologies are impacting on the research process and academic work. There is something wonderful about the reflexive way that the Web began at CERN with the requirements for sharing in big science projects and has subsequently brought about significant changes to science practices across the world. The new digital and networked technologies affect the research process and academic work in several distinct ways. Digital and networked technologies:

- Open up new sources of data (see Chap. 5 for a discussion of 'Big Data' in universities)
- Changes the ways data can be stored, preserved and shared (digital documentation standards and archiving)
- Enable new and more dispersed forms of working (virtual labs, collaboratories)
- Enable new entrants to access the research process (e.g. citizen science)
- Enable new forms of publication (open access, blogs)
- Enable new forms of public engagement and scholarly communication (beyond publication)

The academic diversity associated with different fields of knowledge and the disciplinary and subject divides formalised in the academy are also found in new forms of research. This section examines the topic using two of these terms, e-research and digital humanities and the following sections examine the somewhat different framings of closely related topics in terms of digital scholarship and the 'new' invisible college. Digital scholarship explicitly references back to the work of Boyer and the issues of scholarship, combining teaching with research and focused broadly on the academic role, including the public profile of the academic and the way knowledge is circulated as well as produced (Weller 2011). The idea of a new invisible college points forward and asks questions connected to the nature and forms of validation of knowledge available in relation to new technologies (Wagner 2008).

The development of e-research has implications for the development of academic practices in ways that resemble the discussion about teaching and learning. Some researchers have related these changes to alleged generational differences in the population of younger researchers and their information-searching behaviour (Rowlands et al. 2008), but these kinds of claims about research workers are as disputed as those concerning a net generation of digital native students (see Chap. 8).

Proctor et al. summarise their work examining the relationships between e-research and academic staff in the United Kingdom in this way:

> ...e-Infrastructure is often seen by users (both current and potential) as complex and challenging. It is also clear that current users often experience frustrations, while potential users may be unaware of its benefits and of how to take the first steps towards exploiting them. The findings highlight the scale of problems arising from the failure of the human infrastructure—the networks (both formal and informal) of actors essential to effective exploitation of innovations—to develop and keep pace with the technical infrastructure. (Procter, Voss, and Asgari-Targhi 2013, p. 1668)

E-research requires new large-scale infrastructures and related to this it also required more networked, cooperative and collaborative forms of working (Ribes and Lee 2010). The new academic practices rely on the large-scale use of computational and informational technologies and the Internet, and the standardisation associated with the Internet which makes it possible to deploy tools that are widely accessible for the storage, manipulation, sharing and analysis of the large amounts of data now available (Borgman 2007). The novelty of e-research is the way it affects the research processes from start to finish, beginning with data collection and ending with the dissemination of results and end products. Ribes and Lee describe the new sociotechnical infrastructures in this way:

> Between data collection technologies and users lie the networks, computers, storage and a plethora of more subtle integration technologies that promise to facilitate communication and interoperation across all the boundaries that plague interdisciplinary collaboration: hard technologies such as fiberoptic cables and grid computing, soft technologies such as metadata standards and ontologies, and even softer on-paper agreements between institutions and agencies of science to facilitate the movement of 'siloed' data and findings. (Ribes and Lee 2010, p. 233)

This description reminds the reader that e-research and cyberinfrastructures are not 'things' that are to hand, simply available for study, rather they are the ongoing achievements and outcomes of collective activity by humans and machines. Ribes and Lee propose seven themes for the study of cyberinfrastructure and these themes align closely to the suggestions in this book for the use and development of the idea of infrastructure for research and analysis. The seven themes are:

1. Relationality
2. Integration of heterogeneity
3. Sustainability
4. Standardisation
5. Scaling up or extension of infrastructure
6. The distribution between human work and technological delegation
7. Cyberinfrastruture as always already social (adapted from Ribes and Lee 2010)

This brief listing does not do justice to the work supporting these themes but the reader can find elaboration of several aspects of the themes in other parts of this volume. Importantly in the context of academic work the list points to a changing set of relations between humans and machines and a shift in the appropriate levels needed for understanding the new phenomena. In particular infrastructure suggests a focus that includes mesolevel arrangements and methods that go beyond single site and small-scale interpretive research projects.

> Cyberinfrastructure resides at the intersection of many of these methodological entanglements: it is technical (often doubly so, requiring a handle on information technologies and a domain science); it is distributed (nationally and often internationally); it is long term, at times stretching years into the past and prospecting into a future of decades; and brings together multiple heterogeneous expert actors. (Ribes and Lee 2010, p. 239)

The arrangements for academic research, and academic research practices, change with the deployment of an e-research infrastructure. The skills and practices required of researchers are altered and the possibilities for research are changed by the new capabilities of a cyberinfrastructure.

While the terms e-research and cyberinfrastructure were largely confined to the natural sciences the term 'digital humanities' has become something of a buzzword in recent years (Borgman 2009). Digital humanities are an interesting development because e-science and cyberinfrastructure, were early adopters of new ways of working. Similarly the social sciences, while some distance behind, had some similar elements of basic infrastructure for e-research to build on (Woolgar 2003). Borgman (2009) commented with regard to the developments in the different disciplines that:

> The sciences, arts, and humanities have converged and diverged in various ways over the centuries. In the area of digital scholarship, many interests are in common across the disciplines. It is the pace of adoption that is divergent. The sciences, and to a lesser extent the social sciences, have been successful in developing the technical, social, and political infrastructure for digital scholarship under the rubrics of **cyberinfrastructure**—the term used in the U.S., and **eScience**—the term more widely used in the U.K. and elsewhere … Digital scholarship remains emergent in the humanities, while eScience has become the norm in the sciences. (Borgman 2009 Online para 2)

In the article Borgman (2009) identified a number of challenges facing the development of digital humanities including:

- What are data in the humanities?
- What are the infrastructure requirements?
- Where are the social studies of digital humanities?
- What is the humanities laboratory of the twenty-first century?

The challenges Borgman identifies have significant implications for academic work and have great similarities to the general challenges faced across all aspects of e-research. The disciplinarity noted by Becher and Trowler (2001) affects e-research and digital humanities because the discussions about digital humanities are reconstituting preexisting disciplinary boundaries after the new infrastructure has disrupted them. In particular the terms being used seem to reinforce the two cultures identified by Snow (1959).

Across the various disciplines the development of e-research has implications for the development of academic practices in ways that resemble the discussion about teaching and learning. E-research requires new large-scale infrastructures and networked, cooperative and collaborative forms of working (Ribes and Lee 2010).

However, in addition to these similarities there are also significant differences. The arrangements for research, such as in a 'humanities laboratory', change with the deployment of an e-research infrastructure. The skills required for being a researcher can be affected and the possibilities and, increasingly, the requirements for public engagement by digital scholars may also be radically transformed.

Conclusions

The kinds of measures and measurements applied to academic work are being reviewed and that review is taking place in the context of discussion about what a digital scholar might mean and what incentives can be applied to induce more 'digital' scholarship (Weller 2011). A problem with this kind of argument is the way it re-opens an argument that lay at the heart of Boyer's earlier work. Boyer noted that:

> [at] the very heart of the current debate—the single concern around which all others pivot is the issue of faculty time. What is really being called into question is the reward system and the key issue is this: what activities of the professoriate are most highly prized (Boyer 1990, p. xi)

When Weller introduces ideas about restructured reward schemes he is entering a difficult area about the allocation of academic time. This is in a period in which academic time is being restructured for other reasons. The balance between teaching and research is affected by the massification of higher education and the pressure to teach greater numbers and to do it more efficiently. That is to apply to higher education the commercial pressure of value for money and getting 'more for less'. These pressures do not arise from the technology but they raise important questions about who makes the critical judgments. Boyer was criticised for not really addressing this question:

> Boyer (1990) never fully addresses the questions 'most highly prized by whom?' and 'most highly prized for what?' Nor has he identified the most salient issue concerning change—the organizational (social) structure of the university itself. (Davis and Chandler 1998, p. 24)

Networked learning prizes certain kinds of relationships, and these form the basis of a critical stance in relation to some of the pressures on academic work. Digital scholarship can open a range of possibilities up in terms of new ways of working. However it can also be integrated into new managerial schemes of surveillance and accountability that pressure academic staff to perform in ways that destroy the autonomy that is symbolic of academic freedom.

The growth of the invisible college took place beyond the boundaries of the university. It gave rise to academic practices that are now bedrock formations for academic work within universities. Academic journals, the system of peer review, and experimental research emerged from this ferment. An interesting question for future years is what academic practices might emerge from the new invisible college and in the tension between academic life that stretches out into the new networks and brings into universities the life outside institutional boundaries. Peer review may not be the best form of validation and it has many known weaknesses, but it is possibly the least bad system. Networks enable the widespread circulation of ideas and there is no easy way to discriminate between materials in circulation. Will the 'new' invisible college develop rules of thumb concerning the validation of online materials? In journalism some aspects of these practices are beginning to emerge, for example in the verification procedures used to assess the stream of online material from conflict zones. The work of the blogger Brown Moses was seminal in this development and his work has led to the development of a web site dedicated to citizen journalism, Bellingcat.[2] A new invisible college will need to consider how academic practices can develop to deal with the stream of academic online content and provide methods for effective discrimination between resources. In the next chapter ideas about how students are changing in relation to new technologies are examined. The net generation and digital native discourse suggests young people are naturally attuned to the new technology but empirical work shows that students are often ill-equipped to search for and evaluate materials using the Internet. What are the kinds of academic practices emerging from the 'new invisible college' that we need to develop to manage the availability, and ease of production, of materials circulated via the Internet?

References

Altbach, P. G. (Ed.). (2000). *The changing academic workplace: Comparative perspectives.* Boston: Boston College, Center for International Higher Education.

Altbach, P. G. (2011). The academic profession: The realities of developing countries. In P. G. Altbach (Ed.), *Leadership for world-class universities: Challenges for developing countries* (pp. 205–223). Abingdon, England: Routledge.

Altbach, P. G., Reisberg, L., Yudkevich, M., Androushchak, G., & Kuzminov, Y. (Eds.). (2013a). *The global future of higher education and the academic profession: The BRICs and the United States.* New York: Palgrave Macmillan.

Altbach, P. G., Reisberg, L., & Pacheco, I. F. (2013b). *Academic salaries and contracts: Global trends and American realities. THE NEA 2013 Almanac of higher education.* Washington, DC: The National Education Association.

Andresen, L. W. (2000). A useable, trans-disciplinary conception of scholarship. *Higher Education Research & Development, 19*(2), 137–153.

Barley, S. R., & Orr, J. E. (1997). *Between craft and science: Technical work in US settings.* Ithaca, NY: Cornell University, ILR Press.

Becher, T., & Trowler, P. (2001). *Academic tribes and territories* (2nd ed.). Buckingham, England: SRHE and Open University Press.

Beetham, H. (2000). *Career development of learning technology staff: Scoping study final report.* Retrieved from http://www.jisc.ac.uk/publications/reports/2001/cdssfinalreport.aspx

Beetham, H., & Sharpe, R. (Eds.). (2013). *Rethinking pedagogy for a digital age: Designing for 21st century learning* (2nd ed.). London: Routledge.

Bexley, E., James, R., & Arkoudis, S. (2011). *The Australian academic profession in transition: Addressing the challenge of reconceptualising academic work and regenerating the academic workforce.* Melbourne, Victoria, Australia: Centre for the Study of Higher Education.

---

[2] https://www.bellingcat.com/

Blass, E., Jasman, A., & Shelley, S. (2010). *The future of higher education provision in the UK: Workforce implications: A review of the literature: A report to HEFCE.* Bristol, England: Higher Education Funding Council for England.

Bok, D. (2004). *Universities in the marketplace: The commercialisation of higher education.* Woodstock, NJ: Princeton University Press.

Borgman, C. (2003). *From gutenburg to the global information infrastructure.* Cambridge, MA: MIT Press.

Borgman, C. (2007). *Scholarship in the digital age: Information, infrastructure, and the internet.* Cambridge, MA: MIT Press.

Borgman, C. L. (2009). The digital future is now: A call to action for the humanities. *Digital Humanities Quarterly, 3*(4). Retrieved from http://www.digitalhumanities.org/dhq/

Boyer, E. L. (1990). *Scholarship reconsidered: Priorities of the professoriate.* Princeton, NJ: Carnegie Foundation.

Brown, J. S., & Duguid, P. (2000). *The social life of information.* Boston: Harvard Business School.

Carvalho, L., & Goodyear, P. (Eds.). (2014). *The architecture of productive learning networks.* London: Routledge.

Clark, B. R. (1998). *Creating entrepreneurial universities: Organisational pathways of transformation.* Oxford, England: Pergamon.

Conole, G., White, S., & Oliver, M. (2007). The impact of e-learning on organisational roles and structures. In G. Conole & M. Oliver (Eds.), *Contemporary perspectives in e-learning research* (pp. 69–81). London: Routledge Falmer.

Courant, P. (2008). Scholarship: The wave of the future in the digital age. In R. Katz (Ed.), *The tower and the cloud: Higher education in the age of cloud computing,* Educause. Retrieved from http://www.educause.edu/ir/library/pdf/PUB7202t.pdf

Cowan, W., Cowan, R., & Llerena, P. (2008). *Running the Marathon.* Working papers of BETA 2008-10, Bureau d'Economie Théorique et Appliquée, ULP, Strasbourg, France. Retrieved from http://ideas.repec.org/p/ulp/sbbeta/2008-10.html

Cuban, L. (1986). *Teachers and machines: The classroom use of technology since 1920.* New York: Teachers College Press.

Czerniewicz L., & Wiens, K. (2013). The online visibility of South African knowledge: Searching for poverty alleviation: Building the information society. *African Journal of Information and Communication, 13,* 30–41. Retrieved from http://reference.sabinet.co.za/sa_epublication_article/afjic_n13_a4

Daniel, J. (2012). Making sense of MOOCs: Musings in a maze of Myth, paradox and possibility. *Journal of Interactive Media in Education.* Retrieved from http://jime.open.ac.uk/2012/18

Davis, W. E., & Chandler, T. J. L. (1998). Beyond Boyer's scholarship reconsidered: Fundamental change in the university and the socioeconomic systems. *The Journal of Higher Education, 69*(1), 23–64.

Dearing, R. (1997). *Higher education in the learning society.* Report of the National Committee of Enquiry into Higher Education. London: HMSO. Retrieved from http://www.leeds.ac.uk/educol/ncihe/

Dillenbourg, P., Järvelä, S., & Fischer, F. (2009). The evolution of research on computer supported collaborative learning: From design to orchestration. In N. Balacheff, S. Ludvigsen, T. De Jong, A. Lazonder, S. Barnes, & L. Montandon (Eds.), *Technology-enhanced learning* (pp. 3–19). Berlin, Germany: Springer.

Dougiamas, M., & Taylor, P. C. (2002). *Interpretive analysis of an internet-based course constructed using a new courseware tool called Moodle.* Non refereed paper presented at 25th Conference of HERDSA (The Higher Education Research and Development Society of Australasia), 7–10 July, Perth, Western Australia.

Ellis, R., & Goodyear, P. (2010). *Students experiences of e-learning in higher education: The ecology of sustainable innovation.* New York: Routledge.

Ellison, J., & Eatman, T. K. (2008). *Scholarship in public: Knowledge creation and tenure policy in the engaged university*. Syracuse, NY: Imagining America.

Enders, J. (2006). The academic profession. In J. F. Forest & P. G. Altbach (Eds.), *International handbook of higher education* (pp. 5–22). Dordrecht, The Netherlands: Springer.

Enders, J. (2012). The university and the public and private good. In C. Teelken, G. Ferlie, & M. Dent (Eds.), *Leadership in the Public Sector: Promises and Pitfalls* (pp. 195–213). Abingdon, England: Routledge.

Ferguson, R., Clough, G., & Hosein, A. (2010). Shifting themes, shifting roles: The development of research blogs. In L. Creanor, D. Hawkridge, K. Ng, F. Rennie (Eds.), 'Into something rich and strange': Making sense of the sea-change. *Proceedings of the 17th Association for Learning Technology Conference (ALT-C 2010)* (pp. 111–117), 7–9 September 2010, Nottingham, England. Retrieved from http://repository.alt.ac.uk/797/3/Conference_Proc_webv2_2010121510.pdf

Fuchs, C. (2008). *Internet and society; social theory in the information age*. New York: Routledge.

Goodfellow, R. (2013). The 'literacies' of digital scholarship: Truth and use values. In R. Goodfellow & M. Lea (Eds.), *Literacy in the digital university: Critical perspectives on learning, scholarship, and technology* (pp. 67–78). London: Routledge.

Goodyear, P. (2014). Productive learning networks: The evolution of research and practice. In L. Carvalho & P. Goodyear (Eds.), *The architecture of productive learning networks* (pp. 23–47). London: Routledge.

Harasim, L., Hiltz, S. R., Teles, L., & Turoff, M. (1995). *Learning networks: A field guide to teaching and learning online*. Cambridge, MA: MIT Press.

Hodgson, V. E., De Laat, M., McConnell, D., & Ryberg, T. (Eds.). (2014). *The design, experience and practice of networked learning*. Heidelberg, Germany: Springer.

Holliman, R. (2012). The struggle for scientific consensus: Communicating climate science around COP-15. In B. Wagoner, E. Jensen, & J. A. Oldmeadow (Eds.), *Culture and social change: Transforming society through the power of ideas* (pp. 185–207). Charlotte, NC: Information Age.

Holmes, J. (2005). Designing agents to support learning by explaining. *Computers and Education, 48*(4), 523–547.

Hudson, A. (2009). *New professionals and new technologies in new higher education? Conceptualising struggles in the field*. Ph.D. Thesis, Language: English. Umeå University, Department of Interactive Media and Learning (IML), SE-901 87, Umeå, Sweden. Retrieved from http://www.diva-portal.org/smash/get/diva2:236168/FULLTEXT01.pdf

Jankowski, N. W. (Ed.). (2009). *E-research: Transformation in scholarly practice*. New York: Routledge.

Jones, C. (1999). From the sage on the stage to what exactly? description and the place of the moderator in cooperative and collaborative learning. *The Association for Learning Technology Journal, 7*(2), 27–36.

Jones, C. (2011). Students, the net generation and digital natives: Accounting for educational change. In M. Thomas (Ed.), *Deconstructing digital natives* (pp. 30–45). New York: Routledge.

Jones, C. (2012). Networked learning, stepping beyond the net generation and digital natives. In L. Dirckinck-Holmfeld, V. Hodgson, & D. McConnell (Eds.), *Exploring the theory, pedagogy and practice of networked learning* (pp. 27–41). New York: Springer.

Jones, C., Aoki, K., Rusman, E., & Schlusmans, K. (2009). A comparison of three Open Universities and their acceptance of Internet technologies. M-2009: *Proceedings of the 23rd ICDE World Conference on Open Learning and Distance Education including the 2009 EADTU Annual Conference*, 7–10 June 2009, Maastricht, The Netherlands. Retrieved from http://www.ou.nl/Docs/Campagnes/ICDE2009/Papers/Final_paper_081jones.pdf

King, A. (1993). From sage on the stage to guide on the side. *College Teaching, 41*(1), 30–35.

Laredo, P. (2007). Revisiting the third mission of universities: Toward a renewed categorization of university activities? *Higher Education Policy, 20*, 441–456.

Locke, W., & Bennion, A. (2009). Teaching and research in English higher education: New divisions of labour and changing perspectives on core academic roles. In *The changing academic profession over 1992–2007: International, comparative, and quantitative perspectives*, 13–14 January 2009, Research Institute for Higher Education (RIHE), Hiroshima University, Hiroshima, Japan. Retrieved from http://oro.open.ac.uk/16924/2/EFA2D834.pdf

Locke, W, & Bennion, A. (2010). *The changing academic profession: The UK and beyond*. UK Research Report. London: Universities UK. Retrieved from http://www.universitiesuk.ac.uk/highereducation/Documents/2010/TheChangingHEProfession.pdf

Locke, W., & Teichler, U. (Eds.). (2007). *The changing conditions for academic work and careers in select countries*. Kassel, Germany: International Centre for Higher Education Research.

Mason, R., & Kaye, A. (1990). Towards a new paradigm for distance education. In L. Harasim (Ed.), *Online education: Perspectives on a new environment*. New York: Praeger.

McCluskey, F., & Winter, M. (2012). *The idea of the digital university: Ancient traditions, disruptive technologies and the battle for the soul of higher education*. Washington, DC: Policy Studies Organisation/Westphalia Press.

McConnell, D., Hodgson, V., & Dirckinck-Holmfeld, L. (2012). Networked learning: A brief history and new trends. In L. Dirckinck-Holmfeld, V. Hodgson, & D. McConnell (Eds.), *Exploring the theory, pedagogy and practice of networked learning* (pp. 3–24). New York: Springer.

Meyer, E. T., & Schroeder, R. (2009). Untangling the web of e-research: Towards a sociology of online knowledge. *Journal of Informetrics, 3*(3), 246–260.

Mills, D., & Rath, J. (2012). Academia as a workplace (editorial to a special edition). *Higher Education Quarterly, 66*(2), 129–134.

Mitra, S. (2000). *Minimally invasive education for mass computer literacy*. Paper presented at the CRIDALA 2000 conference, Hong Kong, China, 21–25 June 2000. Retrieved from http://www.hole-in-the-wall.com/docs/Paper01.pdf

Molas-Gallart, J., Salter, A., Patel, P., Scott, A., & Duran, X. (2002). *Measuring third stream activities. Final report to the Russell group of universities, SPRU*. Brighton, England: University of Sussex.

Musselin, C. (2011). The academic workplace: What we already know, what we still Do Not know, and what We would like to know. In D. Rhoten & C. J. Calhoun (Eds.), *Knowledge matters: The public mission of the research university* (pp. 423–456). New York: Columbia University Press.

Nguyen, L., Barton, S. M., & Nguyen, L. T. (2014). iPads in higher education—Hype and hope. *British Journal of Educational Technology*. doi: 10.1111/bjet.12137

Oliver, M. (2002). What do learning technologists do? *Innovations in Education and Teaching International, 39*(4), 245–252.

PA Consulting Group. (2010). *The future workforce for higher education*. A Report to HEFCE by PA Consulting Group February 2010. Retrieved from http://www.hefce.ac.uk/media/hefce/content/pubs/2010/rd0310/rd03_10.pdf

Pearce, N., Weller, M., Scanlon, E., & Ashley, M. (2010). Digital scholarship considered: How new technologies could transform academic work. *Education, 16*, 1. Retrieved from http://ineducation.ca/ineducation/article/view/44

Procter, R., Voss, A., & Asgari-Targhi, M. (2013). Fostering the human infrastructure of e-research. *Information, Communication & Society, 16*(10), 1668–1691.

Rhoades, G. (2005). Cogs in the classroom factory: The changing identity of academic labor. *Journal of Higher Education, 76*(4), 477–479.

Rhoades, G. (2011). Whose educational space? negotiating professional jurisdiction in the high-tech academy. In J. C. Hermanowicz (Ed.), *The American academic profession: Transformation in contemporary higher education* (pp. 92–110). Baltimore: The Johns Hopkins University Press.

Ribes, D., & Lee, C. P. (2010). Sociotechnical studies of cyberinfrastructure and e-research: Current themes and future trajectories. *Computer Supported Cooperative Work, 19*, 231–244.

Rowlands, I., Nicholas, D., Williams, P., Huntington, P., Fieldhouse, M., Gunter, B., et al. (2008). The Google generation: The information behaviour of the researcher of the future. *Aslib Proceedings, 60*(4), 290–310.

Säljö, R. (2010). Digital tools and challenges to institutional traditions of learning: Technologies, social memory and the performative nature of learning. *Journal of Computer Assisted Learning, 26*(1), 53–64.

Sappey, J., & Relf, S. (2010). Digital technology education and its impact on traditional academic roles and practice. *Journal of University Teaching and Learning Practice, 7*:1, Article 3. Retrieved from http://ro.uow.edu.au/jutlp/vol7/iss1/

Sclater, N. (2008a). *Large-scale open source E-learning systems at the Open University (UK).* (Research Bulletin 12). Boulder, CO: EDUCAUSE Center for Applied Research. Retrieved from http://www.educause.edu/ecar

Selwyn, N. (2007). The use of computer technology in university teaching and learning: A critical perspective. *Journal of Computer Assisted Learning, 23*(2), 83–94.

Sfard, A. (1998). On two metaphors for learning and the dangers of choosing just one. *Educational Researcher, 27*(2), 4–13.

Skinner, B. F. (1958). Teaching machines. *Science, 128*(3330), 969–977.

Slaughter, S., & Leslie, L. L. (1997). *Academic capitalism—politics, policies and the entrepreneurial university.* Baltimore: Johns Hopkins University Press.

Snow, C. P. (1959). *The two cultures and the scientific revolution.* Cambridge, England: Cambridge University Press.

Sutherland, K., & Taylor, L. (2011). The development of identity, agency and community in the early stages of the academic career. *International Journal for Academic Development, 16*(3), 183–186.

Trowler, P., & Knight, P. T. (2000). Coming to know in higher education: Theorising faculty entry to new work contexts. *Higher Education Research & Development, 19*(1), 27–42.

Tynan, B., Ryan, Y., & Lamont-Mills, A. (2013). Examining workload models in online and blended teaching. *British Journal of Educational Technology*, Retrieved from Nov 2013, 10.1111/bjet.12111

Vendetti, M., Reale, E., & Leydesdorff, L. (2013). Disclosure of university research to third parties: A non-market perspective on an Italian university. *Science and Public Policy, 40*(6), 792–800.

Wagner, C. S. (2008). *The new invisible college: Science for development.* Washington, DC: Brookings Institution Press.

Weller, M. (2007). *Virtual learning environments: Using, choosing and developing your VLE.* Abingdon, England: Routledge.

Weller, M. (2011). *The digital scholar: How technology is transforming academic practice.* London: Bloomsbury Academic.

Woolgar, S. (2003). *Social shaping perspectives on e-science and e-social science: The case for research support. A consultative study for the economic and social research council (ESRC).* Swindon, England: ESRC.

Zawdie, G. (2010). Knowledge exchange and the third mission of universities: Introduction: The triple helix and the third mission—Schumpeter revisited. *Industry and Higher Education, 24*(3), 151–155.

Chapter 8
The Learner and Digital Networks

Networked learning naturally focuses on learning, but learning is not thought of as an abstract phenomenon it involves real people and organisations. In this chapter the focus is on the learner but I want the focus to be on real embodied students when I use this term rather than broad generalisations. The learner is not something generic, the learner is always a substantial person, embodied and embedded in an assemblage of social and material relations. The early descriptions of the learner and students in networked learning assumed a person connected to others via a fixed computing device (Harasim et al. 1995). Computer networks had allowed communication since the 1960s and email became available in the 1970s but even into the 1990s communication was still largely by way of typed written texts. Contrast that early setting with the situation in the contemporary period. Students and learners generally frequently have access to networked communication in most locations and at all times via a smartphone. The extent of these networks exceeds that of fixed line networks and mobile networks can be found in rural areas in developing economies as well as in the cities and centres of the advanced industrial countries. Wireless networks and telecommunication via mobile cellular phone networks exceed anything envisaged only 20 years ago. In the conclusion of Harasim et al. (1995), p. 280 there is an epilogue set in 2015 described as an 'Email from the Future'. The email envisages a future still dominated by fixed networks of limited capacity in which network access still has to be requested rather than a world in which there is easy access to a variety of networks. The main concerns of the 'Email from the Future' remained focused on the ways that the increasingly 'virtual' world would undermine those institutions based on place and unmediated face-to-face relationships. Some of these concerns remain future-oriented and they are still rehearsed in relation to new developments such as MOOCs (Daniel 2012), however the reality of 2015 is less about the virtual and a binary contrast with the real and more about the pervasive effects that the exposure of young people to networks and digital technologies is likely to have (Thomas 2011). This chapter begins from this changed technological environment for the learner and the ways in which the relationship between the

© Springer International Publishing Switzerland 2015
C. Jones, *Networked Learning*, Research in Networked Learning,
DOI 10.1007/978-3-319-01934-5_8

learner, young people and technologies has been theorised. It concludes by locating the learner in the discourse around the student experience.

In the context of networked learning the learner is always considered in relation to the development of digital and networked technologies, however the chapter also discusses the learner relative to the broader idea of the student or learner experience. The student experience is currently affected by the global financial crisis and the consequent austerity policies adopted by many governments. This age of austerity has had, and continues to have, profound consequences for academic life and the position and experience of students in educational systems, especially in the developed economies. Because of this shift the chapter examines the idea of the learner experience in relation to networked and digital technologies and it locates this historic account in the contemporary context of austerity.

Early Work on Students and Technology

At the beginning of the millennium, two research studies were conducted in the United Kingdom which shed some light on the conditions for student learning at the time when digital and network technologies were becoming embedded in universities. Crook conducted research focused on what was then a novel group of students which he described as 'partially virtualised' learners located in a traditional residential campus (Crook 2002). At about the same time the networked learning in higher education project was also reporting its findings (Goodyear, et al. 2005; Jones and Bloxham 2001; Jones and Asensio 2001). In that period there was relatively little research that examined undergraduate use and experiences of networked and digital technologies in contexts in which networked technologies were supported by face-to-face contact. The assumption was still common that learning would either be face-to-face or virtual rather than an integration of the two forms of learning. The extensive networking of student residences and campuses was relatively new and much of the rhetoric focused on the virtual campus, and the potential threat that such developments posed to place-based and campus-located education.

Crook reported that the use of computer-based collaboration was modest and the joint activity that took place between students was in their study bedrooms or located around routine social interactions, such as over a meal. He found that the majority of students discussed their work in and around time-tabled sessions such as walking between classes and lectures or in chance encounters. Formal meetings with staff and other students were rare and the formal use of discussion boards, text conferencing and email for debate was limited. The heaviest use of networked technology was of ICQ (an Instant Messenger) to exchange short messages, though Crook suggested that 'the use of this tool was largely limited to playful purposes' (2002, p. 302). Crook noted that the focus on the networked computer, and the graphical interface on a screen, which provided a single site for work and social interaction, might lead to greater distraction and that intensive use of a networked computer would not always be focused on the curriculum.

The networked learning in higher education project found that there were no strong links between students' judgments about their experience of networked learning and either their conceptions of learning or their approach to study. A practical implication of this research was that they argued that it was reasonable to expect *all* students to have positive experiences on well-designed and well-managed networked learning courses, and positive experiences were not likely to be restricted to those students with more sophisticated conceptions of learning or deep approaches to study (Goodyear et al. 2003). A key finding was that students' views were generally positive at the start and remained so at the end of each course, though their attitudes became more moderated over time. The structure of students' reported feelings remained relatively stable and there was no evidence to suggest that male or younger students had more positive thoughts about networked learning. The thoroughness with which new technologies were integrated into a networked learning course appeared to be a significant factor in explaining differences in students' opinions and a well-integrated course was associated with more positive experiences (Goodyear, et al. 2005). Both studies provided no evidence in England of a generational divide. The most prominent factor affecting the attitudes and experiences of students was the course context, and the degree to which networked learning was embedded in the course. Crook found little evidence that the practices of lecturers were strengthening a participatory approach. He argued that the question as to whether networks were to become a conduit for delivery, or an arena for participation, depended on a deeper pedagogic discussion amongst university management (Crook 2002).

These projects completed over 10 years ago reported on a population of students that would have been born in the early 1980s at the beginning of the age group that are now frequently described as the net generation or digital natives. Broadband network connections were still a novelty and ADSL, broadband connections using copper wire subscriber lines, was only launched commercially in 2000. When Crook reported the provision of wired broadband in student study bedrooms was still unusual and almost certainly unavailable, beyond some workplaces, for distance learners (see also Jones and Healing 2010b). Mobile phones were relatively new and while Vodafone took the first mobile call in 1985 the GSM 2G phone system, enabling SMS text messaging, was only introduced in the 1990s. Mobile broadband internet connections were only introduced with the 3G networks which were deployed after the millennium. This raises a significant question for generational arguments because it is unclear why if young people are affected by their exposure to new technologies students growing up at the start of this period (around 1980) would be similar to those born later (from the mid-1990s) and exposed to mobile technologies.

Even the most mobile students taking advantage of contemporary mobile communications and broadband networks are still located somewhere. Nardi and O'Day (1999) proposed the idea of 'local habitation' to describe settings in which individuals have: 'an active role, a unique and valuable local perspective, and a say in what happens' (Nardi and O'Day 1999, p. ix). It is in these micro settings that local knowledge and authority allow people to act and to develop different meanings for technologies and services appropriate for divergent local conditions. The way local participants co-construct the identity of technologies resonates with the idea of levels and the way different levels afford different kinds of choices. The capacity to influence the way technologies are appropriated is at its greatest at a microlevel and still quite extensive in the mesolevel, but it becomes very limited when considered in relation to macrolevel factors. Jones and Healing (2010b; Healing and Jones 2011) returned to the work by Crook (2002) and his notion of a 'learning nest' and used more current data to explore how students' use of technologies had altered in subsequent years in relation to the spaces they used. What these two studies showed was that in some ways little had changed with regard to students' locations and uses of space in the decade since Crook's original work. Care should be taken at this point because of the continued speed of change in the years following this research. In the research conducted between 2008 and 2010 there was only limited evidence of change, which may have become more widespread in the following years, specifically because of the increasing use of smartphones in teaching spaces and in the use of broadband mobile phone data connections.

The Net Generation and Digital Natives

Networked learning needs to take account of a persistent argument which suggests that the introduction of digital and networked technologies has changed the lives and attitudes of young people in a fundamental way. This argument emerged from the writings of several US-based authors at the end of the last century at roughly the same time as the empirical studies noted in the section above (Tapscott 1997; Prensky 2001a, b; Howe and Strauss 2000). Tapscott introduced and later developed the term net generation (1997, Prensky 2001a, b), the idea of digital natives, and the term millennials was popularised in the work of Howe and Strauss (2000). All three terms have a slightly different emphasis and a variety of additional terms are constantly being coined to capture new technologies (e.g. i-Generation, Rosen 2010) and slightly different orientations towards similar questions (e.g. Google Generation, Rowlands et al. 2008). One of the most persistent alternatives, more commonly found outside education, is Generation Y (Jorgensen 2003; Weiler 2005), which like the term millennials, is firmly located in a generational sequence with the Y generation following Generation X and preceding the Z generation. The generational argument underpins a large part of this literature and its origins can be traced back to earlier work by Howe and Strauss (1991). This chapter largely restricts itself to using the terms net generation and digital natives to refer to this wider literature, although at various points other terms may be introduced for clarity (for a more detailed review of terms see Jones 2013).

The claims made about a new generation of young people are based on the argument that because young people are growing up immersed in a world that is permeated with networked and digital technologies the entire generation thinks differently, learns differently, exhibits different social characteristics and has different expectations for learning. Prensky has gone further than most by claiming that the brains of young people growing up in these conditions are 'physically different' (Prensky 2001, 2011) and students exposed to digital technologies develop different brain structures. Prensky's account relies on largely non-human studies of animals and a limited number of studies focused on brain changes in humans (2001b). Prensky's argument about the plasticity of the brain is not dealt with in detail in this chapter but for a review of the relevant literature in the field of neuroscience see Bavelier et al. (2010). The new generation of students is portrayed as having a common set of preferences including: wanting to receive information quickly; relying on communication technologies; often multitasking and having a low tolerance for lectures; and preferring active approaches to learning (see for example Tapscott 1999; Oblinger 2003; Oblinger and Oblinger 2005). A characteristic of these approaches is that they suggest a sharp break from previous cohorts of students and Prensky (2001a) argues that there is a 'singularity' separating digital native students from their digital immigrant teachers. This binary way of thinking suggesting that young people are a single identifiable group that is distinct from other older people is a characteristic of all these approaches. It is this central idea that flows through this chapter and links the separate parts. Networked learning is interested in the 'irreducible difference' (Knox 2014) between students not the flattening of diversity and theories that assume a uniform student mass.

It is claimed that digital natives alter the conditions of teaching and learning because 'today's students *think and process information fundamentally differently* from their predecessors.' (Prensky 2001, p. 1 emphasis as in original).

> Digital Natives are used to receiving information really fast. They like to parallel process and multi-task. They prefer their graphics before their text rather than the opposite. They prefer random access (like hypertext). They function best when networked. They thrive on instant gratification and frequent rewards. They prefer games to 'serious' work. (Prensky 2001, p. 2)

A notable feature of this account is the way it describes students in a generic way as 'They' and sets out their supposed characteristics with a degree of certainty. The argument that students' ways of thinking have changed can be found much more widely than Prensky's writing and Dede (2005), for example, claimed that technology was reshaping the mind-set of students of all ages and creating a 'neomillennial' learning style. The net generation and digital native arguments are based on a common set of assumed characteristics which suggest that students of a certain age have a known set of needs which require a change from being 'teacher-centred' to becoming 'learner-centred'. This argument mirrors the assertions identified in the previous chapter making a case for a move 'from the sage on the stage to the guide on the side' (Tapscott 1999). These prescriptions for methods of teaching and learning are not novel and they first emerged following the application of the first wave of Internet technologies to education (see for example Harasim 1990; Harasim et al 1995; Hiltz and Turoff 1978). What was new in the net generation and digital native discourse is the central position of the new generation of students as the agents of change in education.

Tapscott argued that the role of the teacher had to change in response to pressures arising from net generation students and they required the teacher to be a facilitator, creating and structuring what happens in the classroom (Tapscott 1999, p. 10).

The learning preferences of these students were set out in his work as if they were already known and common to all young students. They included bite size learning, the use of new media and high levels of social interaction including collaboration. It was because of these assumed changes among students that teachers were told that they had to modify their teaching practices to accommodate the learning needs of their technologically sophisticated students. It is remarkable that these pressures were not identified by the empirical studies of students reported above which took place at roughly the same time. The generational nature of the argument about students' preference and learning 'style' leads directly to a deficit model of professional development for teachers (Bennett et al 2008). Teachers because they are older and grew up prior to the deployment of ubiquitous digital and networked technologies are described as strangers to the new world, in Prensky's terms they are digital immigrants. Prensky argues that teachers have to try and imitate their digital native students, but however hard they try they will always retain a digital immigrant 'accent'. Other writers are less rigid, for example Tapscott argues that teachers can learn new skills, but notably this is under the guidance of their students.

> Needless to say, a whole generation of teachers needs to learn new tools, new approaches, new skills. This will be a challenge... But as we make this inevitable transition, we may best turn to the generation raised on and immersed in new technologies. Give the students the tools and they will be the single most important source of guidance on how to make their schools relevant and effective places to learn. (Tapscott 1999, p. 11)

From this point of view digital native students just grow up that way and their digital immigrant teachers have relatively fixed characteristics that are already established. The digital native and net generation arguments are a form of standardisation which relies on an excessive and overgeneralised description of the positions and characteristics of both the student and the teacher. This argument introduces a rigidity that leads to an unusual version of the deficit model because teachers are required to change, to learn new skills and approaches, even though they can never be fully successful in this endeavour. There is also an inversion of the teacher–student relationship because it is the digital native students who teach their teachers and become their source of guidance.

Despite the rhetoric of transformation and inevitability the idea that a new generation of students would force change has been slow to have an effect:

> It is inevitable ... that change would finally come to our young peoples' education as well, and it has. But there is a huge paradox for educators: the place where the biggest educational changes have come is not our schools; it is everywhere else but our schools. (Prensky 2010, p. 1)

Slow change despite revolutionary rhetoric is not the only weakness identified by the originators of these ideas and Prensky (2009, 2011) has also recognised that the original distinction he drew between digital natives and digital immigrants might have become less relevant because, since he wrote the original articles, an increasing proportion of society has grown up exposed to digital and networked technology. To accommodate these changes he proposed an alternative way to describe the transformation using the term 'digital wisdom'.

> Although many have found the terms useful, as we move further into the 21st century when all will have grown up in the era of digital technology, the distinction between digital natives and digital immigrants will become less relevant… I suggest we think in terms of digital wisdom. (Prensky 2009, p. 1)

Prensky defined wisdom as '…the ability to find practical, creative, contextually appropriate, and emotionally satisfying solutions to complicated human problems.' (Prensky 2011, p. 20). He uses this definition of wisdom to argue that it is possible to acquire digital wisdom through interaction with technology. This is a significant change which abandons the generational rigidity of the terms natives and immigrants. However Prensky still retains the radical and largely unsupported claim that the 'brains of those who interact with technology frequently will be restructured by that interaction' (2011, p. 18). Prensky has softened his previous position, which he had described in terms of a 'singularity' but he retains many of the key features of his original argument. Overall Prensky's position has moved from a hard form of technological determinism, in which the divide between natives and immigrants is a necessary outcome of their exposure to technology, to a softer form of determinism in which digital enhancement is a necessary development for everyone if they are to succeed.

Palfrey and Gasser (2008) mounted a sustained attempt to reclaim the term digital native as a useful academic term. They suggested that the term generation was an overstatement and preferred to call the new cohort of young people a 'population' (2008, p. 14). They have developed this argument further in a more recent publication (Palfrey and Gasser 2011). Digital natives thought of as a population rather than a generation are defined by their access to technology. The digital native is no longer defined by the deployment of technology in society in general, and the condition of being a digital native comes to depend on a variety of factors such as social class (socioeconomic status) and geographical location and access to new technology also depends on a digital literacy, which needs to be acquired through informal or formal learning. Palfrey and Gasser have moved away from the original argument in which a generation of young people are born digital because they grew up in a world infused with new technology. Their reformulation identifies digital natives as a sub-group of young people whose attributes depend on their access to technology. This attempt to reclaim the term has significant weaknesses and it is not clear what benefits are gained by retaining it. The authors agree that the idea of a generational change needs to be abandoned, but in my opinion the continued use of the term digital native in these circumstances becomes misleading.

An alternative binary metaphor has been proposed as a replacement to the terms natives and immigrants by White and Le Cornu (2011) who have recommended substituting them with 'residents' and 'visitors'. The authors contend that the original arguments made by Prensky pre-date social media and they suggest that this shift in the technologies that are available requires a new metaphor. Their proposed replacement for the generational divide between natives and immigrants follows Palfrey and Gasser by introducing an experiential divide between 'residents' and 'visitors' and like Palfrey and Gasser this is an attempt to salvage some elements from the digital native and net generation debates while acknowledging the strength of some of the opposing evidence and arguments. White and Le Cornu wanted to recognise the usefulness of typologies and retain this potential strength and to acknowledge the importance of the debate and the simple framework that Prensky offered.

> We therefore argue that tools, places and spaces are the three key metaphors that most aptly describe the experience of computer users in a world where social media are becoming more and more prevalent. (White and Le Cornu 2011 Online)

Residents are described as those people who spend a (large) proportion of their lives online and for whom online spaces are 'like a park or a building in which there are clusters of friends and colleagues'. Visitors by contrast are those who use technology as a tool to address their specific needs and inhabit a space 'akin to an untidy garden tool shed'. The spatial metaphor is an improvement on the original but still retains its highly restrictive binary form. It is also unclear to me why the typology used to describe young people and their use of technology still has to adopt this binary. The empirical evidence would suggest that life is far more complex than any binary account would allow for and the oversimplification that simple typologies and binary distinctions lead to result in bad policy decisions and poor practice.

The persistence of the net generation and digital native discourse is a concern for those interested in networked learning because some of the prescriptions for change are familiar to those engaged in networked learning. However the arguments used by proponents of networked learning to support such changes are of a very different type. Networked learning is interested in cooperation and collaboration as a form of dialogue between teachers and learners because it is an effective and desirable pedagogic approach that develops critical thinking (McConnell et al. 2012). The educational reforms proposed by Tapscott and Prensky have very different roots despite the similarity in some if the vocabulary.

A Generational Divide?

A central claim of the digital native and net generation arguments is that there is a generational divide, a sharp break between young people born into a digital world and those older people who were not. Howe and Strauss wrote the book Millennials Rising (2000) several years after they co-authored a book that argued a general case about generations in the United States (Howe and Strauss 1991). Although it would be unreasonable to argue that those who use the term net generation or digital native endorse the cyclical view of generations found in Howe and Strauss it has had a clear influence both directly through Howe and Strauss' later work and through Oblinger and Oblinger who built on Howe and Strauss' work when discussing education (Oblinger and Oblinger 2005). The generational argument can be read as a general case affecting all young people of a certain age, or it can be seen as generalising the experience of the advanced industrial countries and the United States in particular. In other countries different characteristics have been used to define age groups and generations. In China the single child policy and the funnelling of resources from a whole family to one child led to the term 'Little Emperor' to describe the characteristics of the young. In South Africa the end of apartheid led to the description of the young as 'born free' and there is no reason to suggest that responses to technology in South Africa will mirror those in the United States (Brown and Czerniewicz 2008; Thinyane 2010; Brown and Czerniewicz 2010). The generational divide based on technology alone can be thought of as an extrapolation from a narrow cultural and national base.

Empirical research has also found that there are variations among students within the age group identified with the net generation, and that young people in this cohort can be clustered into different user groups with different interests, preferences and lifestyles (Bullen et al. 2011; Jones et al. 2010a; Jones and Hosein 2010; Kennedy et al. 2010; Schulmeister 2010; Van Beemt, et al. 2010b). There is good evidence, even in the rich industrial states, to show that there is no simple generational divide (Bullen et al. 2011; Kennedy et al. 2008, 2010; McNaught et al 2009; Pedró 2009; Salajan et al. 2010; Waycott et al 2009). Pedró's (2009) meta-analysis of studies from countries in the Organisation for Economic Co-operation and Development (OECD) concluded that there were differences in students' technology adoption and use and a variety of digital divides persist between different kinds of students (Pedró 2009; Schulmeister 2009; Hargittai (2010). Hargittai et al. (2010) showed that socioeconomic factors were related to the complexity and variation in people's use of the Internet and students' online skills. Other broad demographic influences affected students' interaction with technology and these included gender and ethnicity alongside social class (Hargittai 2010; Jones et al. 2010a; Smith and Caruso 2010; Kennedy et al. 2010; Selwyn 2008). Research in China has also found evidence that there are variations in information searching and levels of competence amongst the young (Li and Ranieri 2010; Li and Kirkup 2007). Access to technology is still unevenly spread and access relies on young people having the necessary digital literacies rather than simply the availability of new technology (Schulmeister 2010; Palfrey and Gasser 2008). Jones and Shao (2011) concluded their review of international literature by stating that there was no empirical evidence for a new generation of young students entering higher education and the terms net generation and digital native did not capture the processes of change that were taking place.

There are two implications that can be drawn from this. The first is that the alleged divide between native students and immigrant academic staff has been overdrawn. The second is that the use of a generational metaphor and an exaggerated claim for a 'singularity' separating one age defined generation from another obscures the actual age-related changes that are taking place. Jones and Shao (2011) argue that the complex changes identified in extensive empirical work show an age-related component, particularly with regard to newer technologies such as social networking site use (e.g. Facebook), the uploading and manipulation of multimedia (e.g. YouTube) and the use of handheld devices to access the mobile Internet. The relationship to age is itself complex because it is affected by how recently a particular technology has been introduced. Secondly it is influenced by the dynamics of particular age cohorts, for example by the stage of life they are currently passing through. An example of this would be first-year university students at residential universities that take them away from home. Such students show a pattern of social network use that includes contact with home while they are at university and contact with university friends when they return home. Such a pattern is related to the transition from home to university and while it is enabled by the technology of social networks it is not caused by their availability.

A further complicating factor undermining the idea of a generation of digital natives is that demographic factors interact with age to pattern students' responses to new technologies and that the most important of these are gender, socioeconomic background, academic preference (major) and year of study (grade), mode of study (distance or place-based) and the international or home-based status of the student (Brown and Czerniewicz 2008; Caruso and Kvavik 2005; Dahlstrom and Bichsel 2014; Dahlstrom et al. 2013; Gros et al. 2012; Hosein et al. 2010a; Jones et al. 2010a; Kvavik 2005; Krause 2007; McNaught et al. 2009; Selwyn 2008; Smith et al. 2009; Smith and Caruso 2010; Van den Beemt, et al. 2010a). Jones and Shao (2011) concluded their review by stating that there was no evidence that a generation of students was entering university with demands for new technologies that the universities and their teachers could not meet (see also Salajan et al 2010; Waycott et al 2009).

Relationships Between Technology Use in Society and in Education

While there has been considerable growth in students' access to computing technologies and online tools the take-up of these technologies has often been for social and entertainment purposes rather than for learning (Oliver and Goerke 2007; Selwyn 2009). Furthermore students' use of technology for social and leisure purposes has been shown to be different to their use of technologies for academic purposes (Corrin et al 2010; Jones et al. 2010a; Jones and Ramanau 2009; Hosein et al. 2010b). A key distinction needs to be attended to when discussing students' uses of technology and that is that educational use and use more generally for learning has its own characteristics and simply because technologies are used by young people it does not mean that the familiarity with new technology in one area will transition seamlessly into learning and education. The distinction between social uses and educational uses of technology should not be thought of as a separation in relation to the student's live experience. Jones and Healing (2010b) report that students often have multiple applications open at one time, some of them for academic work and some for leisure. Jones and Healing described the ways students managed the distraction that occurred in these circumstances, often involving issues of time management. Gourlay (2014) also noted that students' academic use of the technologies is intertwined with leisure uses and she related this with time issues, the complex relationships between networked devices, digital materials and practices, and the broader questions of course requirements and the curriculum.

Because young people use new technologies and have relatively high general levels of skill using them it should not be assumed that this level of use and skill translates into *preferences* for an increased use of technology in educational contexts. In contrast to net generation and digital native theories researchers report that a large number of students still hold conventional attitudes towards teaching (Kennedy et al. 2007; Gabriel and Wiebe 2009; Garcia and Qin 2007; Lohnes and Kinzer 2007; Margaryan et al. 2011). There is also a consistent and long-standing finding that students prefer a moderate use of technology in the classroom, although care needs to be taken with this finding because the idea of moderate in 2004 may not correspond with current views about what constitutes moderate use (Jones 2012; Kennedy et al. 2007; Kvavik 2005; Salaway and Caruso 2007; Smith and Caruso 2010). More recently it has been claimed that technology has become 'omnipresent in the lives of students' Dahlstrom and Bichsel 2014, p. 34). In relation to the changing technological context early work showed little evidence that students were significant users of either Web 2.0 or the more recent or most advanced technologies (Kennedy et al 2007). There is some evidence that some uses of new technologies in education can be contrary to student wishes (Jones, Blackey et al. 2010). Selwyn (2009) reviewed literature with a particular focus on information sciences, education and media/communication studies and he concluded that young people's engagements with digital technologies were varied and often unspectacular. He also highlighted the misplaced determinism and concluded that while there is a need to keep in mind the changing lifeworlds of young people it would be helpful to steer clear of the excesses of the digital native debate.

Students have a pragmatic and instrumental way of using technologies and they only use those technologies that are useful to them for communication and information searching (Schulmeister 2010). Nagler and Ebner (2009) found that use varied between common services and Wikipedia, YouTube and social networking sites were commonly used while social bookmarking, photo sharing and microblogging were much less popular at that time. Schulmeister (2009) argued that many of the claims about the effects of technology on cognitive development were overstated or unsupported and noted that studies did not always distinguish between the types, contents or functions of media activities or include anything about the motives of the users. However evidence that students do not exhibit a natural take-up of some technologies does not mean students will not make use of similar technologies if they are requirements for their studies (Dahlstrom and Bichsel 2014; Jones, Ramanau, Cross, and Healing 2010a; Smith and Caruso 2010; Kennedy et al. 2007). Taken together this evidence shows significant changes in the technologies that are available and in their use by learners, but the diversity of that use and the active appropriation of technologies informed by a variety of factors contrasts with net generation and digital native rhetoric which claims that a uniform generation of students become advanced users of new technology and force educational change. There is no real evidence of a significant break between young people and the rest of society and educationalists should approach net generation and digital native literature with extreme caution.

Design and Alternative Accounts of Technology

The net generation and digital native arguments are flawed but they have a remarkable persistence. One of the reasons for this persistence is the simplicity of the argument and the way that the prescriptions translate directly to clear answers and locate with key policy agendas, which suggest that actions must be taken and there is one best way to deal with the changes that are taking place amongst students. A further reason for the persistence of these arguments is that commercial interests have been active in perpetuating the idea of a new net generation (Bayne and Ross 2011). A clear danger that flows from this persistent influence is that universities follow the flawed advice and reasoning found in these discourses and frame their actions according to their simplistic agendas. The arguments of this book have been that learning is part of a complex sociotechnical assemblage in which institutions and infrastructures are key actors. This section examines a small number of key issues and theoretical approaches to the questions raised by the changing engagements of young students with new technologies. The intention is to provide alternative approaches to student engagements with technology which can help readers understand the processes of change that are taking place without resorting to the generational and determinist accounts found in the net generation and digital native literature.

Stoerger (2009) proposed one of the more useful alternative metaphors, 'the Digital Melting Pot' with an aim to redirect attention away from 'assigned' generational characteristics to the diverse technological capabilities young people have and to focus on the digital skills they might gain through experience. The Melting Pot metaphor emphasised integration rather than the segregation of digital natives and digital immigrants into distinct populations. Stoerger (2009) went on to argue that by gaining technology experience, those with low levels of competency could be transformed. One of the key findings of the early networked learning in higher education studies had been the moderating effect of exposure to networked technologies in education. Students with little expertise or prior knowledge of new technologies would become more positive, increase their capacity and express more confidence while those who were most enthusiastic about the technology would moderate their opinions (Goodyear et al 2003). Educational experience can play a significant role in developing both capacity and a positive attitude towards new technologies by providing guidance concerning the acquisition and enhancement of technological skills.

> Educators, as well as their corresponding institutions, could be major players in the digital melting pot assimilation process. Together they could provide all individuals the chance to acquire, refine, and update technology skills. The digital native–digital immigrant metaphor serves to place individuals into separate silos based on over–generalized and oftentimes inaccurate characteristics. (Stoerger 2009 Online).

The approach Stoerger takes is an advance on the original argument by Prensky and it takes into account Prensky's revision in terms of the idea of digital wisdom. Stoerger rejects the revision because even those new to technologies who show digital wisdom remain segregated from those who are native to digital settings.

Stoerger also made an important point about the way the technological environments experienced by digital natives were designed and developed by previous generations.

> Someone had to design, build, and upgrade the technologies that have evolved into the electronic spaces that the natives now inhabit. Interestingly, very few educational technology advocates mention that the digital immigrants were the creators of these devices and environments. (Stoerger 2009 Online).

Stoerger position is a clear advance on Prensky because digital technologies are shown to be an outcome of social change and to embody in their design and evolution all age groups and prior social conditions.

Affordance, Agency and Causation

There are potentially two different arguments about the changes that are taking place amongst young people and their relationship to networked and digital technologies (Jones 2011). The first argument and the one, that is most associated with the idea of the Net Generation and Digital Natives, is that:

1. The ubiquitous nature of digital and networked technologies *has affected the outlook of an entire generation* in advanced economies.

   A second related but distinct argument is that:

2. The new digital and networked technologies emerging in the lifetime of young people have particular characteristics that *afford certain types of social engagement.*

My argument is that it is the first of these arguments that we need to abandon in the face of the empirical evidence. First we need to abandon the idea that the changes are generational in character and second we need to abandon the determinist argument that technologies, in and of themselves, cause definite effects in the young. The argument based on affordance tries to retain the rational kernel of an argument about changes in young people related to their exposure and experience of new technologies. It draws attention to the *affordances* of technology as discussed in Chap. 2. One good reason why the net generation and digital native arguments persist is because they draw attention to the ways new technologies are changing the approaches that young people take in ways that are significant and often related to age. The kinds of change that are taking place require careful observation and assessment because technologies do not have effects that can be read off from the features or characteristics of the devices and technologies themselves. Students actively appropriate available technologies and they do so in ways that are related to their understandings of their position as a student and in the world, and their choices are related to the opportunities and constraints that educational institutions and infrastructures place on them. To borrow an idea from Marx—students make their own technological conditions but they do so in circumstances that are not of their own making.

Students' relationships to networked and digital technologies can be understood in terms of agency (Czerniewicz et al. 2009; Jones and Healing 2010a). Czerniewicz et al (2009), p. 86 showed how 'students are influenced by, but not determined by, the barriers they face'. Their research showed how in some circumstances students can make exceptional efforts to overcome their disadvantages with regard to technology. Students' roles in relation to their use of technology can be enforced by sanctions operating at an organisational level which are physical, economic and moral. In my research students provided accounts about the ways that their judgement about the reliability of sources for academic work rested on what they were told by academic staff and what was enforced by assessment regimes and sanctions which enacted a view of what was and was not acceptable academic practice (Jones and Healing 2010a). Czerniewicz et al. (2009) described the relationship with technology as part of a process involving an interplay between social situations and the personal projects of agents. My own view is that it is better understood from a less individualised standpoint, as part of an emergent activity system within which subjects try to achieve their objectives and goals, but in which the activity system cannot be reduced to individuals, their social situation and goal directed actions. The structural conditions that students interact with are to a significant degree the outcomes of the kinds of collective agencies that we have described in Chaps. 5 and 6 using the concepts institution and infrastructure. The implications of this are that I argue for an expansion of the notion of agency to include persons acting not on their own behalf, but enacting roles in collective bodies such as courses, departments, schools and universities. Academic work undertaken by students takes place using available technologies and the availability of these technologies and infrastructures is an outcome of decisions and actions taken elsewhere, either in the wider world or in the university. I argue that aspects of structure and agency are at play at all levels of scale (macro-meso-micro) and that agency needs to be thought of as an emergent property. When considering student academic work the inclusion and exploration of mesolevels are especially important if we are to fully understand the ways students engage with new technologies at university.

Spaces and Places

The importance of location has been understood since the earliest writing about networked learning because learning networks allowed groups of people to use computer-mediated communication 'to learn together, at the time, place, and pace that best suits them and is appropriate to the task.' (Harasim et al. 1995, p. 4). The increasing availability and use of digital and networked technologies since that time has led to an increasing variety of spaces in which students can learn and to a pressure on universities to increase the flexibility of their provision, in terms of both the digital infrastructure and the physical estate of the institution (Ellis and Goodyear 2010). From the early provision of cable-connected computer laboratories and library provision of computers, universities have moved to the establishment of extensive wireless networks, remote access via broadband connections to the Web and more recently making provision for students to bring their own devices (BYOD). In his original conception of indirect design (Goodyear 2001, 2005, see Chap. 3 this volume) space and place were two factors considered in relation to learning, alongside task and activity, and organisation and community. Goodyear argued spaces could be designed but it was the activity of people (students and teachers) in those spaces that enacted the places in which learning took place. I have previously argued for a distinction to be made:

> between space, which is understood as a relatively stable and potentially designed environment, and place, understood as contingent and locally inhabited... fostering a sense of place in networked learning environments is necessary in order to develop a social and emotional context to sustain social interactions and collaboration, whether these interactions are composed of either strong or weak ties. (Jones and Dirckinck-Holmfeld 2009, p. 22)

As the spaces in which learning takes place increase so does the design complexity due to the variety of ways that students can actively appropriate the possibilities and circumvent the constraints that the designed spaces afford them. Carvalho and Goodyear (2014) have analysed the key components of learning networks and illustrated the ways that learning networks have allowed learning to move out into networks and areas of everyday life including both leisure activities and work.

The mobilities paradigm has questioned traditional approaches to society and examined mobility in ways that are important in terms of an understanding of geographical location, space and place (Urry 2007. In particular mobilities research points to the 'fixtures' that allow movement, and the firm, material and located infrastructures that underpin the apparent ease of movement. Think for example of the airports that allow mobility by air and the motorway networks that enable automobility. In educational contexts the mobility of students via digital networks also needs to be located in the infrastructural and material locations through which mobility takes place. On the one hand students have increasing access to various devices, smartphones, tablet computers, e-book readers and a number of hybrid devices that are WiFi enabled and often linked via mobile broadband to the Internet. On the other their use of these devices often hinges on university infrastructures that have already integrated wired communications, and a variety of Internet-based services, but which now face a new range of challenges as staff and students access university networks using their own devices and universal service infrastructures impinge on the institutional setting. The emergent ecology of mobile devices in higher education that results from these changes is complex and poorly understood, even though there has been considerable effort to theorise mobile or m-learning (Kukulska-Hulme and Traxler 2013; Pachler et al. 2010; Sharples et al. 2007; Sharples et al 2009; Roschelle 2003).

Jones and Healing (2010b) found that the common locations for students were still their dedicated work spaces in their term time homes. These were usually either within the student's permanent residence or in a student study bedroom. In some cases these spaces were dedicated to study but in others the spaces were multifunctional, with a study area set aside from the other activities that took place in the larger area. The university library, multimedia centres, lecture theatres and computer labs all remained common spaces in which students did their academic work. Students were well connected and most were connected to their networks all the time, often sleeping next to their phone in order to keep in touch with other students and friends from home. One university involved in the research had equipped an area that was open 24 h a day 7 days a week with access to wireless networking, loan laptop computers and a comfortable and informal working area. This change in the physical campus infrastructure had begun to alter some students' use of mobile technologies on campus. In the period 2008–2010 students already seemed permanently connected to their networks and there was a blurring of activities from their student working life and their social life and leisure.

> The settings that students reported are local habitations in the sense that students have a degree of control in make use of available resources by negotiating the meaning and relevance of a technology within their own life space and the flow of their lives. They are active agents because each student has their own study practices, subject area and network of relationships and they don't act uniformly in relation to the technologies and services they are presented with. (Jones and Healing 2010b, p. 382)

I am convinced that the increasing mobile technologies and the drive to increase the mobility of learning requires a continued strong focus on location, on the spaces that are provided in which learning can take place. This will require a degree of methodological innovation to track and trace learning activity in a wide variety of locations. One possible way of accomplishing this is to adopt the ANT approach and 'follow the actor' via the traces they leave in digital networks and by developing innovative ways for actors to record their own activity. It is also important to recognise that calls for a complete overthrow of traditional forms of place-based learning in the face of 'disruptive' technologies ignore the ways that disruption at one point of time is only one part of a continuing sequence. Campus universities and city-based locations may become reinvigorated as nodes in the wider network which are valued because there are substantial intrinsic attractions to them, even as they are interpenetrated with networked and digital technologies.

Learners at the Interface

The learner is located in physical space but they also stretch outward across digital networks which are re-presented to them at the interface. This process preceded the development of mobile technologies but it is amplified by it.

> In this society, work and leisure activities not only increasingly involve computer use, but they converge around the same interfaces. Both work applications (word processors, spreadsheet programs, database programs) and 'leisure' applications (computer games, informational DVD) use the same tools and metaphors of GUI. The best example of this is a Web browser employee both in the office and at home, both for work and play. (Manovich 2001, p. 65)

Much of the locus of learner interaction is now at the interface and their interaction is often with services supplied via the network. The interface and the device are acting as portals to a network of resources, service and people that reside 'elsewhere'. As Manovich puts it 'we are no longer interfacing with a computer but to culture encoded in digital form' (Manovich 2001 pp. 69–70). Galloway expands on this understanding of the interface in a way that resonates with ANT in the way that it sees 'effects':

> Interfaces are not simply objects or boundary points. They are autonomous zones of activity. Interfaces are not things but rather processes that effect a result of whatever kind. (Galloway 2012 vii)

This interpretation of the interface means that less attention is placed on objects such as screens and keyboards and more on the effects of interfaces both in terms of the way that interfaces change material states and in the way that they are themselves the effects of larger forces that generate them.

The learner appropriates the networked services and the technological devices that are available to them in active way and it has been repeatedly noted that this active interaction with technologies separates out uses for social life and leisure and educational use (Corrin et al. 2010; Kennedy and Judd 2011; Bennett and Maton 2011). Kennedy and Judd (2011) argue that students use of information seeking and communication technologies is driven by a shallow 'satisficing' strategy and that while they use such technologies routinely they are challenged by scholarly uses. The term satisficing is used to suggest a strategy that provides satisfactory results but the results do not have to be the best available. Kennedy and Judd also draw attention to the way 'satisficing' can be linked to the idea of deep and surface learning. Students do not develop sophisticated approaches to information seeking or learning in their interactions with technology 'in the wild', academic and scholarly uses are learned and require educational processes, if not always formal education. The research on students' relationships with digital and networked technologies illustrates a contradictory process in which students are working with technologies relevant to their social life and leisure via the same interfaces that they use for academic and scholarly work. However students actively manage this common interface and discriminate between uses that are for academic purposes and those that are not. The evidence suggests that students do not naturally adopt the most useful approaches to technologies appropriate for academic work, such as information seeking, but that they will take-up new technologies and engage with them if there are good pedagogical reasons to do so. The interface is a critical site as important as the spaces and places for learning because it is at the interface that students navigate their networks and there is a need for researchers to understand the increasingly complex interactions between the embodied location of students and the interfaces that they use to:

a) bring the network connections and resources to them and
b) extend their learning network outwards into the world.

Student Experience and Design

Networked learning has emphasised the way that design attention has moved from direct design of learning to indirect design (Carvalho and Goodyear 2014) and focused on those points indirectly related to learning (often at the mesolevel) where choices can be made between the variety of tools, services and resources because both digital and material forms become available as alternatives (Goodyear 2005). In previous chapters in this volume I have noted how networked learning takes place in learning infrastructures (Chap. 6), which are assemblages of humans, digital and material forms (Chap. 4). I have previously argued that this leads to an increasing complexity of design (Jones and Dirckinck-Holmfeld 2009; Jones and Healing 2010b). The apparently simple choices between online and (offline) face-to-face, or between distance and local, become increasingly complex as educational designs blend a variety of components in what I have described as a variable geometry and others as an ecology (Dillenbourg 2008; Ellis and Goodyear 2010). Ellis and Goodyear argue that the binary distinctions found in the contrast between digital natives and immigrants and between transmission (acquisition) and student-centred (participation) approaches to teaching and learning are not found in practice. Rather the say the reality 'is that beliefs represent a melange of the teacher-centred and the student-centred' (Ellis and Goodyear 2010, p. 187). They propose that an ecology of learning should be informed by a sense of 'good learning' which they define as:

…a set of tensely adjusted beliefs and constructs emerging from the experiences and values of students, teachers, employers, community groups, experts in pedagogy and researchers in the learning sciences. (Ellis and Goodyear 2010, p. 187)

The sense of good learning Ellis and Goodyear speak about is rooted in change and the periods of calm in which universities can share a sense of purpose are described in terms of provisional stabilities. This dynamic and complex picture is more in tune with the early twenty-first century findings about student experiences with technology than the standard simple binaries of digital natives and immigrants. By being located in design processes, and the possibility of managing the risks that come with change and uncertainty, this approach offers a better way of thinking about the relationships between students, their experiences and digital and networked technologies. Within this ecological perspective the student experience is one part of a complex and changing set of relations at all levels. At the macrolevel university leaders are dealing with large infrastructural questions. At the mesolevel the development of design-like practices in departments and educational programmes can help provide iterative adjustments and coordinate a cyclical process of improvement. Finally at the microlevel of day-to-day interaction it is good (successful and effective) learning and the experiences of students in their routine interactions that holds this ecology together and gives it purpose.

The Student/Learner Experience

The early work in networked learning reported earlier in this chapter was connected with the need to include the lived experience of students in the discussion that surrounded the incorporation of network and digital technologies in education.

One of the sources for thinking about networked learning arose from a series of EU and UK-funded projects (Goodyear 2014; McConnell et al. 2012). These projects and in particular the 2-year JISC-funded project concerning students' experiences of networked learning (1999–2000) had a key role in formalising and stabilising the developing field of networked learning in continental Europe and the United Kingdom (Carvalho and Goodyear 2014). That project had as its main aim:

> To help the UK HE sector come to a better understanding of the potential and problems of networked learning, particularly by attending to the student experience and to learning and teaching issues (Goodyear 2000, p. 3)

At this stage there was a clear link between networked learning and the student experience and that understanding was informed by a clear approach based on a relational view of learning and the phenomenographic tradition in particular (see Jones and Asensio 2001).

The phenomenographic tradition (see Chap. 3) has provided something of a bridge between academic research investigating students' experience and more recent policy initiatives. Key individuals have been involved in both academic research and the policy developments in terms of the student experience (e.g. Paul Ramsden[1] and Mike Prosser[2]). The quantitative branch of phenomenographic research had independently developed a number of instruments such as the approaches to study inventory (ASI) and later variants such as the approaches and study skills inventory for students (ASSIST) which provided a starting point for some of the work developing survey instruments with a direct link to national policy (e.g. Entwistle and Ramsden 1983). The fundamental understanding of phenomenography was that there are a limited number of qualitatively different ways to experience a phenomena and that these could be related to each other (often in a hierarchical manner) (Marton and Säljö 1976a, b; Marton 1981, 1994; Marton et al 1993; Marton and Booth 1997). Marton defined the approach as:

> …the empirical study of the differing ways in which people experience, perceive, apprehend, understand, or conceptualize various phenomena in, and aspects of, the world around them. (Marton 1994, p. 4424)

A second key aspect of this approach, which has informed research and policy concerning the student experience, has been the idea that the qualitatively different experiences of learning could be related to different learning outcomes (Prosser and Trigwell 1999). An additional step was also made which argued that some ways of teaching and of experiencing learning led to surface approaches to learning, whereas others led to a deep approach:

> The relation between teachers' experiences and their students' experiences is such that university teachers who adopt a conceptual change/ student-focused approach to teaching are more likely to teach students who adopt a deep approach to their learning, while teachers

---

[1] http://www.heacademy.ac.uk/resources/detail/consultations/paulramsden_teaching_and_student_experience

[2] http://www.heacademy.ac.uk/assets/documents/teachingandresearch/Interpretingstudentsurveys_Nov_2005.doc

who adopt an information transmission/teacher-focused approach to their teaching are more likely to teach students who adopt surface approaches to their study.' (Prosser and Trigwell 1999, p. 162)

As these methods developed, further distinctions were identified and in particular a strategic or achieving approach to learning has been widely adopted as a potential third approach to learning (Biggs 1979; Kember 1996). There has also been extensive discussion on this tradition about students from a 'Confucian' heritage, who it is claimed may appear to have a surface approach to learning, but who may be engaged in deeper processes of learning (Biggs 1998)

In recent years the idea of the student experience has become a mainstream concern with numerous funded projects and a place in policy documentation at both an institutional and governmental level. In a number of countries, national student surveys have become established[3] (see for example BIS 2011) and institutions regularly survey students at a module and course level. In some cases such as the University Experience Survey (UES) in Australia the student experience is linked to performance and funding (Radloff et al. 2012). These surveys generalise across diverse contexts and suggest that it is possible to design for a universalised 'student experience'. From a niche academic area of research, and more or less peripheral concern in the late 1990s, the student experience has moved to centre stage especially in those educational systems most influenced by the introduction of the market into higher education (PA Consulting Group 2014). The concern with students' experiences has moved from an academic interest concerned with giving voice to students, in ways that are varied and nuanced, to a market-driven and consumption-oriented snapshot of generic indicators of satisfaction.

It is in this context that students constitute their relationships with technology. Students experience technology in relation to educational requirements that are mediated by a drive towards achieving positions in international league tables which measure universities and nation states against each other (Jöns and Hoyler 2013). Jöns and Hoyler note that:

First the production of world university rankings in the early 21st century has been shaped by a new era of globalization and neoliberalization in higher education…, Second the highly uneven geographies of higher education that emerge from the analysis mark particular nodes in the global circulation of knowledge and expertise, namely those that conform best to Anglo-American publication cultures… (Jöns and Hoyler 2013, p. 56)

In the competition for league position and status, universities worldwide are drawn into the measurement of the student experience in generic and market-oriented ways. This international competition has been sharpened by the financial crisis of 2008 and the austerity politics that followed in many developed economies.

The student experience is important to a networked learning perspective but it has a very different character because it focuses on the complex empirical makeup of actual student experiences rather than generic notions of 'the' student experience

---

[3] For example in the USA see http://nsse.iub.edu/; in the UK see http://www.hefce.ac.uk/what-wedo/lt/publicinfo/nss/; in Ireland http://studentsurvey.ie/wordpress/about-the-survey/

(See Ellis and Goodyear 2010). From a networked learning perspective researchers are interested in the ways that students engage in learning, through their connections with people, enabled by a variety of media and in relation to material artefacts and the resources they use for learning. One of the ways that technology has changed the kinds of environments in which learning takes place is in the way variety has been increased in both the kinds of devices that students use and in the kinds of networks they have access to. Not only has the technological environment diversified but students engage with universities in different ways, for example on full- or part-time programmes, and with varying provision in terms of distance and online methods of teaching and learning. The idea that there is a clearly defined, singular 'student experience' is clearly nonsense, but it has powerful political and institutional support.

Students and Their Experiences of Technology

Networked learning is defined in terms of connections and while these connections are enabled by networked and digital technologies it is the activity across the network that defines both the learning and the learner. Learning is understood as an emergent process that can be designed for but learning itself cannot be designed. The learner in networked learning develops in an emergent way from interactions with other humans, mediated by language and technology and connected indirectly with earlier activity through the learning resources that others have contributed. Learning can often be mundane but it is deeply connected to civilisation and it is the root of human development, it is at the heart of the process of historical change and progress. Such a view contrasts sharply with the reduction of learning to performance in league tables and a bland and homogenised student experience.

The chapter began by locating student experience with networked technologies and discussing the pervasive and persistent idea that new technologies have led to a generational step change in student attitudes and behaviours. This way of thinking about students and the learning process using technology leads to a flattening of the learner's experience with technology to a simple formula which can be applied to all young people in all settings. Even when the digital native thesis is amended to reduce digital natives to a 'population' described as a subset of a generation the implications are still reductionist and technologically driven (Palfrey and Gasser 2011). Other binary divisions such as residents and visitors (White and Le Cornu 2011) are equally narrow and do not allow for a full expression of the full diversity found in students' and learners' engagements with technology. A key reason for the persistence of these crude binary divisions is the way that they simplify decisions for policy makers and politicians but it is possible to provide more sophisticated alternatives that recognise that technologies while there is diversity and the features of technology afford a limited variety of social engagements. Technologies have their limits and constrain learners from some kinds of connections and engagements and the phenomenographic notion of student experience is helpful here in the discussion of experiences having a limited number of variations. In a similar way technologies afford a wide but ultimately limited range of engagements with them.

This chapter concludes with an attempt to locate the way students engage with technology in relation to research in networked learning and to consider the relationships between students' experiences of technology and students' experiences of networked learning in the relation to the world beyond the academy. This chapter has argued that there are at least four areas that require greater understanding:

1. The experiences of students (not *the* student experience) including the experiences learners and students have with digital and networked technologies.
2. The affordances and constraints of specific technologies and the kinds of social and scholarly engagements that can be enabled by the features of new technologies.
3. The spaces and places in which students work, whether these are campus based, online or at a distance. The more mobile students become the more important it is to understand the kinds of locations they use for learning.
4. The interface has become the mobile threshold for network connections and resources. Wherever students are located, whatever device they are using they will be gathering and distributing their social lives and scholarly and academic work through activity at the interface.

The idea that links the consideration in this chapter of the student and learner's experience with their experiences of digital and networked technologies is that they cannot be reduced to a universalised student 'experience' nor to simplistic binaries such as digital natives and immigrants or residents and visitors. In this I think the notion of 'irreducible difference' used by Knox (2014) proves to be especially important. If networked learning has a view about students and learners and their engagements with technologies it is that they cannot be reduced to simple formulas or dichotomies and their diversity has to be acknowledged. This requires consistent empirical research to examine and analyse the lived experience of students and learners not the creation of new generational myths.

References

Bavelier, D., Green, C. S., & Dye, M. W. G. (2010). Children, wired: For better and for worse. *Neuron, 67*(5), 692–701.

Bayne, S., & Ross, J. (2011). 'Digital native' and 'digital immigrant' discourses: A critique. In R. Land & S. Bayne (Eds.), *Digital difference: Perspectives on online learning* (pp. 159–169). Rotterdam, The Netherlands: Sense.

Bennett, S., & Maton, K. (2011). Intellectual field or faith-based religion: Moving on from the idea of 'digital natives'. In M. Thomas (Ed.), *Deconstructing digital natives: Young people, technology and the new literacies* (pp. 169–185). New York: Routledge.

Bennett, S., Matton, K., & Kervin, L. (2008). The 'digital natives' debate: A critical review of the literature. *British Journal of Educational Technology, 35*(9), 775–786.

Biggs, J. B. (1979). Individual differences in study processes and the quality of learning outcomes. *Higher Education, 8*, 381–394.

Biggs, J. B. (1998). Learning from the Confucian heritage: So size doesn't matter? *International Journal of Educational Research, 29*, 723–738.

BIS (Department for Business and Skills) (2011). *Higher education: Students at the heart of the system*. Department for Business and Skills White Paper. Retrieved from https://www.gov.uk/government/uploads/system/uploads/attachment_data/file/32409/11-944-higher-education-students-at-heart-of-system.pdf

Brown, C., & Czerniewicz, L. (2008). *Trends in student use of ICTs in higher education in South Africa*. Paper presented at the 10th Annual Conference of WWW Applications, Cape Town, South Africa, 3–6 September 2008. Retrieved from http://www.cet.uct.ac.za/files/file/ResearchOutput/2008_wwwApps_UseTrends.pdf

Brown, C., & Czerniewicz, L. (2010). Debunking the 'digital native': Beyond digital apartheid, towards digital democracy. *Journal of Computer Assisted Learning, 26*(5), 357–369.

Bullen, M., Morgan, T., & Qayyum, A. (2011). Digital learners in higher education: Generation is not the issue. *Canadian Journal of Learning Technology*, 37(1).Retrieved from http://www.cjlt.ca/index.php/cjlt/issue/view/71

Caruso, J. B., & Kvavik, R. B. (2005). *ECAR study of students and information technology 2005: Convenience, connection, control and learning: EDUCAUSE*. Retrieved from http://www.educause.edu/ECAR/ECARStudyofStudentsandInformat/158586

Carvalho, L., & Goodyear, P. (Eds.). (2014). *The architecture of productive learning networks*. London: Routledge.

Corrin, L., Lockyer, L., & Bennett, S. (2010). Technological diversity: An investigation of students' technology use in everyday life and academic study. *Learning Media and Technology, 35*(4), 387–402.

Crook, C. (2002). The campus experience of networked learning. In C. Steeples & C. Jones (Eds.), *Networked learning: Perspectives and issues* (pp. 293–308). London: Springer.

Czerniewicz, L., Williams, K., & Brown, C. (2009). Students make a plan: Understanding student agency in constraining conditions. *Research in Learning Technology, 17*, 75–88.

Dahlstrom, E., & Bichsel, J. (2014). *ECAR study of undergraduate students and information technology, 2014*. Research report. Louisville, CO: ECAR. Retrieved from http://www.educause.edu/ecar

Dahlstrom, E., Walker, J .D., & Dziuban, C. (2013). *ECAR study of undergraduate students and information technology, 2013*. Research report. Louisville, CO: ECAR. Retrieved from http://www.educause.edu/ecar

Daniel, J. (2012). Making sense of MOOCs: Musings in a maze of myth, paradox and possibility. *Journal of Interactive Media in Education*. Retrieved from http://jime.open.ac.uk/2012/18

Dede, C. (2005). Planning for 'neomillennial' learning styles: Implications for investments in technology and faculty. In J. Oblinger & D. Oblinger (Eds.), *Educating the net generation* (pp. 226–247). Boulder, CO: EDUCAUSE.

Dillenbourg, P. (2008). Integrating technologies into educational ecosystems. *Distance & Education, 29*(2), 127–140.

Ellis, R., & Goodyear, P. (2010). *Students experiences of e-learning in higher education: The ecology of sustainable innovation*. New York: Routledge.

Entwistle, N. J., & Ramsden, P. (1983). *Understanding student learning*. London: Croom Helm.

Gabriel, M. A., & Wiebe, S. (2009). Net generation expectations for technology-mediated learning at the university level. In A. Mendez-Vilas (Ed.), *Research, reflections and innovations in integrating ICT in education* (Vol. 1, pp. 996–1000). Badajoz, Spain: Formatex.

Galloway, A. R. (2012). *The interface effect*. Cambridge, MA: Polity Press.

Garcia, P., & Qin, J. (2007). Identifying the generation gap in higher education: Where do the differences really lie? *Innovate, 3*(5).

Goodyear, P. (2000). *Final report, volume 1: Networked learning in higher education project (JCALT)*. Retrieved from http://csalt.lancs.ac.uk/jisc/

Goodyear, P. (2001). *Effective networked learning in higher education: Notes and guidelines (Deliverable 9)*. Bristol, England: Joint Information Systems Committee (JISC). Retrieved from http://csalt.lancs.ac.uk/jisc/docs/Guidelines_final.doc

Goodyear, P. (2005). Educational design and networked learning: Patterns, pattern languages and design practices. *Australian Journal of Educational Technology, 21*, 82–101.

Goodyear, P. (2014). Productive learning networks: The evolution of research and practice. In L. Carvalho & P. Goodyear (Eds.), *The architecture of productive learning networks* (pp. 23–47). London: Routledge.

Goodyear, P., Asensio, M., Jones, C., Hodgson, V., & Steeples, C. (2003). Relationships between conceptions of learning, approaches to study and students' judgements about the value of their experiences of networked learning. *The Association for Learning Technology Journal, 11*(1), 17–27.

Goodyear, P., Jones, C., Asensio, M., Hodgson, V., & Steeples, C. (2005). Networked learning in higher education: Students' expectations and experiences. *Higher Education, 50*(3), 473–508.

Gourlay, L. (2014). Creating time: students, technologies and temporal practices in higher education. *E-Learning and Digital Media, 11*(2), 141–153.

Gros, B., Garcia, I., & Escofet, A. (2012). Beyond the net generation debate: A comparison of digital learners in face-to-face and virtual universities. *International Review of Research in Open and Distance Learning, IRRODL, 13*(4). Retrieved from http://www.irrodl.org/index.php/irrodl/article/view/1305/2311

Harasim, L. (Ed.). (1990). *Online education; perspectives on a new environment.* New York: Praeger.

Harasim, L., Hiltz, S. R., Teles, L., & Turoff, M. (1995). *Learning networks: A field guide to teaching and learning online.* Cambridge, MA: MIT Press.

Hargittai, E. (2010). Digital Na(t)Ives? variation in internet skills and uses among members of the 'net generation'. *Sociological Inquiry, 80*(1), 92–113.

Hargittai, E., Fullerton, L., Menchen-Trevino, E., & Thomas, K. Y. (2010). Trust online: Young adults' evaluation of Web content. *International Journal of Communication, 4*, 468–494. Retrieved from: http://ijoc.org/ojs/index.php/ijoc/article/download/636/423.

Healing, G., & Jones, C. (2011). *Learner experience advancement project (LEAP) phase 2, stage 2 final report.* Milton Keynes, England: The Open University.

Hiltz, S. R., & Turoff, M. (1978). *The network nation: Human communication via computer* (1st ed.). Reading, MA: Addison-Wesley [Revised Edition. Cambridge, MA: MIT Press, 1993.].

Hosein, A., Ramanau, R., & Jones, C. (2010a). *Are all Net Generation students the same? The frequency of technology use at University.* Paper presented at the IADIS E-learning Conference July 2010. Retrieved from http://oro.open.ac.uk/24114/

Hosein, A., Ramanau, R., & Jones, C. (2010b). Learning and living technologies: A longitudinal study of first-year Students' frequency and competence in the use of ICT. *Learning Media and Technology, 35*(4), 403–418.

Howe, N., & Strauss, W. (1991). *Generations: The history of America's future and the fourth turning: An American prophecy.* Oxford, England: Oxford University Press.

Howe, N., & Strauss, W. (2000). *Millennials rising: The next greatest generation.* New York: Vintage Books.

Jones, C. (2011). Students, the net generation and digital natives: Accounting for educational change. In M. Thomas (Ed.), *Deconstructing digital natives* (pp. 30–45). New York: Routledge.

Jones, C. (2012). Networked learning, stepping beyond the net generation and digital natives. In L. Dirckinck-Holmfeld, V. Hodgson, & D. McConnell (Eds.), *Exploring the theory, pedagogy and practice of networked learning* (pp. 27–41). New York: Springer.

Jones, C. (2013). The new shape of the student. In R. Huang & J. M. Kinshuk Spector (Eds.), *Reshaping learning—The frontiers of learning technologies in global context* (pp. 91–112). New York: Springer.

Jones, C., & Asensio, M. (2001). Experiences of assessment: Using phenomenography for evaluation. *Journal of Computer Assisted Learning, 17*(3), 314–321.

Jones, N., Blackey, H., Fitzgibbon, K., & Chew, E. (2010a). Get out of MySpace! *Computers & Education, 54*(3), 776–782.

Jones, C., & Bloxham, S. (2001). Networked legal learning: An evaluation of the student experience. *International Review of Law, Computers and Technology, 3*(15), 317–329.

Jones, C., & Dirckinck-Holmfeld, L. (2009). Analysing networked learning practices: An introduction. In L. Dirckinck-Holmfeld, C. Jones, & B. Lindström (Eds.), *Analysing networked learning practices in higher education and continuing professional development* (pp. 1–27). Rotterdam, England: Sense Publishers, BV.

Jones, C., & Healing, G. (2010a). Net generation students: Agency and choice and the new technologies. *Journal of Computer Assisted Learning, 26*(5), 344–356.

Jones, C., & Healing, G. (2010b). Networks and locations for student learning. *Learning Media and Technology, 35*(4), 369–385.

Jones, C., & Hosein, A. (2010). Profiling university students' use of technology: Where is the Net generation divide? *The International Journal of Technology Knowledge and Society, 6*(3), 43–58.

Jones, C., & Ramanau, R. (2009). Collaboration and the net generation: The changing characteristics of first year university students. In C. O'Malley, D. Suthers, P. Reiman & A. Dimitracopoulou (Eds.), *Proceedings of the 9th International Conference on Computer Supported Collaborative Learning: CSCL2009: CSCL Practices* (pp. 237–241). Rhodes, Greece: University of the Aegean.

Jones, C., Ramanau, R., Cross, S. J., & Healing, G. (2010b). Net generation or digital natives: Is there a distinct new generation entering university? *Computers & Education, 54*(3), 722–732.

Jones, C., & Shao, B. (2011). *The net generation and digital natives: Implications for higher education.* New York: Higher Education Academy. Retrieved from http://www.heacademy.ac.uk/resources/detail/evidencenet/net-generation-and-digital-natives

Jöns, H., & Hoyler, M. (2013). Global geographies of higher education: the perspective of world university rankings. *Geoforum, 46*, 45–59.

Jorgensen, B. (2003). Baby boomers, generation X and generation Y?: Policy implications for defence forces in the modern era. *Foresight, 5*(4), 41–49.

Kember, D. (1996). The intention to both memorise and understand: Another approach to learning. *Higher Education, 31*(3), 341–354.

Kennedy, G., Dalgarno, B., Bennett, S., Judd, T., Gray, K., & Chang, R. (2008). Immigrants and natives: Investigating differences between staff and students' use of technology. In *Hello! Where are you in the landscape of educational technology? Proceedings of ascilite Melbourne 2008.* Retrieved from http://www.ascilite.org.au/conferences/melbourne08/procs/kennedy.pdf

Kennedy, G., Dalgarno, B., Gray, K., Judd, T., Waycott, J., & Bennett, S., et al. (2007). The net generation are not big users of Web 2.0 technologies: Preliminary findings. In *ICT: Providing choices for learners and learning. Proceedings ascilite Singapore 2007.* http://www.ascilite.org.au/conferences/singapore07/procs/kennedy.pdf

Kennedy, G. E., & Judd, T. S. (2011). Beyond Google and the 'Satisficing' searching of digital natives. In M. Thomas (Ed.), *Deconstructing digital natives* (pp. 119–136). New York: Routledge.

Kennedy, G., Judd, T., Dalgarno, B., & Waycott, J. (2010). Beyond natives and immigrants: exploring types of net generation students. *Journal of Computer Assisted Learning, 26*(5), 332–343.

Knox, J. (2014). Digital culture clash: 'massive' education in the E-learning and digital cultures MOOC. *Distance Education (Special Issue on Massively Open Online Courses), 35*(2), 164–177.

Krause, K.-L. (2007). Who is the e-generation and how are they fairing in higher education. In J. Lockard & M. Pegrum (Eds.), *Brave new classrooms: Democratic education and the Internet* (pp. 125–139). New York: Peter Lang.

Kukulska-Hulme, A., & Traxler, J. (2013). Design principles for mobile learning. In H. Beetham & R. Sharpe (Eds.), *Rethinking pedagogy for a digital age: Designing for 21ˢᵗ century learning* (2nd ed., pp. 244–257). London: Routledge.

Kvavik, R. (2005). Convenience, communications, and control: How students use technology. In D. G. Oblinger, & J. L. Oblinger (Eds.), *Educating the net generation* (pp. 82–101). Retrieved from http://www.educause.edu/ir/library/pdf/pub7101.pdf.

Li, N., & Kirkup, G. (2007). Gender and cultural differences in internet use: A study of china and the UK. *Computers & Education, 48*(2), 301–317.

Li, Y., & Ranieri, M. (2010). Are 'digital natives' really digitally competent?—A study on Chinese teenagers. *British Journal of Educational Technology, 41*(6), 1029–1042.

Lohnes, S. & Kinzer, C. (2007). Questioning assumptions about students' expectations for technology in college classrooms. *Innovate, 3*(5).

Manovich, L. (2001). *The language of new media.* Cambridge, MA: MIT Press.

Margaryan, A., Littlejohn, A., & Vojt, G. (2011). Are digital natives a myth or reality? University students' use of digital technologies. *Computers & Education, 56*(2), 429–440.

Marton, F. (1981). Phenomenography—describing conceptions of the world around us. *Instructional Science, 10,* 177–200.

Marton, F. (1994). Phenomenography. In T. Husen & T. N. Postlethwaite (Eds.), *The international encyclopedia of education* (2nd ed., pp. 4424–4429). Oxford, England: Pergamon.

Marton, F., & Booth, S. (1997). *Learning and awareness.* Mahwah, NJ: Lawrence Erlbaum.

Marton, F., Dall'Alba, G., & Beaty, E. (1993). Conceptions of learning. *International Journal of Educational Research, 19,* 277–300.

Marton, F., & Säljö, R. (1976a). On qualitative differences in learning 1: Outcome and process. *British Journal of Educational Psychology, 46,* 4–11.

Marton, F., & Säljö, R. (1976b). On qualitative differences in learning 11: Outcome as a function of the learner's conception of task. *British Journal of Educational Psychology, 46,* 115–127.

McConnell, D., Hodgson, V., & Dirckinck-Holmfeld, L. (2012). Networked learning: A brief history and new trends. In L. Dirckinck-Holmfeld, V. Hodgson, & D. McConnell (Eds.), *Exploring the theory, pedagogy and practice of networked learning* (pp. 3–24). New York: Springer.

McNaught, C., Lam, P., & Ho, A. (2009). The digital divide between University students and teachers in Hong Kong. In *Same places, different spaces. Proceedings of Ascilite,* Auckland, New Zealand. Retrieved from http://www.ascilite.org.au/conferences/auckland09/procs/mcnaught.pdf

Nagler, W., & Ebner, M. (2009). Is your university ready for the Ne(x)t-Generation?. In *Proceedings of 21st World Conference on Educational Multimedia, Hypermedia and Telecommunications (EDMEDIA)* (pp. 4344–4351), 22–26 June, Honolulu, HI.

Nardi, B. A., & O'Day, V. L. (1999). *Information ecologies: Using technology with heart.* Cambridge, MA: MIT Press.

Oblinger, D. (2003). Boomers, Gen-xers and millennials: Understanding the new students. *Educause Review, 38*(4), 37–47.

Oblinger, D. G., & Oblinger, J. (2005). *Educating the net generation.* EDUCAUSE Online book. Retrieved from http://www.educause.edu/ir/library/pdf/pub7101.pdf

Oliver, B., & Goerke, V. (2007). Australian undergraduates' use and ownership of emerging technologies: Implications and opportunities for creating engaging learning experiences for the net generation. *Australasian Journal of Educational Technology, 23*(2), 171–186.

PA Consulting Group. (2014). *Charting a winning course: How student experiences will shape the future of higher education.* Retrieved from http://www.paconsulting.com/our-thinking/download-pas-2013-report-charting-the-course/

Pachler, N., Bachmair, B., Cook, J., & Kress, G. (Eds.). (2010). *Mobile learning: Structures, agency, practices.* New York: Springer.

Palfrey, J., & Gasser, U. (2008). *Born digital: Understanding the first generation of digital natives.* New York: Basic Books.

Palfrey, J., & Gasser, U. (2011). Reclaiming an awkward term: What we might learn from 'digital natives'. In M. Thomas (Ed.), *Deconstructing digital natives* (pp. 186–204). New York: Routledge.

Pedró, F. (2009). *New millennium learners in higher education: Evidence and policy implications. Paris: Centre for Educational Research and Innovation (CERI).*

Prensky, M. (2001a). Digital natives, digital immigrants. *On the Horizon, 9*(5), 1–6.

Prensky, M. (2001b). Digital natives, digital immigrants, part 2: Do they really think differently? *On the Horizon, 9*(6), 1–6.

Prensky, M. H. (2009).Sapiens digital: From digital immigrants and digital natives to digital wisdom. *Journal of Online Education, 5*(3). Retrieved from http://www.wisdompage.com/Prensky01.html

Prensky, M. (2010). *Teaching digital natives: Partnering for real learning.* London: Sage.

Prensky, M. (2011). Digital wisdom and homo sapiens digital. In M. Thomas (Ed.), *Deconstructing digital natives* (pp. 15–29). New York: Routledge.

Prosser, M., & Trigwell, K. (1999). *Understanding learning and teaching: The experience in higher education*. Buckingham, England: Society for Research into Higher Education and Open University Press.

Radloff, A., Coates, H., James, R., & Krause, K-L. (2012). *Report on the development of the university experience survey*. Department for Industry, Australian Government. Retrieved from http://www.innovation.gov.au/highereducation/Policy/Pages/Library%20Card/UES_Development_Report.aspx

Roschelle, J. (2003). Unlocking the learning value of wireless mobile devices. *Journal of Computer Assisted Learning, 19*(3), 260–272.

Rosen, L. D. (2010). *Rewired: Understanding the i-generation and the way they learn*. New York: PalgraveMacmillan.

Rowlands, I., Nicholas, D., Williams, P., Huntington, P., Fieldhouse, M., Gunter, B., Withey, R., Jamali, H., Dobrowolski, T., & Tenopir, C. (2008). The Google generation: The information behaviour of the researcher of the future. *Aslib Proceedings, 60*(4), 290–310.

Salajan, F. D., Schönwetter, D. J., & Cleghorn, B. M. (2010). Student and faculty inter-generational digital divide: Fact or fiction? *Computers & Education, 55*(3), 1393–1403.

Salaway, G., & Caruso, J. B. (2007). *The ECAR study of undergraduate students and information technology*. Boulder, CO: EDUCAUSE Center for Applied Research. Retrieved from http://www.educause.edu/ecar

Schulmeister, R. (2009). Is there a net gener in the house? Dispelling a Mystification. *E-learning and Education (Eleed)*, 5. Retrieved from http://eleed.campussource.de/archive/5/1587

Schulmeister, R. (2010). Students, internet, eLearning and Web 2.0. In M. Ebner & M. Schiefner (Eds.), *Looking toward the future of technology-enhanced education: Ubiquitous learning and digital native*. Hershey, PA: IGI Global.

Selwyn, N. (2008). An investigation of differences in undergraduates' academic use of the internet. *Active Learning in Higher Education, 9*(1), 11–22.

Selwyn, N. (2009). The digital native—myth and reality. *Aslib Proceedings: New Information Perspectives, 61*(4), 364–379.

Sharples, M., Arnedillo-Sánchez, I., Milrad, M., & Vavoula, G. (2009). Mobile learning: Small devices, big issues. In N. Balacheff, S. Ludvigsen, T. de Jong, A. Lazonder, S. Barnes, & L. Montandon (Eds.), *Technology enhanced learning: Principles and products* (pp. 233–249). Heidelberg, Germany: Springer.

Sharples, M., Taylor, J., & Vavoula, G. (2007). A theory of learning for the mobile age. In R. Andrews & C. Haythornthwaite (Eds.), *The Sage handbook of E-learning research* (pp. 221–247). London: Sage.

Smith, S. D., & Caruso, J. B. (2010). *The ECAR study of undergraduate students and information technology, 2010* (Research Study, Vol. 6). Boulder, CO: EDUCAUSE Center for Applied Research. Retrieved from http://www.educause.edu/ecar

Smith, S., Salaway, G., & Borreson Caruso, J. (2009). *The ECAR study of undergraduate students and information technology, 2009* (Research Study, Vol. 6). Boulder, CO: EDUCAUSE Center for Applied Research, 2009. Retrieved from http://www.educause.edu/ecar

Stoerger, S. (2009). The digital melting pot: Bridging the digital native-immigrant divide. *First Monday*, 14(7). Retrieved from http://firstmonday.org/ojs/index.php/fm/article/view/2474/2243

Tapscott, D. (1997). *Growing up digital: The rise of the net generation*. New York: McGraw-Hill.

Tapscott, D. (1999). Educating the net generation. *Educational Leadership, 56*(5), 6–11.

Tapscott, D. (2009). *Grown up digital: How the net generation is changing your world*. New York: McGraw-Hill.

Tapscott, D., & Williams, A. (2010). Innovating the 21st century university: It's time. *Educause Review, 45*(1), 17–29.

Thinyane, H. (2010). Are digital natives a world-wide phenomenon? An investigation into South African first year students' use and experience with technology. *Computers & Education, 55*, 406–414.

Thomas, M. (Ed.). (2011). *Deconstructing digital natives*. New York: Routledge.

Urry, J. (2007). *Mobilities*. Cambridge, MA: Polity Press.

van den Beemt, A., Akkerman, S., & Simons, P. R. J. (2010a). The use of interactive media among today's youth: Results of a survey. *Computers in Human Behavior, 26*, 1158–1165.

van den Beemt, A., Akkerman, S., & Simons, P. R.-J. (2010b). Patterns of interactive media use among contemporary youth. *Journal of Computer Assisted Learning, 27*(2), 103–118.

Waycott, J., Bennett, S., Kennedy, G., Dalgarno, B., & Gray, K. (2009). Digital divides? Student and staff perceptions of information and communication technologies. *Computers & Education, 54*(4), 1202–1211.

Weiler, A. (2005). Information seeking behavior in 'Generation Y' students: Motivation, critical thinking, and learning theory. *Journal of Academic Librarianship, 31*(1), 46–53.

White, D.S., & Le Cornu. A. (2011). Visitors and residents: A new typology for online engagement. *First Monday, 16*, 9(5). Retrieved from http://firstmonday.org/ojs/index.php/fm/article/view/3171/3049

Chapter 9
Networked Learning: A New Paradigm?

Change has been a central focus for this book and I am interested in developing the intellectual capacity needed to provide those analytic resources capable of providing some provisional stability amid the constant process of change. The purpose of this focus on provisional stability is to enable systematic and informed interventions in the process of change and to provide some solid ground from which design and development can take place. A central concept I have deployed in this quest for provisional stability is the idea of affordance. A difficult term that always runs the risk of being interpreted as a fixed feature or property of the technology rather than as a dynamic relationship. Nevertheless the relational view of affordance still provides an essential starting point for networked learning research (See Chap. 2). The concept of affordance is inextricably linked to the scale and complexity of contemporary digital networks. The Internet and Web are technologies that are spoken about as if they are simple and singular things and they are also often spoken about as if they caused definite effects. This view has been challenged throughout this book and an alternative way of thinking about such technologies has been elaborated. This alternative view rests on several key ideas, the idea of affordance, the idea of agency and the idea of assemblages.

The Internet and Web and all other technologies at that level of scale are part of the process of change and although it makes sense to talk about the Internet in 1980 and the Internet in 2010, the complex technology being described by the same term has clearly moved on. Researchers have to be constantly careful to treat the 'things' they describe as changing as they move through time. It is for this reason that socio-material approaches and the theories developed from ANT can be so useful because they treat assemblages as dynamic and composed of complex relationships between humans and machines in which both have the capacity to act. The chapters discussing institutions (Chap. 5) and infrastructures (Chap. 6) locate this potentially abstract discussion of assemblages in two of the more persistent patterns of assemblages for networked learning. The university is one of the longest continuous institutions in modern civilisation, but it is in a constant process of change and it has been seriously

© Springer International Publishing Switzerland 2015
C. Jones, *Networked Learning*, Research in Networked Learning,
DOI 10.1007/978-3-319-01934-5_9

affected in the contemporary period by the deployment of digital and networked technologies. I argue that it still makes sense to talk in terms of the university when it is thought of as a dynamic framework of activities, an assemblage in itself of people and material things. Equally infrastructures while constantly in a process of change provide another relatively stable framework that allows researchers to understand the complex processes surrounding the relationships between technologies and the social processes taking place in education and learning. This concluding chapter begins by focusing on three key concepts that have informed this book and provide the basis for a different way of understanding learning in the age of digital networks, affordance, agency and assemblage. It then continues by considering the future of networked learning and a future research agenda.

Key Concept 1: Affordance

An important idea informing this book has been the concept of affordance. In Chap. 2 the idea and its development were explored and the critical voices who have argued against the use of the term in the context of educational technology were considered. In the conclusions I am returning to the idea of affordance to set out what I believe to be a useful development of the idea for use in the context of networked learning. Kaptelinin and Nardi (2012) have argued for a mediated action conception of affordance. They note the developments that have taken place in the understanding of the concept of affordance in relation to design, in particular the ideas presented in Chap. 2 of:

(a) Visible, hidden or false affordances in terms of perception and in hierarchical and temporal terms of nested and sequential affordance (Gaver 1991, 1996)
(b) Degrees of affordance (McGrenere and Ho 2000)
(c) Levels and types of affordance (Kaptelinin and Nardi 2012).

By degrees of affordance McGrenere and Ho meant that the availability of an affordance should be thought of as more or less accessible and more or less discernible. The level and type of affordance discussed by Kaptelinin and Nardi referred to 'webs of mediators' and they argued that affordances are rarely dependent on singe mediators. This argument concerning mediators is of particular importance in the context of this book because it identifies an issue with the aggregation of technological tools into assemblages, either on the fly or as specifically designed composites. It is as assemblages offering various kinds of complex affordances that technologies are most likely to be found in education and learning. A Learning Management System is one such assemblage of various tools and technologies that presents students and teachers with a complex of potential affordances many of which are interdependent. Importantly the same LMS will offer different affordances to staff and students, for example with regard to grading and the submission of marked work. Kaptelinin and Nardi summarise Gibson's view as:

- affordances are perceived directly; their perception is not based on an interpretation of initially meaningless 'raw' sensory data,

- affordances are relational properties; they emerge in the interaction between the animal and environment: the same environment may offer different affordances to different animals,
- affordances are independent of the situational needs of the perceiver,
- natural environments and cultural environments should not be separated from one another, and
- the theory of affordances is concerned with how affordances are perceived rather than affordances per se. (Kaptelinin and Nardi 2012, p. 968)

Kaptelinin and Nardi argue that Gibson's theory of affordances is limited in its support for understanding mediated human actions and to understand the possibilities offered by technology for specifically human action there is a need to employ another theory of affordance to that found in Gibson's work—one with a different research agenda based on activity theory.

My argument in terms of understanding technology built on this notion of affordance is that:

1. Technologies (but also objects and artefacts) are real in the sense that they exist independently of their being used or perceived and their properties extend across space and time.

Technologies possess properties but not affordances and these can be described by analytic processes. This is not a 'view from nowhere' it is an agreed process of judgment, an analytic process of adjudication which takes evidence from more than one source or perspective. A technology, no matter how temporary, no matter how local, becomes a technology because it has properties which stabilise the changing world and make predictable the shifting and contingent. The properties of an iPhone are the same in outer space as they are on earth, even if there is no signal from a telecommunications network. They remain the same from this day until the next and on into the days that come, even if the networks they were designed to integrate with no longer exist.

2. Technological affordances are relational and the array of properties a technology makes available only become affordances in relation to a user.

The properties are likely to be many and varied but they are not infinite in number and an artefact or technology with a range of properties cannot be used beyond that range. For example I am sure that you can think of many inventive ways that a hairclip can be used, many more than I can probably imagine or list, but whatever these potential uses are they will all be constrained by the limits set by the material character of the hairclip. I could not realistically use the hairclip to fly anywhere or to pour concrete. Similarly an educational technology will have an extensive array of properties that can, in relation to a teacher or a student, offer a set of affordances. However these affordances are not an essential property of the technology, and they do not determine how the technology will be mobilised by any particular user or class of users. The possibilities inherent in the properties of a technology entail constraints and particular technologies can only give rise to a restricted range of affordances.

3. Technology is a term that can be used to refer to widely different levels of scale and complexity.

The simplest technologies have properties that are often readily discernible and consensual in character. There may be unusual properties for a hammer, a stove or a brick but generally the properties are well understood and few disagree about them. At a high level of scale technological collectives such as the Internet, Web or the digital are highly complex, their properties are difficult to describe, and descriptions of their properties fail to cohere around a consensus. However even at these high levels of scale and complexity it is useful to think in terms of the properties of a technology and the affordances users appropriate from these properties. To speak sensibly about the Internet or the Web/Web 2.0 we need to have a coherent discussion about the overall properties these technologies have and how these properties can or have been taken up as affordances in relation to specific users or sets and classes of different users.

4. Technological affordances are second-order phenomena and for human actors and assemblages of humans and machines in education they can be dependent on culture and history.

The properties of a technology are real and independent of the observer and affordances are real but relational, but they can depend on understanding and pre-conceptions. Gibson (1977, 1986 [1979]) was clear that he understood affordance as a real relationship not dependent on perception (so an affordance could exist but not be perceived). In this sense affordances are relational and real. However although this might be suitable for an understanding of affordance in general and when considering organisms in their settings, this kind of understanding is limited when applied to humans when they are learning with technology or in a networked learning setting. Gibson's understanding of perception left the second-order nature of meaning understated in his approach. Gibson's approach being based on the idea of direct perception can imply that the active agent has little or no role in interpreting the stimuli received from an external world and this is a limitation for understanding networked learning.

A final point concerning affordances is of particular importance for networked learning. Technologies are often thought of as discrete, bounded elements, separable from social relations and human interaction. This book has taken a different view which stresses the institutional and infrastructural scale at which technologies are used in education. This means that technologies in networked learning are generally composite sociotechnical systems involving a complex interaction of humans and machines.

Key Concept 2: Agency

The idea of infrastructure and the important place of institutions in the account of networked learning disrupt an often binary understanding of structure and agency. As Elder-Vass (2010), p. 4 notes:

> …instead of ascribing causal significance to an abstract notion of social structure or a monolithic concept of society, we must recognize that it is specific groups of people that have

structural power. As I understand it, the social world is composed of many overlapping and intersecting groups, each of which has the causal power to influence human individuals.

In so far as institutions and infrastructures are groups of people this view is close to my own and it is these intermediate levels of action that are important in linking agency with structure. My difference with this approach is that institutions and infrastructures are sociomaterial in character and causality flows not only from groups of people but in addition from the material artefacts and technologies that they produce. Agency and structure is a major issue in social theory and I will not attempt to add to the considerable efforts made in that field. Following Ashwin (2009) I am more interested in how different ways of thinking about structure and agency can be used to explain a complex social world. This view of agency is also focused on process such that agency is seen as achieved rather than possessed (Biesta and Tedder 2007). So structure and agency are discussed in this section as an epistemological question, rather than an ontological question concerning how the world is.

Kaptelinin and Nardi (2006) explicitly position their activity theoretical approach in relation to ANT and the idea of symmetry between humans and machines. They propose a framework to capture different kinds of agencies and different kinds of agents. Importantly they distinguish between action when thought of as simply having an effect, and action involving an intention. This move sharply separates their approach from ANT which includes the actions of the door groom and sleeping policemen (speed humps). Kaptelinin and Nardi argue that their scheme is not dichotomous, dividing agency between human and machine or between human and material agency, rather they consider various kinds of agents. They contend that different kinds of agents can, under certain circumstances, exhibit similar agencies. As for example in the case of delegated agency, which would apply to door grooms and speed humps, which can also be exhibited by animals and humans. There is much to recommend the framework provided by Kaptelinin and Nardi, especially the way it breaks away from a simple binary of human and non-human. However there are still problems of the kind identified in Chap. 4 concerning the emergent nature of intentionality. In Kaptelinin and Nardi's model intention is the key dividing line between things, life forms and humans. In one sense this is a useful set of distinctions because each layer of complexity fits an understood phase change between non-life inanimate forms, life forms and humanity which singularly steps beyond basic physical and biological needs into the realm of culture and society. However the problem for Kaptelinin and Nardi is most exposed in their treatment of social entities.

These collective entities are understood in terms of human needs, either the acting person's or other persons' needs. From an ANT perspective these social entities are clearly heterogeneous, human–material entanglements which express needs that are both human and material. Let's consider a city which clearly has needs, but these needs are not simply those of either one single person or the collective needs of humans. The city might require a sewage system, a power supply or other significant infrastructural requirements, all of which are the 'needs' of the city but only when viewed as a material–human assemblage. Furthermore the growth of computing and computer networks increasingly sees a delegated set of agencies instantiated in complex human–machine networks, and these assemblages hold out the possibility of emergent properties in which cybernetic systems generate processes that allow for the emergence of intentions which are not the property of any one person, nor are they the property of collectives of humans such as committees and organisational structures. It is conceivable that such assemblages will give rise to human–machine configurations that have their own needs, objects and most importantly intentions.

It is also possible to question some of the assumptions behind the simple divisions between thing, life form and human. If we consider those humans that do not exhibit the full expression of human characteristics these distinctions blur. Children that are born with severe deficiencies preventing them from having human intentions may never fully develop in the way other people do, yet we consider them human. This is not just a stance derived from empathy and ethics, it is because we recognise their form as human, even though they do not have all the characteristics we would normally associate with fully developed humanity. This is of course not an absolute divide and there have been historical examples, for example in eugenics, when some people have not been considered fully human or even human at all. For most people this is not ethically acceptable, but it also flies in the face of a human understanding of the proximity of these people to ourselves a kinship that goes beyond the capacity to construct objects and intentions.

I think some of the weakness of the activity theory position articulated by Kaptelinin and Nardi can be corrected by moving away from a simple focus on the divisions between things–life forms–humans by the addition of sociomaterial entities. This addition allows for the existence of various material–human assemblages (sociomaterial entities), which do not have purely human intentions and objects. It accounts for existing structures, which are networked in form and do not have single control centres such as the Internet and Web. Such large-scale collective organisations do not exhibit object-oriented activity such as that described in the abstracted hierarchical structures of firms or governments. Abstract organisational structures, though never accurate, captured the formal ways that intentions and objects could be formed in such organisations. In the large-scale collective structures found in the Internet and Web, there are systems of governance, and they do embed the objects and intentions of organisations, governments and persons, but they also develop emergent objects and intentions out of the complex interweaving of many attempts to govern at different points and levels within the network structure. Note that this also affects some other living non-human forms such as slime mould, swarms and bird flocks in flight. The needs, intentions and objects that emerge from these processes cannot be predicted from an analysis of the parts because they are dynamic, path-dependent outcomes of complex processes, only partially understood by any one of the governing parts. An interesting feature of these kinds of emergent processes is that while they cannot be reduced to their parts they can in some circumstances have describable governing patterns such as the formulae that give rise to fractal patterns.

Key Concept 3: Assemblage

The term assemblage has been used throughout this book to discuss complex systems composed of humans and machines. It was noted in Chap. 4 that assemblage had a particular place in theories inspired by actor-network theory. As part of the conclusion to the book I want to offer a clarification of the concepts that lie behind the use of assemblage and a rationale for its continued use in networked learning research. Attentive readers will have seen an internal struggle in the sections above between a desire on my part to allow for stability and the use of the term assemblage that emphasises change. The sense of change is deeply embedded in Latour's work as Elder-Vass (2014) notes:

> Although he often applies the concept to what we would normally think of as an 'object' or a 'thing,' for Latour, assemblages are not persistent things or, indeed, recurringly instantiated kinds of things or structures; central to this ontology is a denial of natural stabilities and repeatedly instantiated types. (ibid 2014, p. 6)

I have borrowed the notion of black-boxes from ANT and used them positively to suggest a way to analytically account for stability in a system of thinking that leans towards constant flux. I have also made use of the idea of levels, something explicitly criticised by Latour (1996, 2005) and the notion of phase changes to indicate why I think some significant relatively stable patterns emerge with different levels. Within this emergent account in this volume there is something I now wish to stabilise so that the reader can either accept or reject this attempt to tame the dynamic implications of an ANT understanding of assemblage.

Latour's view of assemblage is tied to a more general view related to Deleuze's metaphor of rhizomes.

> Instead of thinking in terms of surfaces—two dimension- or spheres -three dimension- one is asked to think in terms of nodes that have <u>as many dimensions</u> as they have connections. As a first approximation, the AT [actor-network theory] claims that modern societies cannot be described without recognizing them as having a fibrous, thread-like, wiry, stringy, ropy, capillary character that is never captured by the notions of levels, layers, territories, spheres, categories, structure, systems.(Latour 1996 Online, p. 3)

In this way Latour places a network in contrast to the idea of levels, structures and systems, all concepts used throughout this book.

> …:either we follow social theorists and begin our travel by setting up at the start which kind of group and level of analysis we will focus on, or we follow the actors' own ways and begin our travels by the traces left behind by their activity of forming and dismantling groups. (Latour 2005, p. 29)

Latour's methodological prescription is to follow the actor and to ignore the levels that I find so interesting and important. Assemblage is also used in a much less charged way by Arthur (2009), p. 28 when he argues that technology can be thought of in three distinct ways, one of which as 'as an assemblage of practices and components'. Arthur's use of assemblage is more mundane than Latour's and it signifies the use of a singular term 'technology' to cover a plural application such as when it is applied to electronics, which incorporates both singular devices, collections of devices and social practices.

DeLanda (2006) has a strong position with regard to levels and describes them in terms of reductionism. The levels DeLanda discusses include the mesolevel which he associates with the work of Giddens who he describes as 'meso-reductionist' (DeLanda 2006, p. 5). For DeLanda macro-reductionism is associated with theories that provide accounts derived from structure and micro-reductionism with method-ological individualism. The inclusion of meso-reductionism by DeLanda is based on a reading of Giddens which contends that Giddens believes praxis is the core of social reality. It should be noted that while DeLanda regards Giddens as a meso-reductionist he does not exclude the consideration of scale and he personally dis-criminates between assemblages at what I would describe as different 'levels' of scale, e.g. 'large-scale'. DeLanda's rejection of meso-reductionism is not a rejection of a relational understanding of scale and as such it may not apply to the account of levels provided in this volume. DeLanda also makes an argument in relation to the idea of assemblages that provides a direct link to the arguments made above about the notion of affordance.

> We can distinguish ... the properties defining a given entity from its **capacities to interact** with other entities. Whilst its properties are given and may be denumerable as a closed list, its capacities are not given—they may go unexercised if no entity suitable for interaction is around—and form a potentially open list, since there is no way to tell in advance in what ways a given entity may affect or be affected by innumerable other entities. (DeLanda 2006, p. 10)

It is this central idea about what DeLanda following Deleuze calls 'relations of exteriority' that defines my use of affordance and the idea of assemblage. It is because of the importance of these two concepts and the contrasting views of assemblage and their implications for the use of levels in my arguments that it is essential that I clarify my own use of the term.

I do not adopt the radical view of ontology that can be found in Latour and many who have adopted ANT as the framework for their research. There has been a surge of interest in networked learning for research based on this approach in recent years (see for example Wright 2014) and this interest often takes a radical stance in terms of ontology. This radical stance argues that there are multiple realities constituted by practices and that in some cases the realities that are constituted by different practices although they are related to the same object might be incommensurable (see Oliver 2012). For there to be commensurability between different accounts requires work and the bracketing of differences between accounts, and it results in degrees of compatibility rather than a binary either-or outcome. The key step in the radical argument is that there is no reference point against which better or worse accounts can be judged and there is no foundational truth. My preferences remain solidly realist in relation to this question about ontology, although my emphasis is firmly on how we come to know, rather than the nature of reality in itself.

The standard realist view is that there is a reality beyond human practices to which we can refer in order to adjudicate between different accounts. Notice the use of a judicial term applied to this process because it is used advisedly to emphasise a process that does not suggest an absolute truth or a truth that is fixed. The realist point is that reality is not subjective and that the world resists human constructions. In some ways this leaves Latour as a realist too because he would recognise the argument that the world resists, but he would also argue that this resistance can be overcome if a certain price is paid (see Harman 2009). ANT and Latour cannot be reduced to a purely social constructivist argument, but they can give rise to Mol's argument that reality is multiple (Mol 2002). I argue that there is a limit to the negotiation of costs and there is a limit to interpretive flexibility, a limit to use, even if the user is prepared to pay an extreme cost to work against the material and real. For Latour the world is never constituted by stable and solid forms and the appearance of stability and solidity is the outcome of a negotiation between numerous forces. My argument is that for most practical purposes in the study of networked learning provisional stabilities, negotiated as they might be, can be treated as stable and solid, even if we acknowledge that in principle they are dynamic. The degree of permanence of different stabilised entities is also an issue of some importance, and it should not be flattened in such a way that significant differences in the nature and rates of change are ignored. My argument in favour of levels includes the idea that microlevels are more contingent and macrolevels relatively stable and the interest for networked learning is often in mesolevels of organisation and practice, at which change takes place in moderate time scales and with the application of organised effort.

These arguments about stability are important with regard to assemblages and the emergent properties they may give rise to. Institutions and infrastructures are assemblages that have proved to be an important focus for networked learning. A university is famously more than the sum of its parts and it has existed as a recognisable form in many societies over an extended period of time (Collini 2012; Scott 2006). What is it that makes the various entities a university has been in Paris and Bologna, Oxford and Cambridge something that can convincingly be discussed under a single term? Of course this apparent stability entails work and a constant effort to maintain a degree of constancy. Furthermore the stability doesn't simply arise from the internal properties of a 'university', but it is not entirely free of them either. A university is not reducible to its external relations because it does have a degree of dependence on its internal components. The university has a stability that allows it to persist despite changes to its internal composition and to its external relations, but there are times at which a change in either the internal or external relations can lead to a significant overall change—something I have argued is similar to a phase change of the kind that takes place between different phases of matter (gas–liquid–solid). Black-boxes can be seen as such relatively stable entities, screening the black-boxed assemblage from internal and external change at least until a phase change occurs. In the university historians recognise a phase change in the emergence of the modern university, a concept that covers a period of about two hundred years (Wittrock 2012). This makes black-boxed entities treatable as autonomous 'things' that exist as more than their external relations even though these provisional 'things' cannot be reduced to their component parts. The nature of their endurance is an empirical question to be answered by historical enquiries into the development of these entities and it requires an understanding of when black-boxes arise, what internal and external relations are critical for their continuance and what changes have or could threaten their continuation. Such a discussion is needed currently to locate the changes that arise with the integration of digital and net-worked technologies in the digital university (Jones 2013). Embedding an historical discussion of the assemblages implicated in networked learning is important to avoid the kinds of hype that have accompanied MOOCs and the net generation and digital native's debates.

The Future of Networked Learning

This book began by making a case for using the idea of networked learning to frame a research agenda that could inform design and development in educational technology. The idea of networked learning avoids the hype that only sees new technologies in a positive light. Networked learning also avoids the slightly less common but equally overdrawn dystopian view which sees technology as the cause of a decline that undermines education and learning. Networked learning does not sit between these extremes; it takes a quite different approach. Determinedly research-based, networked learning does not presume that technologies cause either progress or regression; instead it looks for evidence of the kinds of changes taking place and assumes that technology is a sociotechnical feature of life involving complex and emergent causation and an assemblage of people and machines.

Networked learning is based on a relational view of learning and the relational understanding of affordance is entirely consistent with this approach. I have argued that there is no specific theory of learning associated with networked learning but there are some basic assumptions about learning that are common across research in this field. Learning is thought of as a social process involving cooperation, collaboration and dialogue but not restricted to strong ties. Learning from a networked learning perspective contains researchers who are interested in individual and psychological explanations of learning within a social context, and networked learning should not be thought of as exclusively social in outlook although some researchers, including the author, have a strongly social conception of learning. Learning is considered a complex social process and one that can only be designed for and not directly designed. This indirect view of learning has been extremely important in defining the strong relationship between networked learning and educational design. It is also consistent with the view of affordance and assemblage that has been drawn on in this volume. Networked learning also draws on a sociomaterial understanding of the ways in which the material form of technology interacts with social processes. Because networked learning is centrally concerned with learning via net-worked and digital technologies the way the material features of technology are taken into account is of critical importance. I should be clear at this point that the material in this sense includes codes, protocols and standards that can be instanti-ated in digital and documentary form, and the material should not be thought of as being limited to obvious artefacts and things.

The place of humans in networked learning has been emphasised throughout and the definition I explored in Chap. 1 included a warning that the use of online materials alone was not a sufficient characteristic to define networked learning. The use of networked technologies has been used to define a form of society, the emergence of new work processes and the kinds of work being done in many sectors of the economy. The idea that new technologies 'informate' work has had a limited impact in learning, but in the era of big data and learner analytics its time may have come for educational research (see Chap. 5 and Zuboff 1988). There is a serious issue emerging about the degree to which agency can be delegated in educational processes to machines and algorithms. There are also questions being asked about the role of the teacher and whether teaching is necessary at all (Mitra 2000). Teaching used to be thought of as a noble vocation, leading out those younger and less experienced, but in current conditions teaching can be framed as invasive and an authoritarian imposition. Let me be clear, networked learning does not see teaching as invasive or as necessarily being an imposition. Most certainly education can be co-opted by authoritarians and it can be invasive in character, but this is not a characteristic of teaching per se. Indeed the tradition of networked learning emphasises the human element and argues that online materials are not sufficient in isolation. By extension neither automated nor semi-automated systems are sufficient and they should not be used to diminish or downgrade pedagogy and the teaching function.

The way that networked learning approaches the ways networked and digital technologies influence teaching is to investigate how the work teachers do is disaggregated and re-composed in new assemblages of humans and machines. Networked learning values the human components of these assemblages, and it is interested in how the key constituents of a teaching and learning relationship might be re-composed. Aspects of this process of recomposition are already well known. The shift to using greater networked and digital technologies increases the need to pre-prepare courses and course materials, to work in teams that often include specialists as well as academic staff and to ensure clear communication between students and their teachers. The groups of new professionals, the para-academics found under job descriptions such as learning technologist and educational developer, are a practitioner audience for much of networked learning research. The growth of team working affects the working lives and arrangements of course teams, departments, schools, faculties and universities. It has an individual aspect but it is part of a large social process associated with the introduction of what used to be called information and communication technologies. The recomposition of academic work is a thread that runs throughout this book (see especially Chaps. 5 and 7) and the new professionals in para-academic roles are one visible aspect of this, but in addition it requires changes to the work of academic staff, administrators and managers.

The Political Nature of Networked Learning

The view of networked learning that has been presented here is one that places weight on politics and history. Networked learning is not about futures determined by technology, nor is it about sudden and inevitable change. Fundamentally the view of networked learning set out in these chapters has been about choices, and more specifically about choices made in complex historical contexts. Technology itself is a site of struggle (Feenberg 1991). The technologies developed in any society have a complex relationship to the social struggles that are taking place in that society. A current example is the struggle around privacy in which large corporations are interested in gathering data from the customers of their products and services to add value to their business. Governments are interested in the possibility of gathering data from their own and other states' citizens, corporations and government agencies. However governments are also responsive to pressure from their citizens to ensure privacy and they have their own governmental concerns in ensuring the safety and security of their government's own critical data. Citizens are torn between their interests as consumers in which they may offset the cost of a service by giving up their own privacy (either unwittingly or knowingly), and their interests as citizens, concerned by security, safety from potential threats, liberty, and being free from oversight and surveillance. These questions are simultaneously fought over in the market, public discourse and in the political arena. The technologies that are developed, the ecology they survive in (including the legal and regulatory framework), and the market success they enjoy, are outcomes of these ongoing struggles. In this complex arena education, and even more so higher education, is a marginal player largely subject to major decisions taken elsewhere with little regard for educational issues.

While education might be a marginal player in terms of the broad sweep of technological development there are key political issues in education that have a bearing on the technologies that are deployed and the ways in which they are deployed. Current issues include the proper role of the state and the market in education, and the place of the individual and their personal advancement in relation to education as a public good. In the United Kingdom, United States and Australia these battles are being fought over university fees and the balance between the price of education to private individuals and the cost of educational provision to the state. This might seem separated from the interests of those concerned with networked learning, but this argument affects the kinds of subjects and disciplines made available by universities as they maximise their market position. It also affects the broad relationship between the university and its students because students are increasingly seen as customers and the university is defined as a business. In terms of technology these issues are influential in the debates that surround openness, Massive Open Online Courses (MOOCs), the provision of infrastructure (Cloud computing), and the support for new devices including tablet computers and smartphones (Bring Your Own Device). None of the above should be taken to mean that there is a social or political determination of the relationship between technology and networked learning. The most unpromising technologies from a networked learning point of view can be deployed in surprising ways that support the pedagogic values that underpin networked learning. The argument that is being made here is that the political and historic nature of educational technology needs to be highlighted, described and understood. Networked learning has a distinct role in this because of its roots in research, educational values, and because of its understanding of the complex sociotechnical networks in which learning takes place.

My own preferences have underpinned much that has been covered in previous chapters. I see education as a public good, the basis of cultural transmission between generations. I do not favour the primacy of markets and I think there is a substantial and necessary role for the state in funding educational provision. I think that international bodies need to regulate and integrate the various national and state arrangements in education because in a network society no nation state, however large (e.g. China) can stand alone. The twenty-first century economy is a contest between new forms of state capitalism and the more obvious dominance of neoliberal market forms. In higher education this contest often takes on the appearance of a dispute between private (globally structured) and public (state localised) bodies. Should education be in the hands of private corporations, e.g. Pearson, Study Group or Laureate or in the hands of nation states, e.g. France, Japan or South Africa—perhaps there is a significant role for transnational actors such as the EU? Perhaps as with Cloud computing, the future is hybrid with an increasing integration between private corporations and state entities. However these options are decided they will have an impact on the kinds of networked learning that can be pursued and even whether networked learning will retain an important place at all.

Suggestions for a Research Agenda

Networked learning has always highlighted its role as a research-led project. Research has been central to the development of networked learning but it is also affected by the politics and history outlined above. There are those who recognise the political nature of research and advocate taking a critical approach (Facer and Selwyn 2013). They propose that the research agenda should be opened out to include community partners in setting the research agenda and in coproducing research alongside academic researchers. I have no objection to this approach but I think it needs to be supported by stable social actors. Criticism has previously formed part of broad social movements, often based on class and nationality, which have nurtured dissident voices. In the recent past Solidarnosc in Poland provided a much more substantial base for dissident voices than other East European movements which lacked such a solid trade union and class basis. My view is that without the re-emergence of large-scale social movements that have a persistent social base, criticism will remain small scale, marginal and largely ineffective. This should sound a cautionary note for any networked learning agenda, because a radical and critical research agenda will require changes in the wider society, even though positive educational reform is not reducible to the agenda of any particular social movement. However networked learning cannot wait for new social movements before setting out its own agenda and in the sections below I will set out some key elements that networked learning will need to focus on in the near future, even if large-scale social change and a major critical agenda are not achievable in the short term.

Data and Educational Infrastructures

The idea that computing technologies naturally gathered information about the processes they were deployed in is not new (Zuboff 1988). Even prior to the development of the Web it was understood that when computing and computing networks were in place they could be used to provide a trace of the activity of which they were a part. This capacity to trace activity holds a research potential but it is one that has to be managed carefully. Analytics are a contemporary focus in education for both research and managerial purposes and they raise serious questions about privacy, data protection and the ethics of data use. As I noted in the discussion of learning analytics in Chap. 5 analytics is one of the sites of struggle involving technology in contemporary higher education. Those interested in analytics include governments, educational institutions, teachers and learners (Ferguson 2012). Their interests do not always coincide and the kinds of data they wish to collect, the level of data they require and the forms of analysis they wish to subject the data to can all vary. It should be noted in this context that 'big' data is not the only kind of data that is of interest. Detailed data that maps a relatively small area of interest is another potential kind of data generated by digital technologies. The term 'small' data has been used to describe this kind of approach but this is also too limited as big and small are relational terms and big data to one user may be small data to another (boyd and Crawford 2012). Networked learning research is interested in the detailed tracings of activity within educational settings and it is interested in these tracings at a number of different levels of scale. Interactions within small groups, modules and courses are of interest and they have previously been studied using a variety of methods. The newer kinds of data analysis currently available mean that there are opportunities for new insights into this level of activity. Data is also available at the level of the institution, so that students can be tracked across their degree and beyond. Perhaps just as importantly senior managers and administrators are interested in developing tools which manage the student 'experience' and manage staff interactions with students (McCluskey and Winter 2012). The tools developed in these processes and the data they generate may be available for redeployment by researchers interested in networked learning. This will not be a simple task and it will require struggle by ethically informed researchers who will need to explore the detail of data collection and data manipulation to ensure that the data they use is fit for research purposes.

Following the Actor in a Digital Ecology

One of the areas in which data collected by digital devices and networks may prove important is in relation to issues of mobility. The interest in mobile learning and mobility were discussed in Chap. 8 and I concluded that even in extremely mobile contexts student location remained important and the relatively fixed infrastructural elements that supported mobility needed careful consideration. Mobility using digital devices and digital networks leaves traces that can be accessed for research purposes but they have similar limitations to early tracings of activity which made use of computer conferencing transcripts. Transcripts of text-based exchanges appeared to hold out the prospect of providing a relatively permanent record of educational interactions that would previously have had no record. The problem was that the transcripts that provided the record were necessarily partial and they could be seriously misleading (Jones and Cawood 1998). In a similar way the data captured by devices and networks illustrating activity and movement will have inbuilt limitations. For example if we consider the ANT injunction to follow the actor in terms of mobility it leads to a number of interesting questions.

Perhaps most importantly following the actor in the context of mobility raises questions about who or what the actor is at any given time. A student accessing university services, for example library services or the LMS (VLE) can do so via a variety of devices. When they access the university service it may be presented differently according to the type of device being used, whether they are using an app or a web browser and both of these ways of accessing will depend on whether the devices operating system is supported by the university. Who then is the actor, is it the student, a hybrid of the student and their device or a hybrid of the student, the device and the network infrastructure? In some stable infrastructures it may be possible to follow a university service, an e-portfolio for example, as an actor in a university setting. These practical considerations about how an actor can be provisionally defined, black-boxed, in an educational setting show how important the idea of assemblage and affordance can be. Even the idea of an agent shows how complex and time dependent the composition of an assemblage can be. Students increasingly work at an interface that integrates a variety of components in a kaleidoscopic way, combining and recombining a limited variety of component elements. Affordances emerge in the relationships between relatively stable entities in these settings and it is not sufficient to know the properties of an entity to be able to describe the affordances that entity can have in relation to another.

Consider a research project that tried to understand the contemporary student and their interactions in a digital and networked environment. It is now possible to set up tracking software on all the devices owned by the student, their phone, tablet computer and their laptop or desktop. Using such software it might be possible to track much of what a specific student does, including when they log in to network services provided by the university. There would be practical issues concerning how long such surveillance could go on and how much data could reasonably be managed. There would also be serious ethical issues about how the kinds of additional data and not relevant to the research would be treated, about who could access the data and about whether informed consent could really be provided by students unfamiliar with the capacity of digital technologies to record their activity. Even after having taken all these features into account major methodological issues would remain. The same or similar patterns of activity could be shown by more than one student, but the underlying motivations might differ radically. Quite simply numbers and data do not speak for themselves; they need to be informed by understanding and such understanding still requires human beings to act as a research instrument. In current circumstances this suggests that despite the new data sources and their undoubted power, they will still need to be supplemented by methods that draw on the ways human beings understand their surroundings. For example once data has been captured and traces of activity have been derived they can be presented back to the person(s) involved and they can be asked what they remember of what they were doing and why they were doing it at the time the data was collected. Sometimes it might be necessary to present data back to entire groups who were involved in the capture processes and to engage the group in teasing out differences in individual activities or to work through issues that emerge from the data and look for alternative ways to deal with questions that the data gives rise to.

These issues are challenges to adopting an approach that follows the actor using the traces they leave behind, but they should not eclipse the potential for such methods to provide new and exciting insights into a networked world. The learner in a networked learning setting can be located almost anywhere where there is a network connection and additionally in places where there is no network available. Similarly academic work is increasingly dispersed across a range of locations and a diverse collection of networked devices such as smartphones, tablet computers, laptops and desktop computers. The self-reported accounts of activity in these networked settings have well-known weaknesses and a standard methodological technique would be to support these accounts with observations of activity that can be compared with the self-report accounts provided. Network communications make classic forms of observation difficult but new technologies open up alternative routes to supporting evidence. With ethical clearance tracking devices can be deployed on the array of devices an actor uses (Judd and Kennedy 2010, 2011). The network can also be traced from an ego-network perspective and research subjects can be enrolled as participants using techniques that encourage actors to capture their own activity using video and other methods which log their day-to-day practices (Jones and Healing 2010). Digital networks disperse activity but they also enable new ways to access traces of the activity and provide alternative sources of evidence that can complement self-reports gathered from interview accounts and surveys.

Future Issues and Developments in Networked Learning

I have argued that forces beyond education and most certainly beyond networked learning are likely to set the conditions in which networked learning will develop. The global financial crisis of 2008 will come to an end and austerity politics will be replaced by new perspectives. The rebalancing of society and the global economy away from the previous centres of power in Europe and the United States will continue. The world is now bourgeois with over half of the population living in urban centres. This is likely to have a profound effect on education as new workforces develop and the culture of the town establishes itself. The explosive growth of networked and digital technologies may surprise observers once again with a new round of fundamental change, but it might be that digital and networked technologies will now develop more intensively by extending their reach to populations currently excluded, and by the refinement of currently existing techniques. The core drive for the development of networked learning as a research field will remain whatever future emerges. This is because networked learning has a distinct relationship with educational technologies. Networked learning is defined by digital and networked technology, but although these technologies are necessary for networked learning's development they are not sufficient to cause it. Networked learning requires these technologies for support, but networked learning is a research field and a praxis, an orientation to practice with technology that is informed by distinct values.

A key issue that will underpin educational choices is the kinds of employees that are thought to be required to staff the 'new' economy. Will education be able to supply the workers for new industries and can judgements be made now about the kinds of work that they will need to carry out in the future? The self-directed, self-disciplined workers imagined by new plate glass universities develop in the late 1960s and early 1970s have turned out to be the last beneficiaries of a now shrinking middle class in advanced industrial economies, replaced by precarious and 'immaterial' labour. Their professional environments have become increasingly controlled, often by the networked and digital technologies that students first encounter at university. Learning analytics and the new student experience may be the gateway to an informated working life of algorithmic control and work that is insecure and portfolio based in which individual performance is key. While future gazing is notoriously difficult it will be important to imagine the near future if education is to be able to develop the citizens and workers of the future. Networked learning has always been interested in equipping people with the capacity to work creatively, to identify and construct problems to work on, to find the resources to deal with the problems identified and to develop workable solutions. This approach is built with flexibility in mind. It is not tied to the details of a curriculum or a testing regime that measures specified outputs, but it builds resilience and the capacity to deal with change.

The overall perspective argued for in this book has discussed networked learning as part of broad social changes and as being integrated in institutional and infrastructural change. The issues identified throughout are concerned with how in the emerging world concerned with issues of mobility and mobile learning some provisional bases of stability can be derived that can allow design to be applied to the complex systems and networked forms the book has described. At root the book has argued for a relational view of learning through which networked learning can deal with the new mobility and from which networked learning can take its next steps by designing educational opportunities for citizens in an increasingly complex network society.

References

Arthur, W. B. (2009). *The nature of technology: What it is and how it evolves*. London: Allen Lane.
Ashwin, P. (2009). *Analysing teaching-learning interactions in higher education: Accounting for structure and agency*. London: Continuum Press.

Biesta, G., & Tedder, M. (2007). Lifelong learning and the ecology of agency: Towards a lifecourse perspective. *Studies in the Education of Adults, 39*(2), 132–149.

boyd, D., & Crawford, K. (2012). Critical questions for big data. *Information Communication & Society, 15*(5), 662–679.

Collini, S. (2012). *What are universities for?* London: Penguin Press.

DeLanda, M. (2006). *A new philosophy of society: Assemblage theory and social complexity.* London: Continuum Press.

Elder-Vass, D. (2010). *The causal power of social structures: Emergence, structure and agency.* Cambridge, MA: Cambridge University Press.

Elder-Vass, D. (2014). Disassembling actor-network theory. *Philosophy of the Social Sciences.* Retrieved 10 May, 2014, from 10.1177/0048393114525858

Facer, K., & Selwyn, N. (2013). Epilogue: Building allegiances and moving forward. In N. Selwyn & K. Facer (Eds.), *The politics of education and technology: Conflicts, controversies, and connections* (pp. 209–219). New York: Palgrave McMillan.

Feenberg, A. (1991). *Critical theory of technology.* New York: Oxford University Press.

Ferguson, R. (2012). Learning analytics: Drivers, developments and challenges. *International Journal of Technology Enhanced Learning, 4*(5/6), 304–317.

Gaver, W. W. (1991). Technology affordances. In *Proceedings of CHI'91* (pp. 79–84). New Orleans, LA, 28 April–2 May 1991. New York: ACM.

Gaver, W. W. (1996). Situating action II: Affordances for interaction: The social is material for design. *Ecological Psychology, 8*(2), 111–129.

Gibson, J. J. (1977). The theory of affordances. In R. Shaw & J. Bransford (Eds.), *Perceiving, acting and knowing.* Hillsdale, NJ: Erlbaum.

Gibson, J. J. (1986). *The ecological approach to visual perception.* Mahwah, NJ: Lawrence Erlbaum Associates. (Original work published 1979).

Harman, G. (2009). *Prince of networks: Bruno latour and metaphysics.* Melbourne, Victoria, Australia: Re. press. Retrieved from http://re-press.org/books/prince-of-networks-bruno-latour-and-metaphysics/

Jones, C. (2013). The digital university: A concept in need of a definition. In R. Goodfellow & M. Lea (Eds.), *Literacy in the digital university: Critical perspectives on learning, scholarship, and technology* (pp. 162–172). London: Routledge.

Jones, C., & Cawood, J. (1998). The unreliable transcript: Contingent technology and informal practice in asynchronous learning networks. In Networked lifelong learning; innovative approaches to education and training through the Internet. *Proceedings of the 1998 International Conference* (pp. 1.9–1.14). Sheffield, England: University of Sheffield. Retrieved from http://www.networkedlearningconference.org.uk/past/nlc1998/Proceedings/Jones-1.9-1.14.pdf

Jones, C., & Healing, G. (2010). Networks and locations for student learning. *Learning Media and Technology, 35*(4), 369–385.

Judd, T., & Kennedy, G. (2010). A five-year study of on-campus internet use by undergraduate biomedical students. *Computers & Education, 55*(1), 564–571.

Judd, T., & Kennedy, G. (2011). Measurement and evidence of computer-based task switching and multitasking by 'Net Generation' students. *Computers & Education, 56*(3), 625–631.

Kaptelinin, V., & Nardi, B. A. (2006). *Acting with technology: Activity theory and interaction design.* Cambridge, MA: MIT Press.

Kaptelinin, V., & Nardi, B. (2012). Affordances in HCI: Toward a mediated action perspective. In *Proceedings of the 2012 ACM annual conference on Human Factors in Computing Systems* (pp. 967–976). New York: ACM.

Latour, B. (1996). On actor-network theory: A few clarifications and more than a few complications. *Soziale Welt, 47*, 369–381. Retrieved from http://www.bruno-latour.fr/sites/default/files/P-67%20ACTOR-NETWORK.pdf

Latour, B. (2005). *Reassembling the social. An introduction to actor-network theory.* London: Routledge.

McCluskey, F., & Winter, M. (2012). *The idea of the digital university: Ancient traditions, disruptive technologies and the battle for the soul of higher education.* Washington DC: Policy Studies Organisation/Westphalia Press.

McGrenere, J., & Ho, W. (2000). Affordances: Clarifying and evolving a concept. In *Proceedings of graphics interface 2000* (pp. 179–186). New York: ACM. Retrieved from http://www.dgp.utoronto.ca/~joanna/papers/gi_2000_affordances.pdf

Mitra, S. (2000). *Minimally invasive education for mass computer literacy*. Paper presented at the CRIDALA 2000 conference, Hong Kong, China, 21–25 June, 2000. Retrieved from http://www.hole-in-the-wall.com/docs/Paper01.pdf

Mol, A. (2002). *The body multiple: Ontology in medical practice*. Durham, NC: Duke University Press.

Oliver, M. (2012). Learning with technology as coordinated sociomaterial practice: Digital literacies as a site of praxiological study. In V. Hodgson, C. Jones, M. De Laat, D. McConnell, T. Ryberg, & P. Sloep (Eds.), *Proceedings of the 8th International Conference on Networked Learning,* 2–4 April 2012, Maastricht, NL (pp. 440–447). Retrieved from http://networkedlearningconference.org.uk/past-proceedings/index.htm

Scott, J. C. (2006). The mission of the university: Medieval to postmodern transformations. *The Journal of Higher Education, 77*(1), 1–39.

Wittrock, B. (2012). The modern university in its historical contexts: Rethinking three transformations. In M. Feingold (Ed.), *History of universities Vol XXVII/1* (pp. 199–226). Oxford, England: Oxford University Press.

Wright, S. (2014). Actor-network theory: Double Symposium. In S. Bayne, C. Jones, M. De Laat, T. Ryberg, & C. Sinclair, (Eds.), *Proceedings of the 9th International Conference on Networked Learning*, Edinburgh, UK, 7–9 April 2014. Retrieved from http://www.networkedlearningconference.org.uk/abstracts/wright_symposium.htm

Zuboff, S. (1988). *In the age of the smart machine: The future of work and power*. New York: Basic Books.

Index

A

Academic
freedom, 111, 173–174, 178, 184, 190
para-academic, 4, 14, 39, 174,
185–186, 235
staff, faculty, 14, 71, 118–119, 138,
184–186, 188, 190, 205, 210, 235
Accessibility, 116, 121, 137, 153–154,
157–158, 160–161, 188, 226
Acquisition, 7, 52, 60, 122, 151, 155, 185,
208, 214
Activity, 5, 9, 12–14, 22, 31, 35, 37, 39,
51–61, 64, 68–71, 96, 110, 114, 116,
125–127, 137–139, 144–147, 149–151,
154–156, 162, 170–174, 176–177,
179–182, 185–186, 188, 190, 198, 207,
210–213, 217–218, 226, 230–231,
238–240
Activity theory, 34–35, 55, 57–60, 64, 71,
95–96, 146–147, 227, 229–230
Actor, 27, 30, 33, 87, 93, 95, 98, 157, 169,
212, 238–240
Actor-network theory (ANT), 13, 27, 55, 64,
66, 79, 86–87, 91, 93–96, 98, 138,
212–213, 225, 229, 231–233, 239
Administration, 2, 47, 113, 117, 119, 125, 132,
170, 172, 181, 185
Affordance, 12, 27, 58, 79, 107, 137,
169, 197, 225
Agency, 11–12, 23, 27, 34, 38–39, 93, 95–96,
99, 131, 140, 159, 170, 186, 188,
209–210, 225–226, 228–230, 236
Agent, 33, 70, 87, 91–98, 147, 157, 201, 210,
212, 228–229, 239

Analytics
learner, 62, 87, 89, 91, 114–117, 235
learning, 13, 39, 51, 112–116, 119–120,
132, 144, 150, 173, 180, 238, 241
ANT. *See* Actor-network theory (ANT)
Approaches to learning, 54–55, 63, 68–69,
201, 215, 235
Approaches to study, 63–64, 199, 215
Approaches to teaching, 68–69, 184, 214
Assemblage, 3, 11–12, 25, 27, 33–34, 66,
92–94, 99, 118, 131–132, 137, 141,
151, 169, 185, 197, 208, 214, 225–226,
228–235, 239
Asynchronous, 5, 11, 154
learning networks (*see* Learning networks)

B

Behaviourism, 49–54, 56–57, 64–65, 94
Big data, 13, 109, 112–114, 119, 131, 187,
235, 238. *See also* Analytics
Blog, 4, 65, 143, 154, 175, 187, 191
Borgman, C., 172, 175–178
Broadband, 199–200, 210–211
Broadcast, 2, 7, 151, 185
Business, 2–3, 22, 108, 113–115, 117–119,
124–125, 127–128, 130–131, 171,
184, 236

C

Campus, 152, 198, 212, 218
Capital, 22, 38, 59, 123, 130, 186
Capitalism, 3, 20–23, 37–38, 125, 237

© Springer International Publishing Switzerland 2015
C. Jones, *Networked Learning*, Research in Networked Learning,
DOI 10.1007/978-3-319-01934-5

Capitalist, 20, 22, 37, 59
Castells, M., 3, 22, 36–38, 40, 41, 87, 90
Change
    social, 19, 23, 26, 35, 38, 175, 176, 209,
        237, 241
    technological, 13, 25, 35, 68, 142, 152,
        170, 178, 180
Classroom, 6, 37, 49, 50, 130, 143, 146, 148,
    150, 180, 201, 207
Coded, 23, 39, 141, 154, 155, 157, 161, 162, 234
Cognitivism, 9, 30, 34, 49, 51–54, 56, 57, 60,
    64, 65, 92, 146, 157, 172, 173, 207
Collaboration, 4, 8, 11, 42, 59–62, 83, 88–90,
    109, 110, 116, 122, 138, 146, 149,
    153–155, 159, 176, 181, 182, 184,
    187–189, 198, 202, 204, 211, 234
Commercial, 1, 120, 122, 127, 155, 158, 159,
    161, 162, 171, 190, 199, 208
Community
    of practice, 58, 59, 90, 139
Complexity, 59, 66, 67, 91, 96, 97, 132, 145,
    205, 211, 214, 225, 227–229
Computer-supported collaborative learning
    (CSCL), 7, 52, 55, 60–62, 83, 90, 146,
    148, 182
Computer-supported cooperative work
    (CSCW), 60, 148, 162, 186
Conferencing
    computer, 88, 138, 143, 150, 153, 154,
        184, 239
Connectivism, 9, 55, 64–66, 84, 88, 126, 127,
    138, 153, 162
Constraints, 27–31, 54, 70, 107, 137, 156, 157,
    185, 209, 211, 218, 227
Constructivism, 26, 34, 49, 52–57, 64, 65, 95,
    123, 182
Constructivist, 26, 32, 53, 57, 185, 233
Cooperation, 4, 22, 59–61, 83, 89, 90, 109,
    148, 149, 182, 204, 234
Corporate, 47, 99, 111, 125, 127, 138, 149,
    159, 161, 184
Corporation, 3, 109, 130, 148, 159, 236, 237
Cost(s), 120, 123, 125, 128–130, 144, 160,
    161, 176, 177, 183, 233, 236
Course management systems (CMS). See
    Learning management system (LMS);
    Virtual learning environment (VLE)
CSCL. See Computer-supported collaborative
    learning (CSCL)
CSCW. See Computer-supported cooperative
    work (CSCW)

D
Data analytics, 89, 119, 130, 173, 238
Data mining, 114, 115, 160, 161
De Laat, M., 12, 49, 87–89, 109, 115, 116
Design
    indirect, 12, 13, 64, 68–71, 156,
        182, 211, 213
    for learning, 13, 68
Determinism
    technological, 12, 25–27, 32, 36, 38, 41,
        203
Digital, 1, 19, 47, 89, 107, 137, 169, 197, 225
    natives, 14, 26, 107, 112, 130, 176, 177,
        187, 191, 199–209, 214, 217, 218, 234
        (see also Net generation)
    scholarship, 14, 107, 112, 172–179, 187,
        189, 190
    university, 13, 112, 119, 234
Dirckinck-Holmfeld, L., 4, 42, 60, 62, 71, 87,
    145, 146, 211, 214
Disability, 152, 157
Disabled, 152, 157, 161
Discourse, 14, 22, 24, 26, 49, 50, 79, 95, 99,
    112, 132, 169, 177, 191, 198, 201, 204,
    208, 236
Distance
    learning, 2, 70, 130, 146, 183, 199

E
Education(al) systems, 22, 131, 170,
    198, 216
E-learning, 4, 7–10, 20, 67, 131, 151, 180
Emergence, 13, 19–20, 39, 96–99, 112, 119,
    127, 147, 156, 173, 179, 185–186, 230,
    233, 235
Engeström, Y., 55, 57–59, 71, 109, 110, 147
Enterprise resource planning (ERP), 114,
    117–120, 150
Epistemology, 9, 26, 29, 32, 42, 53, 54, 56,
    91–92, 229
ERP. See Enterprise resource planning (ERP)
Experience
    student (learner), 5, 63, 113, 115, 152, 157,
        163, 198, 213–218, 241

F
Face-to-face, 152, 197, 198, 214
Fenwick, T., 27, 55, 64, 66, 91, 99
Fox, S., 92

G

Gender, 205, 206
Gibson, J., 28–34, 226–228
Global, 3, 20–22, 37, 38, 42, 83, 90, 97, 98,
  107–109, 123, 127, 128, 139, 140,
  146–148, 150, 160, 162, 172, 174, 175,
  179, 187, 198, 216, 237, 240
Globalisation, 20–22, 37, 107, 127, 128, 179
Goodyear, P., 4, 5, 12, 49, 52, 61–64, 67–70,
  154, 155, 158, 169, 181–183, 198, 199,
  208, 210, 211, 213–215, 217
Governance, 22–23, 89, 111, 119, 120, 156,
  230
Government, 3, 4, 8, 63, 111, 113, 114, 126,
  129, 149–150, 159, 161, 178, 179, 198,
  216, 230, 236, 238

H

Harasim, L., 11, 12, 37, 49–51, 53–55, 60, 68,
  153, 180, 181, 197, 201, 210
Haythornthwaite, C., 6, 8, 12, 49, 67, 87–89
Higher education, 2, 5, 7, 10, 13, 22, 39, 42,
  47, 49, 60, 63, 107, 110, 111, 113, 114,
  119, 122–124, 127–130, 142, 151, 157,
  160, 170, 171, 173, 176, 182, 190, 198,
  199, 205, 208, 211, 216, 236–238
Hiltz, S.R., 11, 36, 90, 152, 153, 201
Hodgson, V., 3, 4, 42, 60, 67, 182
Hybrid
  infrastructure, 14, 158–161, 163

I

ICT. *See* Information and communication
  technology (ICT)
Immaterial
  labour, 39, 40, 125, 241
Indirect design, 12, 13, 64, 68–71, 156, 182,
  211, 213. *See also* Design, for learning
Informating, 38–40, 109, 112
Information, 2, 22, 51, 87, 112, 140,
  172, 201, 235
  infrastructure, 140–144, 148, 176
  processing, 34, 51, 52, 65
  seeking, 213
  searching, 187, 205, 207
  society, 22, 35–37
Information and communication technology
  (ICT), 5, 8, 32
Information society, 22, 35–37
Infrastructure

information, 140–144, 148, 176
  for learning, 3, 13, 145, 149, 150, 214
Institutions, 8, 10, 13, 14, 21, 39, 51, 60, 62,
  70, 71, 107–132, 138–142, 146, 147,
  153, 158, 161–163, 170, 171, 175, 176,
  179, 184, 188, 197, 208, 209, 216, 225,
  228, 229, 233, 238
Intentionality, 13, 27, 95–99, 229
Interface, 2, 29, 150, 153, 154, 186, 198,
  212–213, 218, 239
Internet, 2, 5, 7, 8, 24, 35, 36, 38, 54, 65, 83,
  86, 92, 138, 140, 142, 151–153, 159,
  160, 175, 176, 181, 188, 191, 199, 201,
  205, 211, 225, 228, 230

J

Jones, C., 3, 4, 22, 26, 32, 42, 60–62, 68, 71,
  83, 87, 90, 91, 94, 112, 138, 145, 146,
  156, 158, 159, 177, 182, 198–200,
  205–207, 209–212, 214, 215, 234, 239,
  240

K

Kaptelinin, V., 31, 34, 35, 95, 96, 226, 227,
  229, 230
Knowledge
  society, 37, 48, 173 (*see also* Information
  society)
Koschmann, T., 55–57, 61, 64, 68

L

Latour, B., 26, 92, 93, 98, 138, 231–233
Lave, J., 55, 57–59, 71
Learning analytics, 39, 51, 112–116, 119, 120,
  132, 144, 150, 173, 180, 238, 241
Learning environment(s), 5, 12, 31, 151, 152,
  158, 163, 181, 211
Learning management system (LMS), 94, 114,
  117, 144, 150, 162, 184, 226
Learning networks, 12, 67, 89, 99, 144, 180,
  181, 210, 211, 213, 234
Learning objects, 51, 68, 70, 121, 125
Learning theory, 26, 39, 48, 49, 52–55, 60,
  63–71, 79, 89, 90
Levels, 3, 20, 47, 86, 119, 138, 171, 199, 225
Library, 114, 117, 138, 140, 144, 150, 174,
  210, 211, 239
LMS. *See* Learning management system
  (LMS)

M

Macro (level), 23, 62, 98, 132, 138, 148, 149, 162, 200, 214, 233

Management, 22, 23, 59, 60, 108, 109, 113–115, 117, 119, 120, 124, 162, 170–172, 178, 181, 185, 186, 199, 206

Manager(s), 115, 124, 143, 184, 185, 235, 238

Managerial, 20, 57, 62, 89, 91, 119, 132, 173, 178, 190, 238

Marton, F., 55, 63, 215

Massive open online courses (MOOC)
  cMOOC, 12, 126, 127, 130
  xMOOC, 127, 130

Materials, 5, 27, 120, 121, 123, 125, 150, 151, 183, 185, 191, 206, 234–235

Materiality, 24, 27, 32–34. *See also* Sociomateriality

McConnell, D., 5, 42, 48, 60, 61, 67, 83, 182, 204, 215

Meso (level), 23, 90, 132, 146–149, 162, 172, 188–189, 200, 210, 213–214, 232, 233

Micro (level), 62, 97, 98, 138, 146–149, 200, 214, 233

Mobile, 7, 38, 138, 147, 150, 154, 197, 199, 200, 205, 211, 212, 218, 238, 241

Mobilities, 152, 211, 212, 238–239, 241

MOOC. *See* Massive open online courses (MOOC)

N

Nardi, B., 34, 35, 95, 96, 199, 226, 227, 229, 230

Neoliberal(-ism), 21–23, 107, 122, 128, 184, 185, 237

Net generation, 14, 107, 176, 177, 187, 191, 199–205, 207–209, 234. *See also* Digital, natives

Network, 1, 19, 47, 79, 107, 137, 169, 197, 225
  individualism, 87, 90–91, 176
  learning, 1, 19, 47, 79, 107, 137, 169, 197, 225
  society, 3, 13, 22, 35–38, 40, 41, 87, 90, 93, 163, 180, 237, 241

New public management, 23, 108, 119, 162

O

Oliver, M., 26, 31–34, 68, 70, 94, 174, 206, 232

Online community, 87, 153

Online courses, 11, 13, 89

Online material(s), 120, 191, 235

Ontology, 26, 27, 29, 32, 54, 91, 93, 94, 96, 97, 113, 188, 229, 231, 232

Open, 12, 21, 48, 88, 110, 143, 171, 206, 232

Openness, 112, 120–126, 177, 236

Open University, 2, 115, 120, 121, 124, 130, 143, 145, 182, 183

Orlikowski, W., 24, 25, 71

P

Paradigm, 51, 55, 61, 113, 211, 225–241

Participation, 4, 7, 9, 40, 55, 57, 58, 89, 151, 154, 155, 177, 185, 199, 214

Pedagogy, 13, 25, 42, 48, 67–69, 115, 122–124, 126, 130, 138, 145, 146, 151, 173, 180–185, 199, 214, 235, 236

Peer, 4, 65, 89, 109, 110, 114, 127, 175, 177, 179, 190–191

Personalise
  personalisation, 108, 151, 176

Phenomenography, 55, 63–64, 215, 217–218

Place, 1, 20, 49, 92, 108, 137, 170, 197, 225

Policy, 4, 8, 13, 22, 23, 26, 39, 41, 63, 94, 109, 113, 124, 126–128, 130, 132, 170, 172, 175, 178, 180, 185, 198, 204, 208, 215–217

Political, 3, 11, 13, 19–23, 25, 41, 42, 48, 107, 108, 114, 122, 124, 126, 127, 131, 151, 152, 174, 178, 189, 217, 235–237

Politics, 3, 13, 20–25, 41, 42, 122–124, 155–157, 216, 235, 237, 240

Pollock, N., 27, 117, 118

Power law, 84, 85, 89

Price, 10, 129, 233, 236

Professional
  development, 7, 47, 60, 99, 186, 202

Public, 1, 23, 62, 80, 108, 109, 111, 112, 121, 122, 125–127, 129–131, 152, 156, 157, 159, 160, 163, 175, 177–178, 180, 187, 190, 236, 237

R

Random networks, 81–84

S

Scale-free networks, 81, 83–86, 155, 179

Selwyn, N., 25, 42, 64, 121–125, 147, 185, 205–207, 237

Siemens, G., 55, 64, 65, 113, 114, 127, 132

Situated learning, 55, 57–61, 64

Small worlds, 79, 81–86

Social learning, 48, 57–61, 71

Social network, 11, 37, 58, 82, 87–91, 145,
    155, 157, 175, 205, 206
Social network analysis (SNA), 13, 79, 87–93,
    114–115
Sociomateriality, 7, 11, 12, 27, 32, 39, 40, 55,
    64, 66, 71, 87, 94, 132, 138, 146, 150,
    163, 169, 185, 225, 229, 230, 234
Socio-technical (sociotechnical), 2, 27, 62, 98,
    117, 118, 139–142, 150, 169, 180, 188,
    208, 228, 234, 236
Space, 5, 12, 24, 29, 47, 64, 66, 69,
    141, 149, 156, 163, 200, 204, 209–213,
    218, 227
Standard(s), 24, 49, 52, 54, 55, 57–59, 63–65,
    71, 93, 117, 118, 125, 137, 139–142,
    144, 150, 161, 162, 171, 172, 178–180,
    183, 187, 188, 214, 232, 234, 240
Standardization, 5, 118, 119, 137, 140, 162,
    183, 188, 202
Study
    approaches to study, 63–64, 199, 215
Surveillance, 120, 161, 190, 236, 239

T
Tasks, 12, 36, 40, 68, 69, 83, 112, 115, 139,
    141, 144, 150, 158, 181, 182, 201, 210,
    211, 238
Teaching
    approaches to teaching, 68–69, 184, 214

Technology
    determinism, 12, 25–27, 32, 36,
        38, 41, 203
Technology-enhanced learning (TEL), 4, 7,
    9–11, 182
Text(s), 4–6, 37, 39, 40, 85, 87, 89, 93, 153,
    177, 197–199, 201, 239
Transmission, 8, 47, 59, 130, 151,
    214, 216, 237

U
University
    digital, 13, 112, 119, 234

V
Virtual learning environment (VLE),
    143, 150–152, 181, 184, 185, 239

W
Web
    Web 2.0, 35, 62, 92, 117, 149, 151, 154,
        155, 180, 207, 228
Weller, M., 7, 70, 117, 121, 151, 152, 172,
    174–178, 185, 187, 190
Wenger, E., 49, 55, 57, 58, 71, 90
Wiki, 80, 86, 97, 143, 154, 207
Wireless, 138, 197, 210, 212

Lightning Source UK Ltd.
Milton Keynes UK
UKOW06n0230070915

258142UK00002B/4/P

9 783319 019338